Losing Our Minds

# Oxford Series in Behavioral Neuroendocrinology

# Losing Our Minds

*How Environmental Pollution
Impairs Human Intelligence and
Mental Health*

BARBARA DEMENEIX

OXFORD
UNIVERSITY PRESS

# OXFORD
UNIVERSITY PRESS

Oxford University Press is a department of the University of
Oxford. It furthers the University's objective of excellence in research,
scholarship, and education by publishing worldwide.

Oxford    New York
Auckland    Cape Town    Dar es Salaam    Hong Kong    Karachi
Kuala Lumpur    Madrid    Melbourne    Mexico City    Nairobi
New Delhi    Shanghai    Taipei    Toronto

With offices in
Argentina    Austria    Brazil    Chile    Czech Republic    France    Greece
Guatemala    Hungary    Italy    Japan    Poland    Portugal    Singapore
South Korea    Switzerland    Thailand    Turkey    Ukraine    Vietnam

Oxford is a registered trademark of Oxford University Press
in the UK and certain other countries.

Published in the United States of America by
Oxford University Press
198 Madison Avenue, New York, NY 10016

Library of Congress Cataloging-in-Publishing Data
Demeneix, Barbara.
Losing our minds : how environmental pollution impairs human intelligence
and mental health / Barbara Demeneix.
pages cm. — (Oxford series in behavioral neuroendocrinology)
Includes bibliographical references and index.
ISBN 978–0–19–991751–8 (hardback)
1. Mental illness—Environmental aspects.    2. Mental health—Environmental
aspects.    3. Mental illness—Case studies.    I. Title.
RC455.4.E58D46 2014
362.19689—dc23
2014013286

9 8 7 6 5 4 3 2 1
Printed in the United States of America
on acid-free paper

*To Ariane and Laurent*

# Contents

# Foreword

Fifty years ago Rachel Carson's book *Silent Spring* eloquently described the degradation of the environment due to the introduction of pesticides. She made a compelling case for regulating their use; after years of bruising battles, the US Environmental Protection Agency was created, and some of the chemicals she indicted were banned. As a result of her foresight and pioneering effort, significant improvements in the health of wildlife followed, as exemplified by the increased survival of endangered bald eagles.

About 30 years later, Theo Colborn, Dianne Dumanovski, and Pete Myers in their book *Our Stolen Future* introduced the general public to "endocrine disruptors," namely, environmental chemicals that interfere with the functioning of the endocrine system. Experimental exposure to low doses of these chemicals alters fetal development; increases the propensity to develop diseases, including cancer, diabetes, and obesity; alters behaviors; and decreases fertility. Thereafter, epidemiological studies showed that these traits and diseases were on the rise in inhabitants of developed countries. To infer that decreased fertility would accelerate the extinction of our own species would qualify as a logical consequence.

During the last decade the increasing incidence of congenital hypothyroidism, autism spectrum disorders (ASD), and attention-deficit/hyperactivity disorder (ADHD) suggested a link to endocrine disruptors, particularly those that interfere with thyroid hormone action. Not only may we be accelerating our demise, but if we are indeed "losing our minds," we might soon be unable to take appropriate action to reverse this trend.

Enter Barbara Demeneix, a very accomplished scientist passionately committed to research into fundamental concepts in the endocrinology of development. Her knowledge of thyroid action in brain development provides an optimal perspective to analyze the causes of these trends in humans, a task she accomplishes in this excellent book. Barbara Demeneix has tackled this complex issue with scientific rigor. Thus, she presents her hypotheses and the evidence supporting them, discusses alternatives, every statement backed by a reference, exactly as a scientist would address her peers. This scholarly level of discourse is still compatible with a complementary interpretation, the one that is directed to the lay reader. There is no simplification or patronizing tone here, but instead a purposeful but dispassionate analysis that makes the text intelligible to all. This makes for obligatory reading for any person concerned by the deterioration of our physical environment in our own backyard.

By reaching the lay audience, Barbara Demeneix has fulfilled what I consider the moral duty of scientists whose research is financed by the taxpayer. In the last chapter of this remarkable book, Barbara Demeneix empowers readers with excellent advice to act both at the individual level, by modifying their lifestyle, and as responsible citizens, by collective action through associations aimed at achieving much needed legislation and regulatory action. She writes: "Failure to correct future injustices is also a failure to recognize that human intelligence and ingenuity have been responsible for the creation and production of a vast array of untested and potentially dangerous substances. It should be possible for human intelligence and ingenuity to find the means to control and eliminate their nefarious consequences. If not, then future generations could well find themselves lacking the intelligence and ingenuity ever to do so."

*Losing Our Minds* describes alterations of behavior and the loss of intelligence, ominous and sad outcomes that follow people's exposure to endocrine disruptors. These people are not "others"; they are our own offspring. This message is delivered in cogent, careful, and wisely articulated arguments that do not compromise the scientific truth. In sum, while Barbara Demeneix has fulfilled her duty as a scientist and citizen, she invites us to fulfill our own responsibility as citizens by protecting the health and minds of our children's children.

*—Ana Soto*
*Professor of Integrative Physiology and Pathobiology*
*Tufts University*

# Preface

In 2001, I was asked to represent France on the OECD[1] committee examining the potential to use amphibian metamorphosis as a screening test for chemicals that might disrupt thyroid hormone signaling. Amphibian metamorphosis was chosen as a model system because the whole spectacular process of turning a tadpole into a frog is orchestrated by thyroid hormone. But the assay is not only relevant to frogs; the thyroid hormone that sculptures a frog from a tadpole is exactly the same molecule, exploiting the same molecular signaling systems, that enables human brains to develop and function correctly. Moreover, the same molecule also regulates our energy metabolism, controls our weight, and controls the functions of many organs, including the heart—hence, the importance of thyroid hormone for many aspects of human mental and physical health.

My name was put forward as a scientific expert for the OECD committee as I had been working on different aspects of thyroid hormone signaling since my thesis in Calgary, Canada, in the mid-1970s and again in Paris for more than 20 years. In between, after 4 years lecturing on physiology at the University Mohammed V, Rabat, Morocco, I took a decade-long excursion into researching how membrane signaling by neurotransmitters modulates gene transcription while working at the University of Strasbourg. During this period I spent a summer in the molecular neurobiology laboratory in Cambridge, learning more molecular biology and cloning techniques. Then, after a sabbatical in the Max Planck Institute for Psychiatry in Munich, I had the opportunity to fulfil a dream and set up my own lab in the Natural History Museum in Paris in 1990.

In Paris I set about applying the growing knowledge of gene transcription and the techniques I had developed with colleagues in Strasbourg to understanding the evolution of thyroid hormone signaling in animals such as frogs and mice. Our aim was to be able to visualize gene transcription within the cells and tissues of a living organism and hence to gain understanding into how hormones such as thyroid hormone control gene networks during development. In 2001 our Paris team had just made the cover of the highly respected American scientific journal, *Proceedings of the National Academy of Science*.

---

1 Organization for Economic Cooperation and Development; according to their site, http://www.oecd.org, the OECD is an "international organisation that helps governments tackle economic, social and governance challenges of a globalised economy." As such, the OECD has a major role to play in drafting and ratifying testing systems for chemicals.

The cover illustration showed a green fluorescent frog that we had followed at the cellular level since it had been a green fluorescent tadpole. The person who suggested I attend the OECD meetings hoped that this new knowledge and the techniques we had generated could be put to good use in developing assays that would be more rapid and possibly more sensitive than the Amphibian Metamorphosis Assay. By applying a lot of bench work and brainwork, we have been able to show he was right.

But at that time it was with mixed feelings that I crossed Paris to attend the OECD discussions, considering it was part of my role as an academic, and a citizen, but being reluctant to be away from the lab. I do not regret it now. For it was then that I was introduced to the complex world of endocrine disruption and gradually became aware of the looming threats to health and biodiversity.

Since then the evidence on the numbers of chemicals that affect thyroid hormone signaling has been accumulating inexorably. It was also the better part of a decade before the figures on the increasing incidence of neurodevelopmental disorders and congenital hypothyroidism began appearing on our radar screens. I could not ignore the obvious links between the roles of thyroid hormone in brain development and the potential for disruption of that process by environmental chemicals. It seemed almost inevitable that ongoing chemical pollution, particularly if experienced in the uterus, could interfere with brain development and intellectual capacity. After all, there were many documented cases on a handful of chemicals that had belatedly been legislated against. Yet the number of untested and potentially harmful molecules was still increasing. It seemed urgent to put the ideas down on paper, not just as a scientific publication, but rather in book form to allow room to develop the hypothesis fully and to discuss the implications.

So the initial idea put forward in mid-2011 was to present and discuss the evidence for how chemical pollution could be downgrading general intelligence across populations and what the socioeconomic consequences might be. However, the experts who read the proposal suggested that the work should also cover the links between thyroid hormone–disrupting substances and autism spectrum disorders (ASD) as well as attention-deficit/hyperactivity disorder (ADHD). How right they were!

Not long after I started writing, updates on ASD incidence in the United States appeared, showing ASD to affect 1 in 56 boys, with marked increases in incidence occurring since the early 2000s. The rise in ASD is paralleled by increased incidence of ADHD. The socioeconomic cost of both disorders is enormous, with annual spending on ASD alone in the United States reaching 35 billion US dollars,[2] a figure, moreover, that cannot take into account the personal tragedies of the families concerned. As explained in depth later, we know that changing diagnosis and genetic causes can only account for part of this increase and that environmental factors, often no doubt exacerbating genetic predispositions, must be considered. However, given the hundreds of

2  (http://www.autismspeaks.org).

thousands of chemicals that for the past decades have been produced and released into the environment (without or before being tested for their physiological effects), one hardly knows where to start to unravel the complexity of their interactions.

Here we take a pragmatic approach that has its origin in bringing together two observations, first, that many of these chemicals affect thyroid hormone signaling and, second, that thyroid hormone signaling is absolutely essential for normal brain development in the unborn, newborn, and developing infant. Furthermore, as the scientific community increasingly becomes aware of the importance and vulnerability of early development to later health and disease risk, we are also seeing evidence that thyroid hormone is vital for very early periods of brain development, the first 3 months of pregnancy in women. Hence, the principal tenet of the book: The intelligence and mental health of unborn children are at risk due to continuous exposure to thyroid hormone–disrupting mixtures in the mother's body from conception onward. Today's populations are doubly at risk. Not only is environmental pollution affecting this vital hormone system but also, in many areas, iodine deficiency is aggravating the situation. Iodine is required for the production of thyroid hormone; thus, insufficient iodine will render the body's thyroid system more prone to chemical interference. The need for iodine is even greater during pregnancy.

Starting from a series of epidemiological findings on the presence of different pollutants and from data showing the effects of the same substances on thyroid hormone action and developmental pathways, one is led to the disquieting conclusion that the intellectual capacity of future generations is seriously compromised. Numerous types of chemicals are effectively found in human tissues and fluids (fat or blood/serum) but, most disturbingly, also in amniotic fluid, umbilical cord blood and milk. Many are found at concentrations that could interfere with thyroid hormone signaling and hence neurological development. Problems with neurological development in pregnancy can in turn be linked not only to reduced intelligence but also to behavioral and mental disorders of childhood, such as ASD and ADHD.

However, to be useful, the ideas presented have to overcome dismay and propose actions. One is reminded of the theories of Lin Ostrom, the first woman to receive the Nobel Prize for Economics in 2009. She argued that misuse of common resources, such as the overfishing of the oceans or pollution of the atmosphere, needs to be addressed by polycentric approaches, with individuals acting at community and national levels to change and enforce legislation. Perhaps she was one of the original "think globally, act locally" activists! It is in this logic that the final chapter examines what individuals, associations, policy makers, and governments can do. One of the suggestions made is that our public health system must ensure that women enter pregnancy with sufficient iodine to maintain thyroid hormone supplies for them and the developing fetus. The most efficient means of helping women maintain optimal thyroid function is to ensure adequate intake of iodine with dietary supplements. This simple and cheap measure can significantly contribute to mitigating the effects of chemical pollution on thyroid function and children's brain development. It can be accompanied by ensuring iodination of salt used in the food industry. As less salt is used, iodine content should be correspondingly increased. All governments have a responsibility to safeguard the mental health of future generations by implementing this inexpensive program with immense cost benefits. This simple measure must be accompanied by better legislation in the testing, registration, and use of chemicals of all categories. To improve legislation on chemicals, the European Union introduced REACH[3] in 2006. The United States has a different approach, applying since 2009 a large-scale screening program, TOXCAST, on groups of compounds such as pesticides and substances suspected to disrupt natural endocrine systems, such as thyroid signaling and those governing reproduction. These programs are often described as "too little, too late." And indeed it is too late for those children already affected whose impaired brain development can never be corrected. However, as citizens, we can make our voices heard so that governments recognize the need to apply these chemical screening programs most effectively, thereby ensuring the rights of each child to fulfil his or her potential as a sentient and responsible member of society.

Ana Soto, one of the experts who kindly read and provided valuable criticism on the manuscript, suggested that it might be interesting to mention how much one learns by writing a book. She made a good point: By immersing oneself in the literature not only does one learn more about the science but also about the sociology of the problems, in this case most notably the histories of the chemical industries and their lobbying activities. Reading books by Gerald Markowitz and David Rosner on industrial lobbying (Markowitz & Rosner, 2002), notably by the lead industry (Markowitz, Rosner, & Fund, 2013), made distressingly edifying reading, the distress only tempered by the strength of their knowledge, force of their arguments, and insight. The question of industrial lobbying has piercing pertinence for Europeans in 2013/2014. In mid-2013 the European parliament delayed their decision on whether pesticides should be tested for potential endocrine-disrupting properties. The decision should have been made in November 2013, but it seems that it was postponed that summer due to pressure from toxicologists supported by the chemical industry. One of the most disturbing events was the publication of a common editorial in a number of toxicological journals (Dietrich et al., 2013a, 2013b, 2013c), signed by 18 editors of similar journals. Their short article denounces proposing legislation that is supposedly based on small numbers of publications and approaches that lack scientific robustness. They make reference to a short letter, dated June 2013 summarizing their position, written to Anne Glover, the chief scientific advisor to José Manuel Barroso (current president of the European Commission). This letter provoked a number of strong reactions from scientists and journalists. Two journalists from the French national

---

3  Legislation covering "registration, evaluation, authorization, and restriction of chemical substances."

newspaper *Le Monde* revealed that most of those signing the Dietrich editorials had financial interests, such as consulting positions or research funding from different actors in the chemical industry. Strong responses also came from academic endocrinologists, with a series of major editorials and articles published between September and November 2013 (see, for example, Gore, 2013; Gore et al., 2012a, 2013b, 2013c, 2013d) signed by editors and members of editorial boards of major endocrinology journals. The main arguments were that the position of Dietrich et al. was dismissive of the thousands of studies on low-dose and nonmonotonic responses that are observed in endocrinology and can be induced by endocrine-disrupting chemicals (EDCs), misconstrued the concept of thresholds, and, most important, ignored the possibility of sensitive windows of development.

As a consequence, Anne Glover convened a meeting between small groups of representatives of each position in the autumn. The minutes and conclusions were released in late 2013.[4] The conclusions covered the main points discussed, definitions, thresholds, nonmonotonic dose–response curves, and testing methods. Succinctly, agreement was reached that thresholds for EDC action cannot be easily demonstrated, that nonmonotonic responses can occur, and that testing strategies need to be extended. The debate has provoked much commentary from different sources. Not the least is that from a representative of the Chemicals Unit in the Environment Directorate of the European Commission, who is reported as stating that the chemical industry must stick to facts and not resort to emotional arguments (cited by "Chemical Watch" November 2013) when presenting cases to policy makers. But in the meantime much needed legislation has been blocked.

Returning to the science behind the writing of this book, in this case I started off with a hypothesis. Like all rigorous scientists, I consider that one progresses by testing the hypothesis and readjusting one's original position according to the results and observations made. And progress is made whether or not the observations fit the hypothesis. I was ready to find that some evidence corroborated my hypothesis while other evidence did not. I was suprised to discover that the majority of the data corroborated my original hypothesis. Literature searches revealed that even mercury, which I initially chose as an example of how a metal could affect brain development independently of thyroid hormone signaling, exerted at least some of its neurotoxic effects through disruption of thyroid hormone availability. Similar arguments surfaced for lead petrol with its brominated antiknock agents. Then, in mid-2013, Margaret Rayman's paper on iodine deficiency in young women in England appeared (Bath, Steer, Golding, Emmett, & Rayman, 2013). Her results showed that even in developed countries, such as the United Kingdom, where governments should be aware of the consequences of the risks of iodine lack, many women will be entering pregnancy with insufficient iodine supplies with the risk that their children

4  http://ec.europa.eu/commission_2010-2014/president/chief-scientific-adviser/
   documents/minutes_endocrine_disruptors_meeting_241013_final.pdf

display lower IQs and poorer reading skills than children born to women who have enough iodine to ensure adequate production of thyroid hormone. In her papers, Dr. Rayman notes that prior to studies published on school children in 2011, there had been no analysis of urinary iodine status in UK populations since the 1950s! National statistics were based on calculating iodine intake from information relating to dietary sources. Her results on iodine lack and lower IQ appeared shortly before the OECD published a comparison on adult skills across 24 of the wealthier countries.[5] In this report the literacy and numeracy skills of the younger UK adults (between 16 and 24 years old) was found to be among the lowest. More disquieting was the finding that the United Kingdom was the only developed country in which this group of young adults had lower skills than those reaching retirement age. Clearly, this is a multifactorial situation with a spectrum of causes to be taken into account, from economic changes, size of classes, curricula taught, teacher training, school and home environments, and, of course, nutrition. However, one cannot ignore the findings of Margaret Rayman when considering these results. For optimal improvements in such statistics across populations, one has to start by ensuring healthy pregnancies and early childhood environments, and that includes starting with prenatal nutrition and appropriate supplements where needed, including iodine.

Such reasoning brings us back full circle to Lin Ostrom's observations on misuse of common resources and the necessity to apply polycentric approaches, with individuals acting at community and national levels to bring about changes in legislation. This book has the modest ambition of being one action toward such a goal of controlling environmental pollution in the interests of protecting the potential and promise of future generations.

## REFERENCES

Bath, S. C., Steer, C. D., Golding, J., Emmett, P., & Rayman, M. P. (2013). Effect of inadequate iodine status in UK pregnant women on cognitive outcomes in their children: Results from the Avon Longitudinal Study of Parents and Children (ALSPAC). *Lancet, 382*(9889), 331–337.

Dietrich, D. R., von Aulock, S., Marquardt, H., Blaauboer, B., Dekant, W., Kehrer, J.,...Harvey, A. (2013a). Scientifically unfounded precaution drives European Commission's recommendations on EDC regulation, while defying common sense, well-established science and risk assessment principles. *ALTEX, 30*(3), 381–385.

Dietrich, D. R., von Aulock, S., Marquardt, H., Blaauboer, B., Dekant, W., Kehrer, J.,...Harvey, A. (2013b). Scientifically unfounded precaution drives European Commission's recommendations on EDC regulation, while defying common sense, well-established science and risk assessment principles. *Toxicology In Vitro, 27*(7), 2110–2114.

5   OECD (2013), *OECD Skills Outlook 2013: First Results from the Survey of Adult Skills*, OECD Publishing. http://dx.doi.org/10.1787/9789264204256-en

Dietrich, D. R., von Aulock, S., Marquardt, H., Blaauboer, B., Dekant, W., Kehrer, J.,...Harvey, A. (2013c). Scientifically unfounded precaution drives European Commission's recommendations on EDC regulation, while defying common sense, well-established science and risk assessment principles. *Chemical and Biological Interactions*, *205*(1), A1–A5.

Gore, A. C. (2013). Editorial: An international riposte to naysayers of endocrine-disrupting chemicals. *Endocrinology*, *154*(11), 3955–3956.

Gore, A. C., Balthazart, J., Bikle, D., Carpenter, D. O., Crews, D., Czernichow, P.,...Watson, C. S. (2013a). Policy decisions on endocrine disruptors should be based on science across disciplines: A response to Dietrich et al. *Andrology*, *1*(6), 802–805.

Gore, A. C., Balthazart, J., Bikle, D., Carpenter, D. O., Crews, D., Czernichow, P.,...Watson, C. S. (2013b). Policy decisions on endocrine disruptors should be based on science across disciplines: A response to Dietrich et al. *Hormone Research in Paediatrics*, *80*(5), 305–308.

Gore, A. C., Balthazart, J., Bikle, D., Carpenter, D. O., Crews, D., Czernichow, P.,...Watson, C. S. (2013c). Policy decisions on endocrine disruptors should be based on science across disciplines: A response to Dietrich et al. *European Journal of Endocrinology*, *169*(6), E1–E4.

Gore, A. C., Balthazart, J., Bikle, D., Carpenter, D. O., Crews, D., Czernichow, P.,...Watson, C. S. (2013d). Policy decisions on endocrine disruptors should be based on science across disciplines: A response to Dietrich et al. *Endocrinology*, *154*(11), 3957–3960.

Markowitz, G. E., & Rosner, D. (2002). *Deceit and denial: The deadly politics of industrial pollution.* Berkeley: University of California Press.

Markowitz, G. E., Rosner, D., & Fund, M. M. (2013). *Lead wars: The politics of science and the fate of America's children.* Berkeley: University of California Press.

# Acknowledgments

This book would not have reached the publisher's desk without the help and support of many friends and colleagues.

First and foremost, I must thank those who provided writing sanctuaries, beginning with my mentor and old friend, François Lachiver, whose small house in Burgundy was yet again vital to this endeavour, as it has been to many others. Even today he continues to remind me of the astonishing chemistry of iodine.

My long-standing friends Jacques and Gisou Bremond in Haute Provence, Anne-Marie Jandaud in the Limousin, and Jean-François and Claire in New Zealand provided conviviality, conversation, and refuge from the madding crowds, each in their contrasting but equally idyllic surroundings. Merci beaucoup, je reviendrai!

In May 2012 I was able to accelerate the pace of work within the inspiring environment of the "Fondation des Treuilles." I thank the Foundation for the privilege; I consider myself fortunate to have enjoyed this unique and aesthetic setting.

Joanne Burden, project manager and friend, kept me on track and sane with her never-failing positive attitude, immense organisational skills, intuition and encouragement. Early on the project, her parents loaned me their lovely flat in Dinard, for which I thank them.

Thanks also to Vincent Laudet, who suggested that I contact Oxford University Press. It has been a pleasure to work with Joan Bossert and her colleagues at OUP.

Three expert scientists Andrea Gore (Austin, Texas), Samantha Richardson (Melbourne), and Ana Soto (Boston) took the time in the summer of 2013 to review the text and suggested many valuable improvements. Their different insights were always pertinent and much appreciated.

My team in Paris not only put up with my reduced presence in the lab, but also provided many opportunities for discussion and exchange of key ideas. In particular, I thank Jean-Baptiste Fini and Marie Stephanie Clerget-Froidevaux, the researchers most involved in the endocrine disruption work, but also Sylvie Remaud for her input on novel cell-specific effects of thyroid hormone.

Thanks also to Sylvia Grommen for her seemingly effortless preparation of the illustrations.

Resounding thanks to my friend and most critical, but ever constructive reader, Michael Westlake. It was due time for the reading roles to be reversed.

And last but not least, my sister Louise and my friends Brenda and Pauline for their support.

# Abbreviations

| | |
|---|---|
| Ach | Acetylcholine |
| AChE | Acetylcholinesterase |
| AhR | Aryl hydrocarbon receptor |
| aADHD | Adult Attention-Deficit/Hyperactivity Disorder |
| ADDM | Autism and Developmental Disabilities Network Monitoring |
| ADHD | Attention-Deficit/Hyperactivity Disorder |
| AR | Androgen receptor |
| ASD | Autism spectrum disorders |
| BBP | Butylbenzyl phthalate |
| BDNF | Brain-derived neurotrophic factor |
| BFR | Brominated Flame Retardant |
| BDE | Brominated diphenyl ether |
| BP2 | Benzophenone 2 |
| BPA | Bisphenol A |
| CDC | Center for Disease Control and Prevention |
| CH | Congenital Hypothyroidism |
| CHAMACOS | Centre for the Health Assessment of Mothers and Children of Salinas |
| CNV | Copy number variations |
| DDE | Dichlorodiphenyldichloroethylene |
| DDT | Dichlorodiphenyltrichloroethane |
| DLC | Dioxin-like chemical |
| DES | Diethylstilbestrol |
| DBP | Dibutyl phthalate |
| DEHP | Di(2ethylhexyl) phthalate |
| DEP | Diethyl phthalate |
| DIDP | Di-isododecyl phthalate |
| DINP | Di-isononyl phthalate |
| DMP | Di-methyl phthalate |
| DnHP | Di-n-hexyl phthalate |
| DnOP | Di-n-octyl phthalate |
| DSM | *Diagnostic and Statistical Manual of Mental Disorders* |
| DZ | Dizygotic twins (nonidentical twins) |
| EPA | Environmental Protection Agency (US) |
| ER | Estrogen receptor |
| ERR | Estrogen-related receptor |
| FT3 | Free tri-iodothyronine |

| | |
|---|---|
| FT4 | Free tetra-iodothyronine |
| HBCD | Hexabromochlorodecane |
| HCB | Hexachlorobenzene |
| ICCIDD | International Council for the Control of Iodine Deficiency Disorders |
| IQ | Intelligence Quotient |
| MAO | Monoamine oxidase |
| 4MBC | 4-methylbeneylidene-camphor |
| MBP | Monobutyl phthalate |
| MBP | Myelin basic protein |
| MBzP | Monobenzyl phthalate |
| MCT8 | Monocarboxylate transporter 8 |
| MCT10 | Monocarboxylate transporter 10 |
| MECP2 | Methyl-CpG-binding protein 2 |
| MEHHP | Mono-(2-ethyl-5-hydroxylhexyl) phthalate |
| MEHP | Mono-(2-ethyl hexyl) phthalate |
| MEP | Mono-ethyl phthalate |
| MMI | Methimazole |
| MZ | Monozygotic twins (identical twins) |
| NHANES | National Health and Nutrition Examination Survey (US) |
| NIS | Sodium-iodide symporter |
| NMDRC | Nonmonotonic dose–response curve |
| NOAEL | No observable adverse effect level |
| OC | Organochlorine |
| OP | Organophosphate |
| OMC | Octyl-methoxycinnimate |
| PAN | Pesticide Action Network |
| PBB | Polybrominated biphenyl |
| PCB | Polychlorinated biphenyl |
| PCDD | Polychlorinated-$p$-dioxin |
| PBDE | Polybrominated diphenyl ethers |
| PBT | Persistent, bioaccumulative, and toxic |
| PC | Polycarbonate |
| PCDF | Polychlorinated dibenzofurans |
| PDD/NOS | Pervasive developmental disorder/not otherwise specified |
| PFAC | Perfluoroalkyl carboxylates |
| PFAS | Perfluoroalkyl sulfonates |
| PFC | Perfluorinated compounds |
| PFOA | Perfluorooctanic acid |
| PFOS | Perfluorooctane sulfonic acid |
| PFNA | Perfluorononanoic acid |
| POP | Persistant organic pollutant |
| PPAR | Peroxisome proliferator-activated receptor |
| PTU | Propylthiouracil |
| PVC | Polyvinyl chloride |

| REACH | Registration, Evaluation, Authorisation and Restriction of Chemicals |
| RTH | Resistance to thyroid hormone |
| RXR | Retinoid X receptor |
| SVHC | Substance of very high concern |
| T3 | Tri-iodothyronine |
| T4 | Tetra-iodothyronine |
| TBBPA | Tetra-bromo–bisphenol A |
| TBPH | Bis-(2-ethylhexyl) tetrabromophthalate |
| TBT | Tributyltin |
| TCDD | Tetrachlorodibenzo-*p*-dioxin |
| TDCPP | Tris (1,3, chloro-2 propyl) phosphate |
| THRA | Gene encoding thyroid hormone receptor alpha (official nomenclature is NR1A1) |
| THRB | Gene encoding thyroid hormone receptor beta (official nomenclature is NR1A2) |
| TPO | thyroid peroxidase |
| TT3 | Total tri-iodothyronine |
| TT4 | Total tetra-iodothyronine |
| TTR | transthyretin |
| TH | Thyroid hormone |
| TSH | Thyroid stimulating hormone (or thyrotropin) |
| TR | Thyroid hormone receptor |
| TRα | Thyroid hormone receptor alpha |
| TRβ | Thyroid hormone receptor beta |
| TRE | Thyroid hormone receptor response element |
| TRH | Thyrotropin releasing hormone |
| WHO | World Health Organisation |
| WWF | World Wildlife Fund |

Losing Our Minds

# Chapter 1

# Chemical Pollution and IQ Loss in Children

*Learning From the Past*

CHAPTER OUTLINE

This chapter provides a historical perspective to the main tenet of this book, that disruption of thyroid hormone (TH) signaling during key periods of brain development can cause irreversible damage, compromising intellectual ability. THs regulate gene expression. As numerous environmental factors interfere with TH-dependent pathways and TH signaling regulates gene expression in the brain, TH signaling can be seen as a bridge linking the environment to gene networks involved in brain development. Two well-documented cases demonstrate how environmental contamination can reduce intellectual capacity in children. Although effects on individuals may be difficult to detect and to relate to environmental causes, studies at the level of populations can reveal significant differences and link causes to effects. Both examples chosen involve consumption of contaminated food: polychlorinated biphenols (PCBs) in fish from the American Great Lakes, and mercury in rural populations in Iraq and in Japanese fishing populations. In each case, exposure during pregnancy is seen to be the most critical window, a period of brain development during which TH plays essential roles. Children are always more vulnerable than adults. Early exposure to certain chemicals permanently reduces intellectual ability, as judged by intelligence quotient (IQ). Nearly half of the children diagnosed today with autism spectrum disorder (ASD) are intellectually disabled, with IQ scores under 70. The current, unprecedented rise in incidence of ASD and other mental and behavioral disorders such as attention-deficit/hyperactivity disorder (ADHD) cannot be accounted for by diagnostic change alone and/or genetic factors. Environmental factors must be taken into account. ASD, ADHD, and the permanent loss of intellectual capacity represent immense socioeconomic burdens, in terms of both the lifelong cost for the individuals and their families and the multiple, far-reaching consequences for the structure of our societies.

BACKGROUND

How can our minds apprehend and understand their own complexity and function? This question has haunted philosophers for millennia and was only fully opened up to experimental research in the 20th century. In 2013, two immense, billion-dollar projects were launched in Europe and in the United States to generate knowledge on how the brain develops and how it uses and integrates information from its hundreds of billions of neurons. During the 10 years that it is programmed to run, the European Human Brain Project (http://www.humanbrainproject.eu) aims to apply current information and computing technologies to generate not only better knowledge of brain function and disease but then to exploit the data on how the brain integrates and processes information to derive novel computing methods. In parallel, in April 2013, President Obama announced funding of the "BRAIN Initiative," with the ambition to map all the connections of the human brain (http://www.nih.gov/science/brain/). BRAIN is the acronym for Brain Research through Advanced Innovative Neurotechnologies and is on a similar scale to the Human Genome Project launched more than 20 years earlier. Both projects will exploit the immeasurable potential of combining current imaging techniques with genetic knowledge, broadening understanding and forging new therapeutic and preventive therapies, but they should also drive innovation. The different research projects financed will provide unprecedented insight into the functioning of the circuitry that drives our conscious and unconscious actions and thinking processes, as well as those that integrate our bodily functions. The neuronal networks in the human brain that will be visualized result from the integration of signals from 100 billion neurons and trillions of synaptic connections between them. Put another way, each of our brains has more neurons than the number of people in the world today, each neuron having thousands of contacts with other neurons. Besides the fundamental technological advances, these ambitious projects will allow us to look inside our minds and compare function during development and aging, in health and in disease.

The American endeavor is not irrelevant to another announcement Barack Obama made during his previous mandate. In 2010, he officially changed the terminology of mental retardation to intellectual disability. This statement came 2 years before the publication of US figures showing ASD, which concerns many children with severe intellectual disability, to have reached 1 in 88 children[1] (Anonymous, 2012), nearly a 60-fold increase compared to 1975 (Weintraub, 2011; see also Chapter 7, Fig. 7.1). ADHD affects even greater numbers of children and adults. Hopefully these research initiatives will provide new insight into and therapeutic options for many neurological and mental diseases. But expectations for this project to provide preventive strategies to reverse the frightening trend on incidence of ASD are probably overoptimistic and possibly misdirected.

The main morphological structures of the human brain develop before birth. Then, before and during the first 2 years after birth the brain grows rapidly and the fine structure of connections between different networks is established with hundreds of trillions of synapses forming between the billions of neurons. It is impossible to describe the intricate molecular and cellular interactions that underlie the process that leads from a fertilized egg to

1   Current figures show an incidence of 1 in 68 children.

the formation of early neural structures to the elaboration and organization of the multitude of synapses that interact in a human brain. The neurobiologist Steven Rose provided a striking image of the process (Rose, 1998) by calculating that, if the brain developed at a constant rate during pregnancy, then 4,000 neurons would be born every single second. The brain does not actually develop at a constant rate and neurogenesis, or birth of new neurons, occurs at different rates in different structures. Suffice it to say, that if something goes wrong during those early months of life in the uterus, it cannot be corrected later.

The distressing deformities of thalidomide, a drug prescribed in the 1950s to counteract morning sickness in early pregnancy, illustrates all too clearly that when a chemical affects the development of a visible part of the body, such as hand or limb, it is not difficult to associate a particular drug with an adverse outcome. The example also underlines the particularly sensitive time window of early pregnancy, although the whole of pregnancy is a vulnerable period. However, examining the effects of a given chemical on brain development is much more difficult, even with the advances made in brain imaging applied today. Examining and understanding the effects of a mixture of chemicals on brain development and function is even more so. A former director of the National Institute of Health, David Rall, has been cited as asking: "If thalidomide had caused a 10-point reduction in IQ, would its effects be known?" Today, one can wonder if it did act on the brain, would it be hidden among the 84,000 chemicals currently marketed?

Determining such effects on brain and behavior requires large-scale studies at the population level. Unfortunately, for many children today many such experiments are carried out with them as unwitting participants. Quite justifiably, no scientist can carry out an experiment on any animal or any test on any fellow human without an ethical permit. Arguably, more stringent ethical scrutiny should be brought to the marketing of certain chemicals, many of which end up in the air we breathe or on our plates as food "additives."

The results of these "experiments" cannot be correctly assessed, as there are no controls. Mixtures of dozens of chemicals are found in everyone, precluding the identification of the major suspects. As we will see at the end of Chapter 5, chemicals can be put on the market in a matter of months, but it will require decades of intense international research to demonstrate their adverse effects on wildlife and humans. Often the scientific evidence is criticized because it only shows an association of a given substance with a physiological or pathological endpoint. Associations are not proof, so lobbying by industrial actors can override the precautionary principle and block legislation. Research for mechanisms must use a maximum of non-animal testing methods, but also animal models, and this at a time when public opinion often questions the ethics of using animals in research. These central problems of screening substances for toxic and/or endocrine-disrupting effects, which need to be considered in the context of the justifiable concerns on reducing animal testing, will be discussed in Chapter 8.

Here, with the rather overused, but highly appropriate, aphorism on learning from our past ringing in our ears, we set the stage by looking at cases where after hundreds of children in a given area were examined over several years, it could be shown that mothers' exposure to chemical pollution during pregnancy caused irreversible intellectual damage in their children. Such large-scale studies, backed up by animal studies, contributed to driving legislation and control of the chemicals incriminated.

For the exposed children and their families it was too late. In the case of the polychlorinated biphenols (PCBs) the legacy of the use of these highly persistent chemicals is still with us, with significant levels still found in blood samples worldwide. The range of chemicals present in our blood today makes the problem of identifying which of them might be causing harmful effects more complex but, simultaneously, renders the problem more pressing.

## LAKE MICHIGAN AND POLYCHLORINATED BIPHENOLS

The year 2012 saw the 50th anniversary of the publication of Rachel Carson's *Silent Spring* (Pimentel, 2012). As a US government biologist, Carson had observed population decreases in many animal groups from fish to birds and attributed abrupt declines to the use of the insecticide dichlorodiphenyltrichloroethane (DDT). Carson astutely realized that DDT spraying was not only affecting the insect populations on which they fed, by reducing food availability, but also accumulating in the fish and birds. Carson's prescient work was one of the factors in the campaign that led to the ban on the general use of DDT in 1972. Before the ban, and despite it, metabolites of DDT were found to accumulate in the environment, with effects on reproductive capacity being most serious in birds at the top of the food chain. These adverse reproductive effects seen in wildlife began to cause disquiet among health authorities, who were concerned that DDT might be exerting similar effects in humans. This questioning spurred numerous studies into the amounts of DDT and its metabolites in human milk, and the relationship of the level of the metabolites to breast-feeding duration. One of the pilot studies was in North Carolina (see Rogan & Gladen, 1985 for a review). Analysis of milk found not only the insecticide but also high quantities of polychlorinated biphenols (PCBs), a category of chemicals that we now know to significantly modify TH levels in exposed groups (Zoeller, 2010). In the same time frame, for many reasons, other groups were examining PCB levels in different states. (The chemistry and thyroid hormone–disrupting actions of PCBs are discussed in Chapter 5.)

Like DDT metabolites, PCBs were known to accumulate in animal tissues and, as they are soluble in fat, particularly in adipose tissue. Milk has high fat content and it was logical to check breast milk for PCB content. Michigan was chosen for detailed study not only because of the probability of consumption of contaminated fish from the lake but also because industrial accidents had contaminated local dairy farms in 1973 and 1975, with a similar chemical, polybrominated biphenyl (PBB). The local health authority covered the cost of PBB measurements in nursing mothers' milk and proposed PCB testing as well, but at the mother's expense. Over 1,000 nursing mothers paid to have their breast milk analyzed for PCB content (Wickizer, Brilliant, Copeland, & Tilden, 1981). In 1981, the values of PCBs in these milk samples obtained in 1977 and 1978 were published (Wickizer et al., 1981). Significant contamination was found in 75% of samples. Further, it was estimated that the babies, as they were growing and building tissues, would be assimilating and not eliminating most of the PCBs, so concern was raised for the long-term health effects of this postnatal exposure.

It was, however, not until nearly a decade later, in 1990, that the first associations of PCBs with adverse effects on intelligence and behavior were fully documented by Joseph and Sandra Jacobson (Jacobson, Jacobson, & Humphrey, 1990). The Jacobsons had managed to obtain data on amounts of different species of lake fish eaten by 8,482 mothers who were due to give birth in 1980–1981 in the Michigan area (Jacobson & Jacobson, 1996). Different fish species were known to accumulate greater or lesser amounts of PCBs, and so 339 of the mothers who had reported eating trout or salmon (at the top of the food chain) from Lake Michigan, and 110 control mothers who had not eaten these fish, were requested to join the study. Over 300 agreed. PCB exposure was evaluated at birth by analysis of maternal serum, umbilical cord blood, and, shortly after, breast milk.

Levels of PCBs in breast milk were a hundred times greater than those in any serum sample, whether from maternal or umbilical cord blood. Levels averaged 0.8 μg/g milk fat. For the correlative analysis with children's development, five groups were distinguished: below 0.5 μg/g milk fat, 0.5 to 0.74, 0.75 to 099, 1.0 to 1.24, and above 1.25, not a large range. Despite the fact that maternal levels of PCB were only slightly higher in women who had eaten lake fish compared to those who had not, already at birth significant differences were found in fetal and postnatal growth and in short-term memory during infancy as a function of PCB exposure. The main lesson to be learned from the Jacobsons' study is, as they emphasize, that despite the higher levels in milk, it was the prenatal PCB levels, deduced from umbilical cord values, that showed the largest associations with neurodevelopmental potential, underlining the importance and the vulnerability of this window of brain formation and growth.

When the children reached the age of 11 years, 212 of them participated in a new series of tests, based on reading and arithmetic skills, to see whether the differences between exposed and control groups were still present. The children's blood levels of PCBs were also measured at this time. The average IQ of all the children was 107, but the average IQ of the 30 children in the highest exposure group was 6.2 points lower. This difference may not seem very large. But it was in a total sample of just over 200 children. As many authors have emphasized, just a five-point loss of IQ in a population can have major socioeconomic consequences. As illustrated (Fig. 1.1), such a downward shift

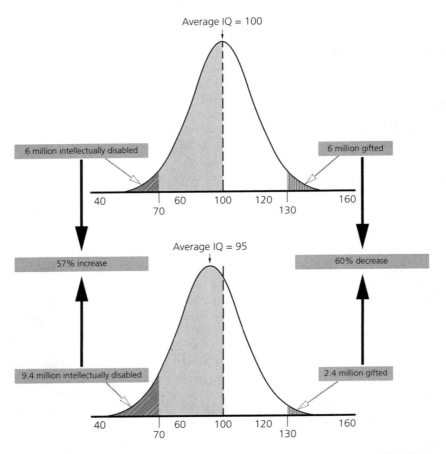

**Figure 1–1.** The consequences of a population-wide 5-point decrease in IQ. If the slight leftward shift in IQ seen in the Michigan study were to occur across a population of 100 million, it would cause an increase of more than 3 million intellectually disabled persons and an equivalent reduction in the proportion of highly intelligent people. The economic cost of losing such a substantial proportion of society's active contributors and the corresponding increase in dependents is enormous. (Adapted from Weiss, 2009.)

in general intelligence in a theoretical population of 100 million will decrease the proportion of gifted people (IQ over 130) from 6 to 2.4 million and increase those of intellectually impaired (IQ below 70) from 6 to 9.4 million. The economic toll of such a downward shift, as seen with the current increase in ASD, is discussed in the section "They Told Us So."

## Mercury and Minamata Disease

The neurotoxic effects of mercury, like those of lead, have been documented since antiquity. Although mercury causes major deleterious effects on brain function at all life stages, in adults as well as children, developing fetuses and infants are the most sensitive. Children are not just reduced-scale versions of adults; their growing brains are particularly prone to pollution that will more often than not cause permanent alterations in brain structure and function. The morphological, cellular, and functional consequences of mercury poisoning have parallels with both TH disorders and ASD, including reduced populations of specialized neurons in the cerebellum and problems with mitochondrial function. Although different authors have underlined the common symptoms and affected pathways between mercury and ASD (see, for instance, Kern et al., 2012), the common traits between mercury toxicity and hypothyroidism (reduced levels of TH) are less often brought together. This oversight could be related to the fact that the direct interference of mercury with TH signaling is not well known. Mercury inhibits production of the active form of TH, thereby producing local and general hypothyroidism (see Chapters 2 and 5). Thus, mercury-induced effects on reduced TH availability (hypothyroidism) will hinder brain development and exacerbate neurotoxic effects of any other environmental factors. Both mercury and PCBs modulate TH levels. THs act through specific nuclear receptors (NRs), the thyroid hormone receptors or TRs. TRs are transcription factors that bind to DNA and modulate gene expression (Box 1.1). The TH modulating actions of mercury and PCBs exemplify how TH signaling can act as a bridge between environmental factors and gene expression patterns and, hence, the cellular processes governing brain development. We will return to this point frequently.

As reviewed by Clarkson (2002), over the past century, mercury exposure could have resulted from three main sources: consumption of organic mercury in the form of methyl mercury, most often from eating contaminated fish; mercury vapor released from mercury-based tooth fillings; and, in some countries up until 2000, use of a mercury-based preservative, thimerosal, in vaccines. This mercury-based component of vaccines is probably the reason that vaccines were sometimes, without any hard evidence, associated with cases of autism (see Chapter 7 for a full discussion). However, in Europe and the United States, thimerosal was withdrawn from use in vaccines in 1999, though whether it is still useful in certain situations, such as tropical countries, is a matter of ongoing debate. Use of mercury in tooth amalgams has also been radically reduced in most countries. Thus, methyl mercury is the main cause of concern today and has been associated with most cases of environmental mercury neurotoxicity.

The most dramatic cases of mercury-induced brain damage seen in the 20th century were those in Minamata, Japan, and in Iraq. In Iraq the cause was human consumption of grain that was destined for planting but was treated with a mercury-based fungicide. The grain had been colored red as a warning against use in food, because of the risk of delivery to people who might not be able to read the instructions. But people thought that washing the grain, thereby removing the red dye, eliminated the risk. Washing did not, however, get rid of the fungicide, and use of contaminated grain in bread caused spates of

Box 1–1. Nuclear Receptors Represent Bridges Between the Environment and Gene Transcription

Nuclear receptors (NRs) are a class of proteins that are found in the nucleus of all cells. All NRs have a modular structure, with a domain that binds to DNA and, in most cases, another domain that forms a pocket allowing a signaling molecule to enter. In physiological situations a specific, natural hormone will occupy this pocket. NRs act as transcription factors by binding to DNA in specific areas of target genes, and many regulate DNA as a function of whether the pocket contains a ligand. This ligand-binding link to transcriptional regulation has driven many pharmaceutical approaches to develop NR-targeting drugs for cancer, metabolism, cardiovascular disorders, contraception, and even performance-enhancing steroids.

In the context of endocrine disruption studies the main NRs studied are the estrogen receptor (ER) and the androgen receptor (AR). As its name suggests, the ligand-binding domain of the thyroid hormone receptor (TR) binds thyroid hormone. Chemicals in the environment can interfere with signaling through NRs either by replacing the natural ligand in the pocket or by modifying the amount of natural hormone that is available to enter the pocket and modulate gene transcription.

ER and AR represent crossroads by which environmental signaling can modulate gene programs and thus the cellular processes that govern reproductive capacity and fertility.

TRs are the highway through which environmental factors can affect gene programs and cellular processes involved in brain development, growth and metabolism.

outbreaks of mercury poisoning between 1950 and 1972. In 1972, the worst outbreak occurred when fungicide-treated grain was distributed to farmers while they were planting or after they had already planted their seeds. Thus, excess grain was used in homes throughout the country for breadmaking (Bakir et al., 1973). No commercially distributed bread was contaminated. The use in homes was so extensive and the poisoning so severe that thousands of rural Iraqis were admitted to hospital and hundreds died (Bakir et al., 1973), with the largest proportion of admissions being young children. Studies were done on levels of exposure of pregnant women and their children exposed as fetuses, and of infants who consumed breast milk of exposed mothers. Newborn children had much higher levels of methyl mercury than their mothers, showing not only that mercury crossed the placental barrier but also that the fetus actually accumulated the metal, and that prenatal exposure rather than breast milk caused the worst contamination. Many of the children born had outward signs of brain damage. Unfortunately, due to circumstances, follow-up of exposed populations, notably those exposed in utero, was not possible. Among the other lessons learned from this outbreak and the detailed study of human exposure that was carried out was the finding that urinary levels could not predict exposure, and blood measures were the most reliable indicators.[2]

The Minamata disaster is probably the most notorious case of mercury poisoning across populations and led to the coining of the eponymous term "Minamata disease." The extensive contamination that occurred on more than one occasion, in at least three different sites, led to thousands of deaths (Eto, 1997; Eto, Marumoto, & Takeya, 2010). The first cases appeared in Minamata Bay in Kumamoto Prefecture, Japan between 1953 and 1956. The history of the outbreak and the time taken to confirm consumption of shellfish and fish as the cause make chilling reading. It is a classic case of industry not only refusing to take responsibility but also taking advantage of scientific debate and arguing lack of proof as a reason for inaction. One of the first doctors to describe the disease worked at the hospital run by the factory causing the contamination, which had been producing vinyl products since the 1930s. In his first reports to the owners, he suggested that contaminated fish might be at the root of the problem, but the employers censored the information and put the blame on rotting fish.

By 1956 the disease was rife, affecting not only humans but also local domestic and wild animals. So a five-man committee was set up to investigate (Eto et al., 2010). They started by carrying out autopsies on humans and examinations of cats showing signs of neuronal disease. The neurological symptoms strongly suggested heavy metal poisoning, and a series of candidates from arsenic to copper were considered, but not mercury, although the very distinctive features of mercury poisoning had been known since the 19th century. It was not until 3 years later that one of the members of the committee made the connection with a description of the neuropathology of work-related mercury poisoning in humans that had been published 5 years earlier by two English toxicologists, Hunter and Russell (1954). Incidentally, the first author on this paper wrote a remarkable treatise on occupational disease, recommended by Clarkson (2002), himself a specialist on mercury toxicology, a recommendation I heartily endorse.

The pathologist, Hosokawa, who made the initial connection with mercury, confirmed mercury as the causative agent by carrying out experiments on cats. The source of the mercury was found to be the local factory, which had been producing vinyl for over 20 years. However, in 1951 the company had changed the manufacturing processes, introducing a mercury-based compound as a catalyst for synthesis for one of the compounds. As was usual at the time, the waste, which contained inorganic mercury, went straight out into the sea, contaminated the fish by a mechanism that was not then understood, and from there entered the bodies and brains of the workers and their families who ate the fish. But it was not until 1968 that the company in Minamata stopped

---

2  Another very interesting piece of information included in the article is that the average weight of an adult living in rural Iraq in 1972 was 51 kg. Small wonder they were reluctant to throw away the grain destined for planting.

dumping the waste in the bay, and mercury contamination dropped slowly. Even after 1968 and after the levels dropped, fish was still not safe for eating. Court cases and political debate dragged on for years, until finally, in 1971, the company started paying some compensation, by which time many victims were dead.

Autopsies carried out on Minamata disaster victims led to detailed characterization of neurological abnormalities according to the age, duration, and extent of methyl mercury exposure. Fetal contamination was characterized by general hypoplasia of the brain. A case of a girl who was exposed for many years as an infant in the early 1950s showed later general loss of coordination and onset of mania and seizures, with the poisoning causing her death at the age of 20. Needless to say, in all cases, brain morphology showed major alterations, especially in the cortex and cerebellum. As related by Grandjean and colleagues (Grandjean, Satoh, Murata, & Eto, 2010), the fact that Japanese parents often keep a piece of their child's umbilical cord for good luck was providential in helping some families prove the connection of their child's disease with the contamination, but it also permitted scientists to determine the relationship between degree of exposure and intellectual disability. Those with the highest levels were severely affected and easily diagnosed with Minamata disease, while those with levels in between controls and high levels had just "standard" intellectual disability. Of course, it would normally have been very difficult to prove that the reason a child who was slower, or even much slower, to learn than other children was because he or she was brain damaged due to environmental exposure. The demonstration relied on the umbilical cord data and unambiguously consolidated the concept that the effects of exposure were most severe if experienced in utero. The particularly sensitive nature of the fetal brain to mercury poisoning was also demonstrated in Swedish studies carried out in the 1950s, again cited by Grandjean et al. (2010). In this case the cause was similar to the Iraq poisonings, grain treated with mercury-based fungicides, but this time used for making porridge. A pregnant mother and one infant ate the porridge regularly, but it was the unborn child who was the most affected.

Among the lessons learned from these and other studies is that methyl mercury exposure can also be continual and surreptitious, and that the earlier the exposure, the worse the effects. Different forms of mercury can be by-products of multiple industrial processes, notably the wood pulp industry and factories that use mercury electrodes. Discharges can enter freshwater and seawater, where bacteria in sediment can transform inorganic mercury to methyl mercury. This methyl mercury can then enter the food chain through fish. This is the process that was causing the accumulation of mercury in Minamata Bay fish, and it is also the process that leads to widespread mercury contamination in most fish today (Fig. 1.2).

In their very readable account of the adverse effects of environmental mercury, including those of the Minamata disease, Phillippe Grandjean and colleagues (2010) describe the clinical symptoms of mercury poisoning, among them the constriction of the visual field (tunnel vision) and deafness. They cite

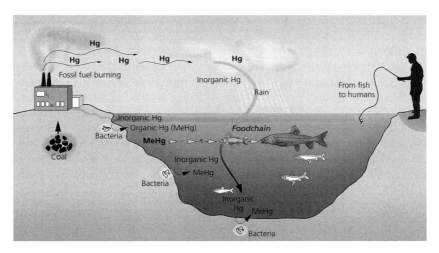

**Figure 1–2.** The cycle of mercury production, organification, and entry into the food chain. Various industrial sites such as coal-fired power plants produce inorganic mercury. Mercury enters the atmosphere and contaminates water supplies. Bacteria in riverbeds and ocean sediment transform inorganic mercury into the organic form, methyl mercury, which is incorporated into the first elements of the food chain. It is then concentrated in tissues of successive predatory fish species and fish consumers, including humans. One of the deleterious actions of mercury in humans (and other vertebrates) is through its interaction with selenium, a substance needed to activate thyroid hormones (see Chapter 2).

a Japanese author who pointed out the remarkable and unfortunate parallels between these and other symptoms of the disease (lack of coordination, forgetfulness, mental retardation) and those displayed by the authorities dealing with the problem. Clearly, today such levels of toxicity as seen in Iraq and Minamata are rare and if found are usually the result of acute, accidental exposure. What is of more current concern are the consequences of long-term exposure to lower levels of different forms of mercury, particularly prenatal exposure. As mentioned earlier and explained in detail in the next chapter, mercury, through interaction with selenium—a component of the enzymes that activate TH—reduces availability of TH, a hormone critically required for all stages of brain development. Thus, mercury, especially methyl mercury, even at low levels, remains a problem today, with coal-fired power plants being major sources (Fig. 1.2).

The economic costs of current prenatal methyl mercury contamination were estimated in a European study published in 2013 (Bellanger et al., 2013). Mercury exposure was calculated from measuring the amounts of the element in samples of hair from nearly 2,000 women of child-bearing age in 17 EU countries. Hair accumulates various metals and metabolites and is often use in forensic, clinical, and research studies as a noninvasive means of assessing exposure. Data from the literature on nearly 7,000 samples were also included. Distinct differences were found in levels of contamination across Europe. The mean level was 0.46 µg mercury/g hair, with the highest levels found in southern countries, particularly Greece and Spain (all with mean levels greater that 1 µg/g) and lowest in countries in Eastern Europe, notably Romania, Bulgaria, and Hungary (means below 0.07 µg/g). Levels in hair allowed the authors to calculate how many children were born with mercury levels in excess of the recommended limits and hence to calculate IQ loss across populations. Detailed analysis on hair, cord blood mercury levels, and IQ loss has been obtained in studies in the Faroe Islands, where occasional consumption of pilot whale meat leads to high intake. These Europe-wide calculations on the economic consequences of IQ loss led to a conservative estimate of between 8 to 9 billion euros per year.

## Lead and Alcohol: The Ever-Present Neurotoxins

By way of introduction to the tremendous social and economic burden of diminished intellectual potential, we discuss two other factors well known to cause irreversible damage to the developing brain, for which economic models have long been available, namely lead and alcohol.

## Lead

The adverse effects of acute and chronic lead poisoning on mental capacity, reasoning, and behavior have been documented since Roman times. The history of human use and misuse of lead is filled with accounts of inadvertent or acknowledged lead poisoning, and current debate focuses on the long-term effects of low-level exposure, particularly in urban settings (Gilbert & Weiss, 2006; Lucchini et al., 2012; Mielke, Gonzales, Powell, & Mielke, 2013). The tale of use of lead containers and pipes as a factor contributing to the fall of the Roman Empire may well be a fallacy, but a sweetening agent, sapa, used in food and wine, was made by prolonged cooking in lead containers producing sweet-tasting lead compounds. Consumption of sapa could have contributed to the various health problems of the Roman elite, including impaired fertility (Riva, Lafranconi, D'Orso, & Cesana, 2012). Moving from conjecture to fact, the negative correlation of higher blood lead levels in children with diminished intellectual capacity has been firmly established in the last decades (Gilbert & Weiss, 2006). There is no safe level for lead exposure. Risk is greatest for children under the age of 7, and lead exposure can be aggravated by malnutrition, particularly lack of calcium. Currently, the US Environmental Protection Agency (EPA) and the Centers for Disease Control and Prevention (CDC) consider that lead blood levels over 10 µg per deciliter (dL) are cause for concern (Patterson, 1965). However, this cutoff level is questioned. Many scientists in the field of neurotoxicity and environmental health have proposed that the level of concern should be reduced to 2 µg/dL (Gilbert & Weiss, 2006), a recommendation that was supported by an advisory committee to the CDC in 2012. Publicly accessible CDC exposure tables show that current national averages in the United States are around or just below that level and have been decreasing since 1999, but exposure varies significantly in rural versus urban areas and within cities (Mielke et al., 2013).

The major environmental causes of lead toxicity in children have been the use of lead in paints and the introduction in the 1930s of lead in gasoline (petrol). Many authors have provided accounts of the discovery of the connection between lead paint and neurological problems linked to exposure, whether from house paint, toys, or even sweets (candy) in the first years of the 20th century (Riva et al., 2012). A riveting account of the decades of battles between the public health authorities and the lead industry is provided by Markowitz, Rosner, and Fund (2013). This book follows on from their earlier one on industrial complicity in marketing products containing known toxins (Markowitz & Rosner, 2002) and analyzes the power play between the different protagonists and how we today can, hopefully, learn from the dramatic story. They relate how a century of lead poisoning from paint and petrol has caused neurotoxicity, brain damage and behavioral problems in generations of children.[3] Their story also reviews many scientific papers showing that even though the effects of low lead exposures may not be as dramatic as acute poisoning, they can induce significant adverse effects on behavior and scholastic achievement, particularly if they occur during early development. They and others have reviewed the history of the introduction of lead into gasoline, the lies from industry producing the (unnecessary) lead-based ethyl additive, and the campaigns driven by the public and scientists to ban it. While working for General Motors (GM), Thomas Midgley Jr. discovered the supposed beneficial effect of adding tetra-ethylene lead (TEL) as an antiknock agent to petrol in 1921. Later, still working for GM but in their Frigidaire department, he developed the use of chlorofluorocarbon (CFC) or Freon as a cooling agent. Of course, Freon and other CFCs became widely used not only in refrigerators but in aerosols and inhalers, and CFCs became one of the major contributors to the ozone hole. For these two inventions Midgley was much lauded in his time and became a member of the National Academy of Science. However, given the disastrous global and long-term consequences of the uses of TEL and Freon, he has posthumously been described by numerous authors as the most damaging single organism to have ever existed. One of the most readable accounts of his life and death, aptly due to his own inventions, is that by Bill Bryson (2003). The toxic properties of TEL were well known to GM; workers died after suffering hallucinations and even Midgley was poisoned while doing a demonstration of the product's supposedly innocuous nature and needed a year's medical leave.

---

3   It is interesting to note that the mechanisms underlying the neurotoxicity of lead are not fully established even today. Certain authors consider, that like mercury, many of the effects could implicate sequestration of selenium, an element needed for production and activation of thyroid hormone (See Chapter 2, Section on Deiodinases and Selenium).

Scientists raised concerns about several issues, and the death of workers in the plant producing the TEL led to a conference led by the US Public Health Department in 1925. But TEL was put on the market and universal lead contamination rose inexorably.

But it was not only lead that was added to the petrol. To stop the accumulation of lead and lead oxide damaging the engine, chemical scavengers had to be added to the mixture. The most appropriate compounds contain reactive halogens, bromine and chlorine, and were added in the form of dicholorethane and dibromoethane. This step could be seen as adding evil to evil. We will return regularly to these halogenated compounds containing bromine, chlorine, and their sister element fluorine, in the context of pesticides, plasticizers, surfactants, and, most notoriously, flame retardants. All of these halogenated chemicals have different capacities to interfere with TH signaling in various ways, as TH is the only naturally occurring biological compound to contain a halogen, iodine. The significance of this point will be discussed in detail in the next chapter.

It has been suggested that the drive to develop brominated flame retardants came from the bromine industry, which needed to find an outlet for its products when the legislation on removing TEL (with its brominated additive) from petrol came into effect. Certainly the phase-out of one was simultaneous with the introduction of the other. The phase-out of lead petrol began in the 1970s. The appearance of brominated flame retardants on the market began at the end of that decade and has since amplified. Brominated flame retardants (BFRs) and their chlorinated relatives are among the most aggressive TH-disrupting chemicals currently accumulating in the environment. Not only do BFRs interfere with TH action in the brain and other parts of the body but bromine released during metabolism can inhibit iodine uptake by the thyroid (Pavelka, 2004), particularly in situations where there is insufficient iodine supply.

Public and governmental awareness of the potential problems of environmental contamination, particularly in urban environments, caused by leaded petrol increased in the 1960s and early 1970s. A decisive publication appeared in 1965 showing that the high levels of lead found in developed nations were of industrial origin and the author argued for controls on lead in petrol and other sources (Patterson, 1965). In the mid-1960s, debates and Congressional hearings were held in the United States (that incidentally led to the creation of the EPA), and international bodies such as the World Health Organization and the Organization for Economic Cooperation and Development published damning reports and data sets on levels of lead exposure. However, as related by the two US public health experts, Markowitz and Rosner (Markowitz et al., 2013), the industrial ploys used to hide incriminating evidence managed to delay significantly the phase-out of leaded petrol, in the same way they had previously, deferring removal of lead paint and denying responsibility. The US government chose to deal with the problems by encouraging, from 1970 on, the development of new car engines that could run on unleaded petrol. Japan, no doubt sensitized by the Minamata scandal, was the first country to put a limit on the use of lead in petrol in 1971, an example followed by the United States, which phased it out between 1972 and 1986. Consequently, lead levels in the US population had dropped by 78% by 1991. The Canadian factory producing TEL closed in 1992. But the European Union did not phase out leaded petrol until 2000, the same year as China (Luo, Ruan, Yan, Yin, & Chen, 2012). Production continues in other parts of the world and motorists can even still buy "lead boosters" to add to their petrol to make it leaded again (http://www.tetraboost.com). Many national and international organizations, such as the Australian anti-lead association (http://www.lead.org.au), are actively campaigning against the sale of this product and that of leaded petrol in countries where it is still legal.

However, removing leaded petrol from the market, although a significant factor in reducing lead pollution and children's exposure, has not eliminated all the risk in industrialized countries. In the United States children in many areas are still exposed to levels above the 10 μg/dL level of concern (Mielke et al., 2012) and such levels can be associated not only with small decreases in intellectual capacity but also with behavioral disorders and social problems. Even in a group of adolescents with lead levels around 2 μg/dL, a twofold increase in blood lead, for instance from 1.5 to 3 μg/dL, was associated with a reduction of 2.4 IQ points (Lucchin et al., 2012). As reported by Luo et al. (2012), in China, children considered "unexposed" have lead levels above 5 μg/dL, whereas children diagnosed with ADHD show an average not that much higher, 8.5 μg/dL, still under the current, 10 μg/dL, level of concern. Mielke and colleagues have analyzed the relationship between changes in atmospheric lead and the incidence of violent crime (aggravated assault) committed by young people exposed as children (Mielke & Zahran, 2012). Their model correlates increases and decreases in atmospheric lead with changing rates of assault committed 22 years later.

Most studies have calculated the benefit of removing lead from petrol and thus reducing exposure, but few have attempted to calculate the cost of the 60 years of maximal exposure in the United States or the 80 or more years in other parts of the world. One of the first cost/benefit analyses was carried out by the EPA and published in 1985.[4] Interestingly, besides the central concern for children's health (especially small children, infants, and the unborn fetus), they mention the potential benefits of reducing hypertension and cardiovascular disorders in adults. The EPA also took into account that reducing lead in petrol should reduce engine corrosion and therefore maintenance and replacement costs to the owner. Not surprising that the car industry was in favor of maintaining lead. To cut a long story short (the report totaled 495 pages!), the net benefit was $35 billion (in 1983 values with the blood pressure and heart disease component included). More recently the United Nations carried out the same exercise on a global scale, taking into account that many countries are still in the grip of leaded petrol. In October 2011,

4  http://yosemite.epa.gov/ee/epa/eerm.nsf/vwan/ee-0034-1.pdf/. . . /ee-0034-1.pdf

they announced the results of a study that had calculated the multiple benefits of a global phase-out, reducing intellectual damage, cardiovascular disease, and criminality, would amount to $2.4 trillion saved per year (4% of global gross domestic product). In their report they refer to WHO statistics showing that in developing countries between 15 and 18 million children were affected by brain damage caused by leaded petrol. It is worth noting that in all these studies on leaded petrol, it is impossible to unravel the effects that are caused by lead itself and those that could be due to the brominated additives that could be targeting TH signaling more directly. Given that the increase in autism seen in the United States has increased most significantly since the removal of leaded petrol from the environment, one has to ask which other environmental pollutants are implicated. Clearly, the increased use of brominated chemicals, such as flame retardants, has to be taken into account. The UN report also underlines that rather than being a burden on economies, taking environmentally favorable actions produces national and international benefits at multiple levels, and hopefully such arguments will inform current governmental decisions.

Alcohol Consumption

Today, the deleterious effects of alcohol in pregnancy are exceedingly well known, and women are continually warned about the risks of drinking alcohol during pregnancy; indeed, fetal alcohol syndrome (FAS) causes distinct craniofacial morphologies and marked intellectual disability. Amazingly, despite the fact that alcohol production is probably as old as the introduction of agriculture in the Neolithic period, and the dangers were known to the Greeks (sources in Rietschel & Treutlein, 2013), and although the thalidomide tragedy brought the concept of fetal vulnerability to light, the consequences of drinking alcohol during pregnancy only became a subject of public health concern in the 1980s (West & Blake, 2005). In the United States an official warning was made in 1981 and pictorial labels were placed on alcoholic drinks contraindicating consumption during pregnancy from 1986 on. Prior to this period, the placenta was erroneously thought by many practitioners to protect the fetus from toxins.

The costs of caring for a child affected with FAS gave rise to the term "million dollar baby." FAS differs from generalized environmental pollution as the effects on the individual can be seen immediately and easily associated with maternal behavior. It is not only the fact that FAS is another well-documented preventable cause of intellectual disability that brings alcohol into the discussion; the second reason is that it has been hypothesized that some of the effects of alcohol on brain development, like PCBs, mercury, and certain pesticides, implicate interference with TH signaling.

Even today, the molecular and cellular mechanisms through which alcohol causes the outwardly recognizable deformations of the head and face and the equally marked intellectual damage are still not clarified. One interesting theory derives from the observation that chronic alcohol consumption reduces circulating TH levels (Zoeller, Fletcher, Simonyl, & Rudeen, 1996). Given that maternal TH levels and then the child's TH are essential for all stages of brain development, this alcohol-induced reduction in TH could be a major contributor to FAS. Furthermore, the symptoms of FAS parallel those of prenatal and postnatal hypothyroidism (lack of thyroid hormone) at every level: behavior, cognition, and neurological changes, including changes in cellular and synaptic organization. One can also draw parallels with the fact that iodine lack, which causes hypothyroidism and intellectual deficits, and FAS are the two most common *preventable* causes of mental retardation.

Eva Redei, working in the Department of Psychiatry and Behavior at the University of Chicago, has been studying similarities between FAS and hypothyroidism for over 10 years. Her team has shown that prenatal TH treatment can reverse some of the behavioral effects of in utero alcohol exposure in rats (Wilcoxon, Kuo, Disterhoft, & Redei, 2005). More recently she has focused on how alcohol could affect the enzymes that determine TH availability in the brain. Her team has shown that alcohol given to gestating rats reduces the amounts of TH generated in specific areas of the brain, including the hippocampus, a structure implicated in memory and learning and one of the brain regions most affected in FAS. More disquieting is that, in the male pups, expression of the genes controlling TH availability in the hippocampus was modified in the long term by epigenetic mechanisms (see Chapter 7). Tom Zoeller, well known for his detailed work on PCBs and TH action in the brain, also examined the effects of alcohol exposure during prenatal development. He observed that giving alcohol to pregnant rats specifically decreased expression of receptors for TH in the hippocampus and cortex of the pups (Scott, Sun, & Zoeller, 1998), providing another link between prenatal alcohol exposure and alteration of TH signaling.

The societal cost of FAS per individual affected varies according to the degree of severity. Some levels of prenatal alcohol exposure (PAE) may not produce the characteristic features of FAS, but the children will still be affected and potentially diagnosed with fetal alcohol spectrum disorder (FASD). The intellectual disability and the health care costs will be largely proportional. A recent US study placed the frequency of FAS or FASD at between 1 and 10 births per thousand. The Canadian government follows FAS statistics and costs closely. In one of the most recent analyses using data from 2008–2009, the authors estimated just the cost of hospital care (emergency and psychiatric services, etc.), services that are disproportionally used by FAS children and adolescents. They underline that both diagnosis and hospital care related to FAS were probably underreported, and taking this into account, estimate costs due to FAS at up to $48 million (Canadian dollars) per year. A calculation taking in factors such as education, medication, social care, and lost productivity brings the estimated total costs to the Canadian government per annum to $5 billion (Stade et al., 2009). Prenatal counseling of vulnerable populations, particularly women who have given birth to a child with FAS, has obvious economic benefits.

Societal Costs of Environmental Pollution Exposure and
Neurodevelopmental Defects and Behavioral Disorders

Moving on from the costs of individual factors (such as lead and alcohol) that
can be modeled from data on blood levels and incidence and severity of symptoms, we address the larger picture of the overall economic and health care burden of environmental pollution on intellectual capacity and behavior. For those
interested in costs specifically related to ASD and ADHD, Chapter 7 (Box 7.1)
provides figures on current spending in the United States and United Kingdom
on these disorders.

Two studies, both published more than 10 years ago, addressed these difficult questions (Landrigan, Schechter, Lipton, Fahs, & Schwartz, 2002; Muir &
Zegarac, 2001). In 2002, Landrigan and colleagues analyzed the percentage of pediatric disease and associated costs that could be attributed to environmental causes. They chose four categories of diseases for which scientific
evidence showed an association with pollution: lead poisoning, asthma, childhood cancer, and neurobehavioral disorders. First of all, they emphasized that
as infectious diseases of childhood have decreased, the main morbidities are
now multifactorial noncommunicative diseases, often with a strong environmental component. As might be expected at that time, the greatest proportion of the overall health costs attributable to pollution was still lead poisoning.
Environmental sources were considered to account for 100% of lead toxicity, at
a cost of $43 billion per annum. For cancer and asthma the environmental con-
tributions were determined to be 3% and 30%, respectively. Using data from
2000, the calculated contribution of environmental factors to neurobehavioral disorders ranged between 5% and 20%, with the best estimate being 10%,
bringing total costs to $9.2 billion. Combining the environmental contribu-
tion to expenditure on all categories came to a figure that the authors said was
a conservative estimate, of over $55 billion, about 3% of total US health care
spending at that time. Landrigan and colleagues stressed in 2002 that unless
something was done to prevent environmental pollution and improve testing
of chemicals that these figures would continue to rise. The figures have indeed
risen, although thorough estimates of current costs are difficult to find.

Muir and Zegarac's paper (2001) was the outcome of an international workshop on Methodologies for Community Health Assessment. The workshop
chose to tackle the problem by taking four main categories of disease with
strong evidence for environmental causation and looking beyond immediate
health care costs at a given age. The first two disorders to be analyzed were
diabetes and Parkinson's disease; the others that could potentially have been
grouped together were neurodevelopmental effects and hypothyroidism on
the one hand and deficits in IQ on the other. They focused their very detailed
data analysis on the United States and Canada. The cumulative costs, which
took into account a spread of economic considerations including impact on
social services and lost GDP, were enormous, reaching between $568 and
$793 billion per year, in the two countries. Grouping hypothyroidism and

neurodevelopmental disorders with IQ loss showed these categories to account for about $500 billion per year for the United States alone, representing the far greater proportion of the total.

It should be noted that their study was published in 2001, analyzing data that were available up until 1999/2000, well before the large increases in various developmental disorders, including ASD, were registered. In fact, although they reveal an interesting statistic, that the number of children with special needs requiring tailored educational programs due to learning disabilities increased by 191% in 15 years up to 1994, and that in Canada approximately 12% of children had some form of cognitive deficit, it is probable that if they were to update their analysis today, the sum would be far greater. Their analytical method allowed them to calculate the economic cost of the "dumbing down" of society by a 5-point loss in IQ (as illustrated in Fig. 1.1). This came out at over a staggering $300 billion per year (for Canada and the United States together). In fact, going further, they went back to data on IQ, education attainment, probability of participation in the workforce, and earnings capacity, and thereby calculated the economic consequence of a loss as a function of single IQ point, arriving at a figure of between $55 and $65 billion per annum/per IQ point (in 1999 US dollars). One of their tables recapitulates the well-documented consequences of small reductions in intellectual capacity on a spread of educational and social outcomes. They cite 3-point IQ reductions as being associated with over 20% increases in childhood poverty and general poverty, high school dropout rates and prison populations. This statistic echoes the example of reduction in atmospheric lead and the correlated decrease in violent crime two decades later (Mielke & Zahran, 2012), and it could be discussed in the light of wider statistics on the disproportionally high representation of people with educational difficulties and behavioral problems in prison populations.

Independently of these figures and analyses, it should be fairly obvious to most people that today, even more so than in the past, a nation's economic potential is largely dependent on its intellectual and educative capacity. Even though manufacturing capital can replace human capital to some extent, it is not limitless. Such arguments date as far back as the 18th century, and probably beyond. John Howard (1726–1790), a British philanthropist active in prison reform and public health, pointed out that the diseases of the poor affect the rich. He pragmatically showed, altruism aside, the rich could benefit by ensuring better social care of the more vulnerable. His arguments can be usefully reiterated today. The current increase in intellectually disabled children with ASD and people dependent on family and society is accompanied by a decrease in those actively contributing to society and innovation. Brain power is a nation's future.

Societal consequences go further than this. Not only are more and more people with intellectual disability or a behavioral disorder dependent on others for their day-to-day needs and care, but we are also continually removing from the work environment low-skilled jobs and manual employment possibilities. Without adopting a Luddite stance against progress, one can argue that some of these job categories could offer constructive means for people with mild to moderate intellectual disabilities to obtain social insertion, providing them with recognition of their role in the social fabric, an essential part of the human condition. Creation or reintroduction of the human element in agriculture, care of animals, and production of goods would have multiple benefits. Besides the increased sense of worth for the persons contributing, the reduction of pesticide use (which can actually increase productivity; Pimentel, 2012) and less intensive production of animals for human consumption, with potential reduction of antibiotic use, would all contribute to both a more resilient environment and a healthier population. Too simplistic and idealistic? Maybe, but the time is ripe for serious debate and decisions to move in these directions.

They Told Us So

The genesis of ideas is difficult to trace. But the notion that environmental pollution is affecting the intellectual potential and behavior of children has been raised repeatedly in the last three decades, sometimes, though not always, in connection with TH signaling. The following list of contributors is deliberately short, and many other important actors will be mentioned in the following chapters as the arguments unfold. I hope I have not offended anyone in the field by not including them in this handful of examples.

Bernard Weiss, now 87 years old, but still very active in the field (2009, 2011), has to be cited as one of the pioneers in demonstrating relationships between neurobehavioral disorders and unnecessary, easily preventable, environmental factors. After studying English literature and psychology, he moved into psychopharmacology and then, neurotoxicity. After mercury and Minamata, food additives became a focal point, and his first papers on the subject date from 1979 (Weiss, Cox, Young, Margen, & Williams, 1979); from the start, they caused a fair bit of debate, even controversy (Weiss, 1980). He refers to his and others' contributions to the field in an exchange of correspondence published in 2008 (Weiss, 2008). The exchange appeared in *Environmental Health Perspectives*, a high-ranking journal supported by many US institutions related to public health and environmental issues, including the National Institutes of Health (NIH) and the National Institute of Environmental Health Sciences (NIEHS). In this commentary he makes reference to his work on food coloring that, although funded by the Food and Drug Administration (FDA), was not taken fully into account in decision making by the FDA and other authorities. On the subject of risks and benefits (which in the case of food coloring are certainly not major), Weiss aptly cites (2009) Philip Handler, a biochemist and nutritionist, who became president of the US National Academy of Science as saying, "A sensible guide would be to reduce exposure to hazard whenever possible, to accept substantial hazard only for great benefit, and no hazard at all when the benefit seems relatively trivial." This is a wise maxim that could well be applied to many environmental contaminants today.

Theo Colborn was one of the driving forces behind bringing together the experts that contributed to the World Wildlife Fund (WWF) Wingspread

Consensus Statement in 1993, which resulted from a workshop organized in 1991. This statement formally articulated the global problem of endocrine disruption, with respect to "alterations in sexual development" in both wildlife and humans. The Wingspread statement was also constructed to emphasize the idea that developmental exposure could lead to disease later in life (Colborn, vom Saal, & Soto, 1993). As most of the original work on endocrine disruption had focused on reproductive problems in wildlife and humans, the principal concern at the time was chemicals that interfere with the two main classes of receptors that control reproduction—the receptors for the steroids estrogen and androgen. Like TH, estrogen and androgen control gene expression by acting through nuclear receptors (NRs) that control gene transcription (see Box 1.1). While co-writing the book *Our Stolen Future*, Theo became aware of the work of the Jacobsons on PCBs and included in the statement the risk of chemical pollution to intellectual achievement and behavior. Since then, regular articles by Philip Landrigan, a public health specialist often co-authoring with Philippe Grandjean (2006), who is particularly knowledgable about mercury and lead pollution, over the last 10 years have been alerting the scientific community and authorities to the neurotoxic actions of environmental chemicals and the consequences for children's behavioral development.

One of the most informed and active critics of flame-retardant policy is Arlene Blum. A scientist and mountaineer, she was one of the first to show the mutagenic effects of a flame retardant back in the late 1970s. At that time she and other chemists demonstrated the mutagenic properties of Tris (TDCPP) (Gold, Blum & Ames, 1978), a product then used in children's pyjamas. Finding out that it is still employed today in household furnishings and articles destined for use around babies and children brought her back into the field. Her contributions are discussed in Chapter 6 on mixtures of flame retardants. Flame retardants will surface regularly in the discussion and are probably some of the major contributors to unnecessary and harmful environmental contamination, particularly in urban settings, but unfortunately, given their persistence, also worldwide.

Take-Home Messages and Future Research Needs

- The exposure data show that the prenatal period of brain growth is exceedingly sensitive to chemical pollution.
- As TH is needed to regulate genes involved in brain development and TH signaling is sensitive to numerous environmental contaminants, TH signaling represents a crossroads between environmental factors and brain gene expression.
- Many cases of chemical pollution affecting TH signaling have been shown to cause brain damage and/or reduction in intellectual capacity in exposed individuals. But it is only by analyzing results across populations, and rarely in individuals, that the relationships can be brought to light.
- Many known causes of loss of intellectual capacity can be prevented.

- A small downward shift in IQ across a population can have major socioeconomic consequences. The benefits of removing lead from petrol in the remaining countries that use it has been estimated at trillions of US dollars per annum, including reduction of criminality, allowing redirection of financial and human potential.
- Some of the major potential culprits, such as lead, that could be associated with intellectual impairment are currently declining. Thus, the central question becomes: Which of the more recently introduced environmental factors are interacting with physiological and genetic regulations, confusing and deflecting brain developmental programs, thereby contributing to the rise in ADHD and ASD?

## REFERENCES

Anonymous. (2012). Prevalence of autism spectrum disorders--Autism and Developmental Disabilities Monitoring Network, 14 sites, United States, 2008. *Morbidity and Mortality Weekly Surveillance Summaries*, *61*(3), 1–19.

Bakir, F., Damluji, S. F., Amin-Zaki, L., Murtadha, M., Khalidi, A., al-Rawi, N. Y.,...Doherty, R. A. (1973). Methylmercury poisoning in Iraq. *Science*, *181*(4096), 230–241.

Bellanger, M., Pichery, C., Aerts, D., Berglund, M., Castaño, A., Cejchanová, M.,...DEMO/COPHES. (2013). Economic benefits of methylmercury exposure control in Europe: Monetary value of neurotoxicity prevention. *Environmental Health*, *12*(1), 3.

Bryson, B. (2003). *A short history of nearly everything*. London, UK: Black Swan.

Clarkson, T. W. (2002). The three modern faces of mercury. *Environmental Health Perspectives*, *110*(Suppl 1), 11–23.

Colborn, T., vom Saal, F. S., & Soto, A. M. (1993). Developmental effects of endocrine-disrupting chemicals in wildlife and humans. *Environmental Health Perspectives*, *101*(5), 378–384.

Eto, K. (1997). Pathology of Minamata disease. *Toxicology and Pathology*, *25*(6), 614–623.

Eto, K., Marumoto, M., & Takeya, M. (2010). The pathology of methylmercury poisoning (Minamata disease). *Neuropathology*, epub ahead of print.

Gilbert, S. G., & Weiss, B. (2006). A rationale for lowering the blood lead action level from 10 to 2 microg/dL. *Neurotoxicology*, *27*(5), 693–701.

Gold, M. D., Blum, A., & Ames, B. N. (1978) Another flame retardant, tris-(1,3-dic hloro-2-propyl)-phosphate, and its expected metabolites are mutagens. *Science*, *20*(200), 785–787.

Grandjean, P., & Landrigan, P. J. (2006). Developmental neurotoxicity of industrial chemicals. *Lancet*, *368*(9553), 2167–2178.

Grandjean, P., Satoh, H., Murata, K., & Eto, K. (2010). Adverse effects of methylmercury: Environmental health research implications. *Environmental Health Perspectives*, *118*(8), 1137–1145.

Hunter, D., & Russell, D. S. (1954). Focal cerebellar and cerebellar atrophy in a human subject due to organic mercury compounds. *Journal of Neurology, Neurosurgery, and Psychiatry*, *17*(4), 235–241.

Jacobson, J. L., & Jacobson, S. W. (1996). Intellectual impairment in children exposed to polychlorinated biphenyls in utero. *New England Journal of Medicine, 335*(11), 783–789.

Jacobson, J. L., Jacobson, S. W., & Humphrey, H. E. (1990). Effects of in utero exposure to polychlorinated biphenyls and related contaminants on cognitive functioning in young children. *Journal of Pediatrics, 116*(1), 38–45.

Kern, J. K., Geier, D. A., Audhya, T., King, P. G., Sykes, L. K., & Geier, M. R. (2012). Evidence of parallels between mercury intoxication and the brain pathology in autism. *Acta Neurobiologiae Experimentalis (Wars), 72*(2), 113–153.

Landrigan, P. J., Schechter, C. B., Lipton, J. M., Fahs, M. C., & Schwartz, J. (2002). Environmental pollutants and disease in American children: Estimates of morbidity, mortality, and costs for lead poisoning, asthma, cancer, and developmental disabilities. *Environmental Health Perspectives, 110*(7), 721.

Lucchini, R. G., Zoni, S., Guazzetti, S., Bontempi, E., Micheletti, S., Broberg, K.,...Smith, D. R. (2012). Inverse association of intellectual function with very low blood lead but not with manganese exposure in Italian adolescents. *Environmental Research, 118*, 65–71.

Luo, W., Ruan, D., Yan, C., Yin, S., & Chen, J. (2012). Effects of chronic lead exposure on functions of nervous system in Chinese children and developmental rats. *Neurotoxicology, 33*(4), 862–871.

Markowitz, G. E., & Rosner, D. (2002). *Deceit and denial: The deadly politics of industrial pollution.* Berkeley: University of California Press.

Markowitz, G. E., Rosner, D., & Fund, M. M. (2013). *Lead wars: The politics of science and the fate of America's children.* Berkeley: University of California Press, Milbank Memorial Fund.

Mielke, H. W., Gonzales, C. R., Powell, E. T., & Mielke, P. W. (2013). Environmental and health disparities in residential communities of New Orleans: The need for soil lead intervention to advance primary prevention. *Environment International, 51*, 73–81.

Mielke, H. W., & Zahran, S. (2012). The urban rise and fall of air lead (Pb) and the latent surge and retreat of societal violence. *Environment International, 43*, 48–55.

Muir, T., & Zegarac, M. (2001). Societal costs of exposure to toxic substances: Economic and health costs of four case studies that are candidates for environmental causation. *Environmental Health Perspectives, 109*(Suppl 6), 885–903.

Patterson, C. C. (1965). Contaminated and natural lead environments of man. *Archives of Environmental Health, 11*, 344–360.

Pavelka, S. (2004). Metabolism of bromide and its interference with the metabolism of iodine. *Physiology Research, 53*(Suppl 1), S81–S90.

Pimentel, D. (2012). Silent Spring, the 50th anniversary of Rachel Carson's book. *BMC Ecology, 12*, 20.

Rietschel, M., & Treutlein, J. (2013). The genetics of alcohol dependence. *Annals of the New York Academy of Science, 1282*, 39–70.

Riva, M. A., Lafranconi, A., D'Orso, M. I., & Cesana, G. (2012). Lead poisoning: Historical aspects of a paradigmatic "occupational and environmental disease." *Safety and Health at Work, 3*(1), 11–16.

Rogan, W. J., & Gladen, B. C. (1985). Study of human lactation for effects of environmental contaminants: The North Carolina Breast Milk and Formula Project and some other ideas. *Environmental Health Perspectives, 60*, 215–221.

Rose, S. P. R. (1998). *From brains to consciousness? Essays on the new sciences of the mind.* Princeton, NJ: Princeton University Press.

Scott, H. C., Sun, G. Y., & Zoeller, R. T. (1998). Prenatal ethanol exposure selectively reduces the mRNA encoding alpha-1 thyroid hormone receptor in fetal rat brain. *Alcohol: Clinical and Experimental Research, 22*(9), 2111–2117.

Stade, B., Ali, A., Bennett, D., Campbell, D., Johnston, M., Lens, C., . . . Koren, G. (2009). The burden of prenatal exposure to alcohol: Revised measurement of cost. *Canadian Journal of Clinical Pharmacology/Journal Canadien de Pharmacologie Clinique, 16*(1), e91–102.

Weintraub, K. (2011). The prevalence puzzle: Autism counts. *Nature, 479*(7371), 22–24.

Weiss, B. (1980). In rebuttal. Food additives and hyperkinesis. *American Journal of Diseases in Childred, 134*(12), 1126–1128.

Weiss, B. (2008). Food additives and hyperactivity. *Environmental Health Perspectives, 116*(6), A240–A241; discussion A241.

Weiss, B. (2009). The first 83 and the next 83: Perspectives on neurotoxicology. *Neurotoxicology, 30*(5), 832–850.

Weiss, B. (2011). Endocrine disruptors as a threat to neurological function. *Journal of the Neurological Sciences, 305*(1–2), 11–21.

Weiss, B., Cox, C., Young, M., Margen, S., & Williams, J. H. (1979). Behavioral epidemiology of food additives. *Neurobehavioral Toxicology, 1*(Suppl 1), 149–155.

West, J. R., & Blake, C. A. (2005). Fetal alcohol syndrome: An assessment of the field. *Experimental Biology and Medicine (Maywood), 230*(6), 354–356.

Wickizer, T. M., Brilliant, L. B., Copeland, R., & Tilden, R. (1981). Polychlorinated biphenyl contamination of nursing mothers' milk in Michigan. *American Journal of Public Health, 71*(2), 132–137.

Wilcoxon, J. S., Kuo, A. G., Disterhoft, J. F., & Redei, E. E. (2005). Behavioral deficits associated with fetal alcohol exposure are reversed by prenatal thyroid hormone treatment: A role for maternal thyroid hormone deficiency in FAE. *Molecular Psychiatry, 10*(10), 961–971.

Zoeller, T. R. (2010). Environmental chemicals targeting thyroid. *Hormones (Athens), 9*(1), 28–40.

Zoeller, R. T., Fletcher, D. L., Simonyl, A., & Rudeen, P. K. (1996). Chronic ethanol treatment reduces the responsiveness of the hypothalamic-pituitary-thyroid axis to central stimulation. *Alcohol: Clinical and Experimental Research, 20*(5), 954–960.

# Chapter 2

# Thyroid Hormone, Iodine, Selenium, and Mercury

CHAPTER OUTLINE

A constant nutritional supply of iodine and selenium is required for brain development in the fetus and child and for normal brain function in the adult. Succinctly put, these elements are essential for the production and activation of thyroid hormone (TH). Iodine is needed to synthesize TH. TH exists in two main forms, thyroxine or $T_4$ (with four atoms of iodine) and the biologically active form, $T_3$ (with three iodine atoms). $T_4$ is transformed into the receptor-binding form, $T_3$, by specialized enzymes, activating deiodinases D1 and D2, which remove an iodine atom from $T_4$. Another deiodinase, D3, can inactivate both $T_4$ and $T_3$. Selenium is a constituent of all three deiodinase enzymes. One of the most common environmental pollutants, mercury, interferes with selenium-based mechanisms and therefore has the potential to interfere with TH signaling by inhibiting deiodinase action. Humans of all ages require TH and therefore need regular supplies of both iodine and selenium. Pregnant women and infants have particularly high requirements for TH and so have even greater needs for iodine and selenium. These increased needs are due to the fact that to develop normally the fetal and postnatal brain needs TH. Pregnant and breast-feeding women should take food supplements that contain iodine. Lack of TH during early development causes mental retardation or intellectual disability. Extreme lack of iodine, and hence lack of TH, causes a particularly severe form of intellectual disability known as cretinism. However, even mild iodine deficiency during pregnancy can have a detrimental effect on the child's cognitive development. As the sea is iodine-rich, many people think that sea salt contains iodine. This idea is totally incorrect. The only form of salt that brings iodine in significant, physiologically useful amounts is iodized salt. These ideas will lead into a concept elaborated in Chapters 3 and 4 that iodine lack can exacerbate the thyroid-disrupting effects of certain chemicals.

Background: Thyroid Hormone, Iodine, and Selenium

TH is produced in the thyroid gland (in humans at the base of the neck) (Fig. 2.1). TH (Fig. 2.2) is formed by the condensation of two aromatic rings (cycles) of tyrosine residues to which iodine atoms are added. The cycle linked to the amino-acid radical is called the inner ring and the other one the outer ring. Each ring can carry two iodine atoms in positions 3 and 5. Two forms of

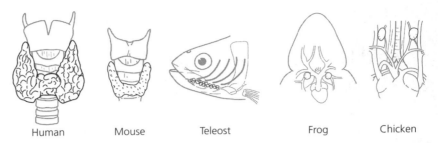

Human          Mouse          Teleost          Frog          Chicken

**Figure 2–1.** Comparative morphology of the thyroid gland. The thyroid gland is a bilobed structure, located at the base of the neck in humans (left). The anatomy of thyroids from a teleost fish, frog, and chicken are shown for comparison.

the hormone are produced by the thyroid gland and both are biologically relevant: thyroxine or 3,5,3′,5′ tetra-iodothyronine also known as $T_4$ that carries four iodine atoms, and the 3,5,3′ tri-iodothyronine or $T_3$ that loses the iodine in position 5′. TH and its derivatives are the only iodine-containing molecules synthetized in vertebrates.

Thyroxine, $T_4$, the major form of TH produced, is considered to be a prohormone and secreted in amounts that largely exceed those of $T_3$. For instance, in humans, it has been estimated that 80% of circulating $T_3$ arises from peripheral deiodination of $T_4$, whereas in rodents it is around 50%.

$T_4$ is converted to the biologically active form, $T_3$, by removal of one iodine atom from the outer ring (see Fig. 2.2). $T_4$ and $T_3$ do not have the same affinity for the thyroid hormone receptors (TRs). $T_3$ has a 10-fold higher affinity than $T_4$ for TRs, hence its consideration as the biologically active compound. $T_3$ binds to TRs in the cell nucleus, where it modifies the expression of target genes. TRs are members of the nuclear receptor family of transcription factors and are encoded by two genes, *THRA* and *THRB* (described in Chapter 3, Fig. 3.1, see Yen, 2001 for review). Deiodination of $T_4$ to active $T_3$ is carried out by highly specific enzymes, deiodinases (see section on "Deiodinases and Selenium"; also see Gereben et al., 2008, for a comprehensive review and Bianco, 2011, for a succinct review). The expression of each of the deiodinases in target tissues is highly regulated, both during development and in the adult according to the cell type and tissue in which they are expressed. Interestingly, as detailed later, all deiodinases contain selenium. Thus, simply put, normal thyroid function requires a constant supply of two rare elements: iodine and selenium.

## Thyroid Hormone Controls Development in All Vertebrates: A Comparative and Historical Perspective

All vertebrates, from fish to amphibians, reptiles, birds, and mammals, including humans, synthesize and use TH. In fact, the appearance of the thyroid gland as an organized follicular structure is coincident with the evolution of the head

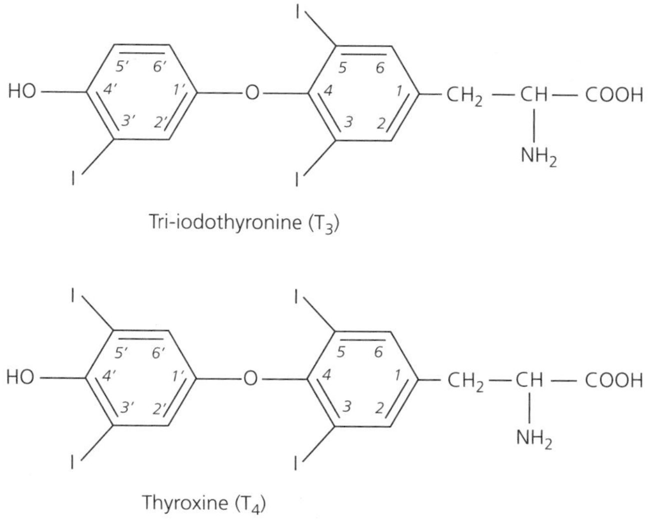

Tri-iodothyronine (T$_3$)

Thyroxine (T$_4$)

**Figure 2–2.** Structure of the thyroid hormones, T$_4$ and T$_3$. The thyroid hormones (THs) have exactly the same chemical structure in all vertebrates (fish, amphibians, reptiles, birds, and mammals, including humans). The two hormones produced by the thyroid, thyroxine (T$_4$) and tri-iodothyronine (T$_3$), are iodinated compounds, iodothyronines. The main iodo-thyronine produced by the thyroid gland is tetra-iodo-thyronine, thyroxine or T$_4$. It has four atoms of iodine. T$_4$ is a prohormone in that to be biologically active, a deiodination step is necessary to remove one iodine atom from the outer thyronine ring, producing tri-iodothyronine or T$_3$.

as seen in the postmetamorphic lamprey, a jawless Craniata. Development of the head in the vertebrates implies not only elaboration of a complex brain structure but also the emergence and coevolution of features that will aid predation. Such characters include compound craniofacial structures such as jaws and myelin to increase speed of nervous transmission along with more complex sensory organs such as eyes and hearing structures. The essential implication of TH in maturation of myelin, bone, and sensory and motor functions in all vertebrates today exemplifies the ancestral role of TH in the development of these cardinal vertebrate structures.

TH is produced and acts in a similar way in each of these animal groups, having exactly the same chemical formula and structure (Fig. 2.2). This common hormone identity is paralleled with high conservation of mode of synthesis, metabolism, action, and regulatory controls throughout all vertebrates. In turn, this high homology of TH signaling across all vertebrate groups has two main consequences. First, any chemical affecting thyroid signaling in one animal group will have a very high probability of exerting detrimental effects in any other species exposed. Second, the high homology means that cells, tissues, and even embryos from one group of vertebrates (e.g., fish or amphibians) can

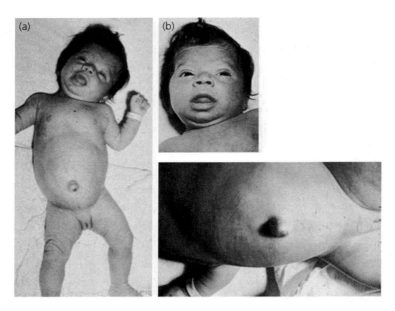

**Figure 2–3.** An example of severe cretinism. (a): A child at age 3 months born with untreated congenital hypothyroidism displaying many features of cretinism including general hypotonicity, affected cranio-facial development (shown in higher detail in b), abdominal swelling and umbilical hernia (shown in higher detail in c). If treatment with thyroxine is not initiated soon after birth, irreversible mental retardation, and permanent skeletal abnormalities result. (Reproduced with permission from Rastogi & LaFranchi, 2010.)

be used as models to test for thyroid signalling-disrupting actions in other groups (e.g., humans).

Throughout vertebrate evolution THs have acquired vital roles in controlling developmental processes and regulating metabolism. The two best examples of the role of TH in development are their actions in controlling brain development in mammals and orchestrating metamorphosis in amphibians. Simply put, without the correct amount of TH at the right moment the human baby becomes (and stays) a cretin (Fig. 2.3) and a tadpole fails to metamorphose into a frog. In adult mammals, TH is also needed to maintain metabolism and to increase heat production in response to cold. A central question for basic research remains that of how exactly the same molecule, TH, can be so essential to development and have such striking, and apparently diverse, effects in different animal groups.

Towards the end of the 19th century some prescient European doctors provided the first demonstrations of the role of the thyroid in controlling both metabolism and brain maturation. In a series of reports, Portuguese and British doctors described the beneficial effects of implanting sheep thyroid, injecting thyroid extract, and later supplying "thyroid tablets" on improving the physical and mental health of patients suffering from severe hypothyroidism, or myxoedema,[1] as it was then called. The links between the thyroid gland and the symptoms these doctors were trying to treat derived from observations of a Swiss surgeon, Kocher, on the negative consequences of surgery to remove large thyroid goiters[2] in patients and from experiments on thyroidectomy in monkeys. In 1891 George Murray injected extract of sheep thyroid into a 46-year-old woman suffering from severe hypothyroidism. Murray describes the mental ("langour"), social ("a disinclination to see strangers"), and physical problems (sensitivity to cold, lack of perspiration and menstruation) of the patient and how the symptoms were reversed by regular injections of sheep thyroid extract. Besides major physical changes, Murray notes that "The speech has become more rapid and fluent. . . She answers questions more readily, the mind has become more active and the memory improved."

These early "clinical trials" were first carried out on adults that had become hypothyroid in later life. Tests were then done on younger subjects who were suffering from cretinism. Cretinism, a severe irreversible condition with mental retardation and physical stunting, is caused by a lack of TH in the first few years of life. The lack of TH itself can be due to untreated sporadic congenital hypothyroidism (CH) (i.e., failure in the fetus to form a fully functional thyroid). However, TH deficiency is often caused by a lack of dietary iodine, iodine being needed to produce TH. Epidemiological data show that both causes are major concerns today. The adolescents first treated by two British doctors in the1890s were probably suffering from CH. Whatever the origin of the lack, the young patients responded well with improvements in growth and mental ability. However, as they had lacked TH in the postnatal period, the period of most rapid brain growth, the mental retardation was irreversible and only moderate improvements in mental ability were seen. One of the doctors reported that giving thyroid tables to a 14-year-old cretin with the "brain condition of a two year-old" had enabled him to be equivalent to a 3-year-old, though he quite rightly predicted that "after the long sleep" his brain had suffered, the damage could never be fully corrected (Railton, 1894). Today we know that the beneficial effects of treating CH with TH are time and dose dependent, increasing as a function of how quickly the condition is detected and treated. Because many babies born with CH will appear normal at birth, the importance of screening for an absent or underactive thyroid gland is vital. Prior to the introduction of screening in the 1980s, about a third of children with CH were not given a diagnosis until months later, and corrective treatment was not begun until after 3 months of age. As a result, most children never reached their full intellectual

---

1 Myxoedema is still used in some instances to describe the effects of severe hypothyroidism in humans and refers to the thickened skin condition that is characteristic of his condition.
2 A goiter is the medical term for a pathological enlargement of the thyroid gland. Goiters can be symptomatic of hypothyroidism and can be due to severe lack of iodine as the thyroid tissue is stimulated to grow under the influence of high levels of TSH produced when thyroid levels are low (see Chapter 4).

potential and had IQ levels under 80. Even those diagnosed and given TH within the first 3 months suffered from residual learning problems. Many older pediatricians active today eloquently compare the immense difference that this major public health measure has made, enabling children who would have otherwise been doomed to an institutionalized or very difficult and limited life to have access to normal schooling and career options. Furthermore, the cost of screening is infinitely less than that of raising and supporting a child (and adult) with intellectual deficiency.

The incidence of reported sporadic CH (i.e., children born without a sufficiently active thyroid gland) is currently increasing in many countries, including the United States (Hinton et al., 2010), Japan (Nagasaki, Asami, Ogawa, Kikuchi, & Uchiyama, 2011), and Mexico (Monroy-Santoyo et al., 2011) (Fig. 2.4), a discussion that we will return to in Chapter 7 in the context of increasing incidence of autism spectrum disorders and attention-deficit/hyperactivity disorders. Mexico has one of the highest documented frequencies

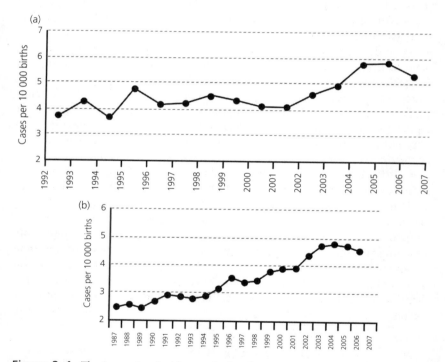

**Figure 2–4.** The increasing incidence of sporadic congenital hypothyroidism in the United States. Data from Texas are given in *a* and the United States (but not including New York State) in *b*. However, the highest incidence is currently found in New York State, where it reached nearly 8 cases per 10,000 births in 2007 (see text). Even though changes in diagnostic methods may account for a part of the increase, current opinion is that environmental factors are implicated. (Redrawn and adapted from Hinton, 2010.)

of CH in the world (Rendon-Macias, Morales-Garcia, Huerta-Hernandez, Silva-Batalla, & Villasis-Keever, 2008) at around 1:2,500 births. In New York State CH incidence has increased by 138% between 1978 and 2005; while across the United States (excluding New York State) the increase was 73% between 1987 and 2002, reaching similar levels to those reported in Mexico, that is, 42.2 cases per 100,000 births (1:2,300 births; Harris & Pass, 2007). Causes of the increasing incidence are debated and include lowered cutoff points for diagnosis, increased frequency of preterm birth and low birth weight (both of which are character-ized by transient hypothyroidism), and environmental factors. However, many authors consider that the increase is not simply attributable to more sensi-tive diagnostic criteria and that the potential risk factors need to be identified (Shapira, Lloyd-Puryear, & Boyle, 2010). In some countries, such as Mexico, the rate of CH is clearly correlated with other birth defects (Monroy-Santoyo et al., 2011), raising the possibility that environmental factors could be impli-cated. In Turkey, a region of mild to moderate iodine deficiency, maternal iodine lack was reported in 88% of the cases of CH in one study (Evliyaoglu, Kutlu, Kara, & Atavci, 2008). Similarly, it has been suggested that there is a causative link between the decrease in iodine nutrition status between 1970 and 2000 and the increase in congenital hypothyroidism over that same period in the United States (Sullivan, 2008). CH occurs in varying degrees and the only treatment is TH replacement. The effects of CH on brain development will depend on the severity of the lack and critically, as mentioned, the rapidity of TH replacement.

Thus, despite the increased incidence of sporadic CH, the severity of the effects of postnatal CH on brain development will be corrected in most devel-oped countries due to neonatal screening for hypothyroidism. However, dif-ferent degrees of iodine lack are still very much present in many countries (see Box 2.1, section on "Cretinism, Iodine Deficiency, and Iodized Salt," and also Chapter 3, section on "Epidemiological Studies in Humans Showing the Importance of TH Signaling for Early Fetal Brain Development") and, as sug-gested earlier, if sufficiently severe in the mother, could not only be affecting the child's neurodevelopment throughout pregnancy but also be implicated in the increased incidence of some transitory forms of CH in newborns.

## Deiodinases and Selenium

Intriguingly, given the chemical energy required to add four atoms of iodine to the $T_4$ molecule, it is the removal of one specific iodine atom, the 5' iodine on the outer ring (Fig. 2.2), that confers biological activity to thyroxine ($T_4$), thereby forming $T_3$. If the iodine at position 5 on the inner ring of $T_4$ is removed, this creates reverse $T_3$ ($rT_3$), an inactive metabolite. Removal of another iodine atom from $T_3$ creates, $T_2$, again an inactive molecule in terms of gene transcription (Fig. 2.5). As introduced earlier, specific enzymes, iodothy-ronine deiodinases, carry out each of these reactions. Thus, cells are not simple recipients of circulating hormone. Cells can tailor TH availability according to developmental and physiological needs. A first control is TH entry into the cells

> **Box 2–1. Iodine and Pregnancy**
>
> A sufficient dietary supply of iodine is required to synthesize thyroid hormone (TH).
>
> As thyroid hormone is needed for brain development during fetal and postnatal growth, all women who are planning a pregnancy, are pregnant, or breast-feeding should ensure they have enough iodine in their diet.
>
> Insufficient iodine intake in mothers has been associated with negative long-term effects on their child's intelligence and learning skills.
>
> Vitamin and folic acid dietary supplements sold for pregnant women should contain iodine (at least 100 μg/day, which would represent about 50% of daily requirements).
>
> Iodine can be found in many marine fish, but sea salt does not contain iodine.
>
> Dairy products are often a good source of iodine.
>
> Iodized salt should be used and only added at the end of cooking or at the table to avoid loss of volatile iodine through during cooking.
>
> Even loss of just a few IQ points across populations can have major socioeconomic consequences (see Chapter 7, Box 7.1). Thus, as iodine deficiency can be a major public health issue in many European countries, governments should take into account these socioeconomic factors and enact appropriate legislation.
>
> Notably, iodine deficiency in vulnerable populations must be corrected by government action to legislate on the use of iodized salt in the food industry and in table salt.
>
> As it is increasingly recommended to reduce salt intake to avoid high blood pressure and cardiovascular disorders, the amount of iodate added to salt used in the food industry and in table salt needs to be adjusted accordingly.

via the TH transporters expressed on the cell membrane (see also Chapter 3). A second control is the temporal and spatial control of expression of the deiodinases that will activate or inactivate different forms of TH. The concept of tissue-specific determination of the amounts of active TH present in a given cell at a given developmental time is central to current thinking in TH function. The relative activities of deiodinases and the presence or absence of specific transporters on defined cell types are key issues. Certain recent comprehensive or focused reviews have addressed the questions of how deiodinase and transporter function contribute to determining intracellular TH levels in spatially and temporally defined manners (Bernal, 2011; Bianco, 2011; Dennert et al., 2011; Dentice & Salvatore, 2011; Köhrle, 2007; Köhrle, Jakob, Contempre, & Dumont, 2005; Salvatore, 2011).

All deiodinase enzymes are selenoproteins (or selenoenzymes); that is, they all contain selenium (Se). The presence of selenium in the enzymes that are

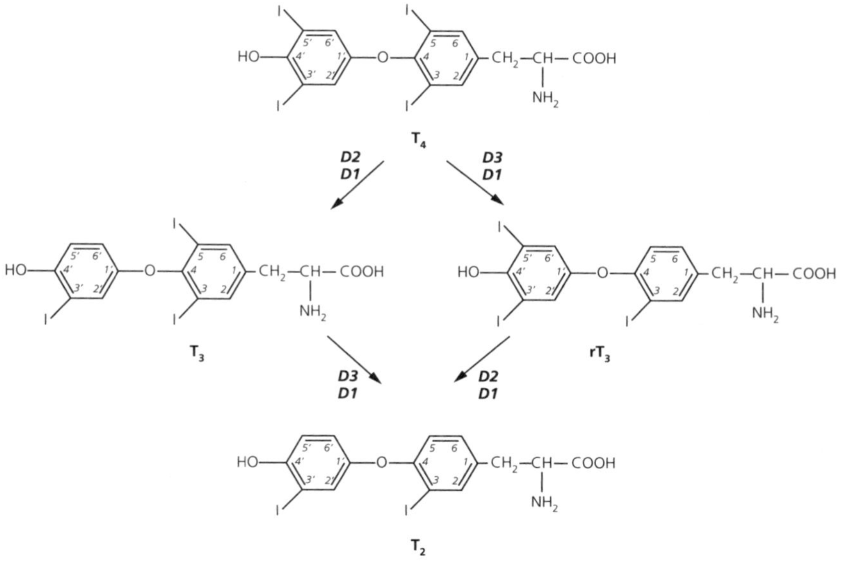

$T_4$

D2
D1

D3
D1

$T_3$

D3
D1

$rT_3$

D2
D1

$T_2$

Figure 2–5. The activating and inactivating deiodinases. Deiodinase 1 (D1) and Deiodinase 2 (D2) are activating deiodinases that remove the 5′ iodine from the outer ring from $T_4$ creating $T_3$. Deiodinase 3 (D3) is an inactivating enzyme that removes iodine at position 5 on the inner ring of $T_4$, forming the inactive metabolite reverse $T_3$ ($rT_3$). D3 can also inactivate $T_3$ by removal of an iodine atom creating $T_2$, again a transcriptionally inactive molecule. D1 can also carry out these inactivating steps. D1 can thus act as an activating or inactivating enzyme according to availability of substrates (different iodothyronines).

required for TH activation (and degradation) explains the fact that selenium lack had long been associated with certain forms of cretinism. The selenium in selenoproteins is present in the form of an unusual amino acid, sometimes referred to as the 21st amino acid,[3] selenocysteine (Sec). In 1973, the first selenoprotein was identified, glutathione peroxidase (GPx; Rotruck et al., 1973), but it was not until 1990/1991 that three groups published reports showing the type 1 deodinase to be a selenoenzyme (Köhrle et al., 2005). Since then approximately 25 different selenium-containing proteins have been identified, though about half of them have no known function. Two main categories of selenoproteins are implicated in thyroid physiology, the deiodinases and certain peroxidases that contribute to protect the cells in the follicular cells in the thyroid gland from the damaging effects of the hydrogen peroxide ($H_2O_2$) generated during synthesis of TH. Thus, the thyroid has a high Se content. Interestingly, some other endocrine glands also have high Se content, namely the adrenals,

3   The vast majority of proteins in plants and animals are composed of 20 main amino acids.

pituitary, testes, and ovary. Besides the roles of the three deiodinases in regulating active TH availability, selenoproteins are implicated in peroxide degradation, control of redox[4] reactions, and spermatogenesis. A group of important
selenoproteins expressed in mitochondria and cytosol of most tissues are the
thioredoxin reductases (TrxRs; Biterova, Turanov, Gladyshev, & Barycki, 2005).
Interestingly, in prokaryotes (such as bacteria) these enzymes do not contain
selenium, so the use of selenocysteine in these enzymes is an evolutionary
novelty. The TrxRs are essential components of the cell's redox homeostasis
system. It is mainly the different actions of selenoproteins in controlling different levels of redox reactions that have linked Se to anticancer actions, in
that they participate in the reduction of reactive oxygen species (ROS). ROS
are associated with cell damage, notably DNA damage. Many authors link this
ROS damage to cancer, cellular senescence, and aging. However, to date there
is no consensus on whether high (or low) Se levels correlate with reduced cancer risk, and a meta-analysis concluded that there was no convincing epidemiological evidence that Se supplementation could prevent cancer in humans
(Dennert et al., 2011). In contrast, it is well documented in animal models
(Köhrle et al., 2005) that lack of Se impairs spermatogenesis, whereas, again in
animal models, an excess of the element may have adverse effects on ovarian
function. Interestingly, in animals deprived of selenium, certain tissues such as
the brain and organs implicated in reproduction and endocrine function are
protected from loss, while other tissues (e.g., muscle, liver, and skin) become
depleted (Köhrle et al., 2005), implying a physiological hierarchy of need.

Each deiodinase enzyme is encoded by a separate gene with distinct regulations and dynamic expression patterns. Current thinking holds that deiodinases,
particularly the widely expressed D2 and D3, are responsible for determining
local concentrations of biologically active $T_3$, thus providing distinct profiles
of TH availability in individual cells and tissues, both during development and
in the adult. D1, highly expressed in the liver, thyroid, and kidney, is considered by many researchers to contribute to supplying systematic, circulating $T_3$
(Marsili, Zavacki, Harney, & Larsen, 2011). Another key idea is that regulatory
controls have evolved to maintain circulating TH levels within a tight range but
that the tissue and cell levels are more variable.

The physiological roles and actions of each deiodinase are discussed separately. Deiodinase type I: D1 catalyzes removal of the iodine atom in the 5′
position from either the prohormone $T_4$ (an activating reaction) or from
the inactive metabolite $rT_3$, as well as from other iodothyronines and their
sulfonated conjugates. In the case of $T_4$, 5′-deiodination produces $T_3$, the
biologically most active form of TH. D1 can also, with lesser efficiency, carry
out deiodination of $T_4$ in 5 position (an inactivating reaction) producing
$rT_3$. In mammals, D1 is the most abundant of the deiodinases, being highly
expressed in liver, kidney, pituitary, and in the thyroid gland itself. D1 is
over 200 times less efficient than D2 (see later) in catalyzing production of

4   Redox reactions involve reversible oxidation-reduction reactions.

$T_3$ from $T_4$. Results from mice bearing mutations in either the D1 or D2 enzymes have led many authors (see for instance, St. Germain, Galton, & Hernandez, 2009) to conclude that the primary physiological role of hepatic D1 is to scavenge and recirculate iodine from $rT_3$ and other iodothyronines. D1 expression in the adult is regulated by numerous hormonal and nutritional factors. The principal substrate ($T_4$) induces its expression, whereas hypothyroidism decreases D1 activity in most sites. D1 expression is modified by other endocrine systems, such as the sex steroids and glucocorticoids, and by different physiological states. For instance, fasting decreases liver D1 activity and, conversely, a diet rich in carbohydrates increases its activity.

*Dio1* (D1) expression besides being spatially constrained in the adult is also highly regulated during development. Notably, much data derived from different animal models show that D1 function is increased following activation of the growth hormone and insulin-like growth factor (GH-IGF1) pathways. This regulation, and its inverse (i.e., down-regulation of D1 and reduced production of circulating $T_3$), has repercussions for endocrine control of aging; many observations from animal studies converge on the concept that lowered GH-IGF1 signaling is favorable for increased life span (List et al., 2011).

Deiodinase type II or D2, like D1, catalyzes the activation reaction of removal of the iodine atom in the 5′ position from the prohormone $T_4$. However, D2 has an affinity for $T_4$ several-hundred-fold higher than D1 (the Km of D2 being around 1- 2nM $T_4$). Intriguingly, the D2 enzyme is inactivated by excess $T_4$, as it is by $rT_3$. Transcription of *Dio2*, the gene encoding D2, is inhibited by its product, $T_3$. Thus, D2 regulation is the reverse of that seen for D1 and for D3, with $T_4$ inhibiting D2 (except in tanycytes, see later) and inducing D1 and D3 in most tissues. Moreover, the enzyme itself has an exceptionally short half-life, less than 40 minutes, as it is rapidly degraded by ubiquitination. Thus, mRNA levels do not reflect functional activity. *Dio2*, is highly expressed in the brain, and its function is critical for brain development and function. Data from different experimental approaches show that normal brain development in the euthyroid rodents requires D2 to provide local production of $T_3$ from $T_4$. Surprisingly, in mice that lack the *Dio2* gene, brain development is not severely compromised, but these animals have double normal levels of $T_4$ and normal circulating levels of $T_3$ that may enter the brain and compensate for the lower levels of brain-derived $T_3$ (St. Germain et al., 2009). In the central nervous system, D2 is expressed mainly in glial cells (astrocytes) and tanycytes (specialized cells lining the brain ventricles in the hypothalamic region). The $T_3$ produced in glia is transported into neighboring neurons, which have much lower levels of, if any, D2. Thus, there is cell-specific production and use of $T_3$ in the different cell types. The presence of different categories of membrane transporters for TH (e.g., OATP1C1, MCT8, and MCT10) on glial cells and neurons allows for efflux of $T_3$ from the glial cells and its uptake by neurons lacking D2 (see Chapter 3; Bernal, 2006; Ceballos et al., 2009; Visser, Friesema, & Visser, 2011). Thyroid status affects D2 production at the level of both transcription and posttranscription, notably in the brain. Many reports describe increased brain D2 in response to hypothyroidism (Bianco, Salvatore, Gereben, Berry, & Larsen, 2002; Guadano-Ferraz, Escamez, Rausell, & Bernal, 1999). Increasing D2 activity in the brain during episodes of hypothyroidism will tend to protect the brain from the exceedingly damaging effects of TH deficiency (see Chapter 3). However, even D2 activation in the brain cannot protect from prolonged severe hypothyroidism, notably if insufficient iodine is present to ensure synthesis of adequate amounts of $T_4$ and hence $T_3$.

An intriguing aspect of D2 physiology relates to its negative feedback regulation by high levels of circulating TH, particularly in the brain. D2 in most parts of the brain (e.g., the cerebral cortex and anterior pituitary; Baqui et al., 2003) is down-regulated by $T_4/T_3$. In contrast, in the mediobasal hypothalamus, where it is expressed in the tanycytes, increased $T_4$ has no effect on D2 activity nor on $Dio2$ expression. Actually, this highly cell-specific lack of negative feedback in tanycytes must have undergone selection during evolution as lack of response to changes in circulating $T_4$ levels ensures that hypothalamic levels of TH are "representative" of circulating, peripheral levels. This lack of response to changing TH supply guarantees appropriate regulatory responses in transcription of TRH, governing the hypothalamic/pituitary/thyroid axis; that is, decreased circulating $T_4/T_3$ levels will abrogate negative feedback on TRH and boost thyroid axis function increasing $T_4/T_3$ production and secretion.

D2 transcription is regulated by several signals besides TH derivatives. Positive regulators include the transcription factors nuclear factor kappa and FoxO3 (Bianco, 2011). In glial cells, thyroid cells, and brown fat (brown adipose tissue), D2 expression is stimulated by cAMP. D2 activation in brown fat increases $T_3$ levels, stimulating the production of uncoupling proteins and, in synergy with catecholamines, driving thermogenesis.

The last deiodinase to be discussed is D3, an inactivating enzyme, inactivating not only the prohormone $T_4$ to $rT_3$, but also inactivating $T_3$, thereby producing metabolites such as $3,5-T_2$. In contrast to D1, D3 does not act on sulfonated forms of $T_4$ or $T_3$. D3 catalyzes deiodination at the 5-position (Fig. 2.2). All of the products of D3 action, the principal product being $rT_3$, are inactive both in TR binding assays and in transcriptional assays. It has been proposed that $rT_3$ could have a physiological role, particularly in the central nervous system, where high levels are found, $rT_3$ inhibiting D2 production (Cettour-Rose, Visser, Burger, & Rohner-Jeanrenaud, 2005) and potentially braking excess formation of $T_3$. D3 itself is expressed at high levels both in the developing brain, in the uterus of the gravid rat, the placenta, and in the fetal liver. In the developing brain, D3 is transiently expressed in areas that are implicated in sexual differentiation (Escamez, Guadano-Ferraz, Cuadrado, & Bernal, 1999).

Generally, D3 appears to play essential roles in limiting $T_3$ availability at crucial developmental time points. In mammalian models, such as mutant mice, this role has been demonstrated in the retina (Marsh-Armstrong, Huang, Remo, Liu, & Brown, 1999; Ng et al., 2010) and the cochlea (Ng et al., 2009). Similarly it has been proposed that high levels of expression of D3 in the placenta and uterus protect the early embryo from excessive $T_3$ exposure. D3 levels and activity are also raised in a series of pathological conditions, including those that implicate hypoxia, notably heart failure and ischemia (Bianco, 2011; Simonides et al., 2008). A new field of intense research interest is the potential role of D3 in cancer cells. Hypoxia is a feature of cancer cells (Brahimi-Horn, Bellot, & Pouyssegur, 2011; Danquah, Zhang, & Mahato, 2011; Goel et al., 2011; Vieira, Alves, & Vercelli, 2011; Wilson & Hay, 2011). A key event in a cell's response to hypoxia is the induction of a transcription factor: hypoxia-induced transcription factor (HIF-1). In turn, among its other targets, HIF-1 induces transcription of D3 (Simonides et al., 2008). D3 activity will limit $T_3$ availability in the tumor cell (Dentice, Ambrosio, & Salvatore, 2009) and potentially favor proliferation over differentiation.

Another important characteristic of the *Dio3* gene is that is an imprinted gene. A gene that is imprinted is subjected to an epigenetic process that determines whether the paternal or the maternal allele of the gene is expressed (Gregg, Zhang, Butler, Haig, & Dulac, 2010). Genetic imprinting is relatively frequent in the brain, and patterns of imprinting of individual genes can vary markedly across brain areas (Bonasio, Tu, & Reinberg, 2010). Epigenetic regulations will be considered in detail in Chapter 7 as endocrine disruption can modulate expression of genes subject to epigenetic mechanisms. Succinctly put, an epigenetic regulation is one that is literally "above" (from the Greek "epi-") the gene. A better way of putting it might be "around" the gene, as these regulations affect the structure of chromatin around the gene and thereby determine whether or not a gene is actively transcribed. Furthermore, the epigenetic state is a form of cell memory, in that the epigenetic state will be determined by the various cues and signals that have been received by the cell. Most definitions of epigenetics incorporate the concept of persistence; that is, an epigenetic mark should be stable, copied, and transmitted with cell division, even in some cases across generations. This feature is responsible for ensuring cell-specific transcription of gene networks, and hence cell phenotypes during development. Epigenetic regulations include modifications (acetylation, methylation, phosphorylation, and ubiquitination) of the histone proteins (components of chromatin) and methylation of DNA (Bonasio et al., 2010).

The *Dio3* gene is part of a large cluster of imprinted genes located in the mouse on chromosome 12 and in humans on chromosome 14 (da Rocha, Edwards, Ito, Ogata, & Ferguson-Smith, 2008). The imprinted domain contains three protein-encoding genes, *Dlk1*, *Rtl1*, and *Dio3*, and many small non-coding RNAs, or micro-RNAs. Comparative analysis of marsupial and mammalian genomes shows that the imprinted status of this gene cluster, like many other imprinted gene clusters, evolved after the divergence of mammals from marsupials and could be related to maternal control of fetal uterine growth (Edwards et al., 2008). The consequences and variations in *Dio3* imprinting and expression have been studied in the context of brain development using rat two strains (Norway and Sprague-Dawley) that have single-nucleotide polymorphisms (SNPs) in *Dio3*. These SNPs allow paternal versus maternal expression patterns of *Dio3* to be determined in different brain areas and as a function

of development (Sittig, Herzing, Shukla, & Redei, 2011). Higher expression of
*Dio3*, and presumably decreased $T_3$, in the hippocampus was associated with
behavioral changes such as increased anxiety. The same group of researchers
(Sittig, Shukla, Herzing, & Redei, 2011) has shown that alcohol exposure during fetal development affects imprinting of *Dio3* with sex-specific and brain
area–specific consequences.

The deiodinases produce other metabolites from further deiodination of $T_4$,
$T_3$, and $rT_3$, while other TH metabolites such as thyronamines (Piehl, Hoefig,
Scanlan, & Köhrle, 2011) are produced by as yet undefined mechanisms. Several
data sets suggest that some of these metabolites, such as 3,5 di-iodothyronine
(3,5-$T_2$; Giudetti, Leo, Geelen, & Gnoni, 2005; Pinna et al., 1998) or some of
the thyronamines may be active in specific conditions or if administered at
high doses may produce quite marked effects, such as induction of deep hypothermia (Scanlan et al., 2004). To date, little is known about if and how these
metabolites play functional roles at physiological concentrations and even less
about whether their production and potential actions are affected by chemical
pollution. Thus, they will not be further discussed here.

## Selenium and Mercury

The problems posed by mercury contamination in the environment will be
a recurrent theme. As seen in Chapter 1, industrial errors caused accumulation of mercury in fish in Minamata, Japan, with population-wide poisoning
and neurotoxicity. In Chapter 5 we will return to the problem of mercury
contamination in the environment and examine the data on levels of mercury in different populations and the associations with TH levels and thyroid
dysfunction.

However, given the essential role of selenium in the structure and function
of all three deiodinases, it is important to discuss mercury–selenium interactions here and the potential for disruption of TH signaling by mercury. As mentioned earlier, selenium is not only required for the synthesis of deiodinases but
also for synthesis of GPx in the thyroid gland and many other tissues. Another
selenoprotein that is relevant to this discussion is selenoprotein P (SePP), where
the "P" indicates its localization in the plasma. In different vertebrate species,
SePP contains between 10 and 17 selenocysteine residues per molecule, with
this high density accounting for the fact that SePP content represents between
50% and 70% of the selenium in human plasma (Köhrle et al., 2005). In cases
of selenium lack, serum GPx levels are restored before those of SPP, suggesting that SPP could be a serum marker of selenium deficiency. The functional
role of SePP is debated (Köhrle et al., 2005; Steinbrenner & Sies, 2013): Its peroxidase function is limited but it has a high affinity for heavy metals such as
cadmium and mercury. It also has a heavy metal response element in its promoter, suggesting that its function could be implicated in heavy metal detoxi-
fication. However, as interesting as this hypothesis seems, it has not yet been
fully established (Burk & Hill, 2005; Mostert, 2000). However, polymorphisms

in the human genes encoding SePP are associated with individual differences in body burden of mercury (Goodrich et al., 2011). SePP is mainly synthesized in the liver, but expression has been reported in the brain and other tissues. Two different models of knockout mice for the *Sepp1* gene show marked neurological dysfunction. It has been proposed that SePP is synthetized by astrocytes and taken up by neurons (Steinbrenner & Seis, 2013), where it could have a role in protecting neurons from oxidative or heavy metal damage. Another brain selenoprotein is SelW (Selenoprotein W), levels of which decrease along with brain GPx proteins in the *Sepp1* knockout mice, probably due to insufficient supply of selenium to the brain, a direct consequence of loss of SePP (Steinbrenner & Seis, 2013).

As introduced in Chapter 1, and detailed in Chapter 5, mercury is found in the environment in three main forms. The main source is methyl mercury, which is produced by various industrial processes such as coal-fired power stations and mining activities. The principal toxicological effects of methyl mercury are on the brain and nervous system, notably the developing brain. The other two sources are related to medical uses that are in decline or banned in most countries: thiomersal, or ethyl mercury, which was used in certain vaccines and mercury amalgams for dental fillings. Organic mercury (such as in methyl or ethyl mercury) can be converted to inorganic mercury by microorganisms in the intestine. Inorganic mercury can persist in the brain for long periods. Inorganic mercury interacts with selenium, forming mercury selenite, HgSe, which is thought to be the form that is retained in the central nervous system.

The study of this mercury–selenium interaction in physiological systems has a long history (see references in Brzeznicka & Chmielnicka, 1981) and has led to the concept that nutritional selenium can protect against mercury toxicity provided it is in molar excess. Both animal studies and epidemiological reports substantiate this idea. For instance, one series of experiments fed rats with diets containing low, medium, or high selenium supplementation and then exposed them to different levels of methyl mercury (Ralston, Blackwell, & Raymond, 2007). The authors found that one of the early symptoms of mercury toxicity in the low-selenium group was growth delay, but if the rats were supplemented with high levels of selenium, not even the high mercury dose produced any effect on growth. Similarly, in a study on Faroese population exposed to high levels of mercury through consumption of whale meat, it was found that because of the surplus levels of selenium in the cohort no deleterious effects of mercury contamination were detected (Choi et al., 2008). These concepts have led to the general recommendation, that despite the risk of consuming mercury in fish, particularly those at the higher end of the food chain such as tuna and swordfish, the very high levels of selenium in these sea fish not only balance the risk but, as they are in large molar excess, they can be beneficial. Interestingly, the study cited revealed that it was not just the selenium in the fish that was providing protection against neurotoxicity (Choi et al., 2008) but that other factors (potentially, omega 3 and other unsaturated lipids) could also be acting positively on brain function. However, the authors also wisely recommend that for pregnant women sources of fish that are low in mercury contaminants should be preferred (Choi et al., 2008). Indeed, the debate on the nutritional advantages of fish versus the potential neurotoxic effects of mercury and other forms of chemical contamination is still raging and much research, clinical and basic, is needed. Another point worth noting on the subject of mercury–selenium interactions is that the neutralizing effects of selenium on mercury can also be seen in plant physiology and agriculture. To cite a recent study, it was found that rice grown in soil that is rich in selenium took up less mercury than that grown in selenium-poor soil (Zhang et al., 2012). This fact can be pertinent to public health issues as certain geographical areas, such as New Zealand, have soils with low selenium content. Certain authors have suggested that soils could be supplemented with selenium to favor its uptake by plants and increase the bioavailability of the element to consumers. Furthermore, in inland China consumption of rice grown in areas with intense smelting and mining activites is a significant pathway for methyl mercury contamination (Zhang, Feng, Larssen, Qiu, & Vogt, 2010). In certain regions daily intake exceeds recommended US doses and in such cases, as rice does not have the neuroprotective properties of fish, the physiological consequences of rice-borne exposure could be greater and this could be an argument for selenium enrichment in the soil or food. However, the biological availability of the selenium from biofortified sources is debatable and, again, more research is needed.

Returning to the biochemical and physiological effects of mercury, surprisingly few studies have examined the effects of mercury, whether organic (such as in methyl mercury) or inorganic mercury, on deiodinase activity. This is more surprising given the common selenocysteine in both the deiodinase enzymes and the antioxidant enzyme found in the thyroid and other tissues, glutathione peroxidase (GPx). However, most of the work on mercury inhibition of selenoproteins has focused on the GPx proteins. Studies on brain GPx expression and the effect of methyl mercury on the developmental profile of the enzyme have been carried out in many vertebrates (such as fish and mice; see, for example, Stringari et al., 2008), but few have examined the effects of the metal in any form on deiodinase activities. Further, to date no epidemiological studies have looked at associations between mercury load and deiodinase activities or mRNA expression levels in humans. One of the few examples of studies in rodents is that of Watanabe and colleagues (1999), who examined the effect of subcutaneous injections into gestating mice of two doses of methyl mercury on the activity of GPx and activating and inactivating deiodinases in placenta and fetal and maternal brain. The levels of selenium were not modified by the treatments, but GPx activity was decreased in both fetal brain and in the placenta, and deiodinase expression was modified, with an increase in the $T_3$-generating deiodinase and inhibition of the inactivating deiodinase. Another example is an early report on mercury inhibition of thyroxine deiodination in rat liver subcellular fractions, but this was in 1976, by a young Theo Visser (Visser, Does-Tobe, Docter, & Hennemann, 1976) before he and others discovered the different types of deiodinases, and well before the first one, D1, was found to be a selenocysteine-containing enzyme.

## Cretinism, Iodine Deficiency, and Iodized Salt

Four atoms of iodine are required to synthesis one molecule of $T_4$. Given the role of TH in brain development (the mechanisms and mode of action of TH on the nervous system are described in Chapter 3), it is not surprising to find that lack of iodine is the world's greatest single, and most easily preventable, cause of mental retardation or intellectual disability. The most damaging effects of iodine deficiency are on brain development, but, given the role of TH in maturation and growth of most tissues, severe cretinism results in stunting with failure to develop the skeletal and muscular systems. In 1990, the World Health Organization (WHO) set the target of eliminating iodine deficiency by 2000. However, despite the progress made, estimates made a decade later suggested that 29% of the world population was still at risk of iodine deficiency, and even in countries that had previously eliminated the risk the problem is reappearing. The resurgence of iodine deficiency can be due to changes in legislation on iodized salt but also to changes in food production methods. For instance, iodine content of cow's milk varies according to methods used for disinfection of udders (Borucki Castro et al., 2010) and whether conventional or organic farming methods are used (Bath, Button, & Rayman, 2011). Iodine content of milk also varies on a seasonal basis (Dahl, Opsahl, Meltzer, & Julshamn, 2003). Given that milk is a vital source of iodine, particularly in areas where use of iodized salt is not legislated and optional, the variation in milk iodine content is becoming a public health issue. Overall, concern about iodine deficiency in the general population is shared by various international bodies.[5]

Clearly the most convenient and consistent form of iodine supplementation is the use of iodized salt, and preferably mandatory use (Pearce, 2011), both in table salt and in the food industry. This position is defended by the International Council for the Control of Iodine Deficiency Disorders (http://www.iccidd.org/) and innumerable experts in the field, clinicians, basic scientists, and epidemiologists (Zimmerman, 2009). Many, but by no means all, developed countries provide access to iodized salt. European countries that do not have obligatory use of iodized salt in the food industry and in table salt include France, Germany, and the United Kingdom, three of the most populous countries in Europe. Even in countries where it is available, its use by individuals is not guaranteed and in some countries it is difficult to buy from the usual outlets. For instance, a recent study in Italy measuring iodine intake in school children showed that only 30% of the households were using iodized salt (Borucki Castro et al., 2010). In the United Kingdom a recent study calculated availability of iodized salt as a function of supermarket offer and found it to be less that 21% of sales (Bath, Button, & Rayman, 2013). These and other

---

5   See, for instance, http://www.who.int/nutrition/publications/micronutrients/iodine_
    deficiency/

factors, such as the need to reduce salt intake to avoid high blood pressure and associated cardiovascular disease, argue for a general increase in the amount of iodine in the salt sold, so as to increase iodine intake through these routes.

Global data on iodine status can be found at http://www.who.int/vmnis/database/iodine/iodine_data_status_summary/en/index.html. Among the various tables that can be consulted on this WHO site, those covering the proportions of populations in different geographical areas that suffer from insufficient iodine intake are particularly eloquent. For instance, comparing the 2004 data on the percentage of population with a urinary iodine (UI) content below 100 μg/L in Africa versus Europe shows that it is in Europe that the greatest percentage of the population is at risk (42.6% risk in Africa versus 56.9% in Europe). This fact is probably related to the lack of legislation on usage of iodized salt in many EU countries (see earlier discussion and Fig. 2.6). Taking a more detailed look at UI values for children aged 6–12 years (data obtained according to samples collected between 1993 and 2006), one finds that urinary iodine levels in children in many European countries (e.g., Belgium, Estonia, France, Italy, and Ireland) are classed as insufficient, with the WHO stating that they are at mild risk of iodine insufficiency. In contrast, children in Egypt, Finland, Germany, and Tunisia have optimal intake. Countries where children's UI levels indicate greatest risk of iodine insufficiency (mean values below 50 μg/L) include Afghanistan, Algeria, Gambia, Kyrgyzstan, and Vietnam. Even in the United States, which is generally considered to be iodine sufficient, there are populations that are mildly iodine deficient. The latest data from the US National Health and Nutrition Examination Survey (NHANES) study show that pregnant women are increasingly iodine deficient, notably in the first two trimesters of pregnancy (Caldwell et al., 2013; Pearce & Leung, 2013). It is important to recall that the first part of pregnancy appears to be the most vulnerable period for TH lack and associated adverse effects on the child's neurodevelopment (Pop et al., 1999). Similarly, recent data from the United Kingdom point to increasingly prevalent iodine deficiency (Bath & Rayman, 2013). This situation seems to be of particular concern for young women of child-bearing age (Bath & Rayman, 2013; Bath, Steer, Golding, Emmett, & Rayman, 2013), as Margaret Rayman's group has shown that even mild maternal iodine deficiency during pregnancy will increase the risk of the child having lower IQ (Bath, Steer, et al., 2013) (see Chapter 3 on iodine, TH, and brain development for more details).

How Much Iodine and Selenium Are Needed Each Day?

Both iodine and selenium are categorized as rare elements and yet all humans require a supply of each. Having underlined the needs for a regular supply of iodine and selenium, it should be pointed out that certain members of the population have higher requirements for iodine as their need for TH is more marked.

Current recommendations for adults are set by different official nutritional authorities at between 90 and 100 μg/day iodine and 55–75 μg/day

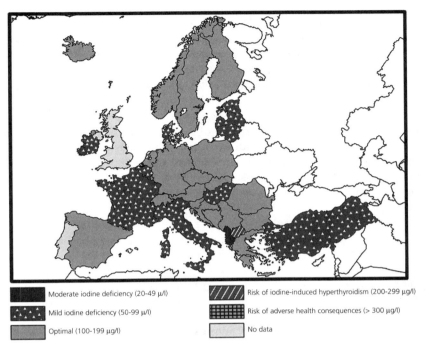

**Figure 2–6.** Map of the iodine status of Europe. It is important to note that even mild iodine deficiency in pregnancy can have significant, negative effects on children's cognitive development. Among others EU countries, France, Italy, and Ireland are in this category of mild deficiency. Further, the fact that no data were available for the United Kingdom most probably masks a similar deficiency (see text for details and references). (Adapted from the World Health Organization http://whqlibdoc.who.int/publications/2004/9241592001.pdf)

selenium. Pregnant and lactating women as well as young children have the greatest needs for iodine, because the rapidly growing brains of unborn and newly born babies and young children require TH for optimal development. Obviously, the fetus is totally dependent on the mother's TH until its own thyroid gland becomes functional, but throughout pregnancy it is dependent on the mother's iodine supply. Maternal iodine deficiency can lead to maternal and fetal hypothyroidism, and the resulting lack of TH can lead to irreversible brain damage in the unborn child. The current recommendations for pregnant and lactating women given by the WHO are 250 µg/day, while officials in the United States (http://www.thyroid.org) recommend 150 µg/day for the same age group. The WHO also suggests 120 µg/day for children aged 6–12 years and 150 µg/day for adolescents. These requirements can only be met by a well-balanced diet rich in suitable sources of iodine, use of iodinized salt, and or use of iodine (and selenium) supplements.

Sea Salt *Does Not* Contain Iodine

Iodine ($I^{127}$) is the heaviest and largest element in the periodic table to be found in a naturally occurring biological molecule. Iodine is a rare element. The major natural source of iodine is seawater that contains 50–60 µg iodine/L. For comparison, tap water contains two orders of magnitude less, with less than 0.1 µg/L.

The fact that seawater contains high levels of iodine leads to a common fallacy: As the sea is the major source of iodine, then sea salt should contain large amounts of iodine. This idea is totally erroneous because iodine is a volatile element (i.e., it evaporates or converts rapidly into gaseous form). Sea salt is produced by evaporating seawater leaving sodium chloride, NaCl. The volatile nature of iodine results in iodine being lost with the water in the evaporation process.

The fact that many people think sea salt is better for them because it is natural and "unmodified" is doubly unfortunate. First, it means that many consumers today are spending significantly more money on speciality sea salts than on standard iodized table salt because they erroneously believe that sea salt is iodine-rich; and, second, they are losing a valuable source of a vital element. Numerous scientific publications have compared the relative amounts of iodine in sea salt and iodized table salt. Fisher and L'Abbe (1980) tested noniodized sea salt, and iodized table salt. The authors found 52.9–84.6 µg iodine/g of salt in iodized table salt and 1.2–1.4 µg iodine/g in noniodized sea salt. Similarly, Aquaron (2000) determined iodine content of natural sea salt, rock salt, and iodized salt. The author found iodine levels of less than 0.71 µg iodine/g of noniodized salt and 7.65–100 µg iodine/g of iodized salt (depending on the country's iodine legislation).

Thus, iodized salt is an excellent source of iodine, and seen from a governmental level, should be considered the easiest way of ensuring iodine supplies for the general population and therefore limiting the most common form of preventable mental retardation. However, many people are on restricted salt diets, including the large numbers of patients with high blood pressure and, of course, many pregnant women whose needs in iodine and selenium are particularly important. Thus, dietary supplementation must be considered for certain categories of the population. One possibility for pregnant women or women who are contemplating pregnancy is to encourage use of supplements that contain iodine. This practice is common for folic acid supplements and could easily be extended to include iodine. The benefits to the individual and society would be enormous, with no risk to either the mother or the child.

It should be recalled that, as mentioned in Chapter 1, bromine is increasingly present in the urban environment, notably in the form of brominated flame retardants, and in some countries it is still used as an addition to leaded petrol. Bromine, a halogen like iodine, competes with iodine for uptake by the thyroid. The negative effects of bromine will be exacerbated by iodine lack.

Table 2–1. Iodine and Selenium Content of Fish and Shellfish

| Seafood | Iodine (μg/100 g) | Selenium (μg/100 g) |
| --- | --- | --- |
| Herring | 29 | 35 |
| Plaice | 33 | 37 |
| Mackerel | 140 | 30 |
| Salmon | 76 | 24 |
| Oyster | 60 | 23 |
| Mussel | 140 | 51 |
| Lobster (boiled) | 100 | 130 |
| Shrimp (boiled) | 100 | 46 |

## Nutritional Sources of Iodine and Selenium

Certain foodstuffs contain reasonable levels of iodine, notably eggs, milk, and certain breads. However, the iodine content of these products will depend on the soil and the grain or cereal, or other foodstuffs, used to feed cattle or poultry. Seaweed (kelp) being a marine product with iodine fixed to proteins is also a good, but very variable source. Undoubtedly, the most reliable sources of both iodine and selenium are sea fish and shellfish. Numerous publications have given results of analysis of iodine and selenium in seafood and other sources. A recent survey of iodine in food in the United Kingdom reported,[6] in accordance with many previous studies, that milk and seaweed were good sources but unfortunately seafood was not analyzed.

However, a reliable reference for the levels of both iodine and selenium in shellfish and different sea fish was published by HMSO[7] in 1993. The authors show that the best sources of iodine are mussels and mackerel (a 100 g serving of either contains about 140 μg iodine, thereby virtually covering the daily requirements of an adult, which is150 μg iodine) with shrimp and lobsters providing 100 μg/100 g. The selenium content of each of these foods is also sufficient for a 100 g serving to nearly cover the average daily needs, with mussels and shrimps averaging 50 μg/100 g and fish averaging 25–30 μg/100 g. For those who can afford to enjoy a serving of lobster from time to time, they can combine the feelings of self-indulgence and gastronomic pleasure that may dispel the financial setback with the comforting idea that each 100 g of lobster covers the better part of 2 days selenium and iodine requirements! (See Table 2.1.)

## Seafood, Iodine, and Theories of Brain Evolution

Although much debated (Broadhurst et al., 2002; Cordain et al., 2005; Cunnane, 2005), it has been proposed that the consumption of iodine-rich foods supplied

6  http://food.gov.uk/news/newsarchive/2008/jun/iodinesurvey
7  British Government publication: Her Majesty's Stationary Office (HMSO).

by a seafood diet could have been a favorable event in the selection processes underlying human brain evolution. As emphasized by Cunnane and colleagues (Broadhurst et al., 2002; Cunnane, 2005), seafood is not only iodine-rich but also rich in polyunsaturated fatty acids (PUFA), notably docosahexaenoic acid (DHA), an omega 3 lipid, also essential for brain development and function. Other authors maintain that both iodine and other essential nutrients for brain development would have been amply supplied by a grain-rich diet supplemented with meat. However, it should be noted here that the iodine content of plants is positively correlated with proximity to the sea.[8] Thus, early hominid populations living near the sea would have benefited from this factor independently of fish consumption. Moreover, the animals they ate as function of a food chain beginning with plant life would also be iodine enriched. Further away from marine coasts, the iodine content of foodstuffs would have been very variable and might only have been sufficient if the thyroid glands of animals were consumed as well as the other tissues. Cunnane emphasizes that PUFAs in seafood were vital for the evolution of the human brain. Cordain and colleagues (2005) argue that aquatic food sources (whether from fresh or marine waters) would have provided only minor contributions to the diets during the critical period of brain expansion in the Early Paleolithic period. However, this argument is countered by the recent work of Braun et al. (2010), which provides strong evidence for lake-sourced crocodiles, turtles, and other animals in the diet 1.95 million years ago. A final point relevant to this debate might be that the protagonists Cunanne and Cordain are overlooking the high selenium content of seafood, which is also central to brain development through its action on TH activation. Even if, as Cordain states, exploitation of marine sources only dates from 110,000 years ago (Middle Paleolithic period), the introduction of marine food could have provided not only iodine and key PUFAs but also selenium in significant quantities.

In the slow process of the evolution of the human brain there would clearly be continual positive feedback between better selection of genes enabling brain development, cognition, and the capacity to develop the tools (Braun et al., 2010), which in turn would increase access to the food supplies rich in various components favorable for brain development. No doubt, parallel increases in each factor (genes/environment/behavior) synergized during the process, that by definition occurred in stages.

Another factor that bolsters the argument that fish consumption was vital for human brain evolution (see Cordain et al., 2005) is that many of the plant products that potentially provided the basis of early hominids' diet have high contents of various goitrogens. Many of the plants domesticated in the Neolithic period (including soy, millet, maize, turnips, and cabbage) contain either propythiouracil derivatives or genistein. Both of these categories of chemicals adversely affect thyroid function at different levels (see Chapter 5).

---

8  This factor still holds today—though, of course, transport of foods from source of production to the consumer means that people living near the sea today do not necessarily benefit from the potentially higher iodine content of locally produced foods.

Therefore, in the context of a goitrogen-rich plant diet, foods rich in readily available iodine (and other micronutrients such as selenium and iron) would be vital to ensure optimal brain development and function. Intriguingly, this requirement for increased iodine supply in the context of goitrogen-rich vegetarian diets may be particularly pertinent in the contemporary context, with increasing numbers of vegetarians in developed countries eating similar diets, rich in goitrogens and low in iodine. Moreover, many of these vegetarians will be choosing to use sea salt because of its theoretically unadulterated nature and the unfortunate fallacy that sea salt is iodine-rich. Such people and their children could be particularly at risk for iodine deficiency and its consequences on thyroid function.

Take-Home Messages and Questions for Future Research

- Thyroid function requires two of the rarer elements, iodine and selenium. Daily requirements for both of these elements increase during pregnancy and in childhood.
- The principal reason that iodine deficiency causes hypothyroidism is that TH contains four atoms of iodine when synthesized as $T_4$ and three atoms of iodine when activated by the selenium-containing deiodinases, forming $T_3$.
- Among the best sources of both iodine and selenium are marine fish, including shellfish such as mussels, clams, shrimp, and lobster. Despite the fact that marine fish, particularly predatory species at the top end of the food chain (such as tuna and swordfish) can have high concentrations of mercury and chemical contaminants, many authorities consider that for children and adults the benefits of fish are greater than the risk. However, pregnant women should only occasionally consume oily fish, and certain fish sources that are notoriously high in contaminants, such as Baltic herring, should be avoided.
- More research is needed on clinical and basic aspects of mercury–selenium interactions so as to better understand the physiology and to provide advice to decision makers and consumers.
- It is important to use iodized salt for cooking and for any salt added to food at the table. When cooking with iodized salt, it should be added at the end of the cooking, for instance, after vegetables have been boiled or baked, to avoid loss of volatile iodine during cooking.
- Although the WHO aimed to eliminate iodine deficiency and the consequent mental retardation by 2000, iodine deficiency is still widespread and is even increasing in certain industrialized countries, including European states. The deleterious effects of mild iodine lack on children's brain development, and the socioeconomic consequences, emphasize the need for iodine supplementation for pregnant women or women of child-bearing age. The cost/benefit of iodine supplementation for the individual and society is enormous, particularly in the light of the potential effects of chemical pollution on the thyroid axis.

## REFERENCES

Aquaron, R. (2000). Iodine content of non iodized salts and iodized salts obtained from the retail markets worldwide. *8th World Salt Symposium, 2*, 935–940.

Bath, S. C., Button, S., & Rayman, M. P. (2011). Iodine concentration of organic and conventional milk: Implications for iodine intake. *British Journal of Nutrition, 107*(7), 935–940.

Bath, S. C., Button, S., & Rayman, M. P. (2013). Availability of iodised table salt in the UK—is it likely to influence population iodine intake? *Public Health and Nutrition, 16*, 1–5.

Bath, S. C., & Rayman, M. P. (2013). Iodine deficiency in the U.K.: An overlooked cause of impaired neurodevelopment? *Proceedings of the Nutrition Society, 72*(2), 226–235.

Bath, S. C., Steer, C. D., Golding, J., Emmett, P., & Rayman, M. P. (2013). Effect of inadequate iodine status in UK pregnant women on cognitive outcomes in their children: Results from the Avon Longitudinal Study of Parents and Children (ALSPAC). *Lancet, 382*, 331–337.

Baqui, M., Botero, D., Gereben, B., Curcio, C., Harney, J. W., Salvatore, D.,...Bianco, A. C. (2003). Human type 3 iodothyronine selenodeiodinase is located in the plasma membrane and undergoes rapid internalization to endosomes. *Journal of Biological Chemistry, 278*(2), 1206–1211.

Bernal, J. (2006). Role of monocarboxylate anion transporter 8 (MCT8) in thyroid hormone transport: Answers from mice. *Endocrinology, 147*(9), 4034–4035.

Bernal, J. (2011). Thyroid hormone transport in developing brain. *Current Opinion in Endocrinology, Diabetes and Obesity, 18*(5), 295–299.

Bianco, A. C., Salvatore, D., Gereben, B., Berry, M. J., & Larsen, P. R. (2002). Biochemistry, cellular and molecular biology, and physiological roles of the iodothyronine selenodeiodinases. *Endocrine Reviews, 23*(1), 38–89.

Bianco, A. C. (2011). Minireview: Cracking the metabolic code for thyroid hormone signaling. *Endocrinology, 152*(9), 3306–3311.

Biterova, E. I., Turanov, A. A., Gladyshev, V. N., & Barycki, J. J. (2005). Crystal structures of oxidized and reduced mitochondrial thioredoxin reductase provide molecular details of the reaction mechanism. *Proceedings of the National Academy of Sciences USA, 102*(42), 15018–15023.

Bonasio, R., Tu, S., & Reinberg, D. (2010). Molecular signals of epigenetic states. *Science, 330*(6004), 612–616.

Borucki Castro, S. I., Berthiaume, R., Laffey, P., Fouquet, A., Beraldin, F., Robichaud, A., & Lacasse, P. (2010). Iodine concentration in milk sampled from Canadian farms. *Journal of Food Protection, 73*(9), 1658–1663.

Brahimi-Horn, M. C., Bellot, G., & Pouyssegur, J. (2011). Hypoxia and energetic tumour metabolism. *Current Opinion in Genetics & Development, 21*(1), 67–72.

Braun, D. R., Harris, J. W., Levin, N. E., McCoy, J. T., Herries, A. I., Bamford, M. K.,...Kibunjia, M. (2010). Early hominin diet included diverse terrestrial and aquatic animals 1.95 Ma in East Turkana, Kenya. *Proceedings of the National Academy of Sciences USA, 107*(22), 10002–10007.

Broadhurst, C. L., Wang, Y., Crawford, M. A., Cunnane, S. C., Parkington, J. E., & Schmidt, W. F. (2002). Brain-specific lipids from marine, lacustrine, or terrestrial food resources: Potential impact on early African Homo sapiens. *Comparative Biochemistry and Physiology Part B: Biochemistry and Molecular Biology, 131*(4), 653–673.

Brzeznicka, E. A., & Chmielnicka, J. (1981). Interaction of alkylmercuric compounds with sodium selenite. I. Metabolism of ethylmercuric chloride administered alone and in combination with sodium selenite in rats. *Environmental Health Perspectives*, 39, 131–142.

Burk, R. F., & Hill, K. E. (2005). Selenoprotein P: An extracellular protein with unique physical characteristics and a role in selenium homeostasis. *Annual Review of Nutrition*, 25, 215–235.

Caldwell, K. L., Pan, Y., Mortensen, M. E., Makhmudov, A., Merrill, L., & Moye, J. (2013). Iodine status in pregnant women in the National Children's Study and in U.S. women (15–44 years), National Health and Nutrition Examination Survey 2005–2010. *Thyroid*, 23(8), 927–937.

Ceballos, A., Belinchon, M. M., Sanchez-Mendoza, E., Grijota-Martinez, C., Dumitrescu, A. M., Refetoff, S.,...Bernal, J. (2009). Importance of monocarboxylate transporter 8 for the blood-brain barrier-dependent availability of 3,5,3'-triiodo-L-thyronine. *Endocrinology*, 150(5), 2491–2496.

Cettour-Rose, P., Visser, T. J., Burger, A. G., & Rohner-Jeanrenaud, F. (2005). Inhibition of pituitary type 2 deiodinase by reverse triiodothyronine does not alter thyroxine-induced inhibition of thyrotropin secretion in hypothyroid rats. *European Journal of Endocrinology*, 153(3), 429–434.

Choi, A. L., Budtz-Jørgensen, E., Jørgensen, P. J., Steuerwald, U., Debes, F., Weihe, P., & Grandjean, P. (2008). Selenium as a potential protective factor against mercury developmental neurotoxicity. *Environmental Research*, 107(1), 45–52.

Cordain, L., Eaton, S. B., Sebastian, A., Mann, N., Lindeberg, S., Watkins, B. A.,...Brand-Miller J. (2005). Origins and evolution of the Western diet: Health implications for the 21st century. *American Journal of Clinical Nutrition*, 81(2), 341–354.

Cunnane, S. C. (2005). Origins and evolution of the Western diet: Implications of iodine and seafood intakes for the human brain. *American Journal of Clinical Nutrition*, 82(2), 483; author reply 483–484.

da Rocha, S. T., Edwards, C. A., Ito, M., Ogata, T., & Ferguson-Smith, A. C. (2008). Genomic imprinting at the mammalian Dlk1-Dio3 domain. *Trends in Genetics*, 24(6), 306–316.

Dahl, L., Opsahl, J. A., Meltzer, H. M., & Julshamn, K. (2003). Iodine concentration in Norwegian milk and dairy products. *British Journal of Nutrition*, 90(3), 679–685.

Danquah, M. K., Zhang, X. A., & Mahato, R. I. (2011). Extravasation of polymeric nanomedicines across tumor vasculature. *Advanced Drug Delivery Reviews*, 63(8), 623–639.

Dennert, G., Zwahlen, M., Brinkman, M., Vinceti, M., Zeegers, M. P., & Horneber, M. (2011). Selenium for preventing cancer. *Cochrane Database of Systematic Reviews* (5), CD005195.

Dentice, M., Ambrosio, R., & Salvatore, D. (2009). Role of type 3 deiodinase in cancer. *Expert Opinion on Therapeutic Targets*, 13(11), 1363–1373.

Dentice, M., & Salvatore, D. (2011). Deiodinases: The balance of thyroid hormone: Local impact of thyroid hormone inactivation. *Journal of Endocrinology*, 209(3), 273–282.

Edwards, C. A., Mungall, A. J., Matthews, L., Ryder, E., Gray, D. J., Pask, A. J.,...Ferguson-Smith, A. C. (2008). The evolution of the DLK1-DIO3 imprinted domain in mammals. *PLoS Biology*, 6(6), e135.

Escamez, M. J., Guadano-Ferraz, A., Cuadrado, A., & Bernal, J. (1999). Type 3 iodothyronine deiodinase is selectively expressed in areas related to sexual differentiation in the newborn rat brain. *Endocrinology, 140*(11), 5443–5446.

Evliyaoglu, O., Kutlu, A., Kara, C., & Atavci, S. G. (2008). Incidence of iodine deficiency in Turkish patients with congenital hypothyroidism. *Pediatrics International, 50*(3), 276–280.

Fisher, P. W. F., & L'Abbe, M. (1980). Iodine in iodized table salt and in sea salt. *Canadian Institute of Food Science and Technology Journal, 13*(2), 103–104.

Gereben, B., Zavacki, A. M., Ribich, S., Kim, B. W., Huang, S. A., Simonides, W. S.,... Bianco, A. C. (2008). Cellular and molecular basis of deiodinase-regulated thyroid hormone signaling. *Endocrine Reviews, 29*(7), 898–938.

Giudetti, A. M., Leo, M., Geelen, M. J., & Gnoni, G. V. (2005). Short-term stimulation of lipogenesis by 3,5-L-diiodothyronine in cultured rat hepatocytes. *Endocrinology, 146*(9), 3959–3966.

Goel, S., Duda, D. G., Xu, L., Munn, L. L., Boucher, Y., Fukumura, D., & Jain, R. K. (2011). Normalization of the vasculature for treatment of cancer and other diseases. *Physiological Reviews, 91*(3), 1071–1121.

Goodrich, J. M., Wang, Y., Gillespie, B., Werner, R., Franzblau, A., & Basu, N. (2011). Glutathione enzyme and selenoprotein polymorphisms associate with mercury biomarker levels in Michigan dental professionals. *Toxicology and Applied Pharmacology, 257*(2), 301–308.

Gregg, C., Zhang, J., Butler, J. E., Haig, D., & Dulac, C. (2010). Sex-specific parent-of-origin allelic expression in the mouse brain. *Science, 329*(5992), 682–685.

Guadano-Ferraz, A., Escamez, M. J., Rausell, E., & Bernal, J. (1999). Expression of type 2 iodothyronine deiodinase in hypothyroid rat brain indicates an important role of thyroid hormone in the development of specific primary sensory systems. *Journal of Neuroscience, 19*(9), 3430–3439.

Harris, K. B., & Pass, K. A. (2007). Increase in congenital hypothyroidism in New York State and in the United States. *Molecular Genetics and Metabolism, 91*(3), 268–277.

Hinton, C. F., Harris, K. B., Borgfeld, L., Drummond-Borg, M., Eaton, R., Lorey, F.,... Pass, K. A. (2010). Trends in incidence rates of congenital hypothyroidism related to select demographic factors: Data from the United States, California, Massachusetts, New York, and Texas. *Pediatrics, 125*(Suppl 2), S37–S47.

Köhrle, J. (2007). Thyroid hormone transporters in health and disease: Advances in thyroid hormone deiodination. *Best Practices and Research Clinical Endocrinology and Metabolism, 21*(2), 173–191.

Köhrle, J., Jakob, F., Contempre, B., & Dumont, J. E. (2005). Selenium, the thyroid, and the endocrine system. *Endocrine Reviews, 26*(7), 944–984.

List, E. O., Sackmann-Sala, L., Berryman, D. E., Funk, K., Kelder, B., Gosney, E. S.,... Kopchick, J. J. (2011). Endocrine parameters and phenotypes of the growth hormone receptor gene disrupted (GHR-/-) mouse. *Endocrine Reviews, 32*(3), 356–386.

Marsh-Armstrong, N., Huang, H., Remo, B. F., Liu, T. T., & Brown, D. D. (1999). Asymmetric growth and development of the Xenopus laevis retina during metamorphosis is controlled by type III deiodinase. *Neuron, 24*(4), 871–878.

Marsili, A., Zavacki, A. M., Harney, J. W., & Larsen, P. R. (2011). Physiological role and regulation of iodothyronine deiodinases: A 2011 update. *Journal of Endocrinological Investigation, 34*(5), 395–407.

Monroy-Santoyo, S., Ibarra-González, I., Fernández-Lainez, C., Greenawalt-Rodríguez, S., Chacón-Rey, J., Calzada-León, R., & Vela-Amieva, M. (2011). Higher incidence of thyroid agenesis in Mexican newborns with congenital hypothyroidism associated with birth defects. *Early Human Development, 88*(1), 61–64.

Mostert, V. (2000). Selenoprotein P: Properties, functions, and regulation. *Archives of Biochemistry and Biophysics, 376*(2), 433–438.

Murray, G. R. (1891). Note on the treatment of myxoedema by hypodermic injections of an extract of the thyroid gland of a sheep. *British Medical Journal, 2*(1606), 796–797.

Nagasaki, K., Asami, T., Ogawa, Y., Kikuchi, T., & Uchiyama, M. (2011). A study of the etiology of congenital hypothyroidism in the Niigata prefecture of Japan in patients born between 1989 and 2005 and evaluated at ages 5–19. *Thyroid, 21*(4), 361–365.

Ng, L., Hernandez, A., He, W., Ren, T., Srinivas, M., Ma, M., . . . Forrest, D. (2009). A protective role for type 3 deiodinase, a thyroid hormone-inactivating enzyme, in cochlear development and auditory function. *Endocrinology, 150*(4), 1952–1960.

Ng, L., Lyubarsky, A., Nikonov, S. S., Ma, M., Srinivas, M., Kefas, B., . . . Forrest, D. (2010). Type 3 deiodinase, a thyroid-hormone-inactivating enzyme, controls survival and maturation of cone photoreceptors. *Journal of Neuroscience, 30*(9), 3347–3357.

Pearce, E. N. (2011). Iodine nutrition in the UK: What went wrong? *Lancet, 377*(9782), 1979–1980.

Pearce, E. N., & Leung, A. M. (2013). The state of U.S. Iodine nutrition: How can we ensure adequate iodine for all? *Thyroid, 23*(8), 924–925.

Piehl, S., Hoefig, C. S., Scanlan, T. S., & Köhrle, J. (2011). Thyronamines--past, present, and future. *Endocrine Reviews, 32*(1), 64–80.

Pinna, G., Hiedra, L., Meinhold, H., Eravci, M., Prengel, H., Brödel, O., . . . Baumgartner, A. (1998). 3,3'-Diiodothyronine concentrations in the sera of patients with nonthyroidal illnesses and brain tumors and of healthy subjects during acute stress. *Journal of Clinical Endocrinology and Metabolism, 83*(9), 3071–3077.

Pop, V. J., Kuijpens, J. L., van Baar, A. L., Verkerk, G., van Son, M. M., de Vijlder, J. J., . . . Vader, H. L. (1999). Low maternal free thyroxine concentrations during early pregnancy are associated with impaired psychomotor development in infancy. *Clinical Endocrinology (Oxford), 50*(2), 149–155.

Railton, T. C. (1894). Sporadic cretinism treated by administration of the thyroid gland. *British Medical Journal, 1*(1744), 1180–1181.

Ralston, N. V., Blackwell, J. L., III, & Raymond, L. J. (2007). Importance of molar ratios in selenium-dependent protection against methylmercury toxicity. *Biological Trace Elements Research, 119*(3), 255–268.

Rastogi, M. V., & LaFranchi, S. H. (2010). Congenital hypothyroidism. *Orphanet Journal of Rare Diseases, 5*, 17.

Rendon-Macias, M. E., Morales-Garcia, I., Huerta-Hernandez, E., Silva-Batalla, A., & Villasis-Keever, M. A. (2008). Birth prevalence of congenital hypothyroidism in Mexico. *Paediatric and Perinatal Epidemiology, 22*(5), 478–485.

Rotruck, J. T., Pope, A. L., Ganther, H. E., Swanson, A. B., Hafeman, D. G., & Hoekstra, W. G. (1973). Selenium: Biochemical role as a component of glutathione peroxidase. *Science, 179*(4073), 588–590.

Salvatore, D. (2011). Deiodinases: Keeping the thyroid hormone supply in balance. *Journal of Endocrinology, 209*(3), 259–260.

Scanlan, T. S., Suchland, K. L., Hart, M. E., Chiellini, G., Huang, Y., Kruzich, P. J.,... Grandy, D. K. (2004). 3-Iodothyronamine is an endogenous and rapid-acting derivative of thyroid hormone. *Nature Medicine, 10*(6), 638–642.

Shapira, S. K., Lloyd-Puryear, M. A., & Boyle, C. (2010). Future research directions to identify causes of the increasing incidence rate of congenital hypothyroidism in the United States. *Pediatrics, 125*(Suppl 2), S64–S68.

Simonides, W. S., Mulcahey, M. A., Redout, E. M., Muller, A., Zuidwijk, M. J., Visser, T. J.,... Huang, S. A. (2008). Hypoxia-inducible factor induces local thyroid hormone inactivation during hypoxic-ischemic disease in rats. *Journal of Clinical0 Investigation, 118*(3), 975–983.

Sittig, L. J., Herzing, L. B., Shukla, P. K., & Redei, E. E. (2011). Parent-of-origin allelic contributions to deiodinase-3 expression elicit localized hyperthyroid milieu in the hippocampus. *Molecular Psychiatry, 16*(8), 786–787.

Sittig, L. J., Shukla, P. K., Herzing, L. B., & Redei, E. E. (2011). Strain-specific vulnerability to alcohol exposure in utero via hippocampal parent-of-origin expression of deiodinase-III. *FASEB Journal, 25*(7), 2313–2324.

St. Germain, D. L., Galton, V. A., & Hernandez, A. (2009). Minireview: Defining the roles of the iodothyronine deiodinases: Current concepts and challenges. *Endocrinology, 150*(3), 1097–1107.

Steinbrenner, H., & Sies, H. (2013). Selenium homeostasis and antioxidant selenoproteins in brain: Implications for disorders in the central nervous system. *Archives of Biochemistry and Biophysics, 536*(2), 152–157.

Stringari, J., Nunes, A. K., Franco, J. L., Bohrer, D., Garcia, S. C., Dafre, A. L.,... Farina, M. (2008). Prenatal methylmercury exposure hampers glutathione antioxidant system ontogenesis and causes long-lasting oxidative stress in the mouse brain. *Toxicology and Applied Pharmacology, 227*(1), 147–154.

Sullivan, K. M. (2008). Increase in congenital hypothyroidism due to inadequate iodine nutrition? *Molecular Genetics and Metabolism, 93*(4), 485.

Vieira, H. L., Alves, P. M., & Vercelli, A. (2011). Modulation of neuronal stem cell differentiation by hypoxia and reactive oxygen species. *Progress in Neurobiology, 93*(3), 444–455.

Visser, T. J., Does-Tobe, I., Docter, R., & Hennemann, G. (1976). Subcellular localization of a rat liver enzyme converting thyroxine into tri-iodothyronine and possible involvement of essential thiol groups. *Biochemical Journal, 157*(2), 479–482.

Visser, W. E., Friesema, E. C., & Visser, T. J. (2011). Minireview: Thyroid hormone transporters: the knowns and the unknowns. *Molecular Endocrinology, 25*(1), 1–14.

Watanabe, C., Yoshida, K., Kasanuma, Y., Kun, Y., & Satoh, H. (1999). In utero methylmercury exposure differentially affects the activities of selenoenzymes in the fetal mouse brain. *Environmental Research, 80*(3), 208–214.

Wilson, W. R., & Hay, M. P. (2011). Targeting hypoxia in cancer therapy. *Nature Reviews Cancer, 11*(6), 393–410.

Yen, P. M. (2001). Physiological and molecular basis of thyroid hormone action. *Physiological Reviews, 81*(3), 1097–1142.

Zhang, H., Feng, X., Larssen, T., Qiu, G., & Vogt, R. D. (2010). In inland China, rice, rather than fish, is the major pathway for methylmercury exposure. *Environmental Health Perspectives, 118*(9), 1183–1188.

Zhang, H., Feng, X., Zhu, J., Sapkota, A., Meng, B., Yao, H.,... Larssen, T. (2012). Selenium in soil inhibits mercury uptake and translocation in rice (Oryza sativa L.). *Environmental Science and Technology, 46*(18), 10040–10046.

Zimmermann, M. B. (2009). Iodine deficiency. *Endocrine Reviews, 30*(4), 376–408.

# Chapter 3

# Thyroid Hormone and Brain Development

*Bridging Environment to Gene Expression*

CHAPTER OUTLINE

The brain is the most complicated and specialized organ in the vertebrate body and arguably the most organized structure known. Possessing the greatest number of different cell types of any tissue, it expresses over 75% of genes identified in the human genome. All of the major cell types in the brain express the nuclear receptors for thyroid hormone (TH), referred to as thyroid hormone receptors (TRs). TRs act as ligand-binding controllers of transcription. As TRs directly regulate gene networks controlling neuronal development, thyroid signaling forms a direct route through which environmental factors can modulate brain development programs. TH-responsive cell types in the brain include the multiple categories of neurons and all of the different types of glial cells (astrocytes, oligodendrocytes, and microglia). As seen in Chapter 2, the primary action of TH and TRs is to regulate gene transcription. Numerous processes in the developing brain require TH regulation of gene networks, including cell division, differentiation to specific neuronal cell types, synaptogenesis, and neuronal plasticity. Most of these processes continue, albeit at reduced rates, in the adult. Thus, TH is required for optimal brain function throughout life. However, there are particularly sensitive windows of development when either insufficient or excess TH will adversely alter the genetic programs underlying brain development and permanently affect function. The best documented sensitive window for TH effects on neurodevelopment is the perinatal period, but increasing focus is being placed on early, intrauterine development.

Background: Lack of Thyroid Hormone Irreversibly Impairs Brain Development

Without the right amount of TH at the right time during your development and growth, you, the person reading these lines, would not be able to make sense of this sentence, let alone the message of this book. Lack of TH due to iodine deficiency (see Chapter 2) is the world's main cause of preventable mental retardation. Iodine deficiency, and hence hypothyroidism during development, has been estimated to lead to a global loss of 10 to 15 IQ points at the population level (see http://www.iccidd.org/). As discussed in Chapters 1 and 7 (see Box 7.1), such a shift in a population's IQ can have devastating socioeconomic consequences, with respectively decreased and increased proportions of gifted individuals and socially dependent people. Severe lack of TH during development in humans causes cretinism. Owing to postnatal testing for congenital hypothyroidism, cretinism due to severe TH deficiency is a disease of the past in developed countries. However, lesser TH deficiencies in fetal development or childhood due to lack of iodine and often compounded by chemical pollution are still present and could be contributing to different brain disorders. Disorders of developmental origin that have been linked to environmental pollution include intellectual disability, autism spectrum disorders (ASD). and attention-deficit/hyperactivity disorder (ADHD), with many of the suspected substances acting on TH signaling.

Although this book addresses the question of how environmental pollution can affect TH control of brain development and function, it should be recalled that TH contributes to the development of many other organs and tissues. This fact is particularly evident in cretinism, where not only intelligence is severely impaired, but also physical growth is stunted, and craniofacial features are affected. In the most marked cases the limb bones fail to form correctly and the patient cannot walk. Such observations are in accordance with the multiple actions of $T_3$ on bone and muscle metabolism, during development and in the adult (Bassett & Williams, 2008). Furthermore, despite the fact that most of the emphasis in endocrine disruption work has focused on signaling implicated in estrogen or androgen signaling and reproduction,[1] the number of potential chemicals that affect thyroid signaling appear to be far greater (Howdeshell, 2002). Also, the spectrum of physiological endpoints controlled by TRs exceed those regulated by estrogen signaling.

Here we address only the effects of TH on brain and the central nervous system. Much of the discussion concerns studies that primarily addressed the question of how thyroid signaling acts on brain development by experimentally modulating TH availability, as opposed to animal models lacking TRs or expressing mutant TRs. Three main arguments justify this emphasis on the ligand, $T_3$, and less on the receptors that transduce the signal. First, developmental effects of TH lack are greater than that of any of the main receptor isoforms, TRα1, TRβ1, or TRβ2 (Fig. 3.1a). Many hypotheses have been proposed to explain this result, which was a very surprising finding to many observers. The model that fits best with current understanding of the molecular mechanisms underlying thyroid signaling argues that effects on transcription induced by the receptor in the absence of ligand is far more detrimental than the modified level of transcription that results from absence of receptor, as seen in mice that lack one or other of the TRs. Another argument for the emphasis on ligand in this chapter is that lack of ligand is much more common in clinical settings than lack of receptor or mutations in receptors. In fact, it was only recently that the first mutation in a human TRα was reported (Bochukova et al., 2012).

---

1 A current PubMed search for "reproductive endocrine disruption" generates about 1,710 citations; "endocrine disruption and thyroid" generates around 480.

Multiple mutations in TRβ have been described in human populations and have been engineered in mice. The phenotypes of mutant mice lacking TRs or bearing mutant TRs have been reviewed (Flamant & Samarut, 2003), with one focusing on brain development (Bernal, 2007). The third, and most important, argument is that the majority of TH-disrupting chemicals modulate TH availability, most often decreasing the amounts of $T_3$ that reach target tissues (see Chapter 5). Chemicals that modify $T_3$ availability at crucial times in development will alter the timing of the genetic programs controlled by $T_3$/TRs that are essential to normal brain development. Interference by environmental factors with $T_3$/TR control of gene transcription provides a mechanism whereby environment can play out effects on gene networks; that is, it can underlie the gene × environment effects that are discussed more in the context of developmental disorders such as ASD (Chapter 7). To aid understanding of this principal mode of action of TH on gene expression via their nuclear receptors, a brief account of how TRs regulate gene transcription is necessary.

### Thyroid Hormones Bind to Thyroid Hormone Receptors, Members of the Nuclear Receptor Family of Ligand-Dependent Transcription Factors

As illustrated in Fig. 3.1, most vertebrate genomes have two genes that code for proteins that can bind the active form of TH, $T_3$. These proteins are called thyroid receptors (TRs) and belong to a larger category of similar nuclear receptors (NRs; see Box 1.1, Chapter 1). All these NRs are transcription factors.[2] The NR family of transcription factors includes the receptors for steroid hormones (e.g., estrogens, androgens, and progesterone) as well as those that bind the stress hormones (glucocorticoids). These receptors have a modular structure with specific parts of the protein that bind DNA (DNA binding domain [DBD]), and other parts that bind the ligand (ligand binding domain [LBD]), while the structure of other regions defines interactions with multiple proteins implicated in controlling gene transcription.

This modular structure allows a part of the receptor that binds a hormone (or ligand) to, in turn, regulate the transcriptional activity of the receptor on target genes. This hormone-dependent gene control system explains why the ligand-binding NRs, such as estrogen receptors (ERs), androgen receptors (ARs), and TRs represent such sensitive and direct routes for environmental factors to interfere with the physiological functions they control: development, reproduction, and homeostasis.

Four main TR proteins are produced from the two TR-expressing genes, originally called *c-erbAa* and *c-erbAb* but more recently renamed thyroid hormone receptors A and B (*THRA* and *THRB*). The international nuclear receptor nomenclature for these genes is NR1A1 and NR1A2. *THRA* gives rise to

2   A transcription factor is a protein that binds to specific sequences in DNA thereby modulating the rate of transcription. Transcription factors interact directly and indirectly with other proteins, such as comodulators and enzymes implicated in the process of transcribing RNA from DNA.

two proteins: TRα1 and TRα2; whereas TRβ1 and TRβ2 are produced from *THRB* (Fig. 3.1a). TRα1, TRβ1, and TRβ2 are all bona fide TRs in that they can bind $T_3$ (and with much lesser affinity, $T_4$) and thereby modulate target gene transcription. In contrast, the TRα2 isoform cannot bind either $T_3$ or $T_4$. However, as the DBD of TRα2 is the same as that of TRα1, it can recognize the DNA sequences in the same gene targets as the other $T_3$-binding receptors. TRα2 can thus block the $T_3$-dependent responses that would otherwise be produced by the bona fide TRs present in the cell. Intriguingly, the brain shows particularly high levels of expression of mRNA encoding the TRα2 isoform, though little research has been directed to understanding its physiological significance.

TRs most often regulate transcription by forming heterodimers with an RXR receptor. These TR/RXR heterodimers act by binding to the TH regulatory elements (TREs) in target genes (Fig. 3.1b). In most vertebrate genomes RXRs are encoded by three genes: RXRα, β, and γ. All three RXR isotypes can act as heterodimeric partners for TRs. As for TRs, each gene produces two major isoforms (RXRα1 and RXRα2, etc.; Germain et al., 2006). All three RXR isotypes are present in the brain, though like the TRs, they show region- and cell-specific expression patterns. Besides forming heterodimers with TRs, RXRs are also partners for other NRs, notably the Vitamin D receptor and the so–called peroxisome proliferating activator receptors (PPARs), of which again there are three types, α, β, and γ. The ligand-binding pockets of the RXR subtypes are larger than that of the TRs and represent confirmed targets for endocrine disruption (le Maire et al., 2009) with many molecules capable of fitting within the pocket.[3]

Returning to the classical, ligand $(T_3)$- binding receptors, TRα1, TRβ1, and TRβ2, it is important to realize that these TRs, like other NRs, form direct physiological links relaying information from the environment, through the production of hormone to the immediate control of gene activity. An example is the effect of cold on heat production by the body. Cold temperatures stimulate the hypothalamus to produce more TRH, which in turn increases production of pituitary TSH and thyroid gland production and release of $T_4$. The prohormone $T_4$ is converted to $T_3$ in target tissues by the enzyme deiodinase 2 (D2). Certain targets tissues, such as brown adipose tissue (BAT), are particularly implicated in the body's response to cold by increasing thermogenesis. In the mitochondria-rich BAT, stimulation by the cold-activated adrenergic system increases the production of signals (cAMP), which in turn stimulates the production of D2, producing even more $T_3$ from the TRH/TSH-driven increased availability of $T_4$. Increased production of D2 and $T_3$ production drive heat production by the mitochondria via increased expression of an uncoupling protein, UCP1 (Martinez de Mena, Scanlan, & Obregon, 2010). Thus, the gene

---

3   The PPAR and RXR receptors have much larger, and more flexible, ligand-binding pockets than TRs. Recent data show that the LBD of PPARs can bind two ligands simultaneously.

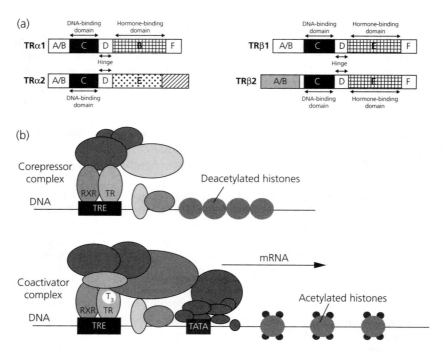

Figure 3–1. Thyroid hormone receptors (TRs) and transcriptional regulation. (*a*) In most vertebrates, two genes encode nuclear thyroid hormone receptors, THRA and THRB. As different promoter start sites can be used to begin transcription and alternative splicing of mRNA can occur, two distinct isoforms can be produced from each of the genes: TRα1 and TRα2 from THRA and TRβ1 and TRβ2 from THRB. TRα1, TRβ1, and TRβ2 all bind $T_3$ and are bona fide receptors. In contrast, TRα2 does not bind $T_3$ but can bind to the same DNA sites (TH response elements [TREs]) as the $T_3$ binding TRs. All four of these isoforms are expressed in the brain, although with markedly distinct expression patterns and levels of production. (*b*) A simplified model of TH and TR regulation of transcription of a positively regulated gene. Upper part: In many situations TR and its heterodimeric partner, an RXR, can bind to regulatory regions (TREs) in the target gene in the absence of ligand. In this case, a gene that is positively regulated by $T_3$/TR, the empty receptor is in a configuration that will associate with corepressor complexes that cause chromatin compaction around the target gene, a state that represses transcription. Lower part: When $T_3$ is bound, a conformational change occurs in the TR, which then associates with a new set of comodulator proteins, coactivators that permit acetylation of the histones in the chromatin, a modification that changes chromatin conformation and permits active transcription and mRNA production (arrow).

response to cold is regulated directly and locally by a central, brain-driven, increased availability of $T_3$ to activate transcription by TRs already present in the target tissue. Heat production is also stimulated in hyperthyroidism. In this case the driver is increased hypothalamic $T_3$, which again stimulates the sympathetic nervous system to activate D2 and hence $T_3$ and heat production in BAT (Lopez et al., 2010).

Virtually every cell in all vertebrate organisms expresses at least one of the TRs. The brain displays cell-specific and developmentally regulated TR expression. For instance, the hypothalamic TRH-expressing neurons express both TRβ1 and TRβ2, whereas few other neurons express both TRβ isoforms. Certain genes show highly TR-specific responses, whereas others can be activated or repressed by any one or other of the TRs. An interesting example of TR-specific gene regulation is $T_3$-dependent repression of TRH transcription in the hypothalamus, where only TRβ1 and TRβ2 induce transcriptional repression of this gene (Dupre et al., 2004) and this despite the fact that TRα1 and TRα2 are expressed in the TRH neuron. Other neural cells may only express one or other of the THR genes. This is the case of the progenitor cells in the subventricular zone of the adult mammalian brain. These cells that generate new neurons throughout life only express the THRA gene and produce TRα1 and TRα2. No TRβ is expressed in these cells. Thus, in each brain area and specific neural cell type, the combination of TRs present and the availability of $T_3$ (which is determined locally by the relative expression of activating and inactivating deiodinases and transporters) will define how target genes are regulated.

It has been suggested that $T_4$ can exert certain biological functions that occur independently of nuclear TRs and without $T_4$ undergoing deiodination to $T_3$. These effects are sometimes referred to as "nongenomic effects" because they seem to be triggered by association with cell membrane proteins such as integrins (Davis, Davis, Mousa, Luidens, & Lin, 2011). The in vitro experiments that have been used to demonstrate such membrane effects require very high concentrations of $T_4$ to induce responses. For instance, in a study (Bergh et al., 2005) where radioactive $T_4$ was displaced by cold $T_4$ or $T_3$ from binding to the integrin αV β3 receptor, the IC50 (50% displacement of the radioactive ligand), corresponded to supraphysiological amounts of $T_4$, close to $10^{-6}$ M, or even higher amounts of $T_3$, over $10^{-4}$ M. The fact that such high amounts are required suggests that to carry out similar functions in vivo, levels of $T_4$ would need to be maintained at levels well over normal. Thus, a physiological relevance for these nongenomic effects seems unlikely, given that total serum $T_4$ levels in euthyroid humans are in the $5.10^{-8}$ M to $10^{-7}$ M range, but values for free $T_4$ (i.e., not bound to distributor proteins) are in the range of $10^{-11}$ M, more that 7 orders of magnitude lower than the concentrations used in many in vitro nongenomic studies. Values of $FT_3$ are even lower (between 2 and $6.10^{-12}$ M).

From here on, in this chapter we take chronological and structural approaches to emphasize the time windows and cellular processes that could be targets of endocrine disruption through TH-dependent mechanisms in brain development.

Early Neurodevelopment

To understand, or at least have a perspective on the numerous processes in which TH can be implicated during the development of the nervous system, a rapid description of neurodevelopment is required.

In vertebrates (the group of animals that includes fish, amphibians, reptiles, birds, and mammals) the nervous system is derived from the ectoderm, the outer layer of the three germ layers (Gilbert, 2010). The ectoderm actually gives rise to three major sets of tissues: the epidermis, the neural crest, and the neural tube (Fig. 3.2). The epidermis then differentiates into tissues that include skin, eye lens and cornea, nails, hair, and tooth enamel. Neural crest derivatives include the peripheral nervous system (neuroglial cells, Schwann cells, and the sympathetic and parasympathetic autonomic nervous systems), the adrenal medulla, and tooth dentine. The brain, spinal cord, and retina derive from the neural tube.

The developmental process that separates the ectoderm into these three sets of tissues is referred to as "primary neurulation." This series of events includes the shaping a specialized area of neuroectoderm, the neural plate, into the neural tube and neural crest. These processes implicate the folding of a flat structure, the neural plate, into a cylinder, the neural tube. Defects in neural tube formation (and especially neural tube closure) are quite frequent, representing up to 1 in 1,000 live births in humans. Prescription of folic acid (often refered to as folate or vitamin B9) has reduced the incidence and economic burden of neural tube defect (Obican, Finnell, Mills, Shaw, & Scialli, 2010; Yi, Lindemann, Colligs, & Snowball, 2011). Although TH has not been implicated in this process per se, environmental contaminants, such as water disinfection by-products or fungal contamination of crops, have been

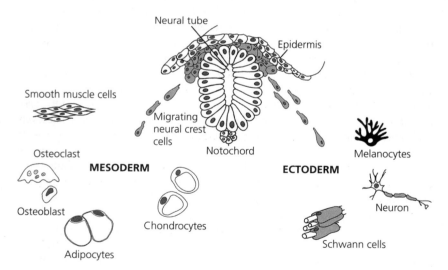

Figure 3–2. The vertebrate ectoderm and its derivatives. The ectoderm is the outer of the three germ layers. The other two layers are the mesoderm and the endoderm (not shown). After differentiation into the epidermis, the neural crest, and the neural tube, the ectoderm becomes the source of multiple neuronal and nonneuronal cell types. On the left part of the figure some of the mesoderm derivatives are illustrated.

associated with increased risk of neural tube closure effect (Klotz & Pyrch, 1999; Marasas et al., 2004; Ren et al., 2011). Also, recent epidemiological studies from China showed that levels of polycyclic aromatic hydrocarbons (PAH) were particularly high in the placentas of fetuses or newborns with neural tube defects (Naufal et al., 2010; Ren et al., 2011). PAH compounds include flame retardants and polychlorinated biphenyls, which can interfere with thyroid signaling (see Chapter 5).

Once formed, the neural tube undergoes differentiation to form the brain and spinal cord and then their main constituent morphological areas (Fig. 3.3). Three overarching mechanisms contribute to this process simultaneously. First, bulges and constrictions sculpt the main chambers, while distinct cell populations are organized into functional areas then, at the level of individual cells, differentiation into nerve cells (neurons) or glia (cells with a more supporting, but still very active, role) begins.

About $10^{11}$ neurons and $10^{12}$ glia cells constitute the human brain (see Box 3.1). The different stages of differentiation of the immense variety of neuronal types and glia cells from a specialized precursor cell in the neuroectoderm are not fully understood. It is, however, well established that during early embryonic development, specialized cells in the lining of the neural tube near the ventricle (or lumen) become radial glial cells that then undergo division to generate neuronal precursors (that will then respond to other cues to give rise to the immense variety of different neurons) and glial cell precursors. As development proceeds, these radial glial cells are somehow set aside, and spared from differentiating signals, to become the neural stem cells of the adult neurogenic niche (Kriegstein & Alvarez-Buylla, 2009; Merkle & Alvarez-Buylla, 2006) (Fig. 3.4).

For decades, it was thought that neurogenesis, implicating the birth of new neurons from stem cells, was limited to early development. During the last two decades of the 20th century numerous highly original research approaches gradually eroded and disproved this dogma. However, before that back in the early 1960s, Joseph Altman had cautiously questioned whether new neurons could arise in the adult rodent brain (Altman, 1962). Interestingly, much of Altman's research concerned effects of hypo- and hyperthyroidism on the developing rat brain (Nicholson & Altman, 1972a, 1972b), although he did not investigate the effects of TH on adult neurogenesis. The main evidence driving the shift in thought on the occurrence of neurogenesis in adult mammals came from work from Nottebohm's group, who observed annual cycles of neurogenesis with testosterone-dependent learning of new songs in canaries (Alvarez-Buylla, 1990; Alvarez-Buylla, Theelen, & Nottebohm, 1988). The younger scientist carrying out this work, Alvarez-Buylla, then went on to demonstrate that the neural stem cells in the adult mouse brain are a very specialized form of astrocyte (a type of glial cell). This work produced a landmark paper in 1999 (Doetsch, Caille, Lim, Garcia-Verdugo, & Alvarez-Buylla, 1999). Two main areas of the adult mammalian brain are now known to harbor neural stem cells, the hippocampus (essential for learning and memory) and the subventricular zone (SVZ) of the lateral ventricle. The importance of

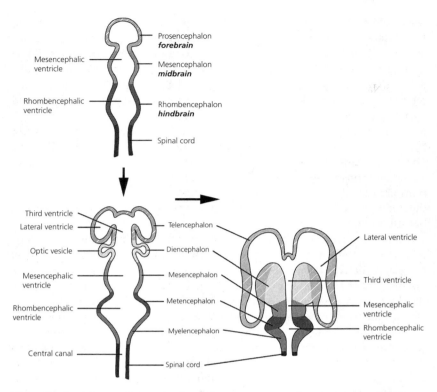

**Figure 3–3.** Schema of neural tube differentiation into the main anatomical brain structures. As development progresses following closure of the neural tube, ballooning and constrictions of the lumen sculpt the chambers of the brain.

---

**Box 3–1. Neurons and Glia**

---

Two main categories of neuronal cells constitute the brain and peripheral nervous system: neurons and glia. Neurons are the specialized cells that transmit electric impulses. They receive input from other neurons via their dendrites and send out axons that synapse with other neurons. Glia cells are frequently described as the supporting cells that nurture neurons, though their active roles in modulating neural transmission are increasingly well documented. Three main types of glial cell are distinguished: astrocytes and the two types of cells that produce myelin, oligodendrocytes in the central nervous system and the Schwann cells in the peripheral nervous system (including the spinal cord). A fourth type of "glia" cell is the microglial cell that has a completely different cellular origin. These brain-specific immune cells are actually derived from bone marrow–derived myelo-monocytic cells that cross the blood–brain barrier and differentiate into the microglia. Like macrophages, microglia have a phagocytic function, engulfing dead cells. They also produce inflammatory signals, cytokines.

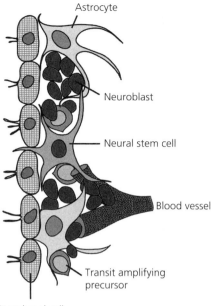

Astrocyte

Neuroblast

Neural stem cell

Blood vessel

Transit amplifying
precursor

Ependymal cell

**Figure 3–4.** The adult neural stem cell niche. In the adult brain the radial glial cell–derived neural stem cells are surrounded by transit amplifying cells in the parenchyma and ependymal cells lining the ventricle. However, the neural stem cells themselves make contact with the ventricle and the cerebrospinal fluid through their cilia that project into the ventricular lumen.

TH signaling in controlling division and differentiation within both of these adult mouse neural stem cell niches is increasingly documented (Kapoor et al., 2010; Kapoor, Ghosh, Nordstrom, Vennstrom, & Vaidya, 2011; Lemkine et al., 2005; Lopez-Juarez et al., 2012).

Less is known about how TH signaling is implicated in the very early stages of neural development in the embryo. However, data from basic research in birds and amphibians and epidemiological evidence from human studies show that TH can have important roles to play during this period. For instance, using the chick embryo as an experimental model, Flamant and Samarut (1998) were able to demonstrate that different areas of the very early embryo and the tissues surrounding the embryo not only had distinct levels of the active form of TH, $T_3$, but also different capacities to degrade or generate $T_3$, no doubt through differential expression of deiodinases. Similarly, using the *Xenopus* embryo, our laboratory recently showed that several genes implicated in early neurogenesis were regulated in a TH-dependent manner (Fini et al., 2012). One of the key genes regulated by TH in the neurogenic regions of the early embryonic brain is *Sox2*, a pluripotency gene controlling neural stem cell division and neuronal commitment in the adult SVZ (Lopez-Juarez et al., 2012). That *Sox2* is a TH target is of major interest as *Sox2* is a key gene governing stem cell identity, not only in neural stem cells but also in other stem cell lineages. Notably, *Sox2* was a member of the quartet of genes used to induce pluripotency in fibroblasts in the initial groundbreaking, and Nobel Prize winning, discovery of Takahashi and Yamanaka (2006). This research opened up wide and novel perspectives for both basic and applied research in stem cell biology. The fact that *Sox2* is a guardian of stem cell pluripotency and is repressed by TH in the neurogenic areas of mice and amphibians underlines the importance of timing of TH availability during neuronal development. Too much TH will limit production of neuronal precursors by pushing the progenitors to rapid differentiation before they can amplify the progenitor pool by multiple divisions. Too little TH will restrain neural production by blocking cell cycle progression and impair neuronal commitment and differentiation.

## Epidemiological Studies in Humans Show the Importance of Thyroid Hormone Signaling for Early Fetal Brain Development

Findings on the role of TH governing gene expression and cell proliferation balance during neurogenesis in the early vertebrate embryo are echoed in epidemiological studies that show the importance of maternal TH levels in early pregnancy for the child's later neurodevelopment and behavior. Even though it is well established in both rodent and humans that TH is absolutely vital for brain development in late gestation and the early postnatal period, it is only recently that the importance of sufficient levels of TH during early pregnancy have become documented and their role in determining the infant's subsequent neurodevelopment accepted. For instance, that a mother's TH levels during pregnancy are correlated with IQ and neurodevelopment was established and underscored by many thorough epidemiological studies (e.g., see Haddow et al., 1999). However, the critical role of TH during the early stages of brain development has come mostly from more recent studies (Henrichs et al., 2010), and this despite the fact that one of the pioneers of this area of research, Gabriela Escobar del Rey, has for a long time argued that maternal TH could have functional significance for the developing fetus in the first months of pregnancy prior to the formation of the fetal thyroid gland (Contempre et al., 1993; de Escobar, Ares, Berbel, Obregon, & del Rey, 2008; de Escobar, Obregon, & del Rey, 2007). Some of the first epidemiological data came from a Dutch group (Pop et al., 1995, 1999), who showed that the lower the maternal TH levels in the first trimester of pregnancy the greater the risk of delay in the child's psychomotor development. More recently, these findings have been consolidated with more data from the Netherlands (Henrichs et al., 2010), arguing for a need for more data and greater prophylaxis of iodine deficiency and monitoring of thyroid status during early pregnancy across different populations and geographical areas. This lack is particularly striking as, although data on maternal iodine and TH levels (and even chemical contamination) in early pregnancy in other countries are slowly accumulating, little epidemiological data, are available on associations of maternal TH levels with neurodevelopmental outcome of the child.

It seems possible that examining maternal iodide levels is a more sensitive method to assess maternal–fetal iodide and TH status than measuring maternal TH or TSH levels. This may be due to the large individual variations in TH and TSH levels. The most recent report to show clear associations between maternal iodide levels in first trimester pregnancy and the child's neurodevelopmental outcome came from the work of Margaret Rayman's group (Bath, Steer, Golding, Emmett, & Rayman, 2013). As the authors argue, the United Kingdom is showing increasing iodide deficiency, notably in young women of child-bearing age and pregnant women. This iodine deficiency can impact neurodevelopment. Children born to mothers with median urinary iodine levels below 150 µg/g in early pregnancy (mean 10 weeks) had a higher probability of being in the lowest quartile for IQ and for reading accuracy and comprehension when measured at 8 years of age (Bath et al., 2013; Bath & Rayman, 2013).

This statistically significant result obtained on a relatively small cohort (1,040 women), but well analyzed longitudinal study over more than 10 years, contrasts with the less marked results arising from a longitudinal study examining correlations on maternal TH parameters and children's neurodevelopment also carried out in the United Kingdom. This study (Lazarus et al., 2012) included a large number of women, over 20,000. All of the women had a blood sample taken around 12 weeks gestation. Half were screened for their $T_4$ and TSH levels immediately, and if needed given $T_4$. The $T_4$ and TSH levels of the others were measured later. The intellectual development of all the children was assessed at 3 years of age. Contrary to the authors' hypothesis, no difference was seen between the two groups. The authors discuss different factors that might have affected the power of the analysis, and one of their conclusions is that future studies should address earlier stages of gestation and concurrently measure iodine status. This suggestion fits with findings of many recent papers that have shown significant effects of iodine lack on cognitive outcome (see earlier and Bath et al., 2013; Hynes, Otahal, Hay, & Burgess, 2013; Loewenthal, 2013), as well as with current ideas about the previously unrecognized role of TH in the early stages of neurogenesis, the first 3 months of pregnancy in humans. One longitudinal study in the United States that is examining TH parameters earlier in gestation (from 8 weeks of pregnancy) aims to correlate maternal TH status at this stage with the neurodevelopmental outcome of the child at different points, with a last measurement at 5 years of age (http://www.clinicaltrials.gov/ct/show/NCT00388297). Results should be published in 2015.

Another paper on iodine supply and neurodevelopment stands out for its prescience and the strength of its findings, albeit again on small populations (Vermiglio et al., 2004). In this study the authors examined the consequences of relatively minor variations in iodine supply and TH levels on IQ scores and the propensity of children to develop attention-deficit/hyperactivity disorder (ADHD). Maternal TH and TSH at 8, 13, and 20 weeks of pregnancy were measured in an inland area of Sicily (with moderate iodine lack) and compared to those of a coastal group (considered as marginally iodine sufficient). As discussed in Chapter 7 on ADHD, the authors found large differences with significantly lower, mean IQ (−18 IQ points) in children born to mothers that were mildly hypothyroid during early pregnancy in the iodine-insufficient area, and this group had a far greater incidence of ADHD in their children.

## Cell-Specific Expression of Thyroid Hormone Transporters

Combinations of extrinsic and intrinsic signals interplay to generate the vast diversity of different interacting neurons and glial cells that make up a brain. These signals control a series of cellular processes that includes cell division, migration, differentiation, selective cell death, synaptogenesis, and plasticity. TH and TRs are well documented to affect each of these processes in different brain areas at all developmental stages, as well as in the mature, adult animal. An exhaustive coverage of how TH affects each of the processes in different brain areas is not known, mainly because research has tended to focus on those areas that show the most marked responses, even though the whole of brain growth and development is globally affected, particularly by hypothyroidism. Here, we will focus on key brain areas and processes, in particular the main events of brain development that could be irreversible targets of endocrine disruption.

One of the first elements in the generation of different neuronal cell types, whether in the embryonic neural tube or in an adult neural stem cell niche, is an asymmetric division that is followed by a phase of amplification of a pool of progenitor cells. In the embryonic neural tube, asymmetric division of precursor cells in the ventricular zone gives rise to another precursor cell and a neuron that then migrates radially to the external layers. In the adult neural stem cell niche, asymmetric division of a neuronal stem cell gives rise to a new daughter stem cell and a rapidly dividing, transit amplifying cell (TAP, Fig. 3.4). The effects of TH on the TAP cell population has been recently analyzed in the adult mouse brain (Lopez-Juarez et al., 2012), where $T_3$ and its alpha receptor, TRα, act as a neurogenic switch allowing precursor cells to differentiate into migratory neuroblasts (Fig. 3.5).

These observations beg the questions of how $T_4$ and $T_3$ availability is governed (1) in terms of entry into the brain and (2) within different brain structures, such as the neural stem cell niche. A major advancement in our understanding of these questions came with the discovery of specific transporters located on the plasma membrane that actively transport selectively $T_4$ and $T_3$ into and out of cells (Friesema, Jansen, & Visser, 2005; Heuer, 2007). Research in this field was pioneered by Theo Visser's group in Rotterdam starting at the end of the 1990s. Their research put an end to yet another erroneous dogma, the idea that TH, given their lipophilic nature, could enter cells by diffusion. Using a classical technique to express mRNA from rat liver in Xenopus eggs and to screen for clones that affect iodothyronine uptake, they identified a number of amino acid transporters with different selectivity for iodothyronines, including $T_4$ and

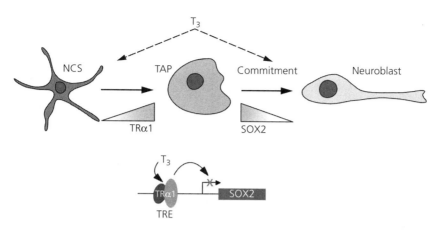

**Figure 3–5.** $T_3$ and TRα1 form a neurogenic switch in the adult neurogenic stem cell niche. As the neural stem cells (NCS) start to express TRα1, this receptor, with $T_3$, down-regulates expression of a pluripotency factor, Sox2. Together this TRα1/T3 combination switches the transit-amplifying cell (TAP) to a committed, migratory neuroblast. (Adapted from Lopez-Jaurez et al., 2012.)

$T_3$ (Friesema et al., 2004). In the brain a number of different transporters are expressed, each with cell-specific expression patterns that will partly determine (along with cell-specific expression of deiodinases) cell-specific availability of active TH.

Two of the most important transporters so far identified for brain development in mammals are the monocarboxylate transporter (MCT)8 and the organic anion transporting polypeptide (OATP)14 (OAT1C1 in humans). The brain also expresses MCT10 and the heterodimeric L-type amino acid transporters (Lat)1 and Lat2. MCT8 is expressed in the choroid plexus (part of the blood–brain barrier), on cells forming the blood–cerebrospinal fluid barrier and on neurons. Lat-1 and Lat-2 are also expressed on neurons in the mature rat brain. OATP14 is also expressed in the rat choroid plexus, but it is not expressed on neurons, only on astrocytes. MCT8, like MCT10, facilitates $T_4$ and $T_3$ uptake and efflux, but apparently it has a higher affinity for $T_3$, whereas OATP14 has higher affinity for $T_4$. As most neurons appear not to express the activating deiodinase, D2, and $T_4$ is present in greater quantities than $T_3$ in the circulation, neurons are largely dependent on production of $T_3$ from $T_4$ in astrocytes (Fig. 3.6).

The importance of MCT8 for neural development in humans is demonstrated by the severe mental retardation in boys that results from mutation of this gene (Friesema et al., 2004). No behavioral abnormalities are found in the phenotypic screens of mice lacking this transporter, suggesting that in mice other transporters can account for $T_3$ transport into neurons during brain development. Indeed, as suggested by Visser (Visser, Friesema, & Visser, 2011), given the complexity of the brain, it would be most surprising

68

Losing Our Minds

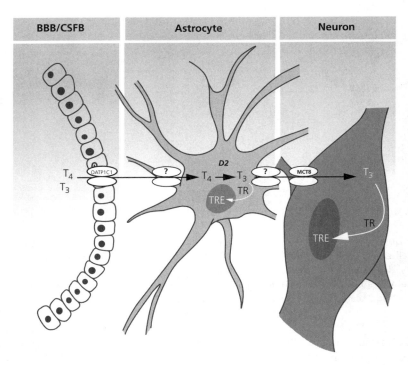

**Figure 3–6.** Schema of transporters controlling thyroid hormone availability and action in the developing brain. Transporters are depicted as homodimers (pairs of ovals). Transporters govern the uptake and efflux of $T_4$ and $T_3$ from the blood into the brain and between different cell types in the brain parenchyma. $T_4$, and to a lesser extent, $T_3$, are transported into the brain across the blood–brain barrier (BBB) or cerebrospinal fluid (CSF) barrier (choroid plexus). In astrocytes deiodinase 2 (D2) produces active $T_3$ from $T_4$. Efflux of $T_3$ from astrocytes and uptake by neurons is necessary for $T_3$ action in neurons. The transporters expressed in the astrocytes are not yet fully characterized (indicated by "?"). All the main cellular components of the brain, neurons, and the glial cells (astrocytes and oligodendrocytes) are responsive to $T_3$. Binding of $T_3$ to its receptors modulates expression of target genes through response elements (TRE) located in regulatory regions of the gene (see Fig. 3.1). (Adapted from Visser et al., 2011.)

if more transporters were not discovered. Current questions in this research area include whether specific transporters account for entry of TH into mitochondria, which transporters are responsible for entry of the hormones into oligodendrocytes, what factors control cell-specific expression of transporters during development, and whether any chemicals affect expression transporter expression during brain development. In this context, given the essential role of MCT8 in human brain development, it has been suggested that mutations or modulation of neuronal TH transporters might be implicated in behavioral disorders such as ADHD.

## Thyroid Hormone Is Needed for Maturation of All Glial Cells

TH modulates the processes of differentiation and maturation of all types of brain glial cells (nonneuronal cells), the astrocytes, oligodendrocytes, and the microglia. Hypothyroid animals have reduced populations of all glial cell types. The microglia are the brain-specific phagocytes that are broadly distributed throughout the brain. During embryogenesis these cells derive from the blood cell lineage and populate the developing brain. After birth a second wave of monocytes enters the brain, contributing to a rapid rise in microglial numbers (Ginhoux, Lim, Hoeffel, Low, & Huber, 2013), after which production of more microglia, such as seen during inflammation, relies on expansion of the resident population. Increasing data show important roles for these cells in immune defense and control of central nervous system homeostasis in normal and pathological states, including ASD (Tetreault et al., 2012). Microglia-based inflammation is observed in most brain pathologies and in response to injury, when microglia migrate to the affected site, release inflammatory signals and engulf degenerating cells and debris (Kettenmann, Hanisch, Noda, & Verkhratsky, 2011). Microglia also participate in normal brain processes, notably synaptogenesis and remodeling of neural networks in the postnatal brain. During the first 3 weeks of postnatal life in the mouse, microglia form complex networks with their processes and the formation of these networks is significantly reduced in hypothyroid pups (Mallat, Lima, Gervais, Colin, & Moura Neto, 2002). TH treatment results in greater production of microglial cells and the density of their processes. The effects of TH on microglia maturation are direct, as the cells express both TRα and TRβ and respond to $T_3$ when grown in culture, in the absence of any other neural cell types.

As to the astrocytes, these cells also express all TRs (Lebel, L'Herault, Dussault, & Puymirat, 1993). Astrocyte maturation is dependent on TH, and their production of extracellular matrix proteins is under control of TH. Most importantly, astrocytes, including the specialized tanycytes lining the brain ventricles, express the activating deiodinase, D2. The astrocytes are thus the main source of the active form of TH, $T_3$, in the brain. Intriguingly, most neurons do not express D2 and are therefore dependent on a supply of $T_3$ from astrocytes. In contrast, neurons can express D3, the inactivating deiodinase (Mohacsik, Zeold, Bianco, & Gereben, 2011).

Oligodendrocytes, the third type of glial cell, are the myelinating cells of the central nervous system, making up the white matter. Unmyelinated axons conduct impulses at a rate directly proportional to the axon diameter, usually between 0.5 and 30 μm, giving propagation rates of around 1 m sec$^{-1}$. Increasing axon size, as in the giant axons of certain invertebrates such as the squid, is one means to increase propagation speed. Myelination, by insulating the axon and preventing dispersal of the electric signal, enables propagation rates of between 50 and 100 m sec$^{-1}$. Certain palaeontologists and biologists consider that the appearance of myelinated axons (that increased speed of nerve conduction, thus decreasing response times) and hinged jaws synergistically provided vertebrates with an unparalleled advantage for predation. Close anatomical examination of the cranial structure and the size of the optic nerve and other brain cavities in fossil Palaeozoic fish led Zalc and collaborators to propose that the myelin sheath evolved with the neural crest (which gives rise to the jaw structures; see Fig. 3.1) and provided vertebrates with a distinct evolutionary advantage (Zalc, Goujet, & Colman, 2008).

A long history of research into the effects of TH on myelination processes (Valcana, Einstein, Csejtey, Dalal, & Timiras, 1975) has resulted in this process becoming one of the best-characterized $T_3$-dependent actions in the brain. Early experiments on the effects of TH on myelination began with rendering rats hypothyroid just after birth and examining myelin accumulation between postnatal weeks two and six, corresponding to the period of most rapid myelin formation and accumulation. Such approaches showed that pups lacking TH during this critical time frame had smaller brains and less myelin, both on a per brain and per total protein basis (Walters & Morell, 1981). These in vivo experiments actually followed earlier in vitro work using cultures of brain cells from mouse embryos at 15 days of embryonic development. Comparing myelin lipid synthesis in cultures grown with hypothyroid calf serum or the same serum supplemented with $T_3$ showed that $T_3$ significantly increased the synthesis of myelin-associated glycolipids. This work therefore showed that $T_3$ had an effect on production of myelin-specific components during embryonic development (Bhat, Sarlieve, Rao, & Pieringer, 1979), prior to the major postnatal phase of myelin accumulation.

Since these studies, many other authors have analyzed how TH acts on myelin protein and lipid formation, showing that $T_3$ regulates oligodendrocyte differentiation and myelin production mainly through transcriptional controls, notably on genes that code for structural proteins, including myelin basic protein (MBP), proteolipid protein (PLP), and myelin-associated glycoprotein (MAG; Ibarrola N & Rodriguez-Pena, 1997; Rodriguez-Pena, 1999; Strait, Carlson, Schwartz, & Oppenheimer, 1997).

Besides the importance of TH for oligodendrocyte protein and lipid production and for the process of differentiation itself, much work has been done on how TH influences the actual timing of the onset of oligodendrocyte differentiation. Much of the groundbreaking work in this area came from the excellent team of Martin Raff in London in the 1990s. In a seminal paper that appeared in 1994 (Barres, Lazar, & Raff, 1994), this group used an immunological method to separate out and purify oligodendrocyte precursor cells from the optic nerve of rats at postnatal day 8. This stage was chosen because they had observed that small numbers of oligodendrocytes begin to appear in the optic nerve soon after birth, but their presence increases most markedly around postnatal day 5 as TH levels start to rise. To test the hypothesis that TH was acting on oligodendrocyte production, the authors compared fates of precursor cells grown in culture with or without $T_3$ and then quantified the differentiated oligodendrocytes or undifferentiated precursor cells in the resulting clones. A dose-dependent effect of $T_3$ on differentiation was found. Closer analysis showed that this induction of differentiation was somewhat indirect, the more direct effect of TH being on the timing of the withdrawal of the precursor from the cell cycle, hence entering differentiation. Furthermore, $T_3$ could actually override the effects of mitogen signaling favoring cycling and push the precursors into the differentiation pathway. This feature of ending precursor cell cycling and permitting progression toward a differentiated phenotype recalls the demonstration cited earlier of the permissive effects of $T_3$ on neural stem cell and progenitor cell progression to a migratory neuroblast in the SVZ (Lopez-Juarez et al., 2012). Interestingly, in both cases, the TRα receptor is responsible for transducing the effects of $T_3$ on the differentiation process (Billon, Jolicoeur, Tokumoto, Vennstrom, & Raff, 2002; Lopez-Juarez et al., 2012), though in the case of the SVZ, TRα/$T_3$ also has an effect of promoting some phases of the cell cycle in the progenitor cell population.

More recently, Ben Barres, who began the work with Martin Raff, has examined which target genes are modulated by TRα and $T_3$ during oligodendrocyte differentiation (Dugas, Ibrahim, & Barres, 2012). He and his colleagues used a large-scale genomic approach to identify genes modulated in oligodendrocyte precursors in the presence of $T_3$. They identified a series of genes but focused on a gene that was previously identified as a very strong and early responder to TH action in brains of mice and amphibians (Denver et al., 1999), *klf9* (or *BTEB*). Earlier work had not identified major defects in myelination during development of mice that lacked this gene, but they found that it was required for remyelination following chemically induced demyelination (Dugas et al., 2012). This finding is important in that, as $T_3$ aids remyelination in this and other models, $T_3$ has been proposed as a possible factor to aid in remyelination strategies for demyelinating diseases such as multiple sclerosis (Silvestroff, Bartucci, Pasquini, & Franco, 2012). However, not only do cardiac complications currently preclude such possible therapeutic approaches, recent work from our team is showing that, at least in the adult mouse, the initial stages of oligodendrocyte commitment require a $T_3$ and TRα-free window. This cell-specific TH-free status in early oligodendrocyte precursors is achieved by a high level of expression of the inactivating deiodinase, D3, combined with at least a transient absence of expression of the TRα receptor in this cell population.

## Thyroid Hormone and Cerebellar Development

The process of division and neuronal migration in different structures within the developing mammalian brain has been given close analysis in a variety of model systems, but some of the best studied are the rodent cerebral cortex, cerebellum, hippocampus, the cochlea (inner ear), and retina. Each of these structures is highly specialized, with functions that are dependent on complex organization and interactions of multiple cell types. TH signaling contributes to the developmental organization of each of these structures. One of the best studied is the cerebellum and within this structure the effects of TH on development of the highly specialized Purkinje cells and the granule cell population have probably been studied in most detail, though TH affects the differentiation and development of the whole structure. Moreover, alterations in cerebellar development and function are frequently observed in ASD patients (Fatemi et al., 2012), hence the choice here to focus on the effects of TH on the development of the cerebellum.

The cerebellum is traditionally thought of as the major control center for coordination and planning of movement and motor learning. However, increasing data show this structure at the base of the brain to have major roles in many other aspects of behavior. Neuronal projections from the cerebellum reach many other brain areas, notably the frontal cortex, thereby contributing to controlling nonmotor behavior functions such as attention, memory, pain, and addiction (Miquel, Toledo, Garcia, Coria-Avila, & Manzo, 2009; Sacchetti, Scelfo, & Strata, 2009; Strick, Dum, & Fiez, 2009). In humans, the cerebellum develops from the cerebellar plate during the seventh and eighth week of gestation (Muller & O'Rahilly, 1990), that is, in the middle of the first trimester of pregnancy. As development proceeds, the cerebellar cortex (or gray matter) divides into three layers: the external or molecular cell layer, the Purkinje cell layer, and the granule cell layer (Fig. 3.7a). Each layer harbors different neuronal types and their interconnecting axons and dendrites. At the interface between the molecular layer, the outermost layer, and the middle layer are the basket cells. These cells represent a main category of GABA-ergic inhibitory interneurons found in the cerebellum. Their name derives from the basket-like network that their axonal outputs form on the Purkinje cells. Purkinje cells (Fig. 3.7b), some of the largest neurons in the brain and the major cerebellar cell type, are the coordinators of cerebellar function. These neurons have enormous dendritic arborizations and more synaptic connections with other neurons than any other neuron identified. They also represent the only output neurons of the cerebellum (Strick et al., 2009) (i.e., the only ones to send information to other brain regions). As such, their development, maturation, and function are vital to innumerable higher brain functions, not only control and coordination of movement.

Numerous extrinsic factors, such as the timing of the arrival of afferent innervations and synapses, affect Purkinje cell differentiation. TH is another extrinsic factor that significantly affects Purkinje cell maturation. Lack of TH in the first weeks of postnatal rodent life strongly reduces development of Purkinje cell morphology and synapses (see also Chapter 7 and Fig. 7.3). Hypothyroidism also causes delay in differentiation of the granule cells that innervate the Purkinje cells. Thus, hypothyroidism during cerebellar development in both humans and rodents is associated with reduced fine motor movement and other neurological symptoms such as ataxia. $T_3$ dose dependently increases dendritic branching of Purkinje cells, with the major receptor implicated being TRα (Heuer & Mason, 2003). Besides their interdependent development, both granule interneurons and Purkinje neurons express TRs, making it exceedingly difficult to dissect the relative contributions of $T_3$ and the different receptors to the differentiation of each cell type. However, mutations in either receptor cause major neurological defects. TRβ mutations introduced

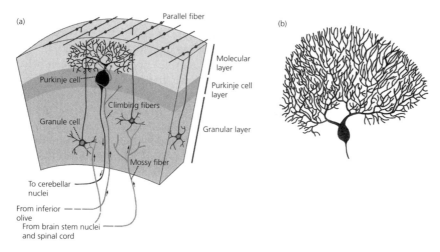

(a)
Parallel fiber

Purkinje cell

Climbing fibers

Granule cell

Mossy fiber

Molecular
layer

Purkinje cell
layer

Granular layer

To cerebellar
nuclei

From inferior
olive

From brain stem nuclei
and spinal cord

(b)

**Figure 3–7.** Schema of the structure of the cerebellar cortex (*a*) and Purkinje cell morphology (*b*). (*a*) The cerebellar cortex is composed of three layers: the innermost granular layer (comprising granule cells and interneurons), the Purkinje cell layer, and the outer molecular layer (where inhibitory neurons, the basket cells, and stellate cells are located). (*b*) The Purkinje cell, one of the largest neurons in the brain, receives multiple synaptic inputs, including multiple inhibitory GABA-ergic afferents. The Purkinje cell is the source of the only output of the cerebellum, sending information to other brain areas, including the cerebral cortex. Purkinje cell development and morphology (notably the richly branched dendritic system) is severely reduced by lack of thyroid hormone.

into mice result in major locomotor deficiencies, smaller cerebellar mass, and reduced molecular and Purkinje cell layers with decreased numbers of Purkinje cells and reduced branching (Hashimoto et al., 2001). Similarly, mice bearing mutations in TRα that reduce ligand binding 10-fold display general neurological and behavioral problems such as extreme anxiety and memory deficiencies (Venero et al., 2005). At the anatomical and molecular level these mice displayed changes in cerebellar structure and Purkinje cell development, but these changes could be corrected just after birth by daily treatment with T₃, and the changes were less marked than those seen in TRβ mutants.

Another group of cerebellar neurons detrimentally and permanently marked by hypothyroidism is the GABA-ergic interneuron population. GABA is the main inhibitory neurotransmitter in the brain. Three types of GABA-expressing interneurons can be distinguished in the cerebellar cortex: the basket and stellate cells in the molecular layer and another group called Golgi II situated in the granule layer. Each is generated from Pax-2-expressing precursors in the cerebellar ventricular zone around gestation day 13 in the rat, though the basket and stellar cells undergo a second round of proliferation in the cerebellar white matter. Using mice lacking TRα and an agonist that is specific for TRβ,

Juan Bernal's group was able to show that both receptors are required for full proliferative capacity of and differentiation of Pax-2-expressing precursors into GABA-ergic interneurons (Manzano, Cuadrado, Morte, & Bernal, 2007).

Not surprisingly, TH regulates multiple genes implicated in cerebellar development and function. One of the first to be studied was the Purkinje cell-specific protein, Pcp-2 (Zou, Hagen, Strait, & Oppenheimer, 1994), but many others have since been identified, including those encoding the nerve growth factors NGF and BDNF (Koibuchi, Yamaoka, & Chin, 2001) and cyclin D2 (Poguet et al., 2003). Two other key cerebellar proteins encoded by genes that, like BNDF, have been implicated in ASD and that are TH targets are RORα and Reelin (see Chapter 7, section on "The Common Ground").

Some of the first studies on the effects of hypothyroidism or hyperthyroidism on the developing brain identified synaptogenesis as one of the highly TH-dependent processes in brain development (Nicholson & Altman, 1972a) (Box 3.2). It has been estimated that the brains of animals that were hypothyroid from birth have about half the synapses of control animals. Again, the cerebellum was identified as one of the major structures in which this process was adversely affected by both states (Nicholson & Altman, 1972b), underlining the fact that either excess or lack of the hormone at that right developmental stage can be equally detrimental. The negative effects of TH lack are easily understood; the adverse effects of excess TH are less well understood. Increased levels of many endocrine signals result in lower physiological responses due, for example, to receptor downregulation or increased metabolism of ligand. Such complex dose responses are exemplified by nonmonotonic dose response curves (see Chapter 6). Other brain areas in which changes in timing of TH availability markedly affects differentiation and synaptogenesis include components of the sensory nervous system—for example, the cochlea (Uziel, Pujol, Legrand, & Legrand, 1983) and retina (Forrest & Swaroop, 2012), and the hippocampus (Rami & Rabie, 1990).

## Timing of Thyroid Hormone Availability and Development of the Retina and Cochlea

Examination of the cretin phenotype indicates that THs act on many aspects of brain development from language acquisition and motor function to memory and learning, but also that they play a role in sensory nervous system maturation and function. Deafness has been associated with reduced thyroid function in children and adults (Trotter, 1960). In rodents, the time window of greatest sensitivity is during postnatal development (Rusch et al., 2001). In a series of very elegant studies, spanning many years and exploiting numerous lines of mutant mice, Doug Forrest's group has focused on how activating and inactivating deiodinases and the different TR isoforms contribute to cochlear development (Forrest, Erway, Ng, Altschuler, & Curran, 1996; Ng et al., 2004, 2009; Rusch et al., 2001). Their work has shown that successive waves of D3 and then D2 characterize cochlea development. In the immature cochlea, cells are

---

Box 3–2. Examples of Thyroid Hormone–Dependent Processes in Brain Development

---

*Proliferation*: Neurogenesis requires amplification of pools of neurogenic precursor cells, prior to commitment to exit from the cell cycle. Studies in rats and amphibians have shown TH to affect proliferation during neurogenesis in embryonic or fetal stages (Mohan et al., 2012; Zhang, Blomgren, Kuhn, & Cooper-Kuhn, 2009) as well as during postnatal and adult neurogenesis (Zhang et al., 2009).

*Commitment*: $T_3$ is required in many contexts for exit from the cell cycle and entry into a differentiation program. For instance, $T_3$ has been shown to be necessary for commitment of different populations of neurons (Lopez-Juarez et al., 2012) and oligodendrocytes (Gao, Apperly, & Raff, 1998).

*Migration*: In many brain areas neuronal precursors migrate long distances to their final differentiation site. In particular, TH has been shown to be required for migration of precursors in the cerebral cortex, hippocampus, and the cerebellum (Bernal, 2005).

*Differentiation and maturation*: TH has repeatedly been demonstrated to have critical roles in the differentiation of multiple neuronal types (Nunez, Couchie, Aniello, & Bridoux, 1992), including the cerebellar Purkinje neurons (Boukhtouche et al., 2010), oligodendrocytes (Billon, Tokumoto, Forrest, & Raff, 2001), astrocytes (Aizenman & de Vellis, 1987), and microglial cells (Mallat et al., 2002). Underlying mechanisms implicate, among others, induction of specific cytoskeletal and structural proteins.

*Synaptogenesis*: Numerous early studies on postnatal brains showed both hypothyroidism and hyperthyroidism to adversely affect formation of synapses (Nicholson & Altman, 1972a & b), and later studies have shown the importance of maternal TH for these processes during fetal growth (Berbel et al., 2010; Madeira & Paula-Barbosa, 1993).

*Myelination*: The requirement of TH for myelination was one of the first roles of TH in the brain to be established, with many myelin components being direct $T_3$ targets, though some indirect mechanisms are also involved (Schoonover et al., 2004). Hypothyroidism significantly delays myelination in most models studied.

---

first protected from the precocious, differentiating effects of $T_3$ and TRβ by the inactivating actions of D3. Later, as development progresses, expression of the activating deiodinase, D2, takes over, allowing $T_3$ action and cochlear maturation. Mice lacking D2 are deaf. These experiments in mice emphasize the tight control of $T_3$ availability that is required during narrow windows of developmental time for correct unfolding of $T_3$-dependent processes in the nervous system and provide an explanation for the hearing problems of children with untreated congenital hypothyroidism.

Although retinal defects are not usually associated with changes in TH availability during development in clinical studies, experiments in rodents have revealed that expression patterns of activating and inactivating deiodinases are subject to tight regulation during retinal development, and changes in their levels affect retinal growth and photoreceptor composition (Brown, 2005; Ng et al., 2010). Notably, the inactivating deiodinase, D3, and the TRβ receptor are specifically required for development of a certain type of cone photoreceptor (Ng et al., 2001), the receptors required for daylight vision. Moreover, in the rat, TH is required for maintenance of opsin expression (a specific light receptor) in the cone cells in the adult retina (Glaschke et al., 2011).

## Thyroid Hormone Control of Hippocampal Development and Function

The hippocampus is one of the main brain structures associated with different forms of memory acquisition and retrieval. One of the major features of adult-onset hypothyroidism is difficulty with memory retrieval (Burmeister et al., 2001), illustrating the constant need for TH to maintain optimal brain function, even in the mature brain. However, as for other brain structures, effects of TH deficiency or excess on hippocampal function are most marked during development.

Like the cerebellum (and many other brain areas) populations of GABA-ergic neurons are implicated in coordinating hippocampal function. However, their function in the hippocampus is not limited to inhibitory inputs and their roles can include excitatory effects on adult neurogenesis (Tozuka, Fukuda, Namba, Seki, & Hisatsune, 2005). Given the effects of hypothyroidism on populations of this interneuron type in the cerebellum, it was not surprising to find that the TRα mutation that reduced $T_3$ binding 10-fold also severely affected the GABA-ergic interneuron population in the CA-1 region of the hippocampus (Venero et al., 2005). However, a more surprising result at first sight was the fact that $T_3$ treatment in adult mice could not only correct this deficit but also the behavioral defects of anxiety and memory problems associated with the cellular impairment. These neurons can be identified in tissue sections by immunochemistry with antibodies against parvalbumin (PV), a calcium-binding protein expressed in both the GABA-ergic interneurons of the hippocampus and cerebral cortex. Immunochemistry showed that $T_3$ given to adult mutant mice restored the density of synaptic terminals of these hippocampal interneurons, providing a demonstration of the sensitivity of the adult hippocampus to TH. The adult hippocampus is also a site of ongoing neurogenesis, a process that like adult neurogenesis in the SVZ is TH dependent (Kapoor et al., 2011).

Hypothyroidism (whether mild or severe) in rats during fetal or early postnatal life permanently affected firing properties and synaptic transmission in the developing hippocampus, changes most probably related to the reductions in populations of PV-reactive GABA-ergic interneurons (Gilbert, 2004; Gilbert et al., 2007) in the hippocampus and in the neocortex (frontal cortex). As in the case for TRα mutant mice, some restoration can occur if TH levels are normalized during postnatal development, but effects on PV-positive cells persist, showing that even small changes in TH availability during development can have permanent effects on brain anatomy and function, notably behavioral function, including learning and memory capacities.

## Thyroid Hormone, Dendritic Spines, and Intellectual Deficiency

The fine extensions of nerve cells that make synaptic contact with the axons of other neurons are called dendrites. Different neural types are characterized by distinct dendritic morphologies and density, with, as already mentioned, the cerebellar Purkinje neuron having the most elaborate dendritic arborization. The dendritic density of a neuron is a direct reflection of its synaptic complexity. Optimal brain function depends on the correct formation of precise synaptic inputs. Dendritic growth and synaptogenesis begin during fetal development and increase markedly during the early postnatal period. Not surprisingly, both processes are modulated by TH and are highly sensitive to disruption. Major disruption of dendritic growth has been associated with certain forms of mental retardation. A first demonstration of abnormal dendritic structure came from studies on children with mental retardation caused by chromosome abnormalities. Following up these studies, and using different morphological techniques to study in detail the brains of mentally retarded children with normal chromosome numbers (e.g., excluding those suffering from Down syndrome with an extra chromosome), Purpura (1974) used the Golgi stain that reveals the fine morphological structure of neurons on either biopsy or autopsy samples. He first observed that dendrites were covered in small stubby projections, or spines, the fine morphology of which varied according to brain area, the type of neuron, and part of the dendrite (apical or proximal to the cell body) examined. His study revealed that the dendrites of severely mentally handicapped children (for whom the cause of handicap was unknown) were very different, being often very thin and entangled and less dense (Fig. 3.8). He observed that the degree of spine abnormality was better correlated with the degree of retardation than with the developmental age of the child.

Early studies on the effect of lack of TH on brain development rapidly revealed effects on dentritic spine density. In pioneering work done by Jacques Legrand's group using the developing chick embryo (Bouvet, Usson, & Legrand, 1987), he and his colleagues observed that a single injection of thiourea (that inhibits TH synthesis) was sufficient to adversely affect dendritic arborization of Purkinje cells and the dendritic spine density. They were among the first to show the correlation between thyroid status of the embryo and/or the young animal and the degree of development of Purkinje neurons. Their observations were followed by work in rodents, revealing adverse effects, in many neuronal types, of either hypothyroidism or hyperthyroidism on dendrite formation during development (Gould, Allan, & McEwen, 1990). Moreover, changes in dendritic spine structure induced by transient modification of neonatal thyroid status persisted in adult brains (Gould et al., 1990). Some authors addressed the question of the

Normal                    Severely retarded

**Figure 3–8.** Dendritic spine structure on dendrites of neurons from the cortex of normal and severely retarded children. Note that the dendrite from the normal child is densely covered with stubby, relatively thick, mushroom-like spines, whereas that from the mentally retarded child has less dense, elongated spines. (Redrawn and adapted from Purpura, 1974.)

mechanisms underlying these developmental morphological defects. Having observed that neurotubule organization was defective in cerebella of hypothyroid rats, Silva and colleagues examined expression of a microtubule protein (microtubule-associated protein-2, MAP2) (Silva & Rudas, 1990). They showed that hypothyroidism delayed MAP-2 expression and affected intracellular distribution of the protein within the Purkinje cell, limiting distribution to the cell body and no further than the most proximal part of the dendrite. These findings can be related to more general effects of TH of cytoskeletal proteins. Using primary cultures of neurons prepared from cerebral cortex of late embryonic rat brains, Biswas et al. (1997) showed that TH acted not only primarily on neural (as opposed to glial cell) morphology and axonal growth but on the relative levels of different categories of cytoskeletal components.

## Brain Metabolism and Thyroid Hormone

A final aspect of TH effects on brain function that could be particularly relevant to the question of how different compounds might disrupt their action is that of brain metabolism. This question has received little attention in the past but could well be brought to the fore as increasingly sophisticated methodologies (such as mass spectrometry) allow new insights into how the metabolome (the spectrum of metabolites in a given tissue or cell population at any time point) responds to different physiological signals. That TH modifies lipid profiles in maturing oligodendrocytes has already been underlined, but other, more recent, studies are showing striking effects of TH status on metabolite profiles in distinct brain areas. One example is the modification of fatty acid profiles in the hypothalamus of hyperthyroid rats or those that received an intrahypothalamic injection of $T_3$ (Lopez et al., 2010). The consequences of modifying TH status during development on brain metabolism have received little attention. However, one early study has shown that hypothyroidism reduces brain glucose utilization (Dow-Edwards, Crane, Rosloff, Kennedy, & Sokoloff, 1986), while a more recent analysis showed that modified metabolism was only found in the brains of mice expressing a mutant TRα receptor, with no effects in mice with targeted mutations in TRβ (Esaki et al., 2003). Changes in metabolic profiles will have multiple downstream effects. For instance, changes in fatty acid profiles in defined brain areas will not only affect signaling through other nuclear receptor pathways (e.g., LXR and PPAR isoforms) but can also affect membrane properties locally and the metabolic responses of the whole animal, as seen for increased hypothalamic $T_3$ concentrations that stimulate heat production by BAT (Lopez et al., 2010).

## Preterm Delivery, Hypothyroidism, and Neurodevelopment

Preterm delivery (before 32 weeks pregnancy) is frequently associated with neurodevelopmental disorders in childhood, particularly for babies born before 26 weeks gestation (Leversen et al., 2011). Many studies have associated either low birth weight (<1.5 kg) and/or preterm birth with both ASD and ADHD (Johnson & Marlow, 2011). Transient low $T_4$ and $T_3$ levels are characteristic of preterm infants, and it is only recently that these low levels, despite their transience, have been shown to result in persistent impaired motor skills and cognitive performance in later childhood (see Williams et al., 2004 and references therein). Given the continually earlier viability of preterm babies, reaching 23 weeks gestation in some countries, the immature state of the thyroid axis and the consequences for the child's future neurodevelopment need to be taken into consideration in care options. Furthermore, even mild maternal hypothyroidism can have negative effects on the neurodevelopment on infants born before 34 weeks gestation (Williams et al., 2012), with small increases in maternal TSH levels being associated with significant decreases in the child's cognitive and verbal ability.

Take-Home Messages and Future Research Questions

- Modification of TH availability and action has pronounced effects on brain development in mammals in the postnatal period, the time of most rapid brain growth.
- Environmental factors that interfere with TH availability and hence $T_3$/TR control of gene transcription demonstrate how environmental effects can be played out at the level of gene programs (gene × environment effects)
- Experimental studies in animals and epidemiological data suggest that another period of sensitivity to TH is early brain development; in humans this is during the first 3 months of pregnancy.
- Iodine deficiency during pregnancy will affect the mother's capacity to synthesize enough TH to ensure optimal development of her child's brain. Even mild iodine deficiency in pregnancy can increase the risk of the child having learning difficulties and lower IQ.
- Within these developmental periods, certain areas have narrow time windows that display marked sensitivity to either excess or lack of active TH. In some cases excess can be more detrimental than deficiency (e.g., the cochlea). This feature underlines that we must not only be concerned about chemicals that antagonize TH signaling but about chemicals that act in a TH-like manner, which can be equally damaging.
- The active form of TH, $T_3$, and its receptors act on all types of brain cells, neurons, all three forms of glial cells, and on the neuronal stem cell and progenitor cell populations. TH affects multiple neuronal processes, with lack of hormone affecting most markedly overall brain growth, cerebellar and hippocampal structure and function, myelination, dendritic morphology, synaptogenesis, and electrical properties of neurons.
- Future research in terms of endocrine disruption and thyroid signaling could be usefully directed to two areas that have received little or no attention so far: examining the effects of modification of TH signaling on development of cerebellar output to the frontal cortex and analyzing how iodine deficiency during key developmental periods affects TH availability and vulnerability to disruption by chemicals.

REFERENCES

Aizenman, Y., & de Vellis, J. (1987). Synergistic action of thyroid hormone, insulin and hydrocortisone on astrocyte differentiation. Brain Research, 414(2), 301–308.

Altman, J. (1962). Are new neurons formed in the brains of adult mammals? Science, 135(3509), 1127–1128.

Alvarez-Buylla, A. (1990). Mechanism of neurogenesis in adult avian brain. Experientia, 46(9), 948–955.

Alvarez-Buylla, A., Theelen, M., & Nottebohm, F. (1988). Birth of projection neurons in the higher vocal center of the canary forebrain before, during, and after song learning. *Proceedings of the National Academy of Sciences USA, 85*(22), 8722–8726.

Barres, B. A., Lazar, M. A., & Raff, M. C. (1994). A novel role for thyroid hormone, glucocorticoids and retinoic acid in timing oligodendrocyte development. *Development, 120*(5), 1097–1108.

Bassett, J. H., & Williams, G. R. (2008). Critical role of the hypothalamic-pituitary-thyroid axis in bone. *Bone, 43*(3), 418–426.

Bath, S. C., & Rayman, M. P. (2013). Iodine deficiency in the U.K.: An overlooked cause of impaired neurodevelopment? *Proceedings of the Nutrition Society, 72*(2), 226–235.

Bath, S. C., Steer, C. D., Golding, J., Emmett, P., & Rayman, M. P. (2013). Effect of inadequate iodine status in UK pregnant women on cognitive outcomes in their children: Results from the Avon Longitudinal Study of Parents and Children (ALSPAC). *Lancet, 382*(9889), 331–337.

Berbel, P., Navarro, D., Ausó, E., Varea, E., Rodríguez, A. E., Ballesta, J. J., . . . de Escobar, G. M. (2010). Role of late maternal thyroid hormones in cerebral cortex development: An experimental model for human prematurity. *Cerebral Cortex, 20*(6), 1462–1475.

Bergh, J. J., Lin, H. Y., Lansing, L., Mohamed, S. N., Davis, F. B., Mousa, S., & Davis, P. J. (2005). Integrin alphaVbeta3 contains a cell surface receptor site for thyroid hormone that is linked to activation of mitogen-activated protein kinase and induction of angiogenesis. *Endocrinology, 146*(7), 2864–2871.

Bernal, J. (2005). Thyroid hormones and brain development. *Vitamins and Hormones, 71*, 95–122.

Bernal, J. (2007). Thyroid hormone receptors in brain development and function. *Nature Clinical Practice Endocrinology and Metabolism, 3*(3), 249–259.

Bhat, N. R., Sarlieve, L. L., Rao, G. S., & Pieringer, R. A. (1979). Investigations on myelination in vitro. Regulation by thyroid hormone in cultures of dissociated brain cells from embryonic mice. *Journal of Biological Chemistry, 254*(19), 9342–9344.

Billon, N., Jolicoeur, C., Tokumoto, Y., Vennstrom, B., & Raff, M. (2002). Normal timing of oligodendrocyte development depends on thyroid hormone receptor alpha 1 (TRalpha1). *EMBO Journal, 21*(23), 6452–6460.

Billon, N., Tokumoto, Y., Forrest, D., & Raff, M. (2001). Role of thyroid hormone receptors in timing oligodendrocyte differentiation. *Developmental Biology, 235*(1), 110–120.

Biswas, S. C., Pal, U., & Sarkar, P. K. (1997). Regulation of cytoskeletal proteins by thyroid hormone during neuronal maturation and differentiation. *Brain Research, 757*(2), 245–253.

Bochukova, E., Schoenmakers, N., Agostini, M., Schoenmakers, E., Rajanayagam, O., Keogh, J. M., . . . Chatterjee, K. (2012). A mutation in the thyroid hormone receptor alpha gene. *New England Journal of Medicine, 366*(3), 243–249.

Boukhtouche, F., Brugg, B., Wehrlé, R., Bois-Joyeux, B., Danan, J. L., Dusart, I., & Mariani, J. (2010). Induction of early Purkinje cell dendritic differentiation by thyroid hormone requires RORalpha. *Neural Development, 5*, 18.

Bouvet, J., Usson, Y., & Legrand, J. (1987). Morphometric analysis of the cerebellar Purkinje cell in the developing normal and hypothyroid chick. *International Journal of Developmental Neuroscience, 5*(4), 345–355.

Brown, D. D. (2005). The role of deiodinases in amphibian metamorphosis. *Thyroid, 15*(8), 815–821.

Burmeister, L. A., Ganguli, M., Dodge, H. H., Toczek, T., DeKosky, S. T., & Nebes, R. D. (2001). Hypothyroidism and cognition: Preliminary evidence for a specific defect in memory. *Thyroid, 11*(12), 1177–1185.

Contempre, B., Jauniaux, E., Calvo, R., Jurkovic, D., Campbell, S., & de Escobar, G. M. (1993). Detection of thyroid hormones in human embryonic cavities during the first trimester of pregnancy. *Journal of Clinical Endocrinology and Metabolism, 77*(6), 1719–1722.

Davis, P. J., Davis, F. B., Mousa, S. A., Luidens, M. K., & Lin, H. Y. (2011). Membrane receptor for thyroid hormone: Physiologic and pharmacologic implications. *Annual Review of Pharmacology and Toxicology, 51*, 99–115.

de Escobar, G. M., Ares, S., Berbel, P., Obregon, M. J., & del Rey, F. E. (2008). The changing role of maternal thyroid hormone in fetal brain development. *Seminars in Perinatology, 32*(6), 380–386.

de Escobar, G. M., Obregon, M. J., & del Rey, F. E. (2007). Iodine deficiency and brain development in the first half of pregnancy. *Public Health and Nutrition, 10*(12A), 1554–1570.

Denver, R. J., Ouellet, L., Furling, D., Kobayashi, A., Fujii-Kuriyama, Y., & Puymirat, J. (1999). Basic transcription element-binding protein (BTEB) is a thyroid hormone-regulated gene in the developing central nervous system. Evidence for a role in neurite outgrowth. *Journal of Biological Chemistry, 274*(33), 23128–23134.

Doetsch, F., Caille, I., Lim, D. A., Garcia-Verdugo, J. M., & Alvarez-Buylla, A. (1999). Subventricular zone astrocytes are neural stem cells in the adult mammalian brain. *Cell, 97*(6), 703–716.

Dow-Edwards, D., Crane, A. M., Rosloff, B., Kennedy, C., & Sokoloff, L. (1986). Local cerebral glucose utilization in the adult cretinous rat. *Brain Research, 373*(1–2), 139–145.

Dugas, J. C., Ibrahim, A., & Barres, B. A. (2012). The T3-induced gene KLF9 regulates oligodendrocyte differentiation and myelin regeneration. *Molecular and Cellular Neuroscience, 50*(1), 45–57.

Dupre, S. M., Guissouma, H., Flamant, F., Seugnet, I., Scanlan, T. S., Baxter, J. D., ... Becker, N. (2004). Both thyroid hormone receptor (TR)beta 1 and TR beta 2 isoforms contribute to the regulation of hypothalamic thyrotropin-releasing hormone. *Endocrinology, 145*(5), 2337–2345.

Esaki, T., Suzuki, H., Cook, M., Shimoji, K., Cheng, S. Y., Sokoloff, L., & Nunez, J. (2003). Functional activation of cerebral metabolism in mice with mutated thyroid hormone nuclear receptors. *Endocrinology, 144*(9), 4117–4122.

Fatemi, S. H., Aldinger, K. A., Ashwood, P., Bauman, M. L., Blaha, C. D., Blatt, G. J., ... Welsh, J. P. (2012). Consensus paper: Pathological role of the cerebellum in autism. *Cerebellum, 11*(3), 777–807.

Fini, J. B., Le Mével, S., Palmier, K., Darras, V. M., Punzon, I., Richardson, S. J., ... Demeneix, B. A. (2012). Thyroid hormone signaling in the Xenopus laevis embryo is functional and susceptible to endocrine disruption. *Endocrinology, 153*(10), 5068–5081.

Flamant, F., & Samarut, J. (1998). Involvement of thyroid hormone and its alpha receptor in avian neurulation. *Developmental Biology, 197*(1), 1–11.

Flamant, F., & Samarut, J. (2003). Thyroid hormone receptors: Lessons from knockout and knock-in mutant mice. *Trends in Endocrinology and Metabolism, 14*(2), 85–90.

Forrest, D., Erway, L. C., Ng, L., Altschuler, R., & Curran, T. (1996). Thyroid hormone receptor beta is essential for development of auditory function. *Nature Genetics, 13*(3), 354–357.

Forrest, D., & Swaroop, A. (2012). Minireview: The role of nuclear receptors in photoreceptor differentiation and disease. *Molecular Endocrinology, 26*(6), 905–915.

Friesema, E. C., Grueters, A., Biebermann, H., Krude, H., von Moers, A., Reeser, M.,... Visser, T. J. (2004). Association between mutations in a thyroid hormone transporter and severe X-linked psychomotor retardation. *Lancet, 364*(9443), 1435–1437.

Friesema, E. C., Jansen, J., & Visser, T. J. (2005). Thyroid hormone transporters. *Biochemical Society Transactions, 33*(Pt 1), 228–232.

Gao, F. B., Apperly, J., & Raff, M. (1998). Cell-intrinsic timers and thyroid hormone regulate the probability of cell-cycle withdrawal and differentiation of oligodendrocyte precursor cells. *Developmental Biology, 197*(1), 54–66.

Germain, P., Chambon, P., Eichele, G., Evans, R. M., Lazar, M. A., Leid, M.,... Gronemeyer, H. (2006). International Union of Pharmacology. LXIII. Retinoid X receptors. *Pharmacology Reviews, 58*(4), 760–772.

Gilbert, M. E. (2004). Alterations in synaptic transmission and plasticity in area CA1 of adult hippocampus following developmental hypothyroidism. *Brain Research and Developmental Brain Research, 148*(1), 11–18.

Gilbert, M. E., Sui, L., Walker, M. J., Anderson, W., Thomas, S., Smoller, S. N.,... Goodman, J. H. (2007). Thyroid hormone insufficiency during brain development reduces parvalbumin immunoreactivity and inhibitory function in the hippocampus. *Endocrinology, 148*(1), 92–102.

Gilbert, S. F. (2010). *Developmental biology.* Sunderland, MA: Sinauer Associates.

Ginhoux, F., Lim, S., Hoeffel, G., Low, D., & Huber, T. (2013). Origin and differentiation of microglia. *Frontiers in Cellular Neuroscience, 7*, 45.

Glaschke, A., Weiland, J., Del Turco, D., Steiner, M., Peichl, L., & Glösmann, M. (2011). Thyroid hormone controls cone opsin expression in the retina of adult rodents. *Journal of Neuroscience, 31*(13), 4844–4851.

Gould, E., Allan, M. D., & McEwen, B. S. (1990). Dendritic spine density of adult hippocampal pyramidal cells is sensitive to thyroid hormone. *Brain Research, 525*(2), 327–329.

Haddow, J. E., Palomaki, G. E., Allan, W. C., Williams, J. R., Knight, G. J., Gagnon, J.,... Klein, R. Z. (1999). Maternal thyroid deficiency during pregnancy and subsequent neuropsychological development of the child. *New England Journal of Medicine, 341*(8), 549–555.

Hashimoto, K., Curty, F. H., Borges, P. P., Lee, C. E., Abel, E. D., Elmquist, J. K.,... Wondisford, F. E. (2001). An unliganded thyroid hormone receptor causes severe neurological dysfunction. *Proceedings of the National Academy of Sciences USA, 98*(7), 3998–4003.

Henrichs, J., Bongers-Schokking, J. J., Schenk, J. J., Ghassabian, A., Schmidt, H. G., Visser, T. J.,... Tiemeier H. (2010). Maternal thyroid function during early pregnancy and cognitive functioning in early childhood: The generation R study. *Journal of Clinical Endocrinology and Metabolism, 95*(9), 4227–4234.

Heuer, H. (2007). The importance of thyroid hormone transporters for brain development and function. *Best Practice and Research Clinical Endocrinology and Metabolism, 21*(2), 265–276.

Heuer, H., & Mason, C. A. (2003). Thyroid hormone induces cerebellar Purkinje cell dendritic development via the thyroid hormone receptor alpha1. *Journal of Neuroscience, 23*(33), 10604–10612.

Howdeshell, K. L. (2002). A model of the development of the brain as a construct of the thyroid system. *Environmental Health Perspectives, 110*(Suppl 3), 337–348.

Hynes, K. L., Otahal, P., Hay, I., & Burgess, J. R. (2013). Mild iodine deficiency during pregnancy is associated with reduced educational outcomes in the offspring: 9-year follow-up of the gestational iodine cohort. *Journal of Clinical Endocrinology and Metabolism, 98*(5), 1954–1962.

Ibarrola, N., & Rodriguez-Pena, A. (1997). Hypothyroidism coordinately and transiently affects myelin protein gene expression in most rat brain regions during postnatal development. *Brain Research, 752*(1–2), 285–293.

Johnson, S., & Marlow, N. (2011). Preterm birth and childhood psychiatric disorders. *Pediatric Research, 69*(5 Pt 2), 11R–18R.

Kapoor, R., Ghosh, H., Nordstrom, K., Vennstrom, B., & Vaidya, V. A. (2011). Loss of thyroid hormone receptor beta is associated with increased progenitor proliferation and NeuroD positive cell number in the adult hippocampus. *Neuroscience Letters, 487*(2), 199–203.

Kapoor, R., van Hogerlinden, M., Wallis, K., Ghosh, H., Nordstrom, K., Vennstrom, B., & Vaidya, V. A. (2010). Unliganded thyroid hormone receptor alpha1 impairs adult hippocampal neurogenesis. *FASEB Journal, 24*(12), 4793–4805.

Kettenmann, H., Hanisch, U. K., Noda, M., & Verkhratsky, A. (2011). Physiology of microglia. *Physiological Reviews, 91*(2), 461–553.

Klotz, J. B., & Pyrch, L. A. (1999). Neural tube defects and drinking water disinfection by-products. *Epidemiology, 10*(4), 383–390.

Koibuchi, N., Yamaoka, S., & Chin, W. W. (2001). Effect of altered thyroid status on neurotrophin gene expression during postnatal development of the mouse cerebellum. *Thyroid, 11*(3), 205–210.

Kriegstein, A., & Alvarez-Buylla, A. (2009). The glial nature of embryonic and adult neural stem cells. *Annual Review of Neuroscience, 32*, 149–184.

Lazarus, J. H., Bestwick, J. P., Channon, S., Paradice, R., Maina, A., Rees, R., . . . Wald, N. J. (2012). Antenatal thyroid screening and childhood cognitive function. *New England Journal of Medicine, 366*(6), 493–501.

le Maire, A., Grimaldi, M., Roecklin, D., Dagnino, S., Vivat-Hannah, V., Balaguer, P., & Bourguet, W. (2009). Activation of RXR-PPAR heterodimers by organotin environmental endocrine disruptors. *EMBO Reports, 10*(4), 367–373.

Lebel, J. M., L'Herault, S., Dussault, J. H., & Puymirat, J. (1993). Thyroid hormone up-regulates thyroid hormone receptor beta gene expression in rat cerebral hemisphere astrocyte cultures. *Glia, 9*(2), 105–112.

Lemkine, G. F., Raj, A., Alfama, G., Turque, N., Hassani, Z., Alegria-Prévot, O., . . . Demeneix, B. A. (2005). Adult neural stem cell cycling in vivo requires thyroid hormone and its alpha receptor. *FASEB Journal, 19*(7), 863–865.

Leversen, K. T., Sommerfelt, K., Rønnestad, A., Kaaresen, P. I., Farstad, T., Skranes, J., . . . Markestad, T. (2011). Prediction of neurodevelopmental and sensory outcome at 5 years in Norwegian children born extremely preterm. *Pediatrics, 127*(3), e630–638.

Loewenthal, L. (2013). Study links iodine deficiency in pregnancy with poor cognitive outcomes in children. *BMJ, 346*, f3365.

Lopez, M., Varela, L., Vázquez, M. J., Rodríguez-Cuenca, S., González, C. R., Velagapudi, V. R., ... Vidal-Puig, A. (2010). Hypothalamic AMPK and fatty acid metabolism mediate thyroid regulation of energy balance. *Nature Medicine, 16*(9), 1001–1008.

Lopez-Juarez, A., Remaud, S., Hassani, Z., Jolivet, P., Pierre Simons, J., Sontag, T., ... Demeneix, B. A. (2012). Thyroid hormone signaling acts as a neurogenic switch by repressing Sox2 in the adult neural stem cell niche. *Cell Stem Cell, 10*(5), 531–543.

Madeira, M. D., & Paula-Barbosa, M. M. (1993). Reorganization of mossy fiber synapses in male and female hypothyroid rats: A stereological study. *Journal of Comparative Neurology, 337*(2), 334–352.

Mallat, M., Lima, F. R., Gervais, A., Colin, C., & Moura Neto, V. (2002). New insights into the role of thyroid hormone in the CNS: The microglial track. *Molecular Psychiatry, 7*(1), 7–8.

Marasas, W. F., Riley, R. T., Hendricks, K. A., Stevens, V. L., Sadler, T. W., Gelineau-van Waes, J., ... Merrill, A. H., Jr. (2004). Fumonisins disrupt sphingolipid metabolism, folate transport, and neural tube development in embryo culture and in vivo: A potential risk factor for human neural tube defects among populations consuming fumonisin-contaminated maize. *Journal of Nutrition, 134*(4), 711–716.

Martinez de Mena, R., Scanlan, T. S., & Obregon, M. J. (2010). The T3 receptor beta1 isoform regulates UCP1 and D2 deiodinase in rat brown adipocytes. *Endocrinology, 151*(10), 5074–5083.

Manzano, J., Cuadrado, M., Morte, B., & Bernal, J. (2007). Influence of thyroid hormone and thyroid hormone receptors in the generation of cerebellar gamma-aminobutyric acid-ergic interneurons from precursor cells. *Endocrinology, 148*(12), 5746–5751.

Merkle, F. T., & Alvarez-Buylla, A. (2006). Neural stem cells in mammalian development. *Current Opinion in Cell Biology, 18*(6), 704–709.

Miquel, M., Toledo, R., Garcia, L. I., Coria-Avila, G. A., & Manzo, J. (2009). Why should we keep the cerebellum in mind when thinking about addiction? *Current Drug Abuse Reviews, 2*(1), 26–40.

Mohacsik, P., Zeold, A., Bianco, A. C., & Gereben, B. (2011). Thyroid hormone and the neuroglia: Both source and target. *Journal of Thyroid Research, 2011*, 215718.

Mohan, V., Sinha, R. A., Pathak, A., Rastogi, L., Kumar, P., Pal, A., & Godbole, M. M. (2012). Maternal thyroid hormone deficiency affects the fetal neocorticogenesis by reducing the proliferating pool, rate of neurogenesis and indirect neurogenesis. *Experimental Neurology, 237*(2), 477–488.

Muller, F., & O'Rahilly, R. (1990). The human brain at stages 21–23, with particular reference to the cerebral cortical plate and to the development of the cerebellum. *Anatomy and Embryology (Berlin), 182*(4), 375–400.

Naufal, Z., Zhiwen, L., Zhu, L., Zhou, G. D., McDonald, T., He, L. Y., ... Donnelly, K. C. (2010). Biomarkers of exposure to combustion by-products in a human population in Shanxi, China. *Journal of Exposure Science and Environmental Epidemiology, 20*(4), 310–319.

Nicholson, J. L., & Altman, J. (1972a). The effects of early hypo- and hyperthyroidism on the development of the rat cerebellar cortex. II. Synaptogenesis in the molecular layer. *Brain Research, 44*(1), 25–36.

Nicholson, J. L., & Altman, J. (1972b). Synaptogenesis in the rat cerebellum: Effects of early hypo- and hyperthyroidism. *Science, 176*(4034), 530–532.

Ng, L., Goodyear, R. J., Woods, C. A., Schneider, M. J., Diamond, E., Richardson, G. P.,...Forrest, D. (2004). Hearing loss and retarded cochlear development in mice lacking type 2 iodothyronine deiodinase. *Proceedings of the National Academy of Sciences USA, 101*(10), 3474–3479.

Ng, L., Hernandez, A., He, W., Ren, T., Srinivas, M., Ma, M.,...Forrest, D. (2009). A protective role for type 3 deiodinase, a thyroid hormone-inactivating enzyme, in cochlear development and auditory function. *Endocrinology, 150*(4), 1952–1960.

Ng, L., Hurley, J. B., Dierks, B., Srinivas, M., Saltó, C., Vennström, B.,...Forrest D. (2001). A thyroid hormone receptor that is required for the development of green cone photoreceptors. *Nature Genetics, 27*(1), 94–98.

Ng, L., Lyubarsky, A., Nikonov, S. S., Ma, M., Srinivas, M., Kefas, B.,...Forrest, D. (2010). Type 3 deiodinase, a thyroid-hormone-inactivating enzyme, controls survival and maturation of cone photoreceptors. *Journal of Neuroscience, 30*(9), 3347–3357.

Nunez, J., Couchie, D., Aniello, F., & Bridoux, A. M. (1992). Thyroid hormone effects on neuronal differentiation during brain development. *Acta Medica Austriaca, 19*(Suppl 1), 36–39.

Obican, S. G., Finnell, R. H., Mills, J. L., Shaw, G. M., & Scialli, A. R. (2010). Folic acid in early pregnancy: A public health success story. *FASEB Journal, 24*(11), 4167–4174.

Poguet, A. L., Legrand, C., Feng, X., Yen, P. M., Meltzer, P., Samarut, J., & Flamant, F. (2003). Microarray analysis of knockout mice identifies cyclin D2 as a possible mediator for the action of thyroid hormone during the postnatal development of the cerebellum. *Developmental Biology, 254*(2), 188–199.

Pop, V. J., de Vries, E., van Baar, A. L., Waelkens, J. J., de Rooy, H. A., Horsten, M.,...Vader, H. L. (1995). Maternal thyroid peroxidase antibodies during pregnancy: A marker of impaired child development? *Journal of Clinical Endocrinology and Metabolism, 80*(12), 3561–3566.

Pop, V. J., Kuijpens, J. L., van Baar, A. L., Verkerk, G., van Son, M. M., de Vijlder, J. J.,...Vader, H. L. (1999). Low maternal free thyroxine concentrations during early pregnancy are associated with impaired psychomotor development in infancy. *Clinical Endocrinology (Oxford), 50*(2), 149–155.

Purpura, D. P. (1974). Dendritic spine "dysgenesis" and mental retardation. *Science, 186*(4169), 1126–1128.

Rami, A., & Rabie, A. (1990). Delayed synaptogenesis in the dentate gyrus of the thyroid-deficient developing rat. *Developmental Neuroscience, 12*(6), 398–405.

Ren, A., Qiu, X., Jin, L., Ma, J., Li, Z., Zhang, L.,...Zhu, T. (2011). Association of selected persistent organic pollutants in the placenta with the risk of neural tube defects. *Proceedings of the National Academy of Sciences USA, 108*(31), 12770–12775.

Rodriguez-Pena, A. (1999). Oligodendrocyte development and thyroid hormone. *Journal of Neurobiology, 40*(4), 497–512.

Rusch, A., Ng, L., Goodyear, R., Oliver, D., Lisoukov, I., Vennstrom, B.,...Forrest, D. (2001). Retardation of cochlear maturation and impaired hair cell function caused by deletion of all known thyroid hormone receptors. *Journal of Neuroscience, 21*(24), 9792–9800.

Sacchetti, B., Scelfo, B., & Strata, P. (2009). Cerebellum and emotional behavior. *Neuroscience, 162*(3), 756–762.

Schoonover, C. M., Seibel, M. M., Jolson, D. M., Stack, M. J., Rahman, R. J., Jones, S. A.,...Anderson, G. W. (2004). Thyroid hormone regulates oligodendrocyte accumulation in developing rat brain white matter tracts. *Endocrinology, 145*(11), 5013–5020.

Silva, J. E., & Rudas, P. (1990). Effects of congenital hypothyroidism on microtubule-associated protein-2 expression in the cerebellum of the rat. *Endocrinology, 126*(2), 1276–1282.

Silvestroff, L., Bartucci, S., Pasquini, J., & Franco, P. (2012). Cuprizone-induced demyelination in the rat cerebral cortex and thyroid hormone effects on cortical remyelination. *Experimental Neurology, 235*(1), 357–367.

Strait, K. A., Carlson, D. J., Schwartz, H. L., & Oppenheimer, J. H. (1997). Transient stimulation of myelin basic protein gene expression in differentiating cultured oligodendrocytes: A model for 3,5,3'-triiodothyronine-induced brain development. *Endocrinology, 138*(2), 635–641.

Strick, P. L., Dum, R. P., & Fiez, J. A. (2009). Cerebellum and nonmotor function. *Annual Review of Neuroscience, 32*, 413–434.

Takahashi, K., & Yamanaka, S. (2006). Induction of pluripotent stem cells from mouse embryonic and adult fibroblast cultures by defined factors. *Cell, 126*(4), 663–676.

Tetreault, N. A., Hakeem, A. Y., Jiang, S., Williams, B. A., Allman, E., Wold, B. J., & Allman, J. M. (2012). Microglia in the cerebral cortex in autism. *Journal of Autism and Developmental Disorders, 42*(12), 2569–2584.

Tozuka, Y., Fukuda, S., Namba, T., Seki, T., & Hisatsune, T. (2005). GABAergic excitation promotes neuronal differentiation in adult hippocampal progenitor cells. *Neuron, 47*(6), 803–815.

Trotter, W. R. (1960). The association of deafness with thyroid dysfunction. *British Medical Bulletin, 16*, 92–98.

Uziel, A., Pujol, R., Legrand, C., & Legrand, J. (1983). Cochlear synaptogenesis in the hypothyroid rat. *Brain Research, 283*(2–3), 295–301.

Valcana, T., Einstein, E. R., Csejtey, J., Dalal, K. B., & Timiras, P. S. (1975). Influence of thyroid hormones on myelin proteins in the developing rat brain. *Journal of the Neurological Sciences, 25*(1), 19–27.

Venero, C., Guadaño-Ferraz, A., Herrero, A. I., Nordström, K., Manzano, J., de Escobar, G. M.,...Vennström, B. (2005). Anxiety, memory impairment, and locomotor dysfunction caused by a mutant thyroid hormone receptor alpha1 can be ameliorated by T3 treatment. *Genes and Development, 19*(18), 2152–2163.

Vermiglio, F., Lo Presti, V. P., Moleti, M., Sidoti, M., Tortorella, G., Scaffidi, G.,...Trimarchi, F. (2004). Attention deficit and hyperactivity disorders in the offspring of mothers exposed to mild-moderate iodine deficiency: A possible novel iodine deficiency disorder in developed countries. *Journal of Clinical Endocrinology and Metabolism, 89*(12), 6054–6060.

Visser, W. E., Friesema, E. C., & Visser, T. J. (2011). Minireview: Thyroid hormone transporters: the knowns and the unknowns. *Molecular Endocrinology, 25*(1), 1–14.

Walters, S. N., & Morell, P. (1981). Effects of altered thyroid states on myelinogenesis. *Journal of Neurochemistry, 36*(5), 1792–1801.

Williams, F. L., Simpson, J., Delahunty, C., Ogston, S. A., Bongers-Schokking, J. J., Murphy, N.,...Collaboration from the Scottish Preterm Thyroid Group. (2004). Developmental trends in cord and postpartum serum thyroid hormones in preterm infants. *Journal of Clinical Endocrinology and Metabolism, 89*(11), 5314–5320.

Williams, F., Watson, J., Ogston, S., Hume, R., Willatts, P., Visser, T., & Scottish Preterm Thyroid Group. (2012). Mild maternal thyroid dysfunction at delivery of infants born </=34 weeks and neurodevelopmental outcome at 5.5 years. *Journal of Clinical Endocrinology and Metabolism, 97*(6), 1977–1985.

Yi, Y., Lindemann, M., Colligs, A., & Snowball, C. (2011). Economic burden of neural tube defects and impact of prevention with folic acid: A literature review. *European Journal of Pediatrics, 170*(11), 1391–1400.

Zalc, B., Goujet, D., & Colman, D. (2008). The origin of the myelination program in vertebrates. *Current Biology, 18*(12), R511–R512.

Zhang, L., Blomgren, K., Kuhn, H. G., & Cooper-Kuhn, C. M. (2009). Effects of postnatal thyroid hormone deficiency on neurogenesis in the juvenile and adult rat. *Neurobiology of Disease, 34*(2), 366–374.

Zou, L., Hagen, S. G., Strait, K. A., & Oppenheimer, J. H. (1994). Identification of thyroid hormone response elements in rodent Pcp-2, a developmentally regulated gene of cerebellar Purkinje cells. *Journal of Biological Chemistry, 269*(18), 13346–13352.

# Chapter 4

# Thyroid Hormone Signaling as a Target of Multiple Pollutants

## CHAPTER OUTLINE

This chapter provides a physiological framework for understanding why chemicals that interfere with thyroid hormone (TH) signaling are such a cause for concern. The importance of TH for brain development, and how it forms a direct bridge between the environment and gene expression, has been underlined in the previous chapter. Here, the different levels of regulation of TH production, distribution, metabolism, entry into cells, and activation are explained. Each can be a target of disruption. A priority is to identify chemicals that interfere with TH signaling during developmental windows of vulnerability when control mechanisms are being forged and when modulation of gene networks will be particularly harmful. Initial focus is placed on development of the hypothalamic/pituitary axis that regulates the production of TH by the thyroid gland, identifying components of regulatory mechanisms that could be targets of disruption. One such key physiological system that is highly dependent on TH homeostasis is energy balance and body weight regulation. A second idea is the complexity of the thyroid gland itself and the many processes required for uptake and incorporation of iodine into TH. A third level groups the proteins with which TH interacts as it is distributed and transported through the body, providing more targets for disruption. Two main causes contribute to the disquieting fact that there are probably more chemicals affecting TH signaling than any other endocrine pathway. The first is the complexity of TH signaling, from iodine uptake, TH synthesis and activation, to the multiple regulatory pathways controlling TH production and metabolism. The second is the structural similarity of TH to multiple categories of halogenated chemicals in the environment. The principal chemical categories affecting TH signaling are discussed in the next chapter.

## BACKGROUND

Chapter 1 described past cases illustrating how brain development can be affected by a series of well-documented environmental pollutants. Examples chosen included effects of mercury poisoning on children in Japanese fishing communities, the consequences of maternal consumption of polychlorinated biphenyl (PCB) contaminated fish around the North American Great Lakes and lead exposure. In the cases of PCBs and lead contamination we saw that small changes in exposure levels had significant consequences on neurodevelopment and intellectual capacity. Similarly, we know that even transient hypothyroidism during development can have irreversible effects on brain development. These ideas underline the exquisite sensitivity of the genetic programs underlying neuronal development, sensitivity not only to determined amounts of TH in specific developmental windows but also to environmental influence. The coupling of TH availability to thyroid receptors (TRs), ligand-dependent transcription factors, is a direct entry point for environmental modulation of gene networks.

Here the aim is to dissect the multiple regulatory levels that evolution has set up to ensure a tight control of delivery of the right amount of TH to the right tissues at the right time. As is only too well known to the scientific and medical communities, interference with this closely adjusted supply mechanism, either too much or too little, is associated with major pathologies. The aim is to provide a basic understanding of the physiology of TH signaling and how its particularities make it a major target of chemical pollution and endocrine disruption. Many factors need to be brought forward for discussion. The first major concern is, as described in Chapter 3, that thyroid signaling is implicated in multiple genetic regulations that participate in the cellular processes governing brain development and maturation. The second, the main subject of this chapter, is that the physiology and biochemistry of thyroid signaling is extremely complex with many layers of regulation and action, each with a potential for disruption by endocrine disrupting chemicals (EDCs). The third is that there are numerous categories of chemicals that interfere with different aspects of thyroid signaling, probably more than with any other endocrine system. These chemical categories will be discussed in the next chapter. A final, vital point is that the effects of chemicals will be exacerbated by iodine deficiency, a continual threat and even an increasing concern in certain Western countries (Stagnaro-Green, & Pearce, 2013).

To this list can be added the fact that even in adolescents and adults TH is needed to maintain many aspects of brain function and general health, notably energy balance and body weight. We have seen that the main adverse effect of hypothyroidism, or lack of TH, in the newborn baby is on the brain that fails to develop properly. In children, adolescents, and adults, hypothyroidism is associated with a spectrum of disorders, which can include one or more of the following: depression, anxiety, mood and memory problems, weight gain, increased sensitivity to cold, dry skin, and constipation. In contrast, hyperthyroidism or an overactive thyroid is associated with cardiac disorders, weight loss, irritability, and sleep problems. Thus, changes in TH availability and action will modulate gene transcription and cellular responses in all the body organs, from the brain to muscle, bones, intestine, fat tissue, and heart. These wide-ranging effects can be partly explained by the fact that virtually all the cells in the human body express the nuclear receptors for TH, TRs. TRs are ligand-dependent transcription factors that modulate the function of numerous gene networks implicated in many developmental and physiological processes.

Thus, given the vital role for TH at all life stages, and the need to maintain circulating levels within a physiological range, evolution has fashioned a system of checks that counterbalance the feedforward drives from the hypothalamus and pituitary that maintain production. These controls in production and genetic response can be adjusted at all life stages by environmental factors such as temperature and food supply. For instance, cold exposure stimulates the hypothalamus-pituitary-thyroid axis, stimulating gene networks that produce heat. Inversely, lack of food or fasting immediately represses TH production to save energy stores. Thus, TH signaling has evolved as a natural communication route to enable gene expression and physiological responses to adapt to environmental signals. The concern today is that a number of extraneous chemicals in our bodies are confusing these communication and adaptation systems, changing TH levels and altering genetic and physiological responses both during development and in maturity.

### Regulation of Thyroid Hormone Production: The Hypothalamic/Pituitary/Thyroid Axis

Circulating TH levels are maintained within narrow ranges in a given individual. Either prolonged excess or lack of $T_3$ can be fatal, but even moderate increases or decreases in circulating levels can have marked physiological consequences. The principal actors governing TH production within the normal physiological range are the thyrotropin-releasing hormone (TRH) neurons of the hypothalamus and the thyrotropin (thyroid-stimulating hormone [TSH])-producing cells of the anterior pituitary (or hypophysis) (Fig. 4.1).

Excess or lack of TH at any life stage is associated with a number of pathological features. Further, given the essential contribution of TH to many developmental processes (the most marked being brain development), the need for maintaining circulating and tissue levels of TH within a limited range is crucial. Having described the consequences of lack of TH on brain development in the previous chapter, here we consider briefly the clinical conditions of hyperthyroidism and hypothyroidism, respectively.

Hyperthyroidism, hyperthyroxinemia, or thyrotoxicosis, to use the clinical terms, is most often a result of untreated Grave's disease. Grave's disease, an autoimmune disease,[1] is the most usual form of hyperthyroidism, with antibodies that act on the TSH receptors, stimulating production and secretion of TH in the same manner as TSH, but without being subject to the negative feedback

---

1   An autoimmune disease is a pathological condition caused by the production of antibodies against one's own body. About 150 autoimmune diseases are known, the large majority being much more common in women than in men. Examples of autoimmune disease include Type 1 diabetes (due to destruction of the insulin-producing β-cells in the pancreas) or different forms of thyroid disease, such as Grave's disease (hyperthyroidism) or Hashimoto's disease (hypothyroidism), each due to different types of antibodies that act on various proteins expressed in or on the thyroid gland.

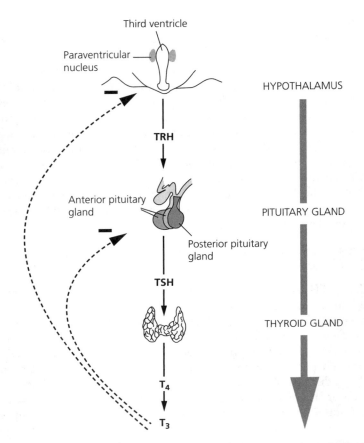

**Figure 4–1.** The hypothalamic/pituitary/thyroid (HPT) axis. TH ($T_4$ and $T_3$) production by iodination of tyrosine residues in the thyroid gland is stimulated by thyrotropin (or thyroid-stimulating hormone [TSH]) produced in and secreted from specialized cells (thyrotrophs) in the anterior pituitary or hypophysis. In turn, TSH production is stimulated by a peptide, TSH-releasing hormone (TRH) produced in a small set of neurons localized in the paraventricular nucleus (PVN) of the hypothalamus. To balance these two positive feedforward mechanisms and to maintain circulating TH levels within physiological range, $T_3$ exerts negative feedback on both TRH and TSH transcription. Each of these central regulatory levels, hypothalamus and pituitary, integrates information from the periphery and central sources (brain).

that down-regulates TSH. Many forms of hypothyroidism are also autoimmune disorders, in this case with antibodies produced against thyroid-specific proteins.

Hyperthyroidism is easily diagnosed by its multiple symptoms (rapid weight loss and bulging eyes) and so it is usually treated rapidly with drugs that block the thyroid gland and production of TH. If severe or recurrent, the thyroid is removed and thyroxine ($T_4$) replacement therapy is instituted. However, if hyperthyroidism is left untreated, it can result in a severe condition, referred to in the medical literature as thyroid storm (Nayak & Burman, 2006), that can be life threatening. Intriguingly, thyroid storm can also, on rare occasions, result from acute trauma (Yoshida, 1996). The most common cause of death from the excess $T_3$ that characterises thyroid storm is from heart complications such as tachycardia (too rapid heartbeat) and atrial fibrillation (problems of cardiac conduction and arrhythmia). It should be noted that cardiac complications are the main reason why $T_3$ should not be prescribed to obese patients who wish to use the metabolism-stimulating and fat-burning properties of the hormone to facilitate weight loss. However, in some countries unscrupulous doctors will prescribe the hormone, often with dire consequences (Kaufman, Gross, & Kennedy, 1991).

Similarly, prolonged and severe hypothyroidism can in exceptional circumstances prove fatal if not treated urgently. A rare clinical condition characteristic of severe lack of TH is myxedema coma (Mathew et al., 2011). The symptoms include edema (accumulation of fluid in the limbs), cardiac problems, respiratory distress, hypothermia, and coma (loss of consciousness) and require immediate administration of $T_3$ or $T_4$.

Today, the cause of myxedema coma will most often be failure to take prescribed thyroxine ($T_4$). However, there is an intriguing case of the pathology in the medical literature, describing the condition of a woman who ate more than a kilo per day of raw cabbage (Chu & Seltzer, 2010)! As the authors of the report underline, Chinese cabbage (and many other related vegetables of the cabbage Brassicae family) contains an enzyme, myrosinase, which is released into the body if the vegetables are eaten raw but is destroyed on cooking. This enzyme causes the breakdown of other substances found in cabbage, glucosinolates, which can generate a series of compounds (e.g., thiocyanates, nitriles, and oxazoldines) that inhibit iodine uptake by the thyroid. This medical case echoes experiments performed nearly a century ago when rabbits fed a diet of cabbage were observed to develop goiter (see references in Chu & Seltzer, 2010 and Webster, Marine, & Cipra, 1931). *Goiter* is the medical term for a pathological enlargement of the thyroid gland. Goiters can be symptomatic of hypothyroidism and lack of iodine as the thyroid tissue is stimulated to grow under the influence of high levels of TSH produced when thyroid levels are low. Studies on the thyroid-inhibiting properties of cabbage (Altamura, Long, & Hasselstrom, 1959) led to the isolation of goitrins or goitrogens (substances that inhibit thyroid gland function) from a number of foodstuffs (Elfving, 1980).

## Maturation of the Hypothalamic/Pituitary/Thyroid Axis in Humans and Rodents: The Development of the Thyroid Gland

In mammals the thyroid is a bilobed structure, with one lobe on either side of the larynx. The thyroid gland, the largest endocrine gland in humans, is composed principally of follicular cells that are derived from embryonic endoderm. In the mature gland, these follicular cells, or thyrocytes, are organized in a single layer around the TH-containing colloid (see Fig. 4.4). The thyroid gland also contains some neural crest–derived cells, the parafollicular or C-cells that secrete calcitonin, a hormone that controls calcium uptake and mineralization. However, these C-cells represent less than 10% of the total thyroid mass.

The main events determining thyroid morphogenesis occur early in gestation, in the first 2 months in humans and in the first 15 days in rodents (Fig. 4.2). In humans, the thyroid gland begins to develop during the third week of pregnancy (Shepard, 1967, 1968). Thyroid development starts at this time as an outgrowth of the endoderm in the primitive buccal cavity that will become the future pharynx. From the initial site of development, between the first and second branchial arches, the developing gland migrates caudally. The developing thyroid is closely associated by its location and migration with the developing heart and in some rare cases extrathyroidal tissue is found in intracardiac sites, and more commonly in other sites along the migratory path, including under the tongue.

The organization of the thyrocytes into the characteristic follicular structure of the thyroid occurs in three stages between weeks 7 and 14 in humans. It is during these stages that the expression of a number of thyroid-specific or thyroid-characteristic proteins involved in synthesis and secretion of TH, $T_4$ and $T_3$, begins. Besides the major TH stocking protein of the colloid, thyroglobulin (TG), synthesis also begins of the sodium-iodide ($Na^+/I^-$) symporter (NIS), the protein responsible for transporting iodide from blood into the thyroid cells. NIS is located on the basolateral membrane of the follicle cells. Other transporters, such as pendrin, an iodide/chloride transporter, which are located on the colloid side of the follicle cells, are required to transport iodide into the colloid. In the colloid, iodide is oxidized and bound to the tyrosine residues of TG. This reaction and that of coupling of iodotyrosines to form $T_3$ and $T_4$ is catalyzed by thyroid peroxidase (TPO). TPO requires hydrogen peroxide ($H_2O_2$) to function. $H_2O_2$ is generated in the thyroid by two related enzymes, the thyroid oxidases THOX-1 (DUOX1) and THOX2 (DUOX2), located at the apical, colloid-abutting membrane.

The main activator of TH production and secretion is TSH. Receptors for TSH are G-protein-coupled receptors that are linked to cyclic AMP (cAMP) production. cAMP stimulates a number of pathways and thyroid tissue differentiation. However, TSH and its receptor are not required for initial thyroid development and do not appear until the 16th embryonic day in rodents. A combination of two thyrocyte-specific transcription factors is required for development of the embryonic follicle cells Nkx2-1, a homedomain transcription factor (in early papers referred to as thyroid transcription factor-1, TTF-1 or Titf1), and paired box gene 8 (Pax8; De Felice & Di Lauro, 2011). Two other transcription factors are coexpressed with Nkx2-1 and Pax8: Hhex and Foxe1. Loss of either *Nkx2-1* or *Pax8* compromises follicular cell survival and differentiation during organogenesis. All factors are expressed in other tissues, but their coexpression determines thyroid differentiation. An elegant, groundbreaking demonstration of the importance of two of these factors, *Nkx2-1* and *Pax8*, in determining thyroid lineage used genetic engineering to drive transient, simultaneous expression of their mRNA in embryonic stem (ES) cells (Antonica et al., 2012). Overexpression of *Nkx2-1* and *Pax8* induced expression of Foxe1 and then functional markers of thyroid differentiation, including the TSH receptor, NIS, and TG. Full differentiation into follicular structures required the presence of TSH.

In the mouse, *Nkx2-1* is first expressed between embryonic days 8.5 to 10 in the endoderm cells of the early pharynx where the thyroid will form, the thyroid anlage or placode. However, its expression is not limited to this area and expression is found also in regions that give rise to parts of the pituitary gland and hypothalamus. *Pax8* also appears at this time, with expression detected in the future thyroid, kidney, and some neural tissue. *Pax8* expression continues in the adult thyroid. Mutant mice with no *Pax8* have virtually no thyroid tissue and the small amount present is largely composed of C-cells.

The contribution of maternal factors to fetal thyroid development has been difficult to address in mammals. It is thought that neither TRH nor TSH passes the placental barrier in sufficient amounts to affect embryonic fetal growth under normal circumstances. However, despite the high expression of the inactivating deiodinase, D3, in the placenta, both $T_4$ and $T_3$ reach the developing embryo as even infants that are born without a thyroid gland have TH levels that can reach 50% of normal levels (Vulsma, Gons, & de Vijlder, 1989) and both $T_3$ and $T_4$ are found in fetal and embryonic fluids prior to the development of the embryonic thyroid (Calvo et al., 2002). Such findings underline the fact that fetal tissues are exposed to physiologically relevant levels of TH well before the fetal thyroid becomes active (see also Chapter 3 and the section on "Early Neurodevelopment"). Another important role of the placenta is provision of sufficient iodide for synthesis of TH once the fetal thyroid has formed. Iodide is actively transported across the placenta. Early studies in rodents show that administering inorganic iodide to pregnant rabbits, rats, and guinea pigs resulted in higher iodide levels in fetal serum than in maternal serum. The movement of iodide across the placenta was inhibited by thiocyanate, indicating a transport mechanism (Logothetopoulos & Scott, 1956). Since then, the transport mechanism has been shown to be dependent on the sodium–iodide symporter (NIS) and to be inhibited by perchlorate and nitrate as well as by thiocyanate (Blount et al., 2009) in humans and animal models. Given the high levels of nitrate and perchlorate in drinking water, some studies have addressed their effects on iodide transport and accumulation in the fetal compartment during pregnancy. In the study cited (Blount et al., 2009), the authors found that, despite high levels of different thyroid inhibitors in maternal urine, accumulation of iodide in the fetal compartment (measured in amniotic fluid at caesarean section) was still higher than in maternal fluids. Inversely, fetal levels of perchlorate were lower than in maternal fluids. The measures were obtained on a small cohort of 150 women from a New Jersey population that was not iodine deficient, probably due to adequate prenatal vitamin supplementation. It is probable that these factors, small cohort size and iodine supplementation, accounted for the fact that there was no association found between any of the thyroid inhibitors and physical parameters of the newborns, though no measures of later neurodevelopment were made.

Insufficient development of the fetal thyroid results in significantly lower TH levels at birth, a condition classified as congenital hypothyroidism (CH). Most cases of CH are due to problems with thyroid gland development, but some are the result of defective hormone synthesis mechanisms. Less than 2% of CH can actually be attributed to mutations in genes involved in thyroid gland morphogenesis and no more that 15% are thought be due to mutations in genes affecting development of the hypothalamic-pituitary-thyroid axis. As discussed in Chapters 2 and 7, many authors consider that the remaining, overwhelmingly larger, proportion of cases not obviously related to genetic causes could implicate environmental factors modulating genes involved in thyroid development. Suffice it here to recall that diagnosis of CH is increasing in many populations. For instance, in the United States the incidence of CH has increased by 138% between 1978 and 2005 and by over 70% in the 15 years between 1987 and 2002 (Harris & Pass, 2007).

## Development of Pituitary Thyroid-Stimulating Hormone–Expressing Thyrotrophs and the Hypothalamus

Development of the pituitary gland and hypothalamus are tightly linked, reflecting their intrinsic coordinated functions throughout life (Fig. 4.2). However, despite much research effort, mainly exploiting mutant mouse models (see Andersen & Rosenfeld, 2001 for review), the details of their complex embryonic determination are not fully elucidated. The anterior pituitary contains six main types of cells that produce and secrete different trophic hormones in response to hypothalamic signals. Thyrotrophs produce TSH (in response to TRH), the somatotrophs produce growth hormone (GH), and lactotrophs produce prolactin. The fourth main group of pituitary cells are the gonadotrophs, implicated in reproduction, that produce either follicule-stimulating hormone (FSH) or lutenizing hormone (LH). Finally, two types of pituitary cells express pro-opiomelanocortin (POMC), which is processed to produce mainly adrenocorticotrophin (ACTH) in corticotrophs and α-melanocyte-stimulating hormone (α-MSH) in melanotrophs.

The anterior pituitary develops from an outgrowth of a group of ectodermal cells (Rathke's pouch) in the buccal cavity below the midbrain (diencephalon) region that will give rise to the hypothalamus. In humans, this occurs around gestational week 4, with pituitary cell differentiation occurring over the next 3–4 weeks, with thyrotrophs being detected around week 8 of gestation. Pituitary morphogenesis is determined by successive expression of a series of transcription factors (Andersen & Rosenfeld, 2001), the most important for thyrotroph determination and TSH expression being Pit-1, Prophet of Pit-1 (Prop-1), and thyrotroph embryonic factor (TEF). Expression of TEF coincides with the expression of the β-subunit of TSH, followed by the expression

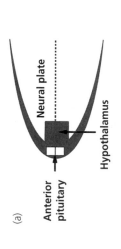

(a)

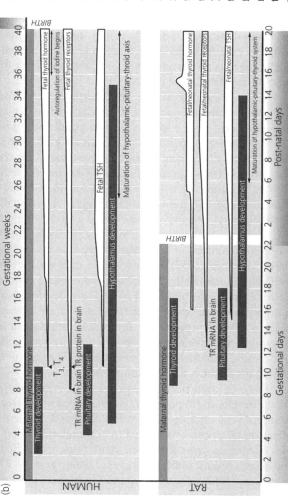

Figure 4–2. Development of the hypothalamic/pituitary/thyroid axis. (*a*) The hypothalamus and the pituitary are intimately linked both developmentally and functionally (see text for details). (*b*) Schema of the parallel developmental timing of the human and rodent hypothalamic/pituitary/thyroid axes. In humans and rodents the formation of the thyroid gland is followed closely by that of the pituitary, after which hypothalamic controls begin to mature. The whole period of axis maturation covers the intrauterine period in humans and in rodents (largely based on rats models but mainly transposable to mice). In rodents this represents the period of midgestation to weaning (20–21 days postnatal). Note that in both rodents and humans the embryo is entirely dependent for the first third of gestation on maternal thyroid hormone supplies prior to formation of the fetal thyroid gland. (Panel B was adapted from Howdeshell, 2002.)

of Pit-1. Continued expression of Pit-1 is necessary for thyrotroph survival and maintenance of TSH expression. Pit-1 is also required for differentiation of somatotrophs and lactotrophs, respectively.

As mentioned earlier, hypothalamic development is intimately linked with that of the pituitary, the close apposition of their presumptive zones suggesting that mutually inductive signals are required for their development and differentiation. The hypothalamus derives from the diencephalon around the fifth or sixth week of pregnancy in humans. Two main neuroendocrine systems are organized within what will become the paraventricular nucleus of the developing hypothalamus: the magnocellular neurons (producing oxcytocin and vasopressin), the axons of which will form the posterior pituitary, and the parvocellular neurons, including the TRH-producing neurons that project to the median eminence and stimulate TSH production.

Impaired pituitary development affecting TSH producing thyrotrophs can be a causal factor in CH. However, in contrast to the increasing incidence of CH, due potentially in some cases to lack of maternal iodine (Harris & Pass, 2007), there is no current epidemiological evidence for environmental effects on pituitary development.

Similarly, there is insufficient knowledge and research on hypothalamic development and the intricate neuronal circuitry that controls metabolism and feeding, including the specific neuron populations governing TH production, the TRH neurons. A number of enigmas exist. For instance, during mouse development circulating $T_3$ and $T_4$ levels gradually rise in the first two postnatal weeks (Hadj-Sahraoui, Seugnet, Ghorbel, & Demeneix, 2000), then drop slightly, reaching adult levels around weaning, at the end of the third week. How *Trh* (and *Tsh*) transcription is regulated during this time, before the negative feedback system matures, is not known. Some authors have addressed the question either using pharmacological tools (Taylor, Gyves, & Burgunder, 1990) or cultures of embryonic neurons (Carreon-Rodriguez, Charli, & Perez-Martinez, 2009), but very little data on the ontology of feedback are available. Theoretically, the rising $T_3$ and $T_4$ levels should inhibit production of both TH and re-equilibrate $T_3$ and $T_4$ production, but feedback is apparently put on hold until weaning when set points are established. Given the importance of these set points for future TH (and whole body) homeostasis, it is important to consider the molecular mechanisms underlying their control, to understand potential actions of endocrine disruption on these processes, both during development and in adulthood.

Only one study, from our own laboratory, looked at the impact of chemicals on the developing hypothalamus in newborn mice (Decherf & Demeneix, 2011; Decherf, Seugnet, Fini, Clerget-Froidevaux, & Demeneix, 2010). We examined effects of two pollutants linked to accumulation of fat in the periphery. These two chemicals, one a flame retardant, tetra bromo bisphenol A (TBBPA), and the other a marine antifouling agent (Tributyl tin, TBT), are classed as potential obesogens. Both were found to modify the set points of metabolic genes in the TRH neurons. Their actions are discussed in the section on "The TRH Neuron."

## The Mature Thyroid Gland

De novo synthesis of the iodothyronines $T_4$ and $T_3$ results from the coupling of two iodotyrosines, a process that is restricted to the thyroid gland in most vertebrates. As explained in Chapter 2, without iodine (or iodide, $I^-$, in its ionized form) no synthesis of TH can occur; therefore, highly sophisticated and efficient means for the uptake, concentration, and organification of iodine in the thyroid gland have evolved. The thyroid is composed of colloid-containing follicles that represent the functional subunit of thyroid tissue. A single epithelial cell layer forms the follicle (Fig. 4.3a), these specialized follicular cells being the thyrocytes that secrete the thyroglobulin (TG)-containing colloid. The height of the follicular cell layer and the density of the colloid change as a function of thyroid activity and can be used, by trained histologists, to determine the general status of thyroid gland function. A dense network of capillaries that irrigates each individual follicle ensures adequate blood supply. Iodide uptake from the bloodstream is a rate-limiting step in iodotyrosine biosynthesis, and this dense vascularization has no doubt evolved to ensure maximal uptake of iodide, the thyroid gland displaying one of the densest vascularizations of any tissue. Iodide, $I^-$, is concentrated in thyrocytes by an active transport system that works against the electrochemical gradient, concentrating $I^-$ by a factor of 20 to 40 over blood plasma concentrations (Dohan et al., 2003). That an enzyme was responsible for this active process was inferred from a number of physiological studies carried out in the 1960s and 70s (see Dohan et al., 2003 for review) and the actual symporter, NIS, identified in the late 80s (Vilijn & Carrasco, 1989) and cloned in 1996 (Dai, Levy, & Carrasco, 1996). The localisation of the NIS glycoprotein on the basolateral membrane of the follicle situates it in intimate association with capillaries; it thus ensures the first, vital step of supplying $I^-$ to the thyroid ($I^-$ influx). The next step is translocation of $I^-$ across the apical membrane in the follicular lumen or space ($I^-$ efflux). A number of researchers have tried to identify the factor responsible for $I^-$ efflux. Two candidates have been suggested, Pendrin and apical iodide transporter (AIP), though neither has been conclusively demonstrated to carry out physiological $I^-$ efflux. Organification of iodide takes place at the interface with the colloid on the thryocyte apical membrane, and this is carried out by another specialized enzyme, thyroid peroxidase (TPO). TPO catalyzes iodination of tyrosyl residues within the TG polypeptide chain, producing monoiodotyrosine (MIT) and diiodotyrosine (DIT) (Fig. 4.3c). TG is a large (660 kDa) glycoprotein dimer; it is produced by the follicle cells and secreted into the lumen, where it serves as the matrix for TH synthesis by TPO. TPO, besides oxidizing $I^-$, enabling its incorporation into iodotyrosine, is also responsible for the subsequent coupling, on the TG matrix, of iodotyrosine residues, either MIT or DIT, to produce $T_3$ and $T_4$. In addition to TG and $I^-$, TPO requires the cofactor hydrogen peroxide ($H_2O_2$), without which TPO has no biological activity. Thus, $H_2O_2$ production is likely a rate-limiting step for TH synthesis (Song et al., 2007). $H_2O_2$ production is ensured by two thyroid-specific NADPH-dependent oxidoreductases referred to as dual oxidases (commonly named THOX1 and THOX2, though their official nomenclature is DUOX1 and DUOX2). The thyroid follicle cells express high levels of the selenoenzyme glutathione peroxidase, GPx. It is thought that the production of $H_2O_2$ by the thyroid would produce significant free radical damage if not reduced to $H_2O$ by GPx and other protective enzymes such as superoxide dismutases. GPx, like the deiodinases, is a sensitive target of mercury pollution because mercury interacts avidly with selenium (see Chapter 2, section on "Selenium and Mercury" and Chapter 5, section on "Mercury").

Iodinated Tg is stored extracellularly in the colloidal compartment, but in response to TSH stimulus and consequent cAMP production, thyroglobulin (TG) is endocytosed from the colloid, enzymatically cleaved within the thyrocytes and free TH secreted into the bloodstream (Dunn & Dunn, 2001). TSH also stimulates the expression of NIS, TG, TPO, and its own receptor (TSH-R) through production of cAMP. Recently, a process related to intrathyroidal iodide recycling was described at the molecular level. Iodotyrosine dehalogenase (DEHAL) mediates the deiodination of MIT and DIT, two iodotyrosines that are released upon lyzosomal proteolysis of mature TG. In fact, despite the fact that there is more MIT and DIT than $T_3$ and $T_4$ in the colloid, only minimal amounts of MIT and DIT are actually released into the blood. Thus, recuperation of I⁻ from these iodotyrosines during TG cleavage provides a physiologically important means of intracellular iodide salvaging and recycling.

Thus, a number of specialized enzymatic processes are implicated in the TH biosynthetic pathway enabling efficient uptake and organification of iodide to ensure TH biosynthesis. Patients carrying mutations of genes encoding for different enzymes implicated in TH biosynthesis, such as NIS, TPO, DUOX2, DEHAL, and TSHR, suffer from different forms of hypothyroidism and goiter.

A number of chemicals affect different aspects of thyroid gland physiology. The main ones studied include perchlorate (which inhibits NIS and therefore iodide uptake) or the thiocarbamide drugs used clinically to treat hyperthyroidism, such as carbimazole (CBZ), methimazole (MMI), or propylthiouracil (PTU), which inhibit TPO. Thus, it is logical to think that besides these well-characterized (and much used) chemicals, other molecules could well cause thyroid gland dysfunction. Besides the complex enzymatic synthesis of THs, two other factors also make the thyroid gland particularly vulnerable to chemical disruption. The first is a rich vascular system, already mentioned, that is extremely sensitive to TSH stimulation. This rich irrigation, which increases in response to iodine deficiency (Gerard, Poncin, Audinot, Denef, & Colin, 2009), means that thyrocytes are relatively more exposed than other tissues to EDCs in blood. The second exacerbating factor is the thyroid-specific long-term production of hydrogen peroxide ($H_2O_2$) with its by-products, reactive oxygen species (ROS), a situation that, again, is exacerbated by fluctuating iodine supplies (Poncin et al., 2008). This endogenous peroxidase activity makes the thyroid particularly vulnerable to the action of low molecular weight agents which can be substrates for $H_2O_2$-catalyzed oxidation and activation (Köhrle, 2008).

As mentioned in Chapter 1, bromine can inhibit iodine uptake by the thyroid (Pavelka, 2004), particularly in situations of iodine deficiency. As bromine is still present in the environment in leaded petrol in some countries and is increasingly present in the form of multiple brominated flame retardants (BFRs), the TH-disrupting potential and consequent neurodevelopmental effects of this element are continually amplifying.

What is more, unknown to many, the bread industry in many countries actually adds bromine to bread rather than iodine. In the United States, bromine, used as a yeast additive, can be added to flour at up to 24 mg/kg, in baking products up to 36 mg/kg, and in malted barley to 75 mg/kg (Anderson, 2009). The public health issues of the concurrent reduction in use of iodized salt and increased use of bromine additives by the food industry need to be revisited in the context of amplified use of BFRs. The urgency of this issue becomes more evident in the light of the recent data on iodine-deficient populations and the effects of even mild iodine deficiency on children's neurodevelopment (Bath, Steer, Golding, Emmett, & Rayman, 2013).

## The Mature Thyrotroph and Thyroid-Stimulating Hormone Production

The thyrotropin (TSH)-producing cells of the human pituitary represent only 1% to 5% of the total cells, but they are all grouped in a distinctly defined anterior region of the gland. These cells synthesise the α- and β-subunits that make up TSH. Some TSH-positive cells contain small amounts of GH, reflecting the common developmental lineage of somatotrophs and thyrotrophs. This common developmental origin can allow transdifferentiation of somatotrophs to thyrotrophs, such progression having been observed under prolonged hypothyroidism. Numbers of thyrotrophs do not differ between genders, but some increase is seen during aging in humans. This increase may reflect the higher incidence of subclinical hypothyroidism in the aging population, a problem that presents a number of difficulties for diagnosis and therapy.

TSH production and secretion, like that of TRH, is very sensitive to $T_3$ feedback, with increased levels of $T_3$ repressing transcription. In contrast to the transcriptional repression of the *Trh* gene that is highly TRβ specific, both TRα and TRβ are involved in $T_3$-dependent repression of *Tsh* (Gauthier et al., 1999).

In terms of endocrine disruption of pituitary thyrotroph function and the exquisite sensitivity of TSH regulation by $T_3$ levels, it follows that any changes in $T_4$ or $T_3$ availability will have major repercussions on TSH production. Moreover, as many selenoproteins are expressed in the pituitary (Köhrle, Jakob, Contempré, & Dumont, 2005), mercury contamination can potentially interfere with thyrotroph function, as could any pollutant affecting RXR action, the heterodimeric partner of TRs, essential for negative $T_3$ feedback on TSH production.

## The TRH Neuron: A Central Regulator of Energy Balance, Thyroid Homeostasis and a Link to the Obesogen Hypothesis

Moving up from the pituitary to the hypothalamus, the TRH neurons that control the pituitary TSH-producing thyrotrophs are only found in the paraventricular nucleus of the hypothalamus, on either side of the third brain ventricle (Fig. 4.4). The TRH neurons govern not only TH production, and therefore development and metabolic rate, but are also major players in determining appetite and feeding activity. Succinctly put, to ensure metabolic homeostasis, TRH production is governed by a number of factors that are implicated in integrating information on energy balance (i.e., energy stores and energy expenditure). The TRH neuron receives information from the circulation and from a dense network of neuronal afferents. The main peripheral signals are $T_4$, which is converted to $T_3$ by the cells lining the third ventricle, and leptin, produced by adipose tissue.

$T_3$ exerts negative feedback on *Trh* transcription and translation. The effect of $T_3$ is played out at the transcriptional level through interaction with either TRβ1 or TRβ2 (Guissouma et al., 2002, Guissouma, Ghorbel, Seugnet, Ouatas, & Demeneix, 1998; Lezoualc'h et al., 1992). Both TRβ2 and TRβ1 induce $T_3$-dependent repression of *Trh* transcription but TRβ1 also has a role in $T_3$-independent activation of transcription (Abel et al., 1999; Abel, Ahima, Boers, Elmquist, & Wondisford, 2001; Guissouma, Froidevaux, Hassani, & Demeneix, 2006). The TRH neurons are, like the thyrotrophs of the anterior pituitary, one of the rare cell types that express high levels of TRβ2. It was this privileged level and highly localized expression that was a first clue as to the role of TRβ, and particulary TRβ2, in $T_3$-dependent repression of transcription of the *Trh* gene. Even though TRα1 and TRα2 are also expressed in the TRH neuron, they do not play a major role in negative feedback of $T_3$ on *Trh* transcription. However, it should be recalled that the TRH neuron does not express the activating deiodinase, D2, that converts $T_4$ to $T_3$. The $T_3$ that determines regulation of *Trh* production through TRβ2 is generated in the neighboring tanycytes that do express D2. The tanycytes are specialized cells surrounding the third ventricle. They make contact with the cerebrospinal fluid as well as with the brain blood supply. $T_3$ produced in the tanycytes reaches the TRH neuron through membrane-located transporters (OATP14 and MCT8, see Chapter 3). The major role of D2 in the rest of the brain is to ensure local production of $T_3$ from $T_4$, as $T_4$ enters the brain more readily than $T_3$. To guarantee sufficient production of $T_3$ during episodes of hypothyroidism, low $T_4$ levels increase D2 activity, notably in the most $T_3$-sensitive areas such as the cerebellar cortex and hippocampus (Hollenberg, 2008). However, unlike D2 in other brain areas, D2 expression in the hypothalamic tanycytes is not up-regulated by low $T_4$ levels (Broedel et al., 2003). This lack of regulation in the hypothalamus is of course vital to ensure that the hypothalamic neurons integrate information that is a direct reflection of the peripheral thyroid status and respond accordingly. Were the tanycytes to stimulate D2 production in response to low $T_4$ levels, the PVN neurons would not be "informed" of changing circulating TH levels.

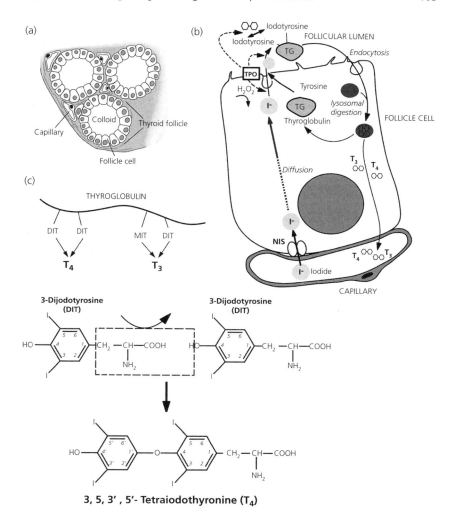

**3, 5, 3', 5'- Tetraiodothyronine (T$_4$)**

**Figure 4–3.** Schema of thyroid gland structure and function. (*a*) Basic structure of the thyroid gland. (*b*) Schematic representation of the thyroid hormone synthesis in the thyroid. The thyroid follicle cell, or thyrocyte, expresses sodium-iodide (Na$^+$/I$^-$) symporter (NIS) on the basolateral membrane that transports inorganic iodide (I$^-$). Following I$^-$ efflux into the colloid, thyroid peroxidase (TPO) ensures organification on thyroglobulin tyrosine residues, producing thyroid hormone that is stocked in the colloid. (*c*) Thyroglobulin dimerization and subsequent iodination by TPO on tyrosine residues is followed by condensation and cleavage to produce T$_4$ (or T$_3$). Under thyroid-stimulating hormone stimulation, the thyroid synthesizes and secretes thyroid hormone, principally in the form of T$_4$ and to a lesser extent T$_3$.

The other peripheral signal of major metabolic importance, besides $T_3$, for which the TRH neurons receive direct and indirect input is leptin (Fig. 4.4). As leptin is produced by adipocytes, its circulating levels are a direct reflection of amounts of adipose tissue. The direct input is through expression of leptin receptors on the TRH neuron itself, although the contribution of these receptors to leptin regulation of metabolism is thought to be less important than the indirect pathway (Fekete & Lechan, 2007). The indirect input is through leptin receptors that are expressed on the cell bodies of neurons that project onto the TRH neurons from the arcuate nucleus (ARC). Two main sets of

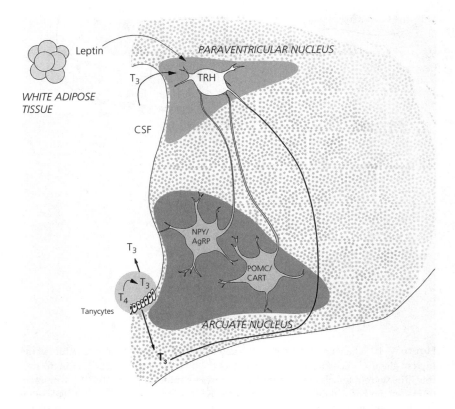

**Figure 4–4.** Simplified schema of the thyrotropin-releasing hormone (TRH) neuron as an integrator of information on energy balance. The two major inputs from the circulation are $T_4$ (converted to $T_3$ in tanycytes) and leptin (produced in white adipose tissue). Leptin is thought to act through direct and indirect mechanisms. The major neuronal afferents arise in the arcuate nucleus (ARC). They include two classes of neurons: those expressing pro-opiomelanocortin (POMC) and cocaine and amphetamine-regulated transcript (CART) and those expressing Neuorpeptide Y (NPY) and Agouti-Related Protein (AgRP). These neuronal outputs affect appetite and feeding. CSF: cerebrospinal fluid.

leptin-sensitive afferent neurons impinge on the TRH neuron from the ARC. One group of these neurons, which coexpresses pro-opiomelanocortin-stimulating hormone (POMC) and cocaine and amphetamine-regulated transcript (CART), has a negative effect on energy balance. By releasing αMSH and CART, *Trh* expression is stimulated and feeding responses inhibited, thus increasing energy expenditure through $T_3$ production and reducing energy intake. The other principal set of ARC-originating neurons are inhibitory on *Trh* and have an overall positive, anabolic effect on energy balance. These neurons coexpress Agouti-Related Protein (AgRP) and Neuropeptide Y (NPY), which inhibit *Trh* production and modulate appetite and feeding responses. POMC is the precursor protein of a number of peptides (Dores & Baron, 2011; Wardlaw, 2011), but the POMC-derived peptide released by the synapses that make contact with the TRH neuron is αMSH. The principal αMSH receptor expressed by the TRH neuron is MC4R. MC4R activity is stimulated by αMSH and inhibited by AgRP (Fekete & Lechan, 2007). MC4R is encoded by one of the few genes in which mutations have been directly associated with cases of extreme obesity in humans (Farooqi & O'Rahilly, 2006). Similarly, in mutant mice, loss of *Mc4r* causes severe obesity (Huszar et al., 1997). MC4R, like adrenaline, activates cAMP, CREB, and *Trh* transcription, thus activating the thyroid axis. Expression of *Mc4r* is under negative feedback by $T_3$, in a parallel manner to negative feedback of $T_3$ on *Trh* (Decherf et al., 2010b). The regulation is direct, involves a negative TRE half-site, but both TRα and TRβ isoforms are able to exert $T_3$-dependent repression of *Mc4r* transcription (whereas only TRβ can repress transcription from the *Trh* promoter; Guissouma et al., 1998).

Cold exposure is another physiological stressor that increases *Trh* production and increases thyroid axis activity. In this case, the stimulatory signal modifying the set point comes from the ascending input of adrenergic neurons from the brainstem. Adrenaline released by the terminals of these neurons stimulates intracellular cAMP production. In turn, this signal phosphorylates the CREB transcription factor that binds to the *Trh* promoter at a CREB response element (CRE) close to the TH receptor response element (TRE) site at which TRβ binds (Decherf et al., 2010b).

Given the major roles of the TRH neurons as metabolic sensors (Hollenberg, 2008), it is not surprising to find that chemicals that interfere with TH signaling in the different parts of the body could also have detrimental effects on energy homeostasis and body weight. Such chemicals could be implicated in the current epidemiology of obesity and have been called "obesogens" (Grün & Blumberg, 2006). At first the term was coined to describe a group of chemicals that had been identified for their actions on the production of adipose tissue (fat). Thus, most work over the last 10 years has emphasized obesogen activity in the periphery, outside the brain. However, recently, the concept has been extended to include substances that may modify metabolic balance at the central, hypothalamic level (Decherf & Demeneix, 2011; Grün, 2010), notably by acting on TRH production, directly or indirectly (Decherf et al., 2010a). As explained earlier, TRH production and secretion are the core mechanisms of central control, not only of $T_3$ production, but they also participate in regulating food intake. Succinctly put, the obesogen concept proposes that the obesity epidemic with its related pathologies, including metabolic disorders such as Type 2 diabetes, hypertension, and cardiovascular disease, could implicate different environmental contaminants.

The obesogen concept appeared in the early 2000s and was reviewed in 2009 (Grün & Blumberg, 2009). The basic hypothesis is that the observed correlation between increasing incidence of obesity and that of industrial chemical production is not just a coincidence but potentially causally related. As mentioned, the term "obesogen" was originally used to describe an environmental pollutant that affects the most direct link with obesity (i.e., increased fat accumulation). Thus, connections were sought between pollutants that could adversely affect various aspects of adipose tissue function, particularly its early development (Janesick & Blumberg, 2011; Newbold, Padilla-Banks, Snyder, & Jefferson, 2007). Nuclear receptors, as ligand-binding transcription factors, have always been in the frontline as potential targets. Emphasis has been placed on substances that interfere with or mimic estrogen and ER signaling, but given the pivotal role of PPARγ in adipose tissue determination, also on chemicals that can interact with this signaling pathway. One should note that both signaling pathways are privileged routes of crosstalk with TH signaling, both in the periphery and in the brain. Examples of estrogen receptor (ER) and TR crosstalk can be found at the level of integrated physiology, with TH levels modulating reproductive behavior in rodents and birds (Morgan, Dellovade, & Pfaff, 2000) and, at the other extreme, at the level of regulation of transcription of individual genes (Pfaff et al., 2000; Vasudevan, Ogawa, & Pfaff, 2002). The same arguments hold for PPARγ and TR interactions, with crosstalk between these signaling pathways modulating physiological processes impinging on metabolic switches both in the periphery (Mishra, Zhu, Ge, & Cheng, 2010) and hypothalamus (Kouidhi et al., 2010). In the case of PPARγ and TR, interactions are not only found at the level of genes and physiological processes that are coregulated but also at the level of molecular partners. All TRs and PPARs use RXR isotypes as their heterodimeric partners in gene regulation, and each can share coactivator or comodulator complexes. Moreover, PPARγ and certain RXR isotypes can be targets of the same EDCs (e.g., TBT [le Maire et al., 2009], see also Chapter 5, section on "Examples of Chemicals Interfering With the Thyroid Receptor Heterodimeric Partner, RXR"). Thus, there is accumulating evidence that obesogens can affect multiple nuclear receptor signaling pathways, including TR-dependent pathways.

## Peripheral Regulation of Thyroid Hormone Distribution and Activity

During evolution a number of processes have undergone selection ensuring that levels of the precursor hormone, $T_4$, and that of the biologically active form, $T_3$, are maintained within narrow ranges. These regulatory systems include positive and negative feedback rheostats determining hormone production and secretion, at the levels of the hypothalamus and pituitary (described earlier, see Fig. 4.1); regulation of iodine uptake and organification (required to form $T_4$ and $T_3$), production of distributor proteins in serum that bind the hormones allowing their even distribution throughout the body, the deiodinases that activate and degrade $T_4$ and $T_3$ in target tissues, transporter proteins expressed on the plasma cell membrane that permit entry (and exit) of $T_4$ and $T_3$ (see Chapter 3), and liver enzymes that enable metabolism and secretion of excess hormone (Fig. 4.5). Each of these systems is subject to adjustment by different physiological parameters, often TH being one of the players.

The essential roles of the selenoenzymes, the activating and inactivating deiodinases, in maintaining local and whole-body TH homeostasis have been described in Chapter 2 (in the section Deiodinases and Selenium), where their propensity to be disrupted by mercury contamination is also discussed. Similarly, the membrane transporter proteins, including MCT8 and OATP14, were introduced in Chapter 3 when discussing their roles in brain development. So here we focus on the main TH distributor proteins in the blood and then on the liver enzymes that carry out conjugation of THs and facilitate their excretion in bile.

Three distributor proteins, transthyretin (TTR), thyroxine-binding globulin (TBG), and albumin carry TH in the blood. A first point to be raised when referring to these proteins, mainly to avoid confusion, is that these proteins used to be called TH transporter proteins or thyroid (hormone) binding proteins (Richardson, 2007). However, two principal factors have led to their renaming. The first reason is more related to their primary function, that of ensuring even distribution of TH around the body, so the term "distributor" is

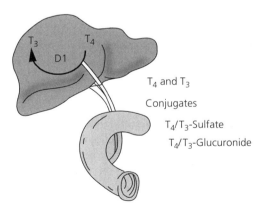

Figure 4–5. The liver is a major site of thyroid hormone metabolism. The liver is the main site of expression of Deiodinase 1, which acts as an activating deiodinase contributing to circulating $T_3$. The liver is also the site of the final stages of $T_3$ metabolism through conjugation (sulfation and glucuronidation) and biliary secretion.

more appropriate. The second was to distinguish between these serum proteins and the cell membrane-located transporters (e.g., MCT8) that were discovered in the early 2000s. To these arguments one could add the need to distinguish between them another class of thyroid-binding proteins, the cytosolic-binding proteins (Osty, Rappaport, Samuel, & Lennon, 1988; Yamauchi, Nakajima, Hayashi, Horiuchi, & Tata, 1999). The functions of these intracellular proteins have not received much attention. However, a number of observations argue for their physiological importance (and potentially their disruption by EDCs). Such data include that related to their affinity to bind $T_3$ (and other iodothyronines), which lies within a reasonable physiological range (in the order of $10^{-8}$M) and their expression levels that vary as a function of thyroid status, development, and tissue, as does their maximal binding capacity (Osty et al., 1988). Work on mouse and Xenopus (Graham, Brocklehurst, Pickersgill, & Warren, 2006; Yamauchi et al., 1999) has shown these proteins to be members of the aldehyde dehydrogenase and retinaldehyde dehydrogenase family that bind NAD+ and NADH and/or NADP+ and NADPH as well as $T_3$. Members of the retinaldehyde dehydrogenase family were initially identified in the retina, where they carry out the $NAD^+$-dependent oxidation of all-*trans*- or 9-*cis*-retinal to all-*trans*- or 9-*cis*-retinoic acid, respectively, but have since been found in many other tissues. This function in retinoic acid (RA) metabolism provides a link between RA and TH signaling, a link that can be found at many other levels, notably in coregulation of developmental processes and gene transcription. Another level of RA/TH interaction is at the level of shared distributor proteins, notably through the interaction of retinol (Vitamin A-precursor) with retinol-binding protein, which in turn interacts with TTR (Monaco, 2000; Smith et al., 1994).

In human blood, respectively, 99.97% and 99.7% of the $T_4$ and $T_3$ are bound to one of the three distributor proteins: TTR, TBG, or albumin (Mendel, 1989). Each of these proteins is synthesized by the liver, but TTR is also synthesized in the choroid plexus (the brain-cerebrospinal fluid [CSF] barrier) where it has a role in transferring $T_4$ to the brain. As shown by the elegant experimental demonstrations of Mendel over 30 years ago (Mendel, 1989) (Fig. 4.6), the principal physiological role of distributor proteins is to maintain a circulating pool of TH in physiological fluids such as blood or CSF, thus enabling an even delivery of TH throughout the body.

Each of the distributor proteins has different affinities for $T_4$ and $T_3$. TBG has the highest affinity for both, TTR affinities are intermediate, and albumin exhibits the lowest. In mammals, each of these distributor proteins has a greater affinity for $T_4$ than for $T_3$, being (for $T_4$) in the order of $1.0 \times 10^{10}$ $M^{-1}$ for TBG, $7.0 \times 10^7$ $M^{-1}$ for TTR, and $7.0 \times 10^5$ $M^{-1}$ for albumin. Birds, reptiles, amphibians, and teleost fish do not have TBG, and in these groups TTR displays greater affinity for $T_3$ than $T_4$.

In all vertebrates, the relative amounts of distributor proteins can be quite distinct. However, the physiological significance of their relative contributions to TH homeostasis depends on the dissociation rates of TH from the proteins

**TH in buffer**

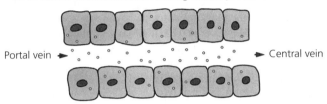

**TH in buffer with hormone-binding serum proteins**

**Figure 4–6.** Schematic representation of the importance of distributor proteins for even apportioning of thyroid hormone (TH). As demonstrated by experiments reported in Mendel et al. (1987), (Upper part) when perfusing rat liver with radioactive (*)T4 in aqueous buffer, most *T4 partitions into the first cells reached; (Lower part) perfusion of liver with *T4 in aqueous buffer supplemented with a mixture of transporter proteins (see text) provides an even distribution of *T4 throughout the liver lobule and in the perfusate. This demonstration underlines the role of distributor proteins in maintaining a circulating pool of TH in physiological fluids such as blood or cerebrospinal fluid, thus enabling an even delivery of TH throughout the body. *, radioactive [$^{125}$I]T4. (Adapted from Schreiber, 2002.)

and the capillary transit times (Richardson, 2007). Taking such factors into account, it appears that, in humans, TTR is the main player in immediate delivery of TH to tissues, whereas TBG acts more as a reserve.

Besides its synthesis in the liver and choroid plexus, TTR is also produced in the placenta (Mortimer et al., 2012; Richardson, 2009), where it is involved in maternal to fetal transport of TH. Thus, interference of xenobiotics with the placental TTR transfer role may have important implications for materno-fetal supply not only of TH but also of retinol/retinol binding protein and hence RA. Placental TTR can be implicated in the transfer of xenobiotics to the fetal compartment (Mortimer et al., 2012).

Unfortunately, many hydroxylated metabolites of persistent organic pollutants show high binding affinity for TTR that can be even higher than those of the endogenous ligand $T_4$ (Hamers et al., 2006; Lans et al., 1993; Meerts et al., 2002). This results in inhibition of $T_4$-binding to TTR, in disruption of the TTR-retinol binding protein (RBP) complex and, as a consequence, elevated plasma levels of TH and reduced retinol levels. At first sight, increased circulating TH levels might seem less worrying than their decrease and lack, but besides increased cellular uptake and enhanced intracellular TH action (which can be detrimental during development with tightly determined windows of TH availability and in mature states where it can induce local hyperthyroidism), raised free TH serum concentrations will activate TH metabolism in the liver and kidney and stimulate TH excretion through biliary, fecal, and urinary routes. Therefore, the presence of, and particularly long-term exposure to TH-disrupting chemicals (and there are dozens) that displace the hormone from TTR, will not only interfere with peripheral and central $T_3$ signaling but also amplify TH elimination and potentially contribute to negative iodine balance (Köhrle, 2008; van der Heide, Kastelijn, & Schroder-van der Elst, 2003). Xenobiotic load can also diminish TTR-dependent transfer of TH across the blood–brain barrier or the placenta but reciprocally increase that of other substances (Köhrle, 2008; Meerts et al., 2002; Morse, Wehler, Wesseling, Koeman, & Brouwer, 1996; Schreiber, Southwell, & Richardson, 1995).

Turning now to hepatic TH metabolizing enzymes, deiodination is the major metabolizing process for iodothyronines, with hepatic D1 being a major contributor, along with the D1 and D3 expressed in most tissues (though D1 has only limited expression in the brain). However, a number of other pathways for TH metabolism exist, notably for sulfation and glucuronidation in the liver. These two enzyme systems facilitate biliary, fecal, and urinary excretion by the production of more hydrophilic derivatives of TH. Another modification, this time resulting in metabolically derivatives, is decarboxylation of the TH alanine side chain. This reaction produces iodothyronamines, 3-iodothryonine (T3AM) and 4-iodothryonine (T4AM). A few papers on the physiological effects of such iodothyronamines were published between 1950 and the 1980s, but it is only recently, from 2004 onward, that more stringent experiments have shown them to have potentially interesting, generally metabolism-slowing, effects on reducing body temperature, heart rate, and respiratory quotient (for review, see Piehl, Hoefig, Scanlan, & Köhrle, 2011). Given the relatively novel research domain, little is known about their potential deregulation by endocrine disruptors.

More is known about the effects of xenobiotics on liver metabolism of THs, though much is derived from data on rodents and the pertinence for human physiology is often unknown. Liver metabolism of $T_4$ by glucuronidation is increased by various groups of drugs, such as barbiturates, antiepilectics, and fibrates, as well as by the widespread PCBs and their derivatives (Hood, Allen, Liu, Liu, & Klaassen, 2003; Morse et al., 1996; Visser et al., 1993).

Iodothyronines containing two iodine atoms on each phenol ring (i.e., principally $T_4$) are preferentially conjugated with glucuronic acid, whereas those with only one per phenol ring (e.g., $T_3$ and $rT_3$ or $T_2$ and $T_1$) are preferentially sulphated. Glucuronidation is the first step in the entero-hepatic recycling of TH (mainly $T_4$) through the liver and bile, where it can either be excreted in the feces or reabsorbed in the colon.

Take-Home Messages and Future Research Questions

- Evolution has elaborated a number of control systems to govern TH signaling and availability, from the brain's central regulation of TRH production in the hypothalamus, to the pituitary, to the thyroid gland itself. Little research has been addressed toward understanding how central, hypothalamic set points are established during development, and even less on analyzing how they could be modified by intrauterine or perinatal exposure to EDCs. Clearly, these areas require more research.

- Peripheral regulators include distributors and transporters that ensure delivery of the hormone to target tissues, where deiodinases and metabolizing enzymes determine precise tissue levels of available active hormone, $T_3$. EDCs can affect the functioning of each of these systems, often inducing marked effects of TH levels in the blood and brain. More research is required on how chemicals modify their activity, thereby impacting TH homeostasis, notably in cases of early and/or long-term exposures that could, respectively, alter hypothalamic set points and override homeostatic mechanisms of adaptation.
- Many EDCs displace TH from the distributor protein, TTR. Placental TTR has a vital role in transferring TH (and RA) to the fetus. Not only do numerous chemicals modify this process, but some can also be carried into the fetal compartment by this mechanism.
- In conclusion, any chemical that interferes with any one of these processes that are required to maintain TH levels within narrow ranges, including central control and feedback, hormone synthesis, distribution throughout the body, activation, and even degradation, will have the potential to imbalance the system, either acutely or in the longer term. Such environmental interference will modulate the gene networks and physiological responses regulated by TH, both during development and in the adult.

## REFERENCES

Abel, E. D., Ahima, R. S., Boers, M. E., Elmquist, J. K., & Wondisford, F. E. (2001). Critical role for thyroid hormone receptor beta2 in the regulation of paraventricular thyrotropin-releasing hormone neurons. *Journal of Clinical Investigation, 107*(8), 1017–1023.

Abel, E. D., Boers, M. E., Pazos-Moura, C., Moura, E., Kaulbach, H., Zakaria, M.,... Wondisford, F. (1999). Divergent roles for thyroid hormone receptor beta isoforms in the endocrine axis and auditory system. *Journal of Clinical Investigation, 104*(3), 291–300.

Altamura, M. R., Long, L., Jr., and Hasselstrom, T. (1959). Goitrin from fresh cabbage. *Journal of Biological Chemistry, 234*(7), 1847–1849.

Andersen, B., & Rosenfeld, M. G. (2001). POU domain factors in the neuroendocrine system: Lessons from developmental biology provide insights into human disease. *Endocrine Reviews, 22*(1), 2–35.

Anderson, D. L. (2009). Determination of bromine in regulated foods with a field-portable X-ray fluorescence analyzer. *Journal of AOAC International, 92*(2), 502–510.

Antonica, F., Kasprzyk, D. F., Opitz, R., Iacovino, M., Liao, X. H., Dumitrescu, A. M.,...Costagliola, S. (2012). Generation of functional thyroid from embryonic stem cells. *Nature, 491*(7422), 66–71.

Bath, S. C., Steer, C. D., Golding, J., Emmett, P., & Rayman, M. P. (2013). Effect of inadequate iodine status in UK pregnant women on cognitive outcomes in their children: Results from the Avon Longitudinal Study of Parents and Children (ALSPAC). *Lancet, 382*(9889), 331–337.

Blount, B. C., Rich, D. Q., Valentin-Blasini, L., Lashley, S., Ananth, C. V., Murphy, E.,...Robson, M. (2009). Perinatal exposure to perchlorate. thiocyanate, and nitrate in New Jersey mothers and newborns. *Environmental Science and Technology, 43*(19), 7543–7549.

Broedel, O., Eravci, M., Fuxius, S., Smolarz, T., Jeitner, A., Grau, H.,...Baumgartner, A. (2003). Effects of hyper- and hypothyroidism on thyroid hormone concentrations in regions of the rat brain. *American Journal of Physiology, Endocrinology and Metabolism, 285*(3), E470–480.

Calvo, R. M., Jauniaux, E., Gulbis, B., Asunción, M., Gervy, C., Contempré, B., & Morreale de Escobar, G. (2002). Fetal tissues are exposed to biologically relevant free thyroxine concentrations during early phases of development. *Journal of Clincial Endocrinology and Metablosim, 87*(4), 1768–1777.

Carreon-Rodriguez, A., Charli, J. L., & Perez-Martinez, L. (2009). T3 differentially regulates TRH expression in developing hypothalamic neurons in vitro. *Brain Research, 1305*, 20–30.

Chu, M., & Seltzer, T. F. (2010). Myxedema coma induced by ingestion of raw bok choy. *New England Journal of Medicine, 362*(20), 1945–1946.

Dai, G., Levy, O., & Carrasco, N. (1996). Cloning and characterization of the thyroid iodide transporter. *Nature, 379*(6564), 458–460.

Decherf, S., & Demeneix, B. A. (2011). The obesogen hypothesis: a shift of focus from the periphery to the hypothalamus. *Journal of Toxicology and Environmental Health Part B: Critical Reviews, 14*(5–7), 423–448.

Decherf, S., Seugnet, I., Fini, J. B., Clerget-Froidevaux, M. S., & Demeneix, B. A. (2010a). Disruption of thyroid hormone-dependent hypothalamic set-points by environmental contaminants. *Molecular and Cellular Endocrinology, 323*(2), 172–182.

Decherf, S., Seugnet, I., Kouidhi, S., Lopez-Juarez, A., Clerget-Froidevaux, M. S.,...Demeneix, B. A. (2010b). Thyroid hormone exerts negative feedback on hypothalamic type 4 melanocortin receptor expression. *Proceedings of the National Academy of Sciences USA, 107*(9), 4471–4476.

De Felice, M., & Di Lauro, R. (2011). Minireview: Intrinsic and extrinsic factors in thyroid gland development: An update. *Endocrinology, 152*(8), 2948–2956.

Dohan, O., De la Vieja, A., Paroder, V., Riedel, C., Artani, M., Reed, M.,...Carrasco, N. (2003). The sodium/iodide Symporter (NIS): Characterization, regulation, and medical significance. *Endocrine Reviews, 24*(1), 48–77.

Dores, R. M., & Baron, A. J. (2011). Evolution of POMC: Origin, phylogeny, posttranslational processing, and the melanocortins. *Annals of the New York Academy of Sciences, 1220*, 34–48.

Dunn, J. T., & Dunn, A. D. (2001). Update on intrathyroidal iodine metabolism. *Thyroid, 11*(5), 407–414.

Elfving, S. (1980). Studies on the naturally occurring goitrogen 5-vinyl-2-thiooxazolidone. Metabolism and antithyroid effect in the rat. *Annals of Clincial Research, Suppl 28*, 1–47.

Farooqi, S., & O'Rahilly, S. (2006). Genetics of obesity in humans. *Endocrine Reviews*, *27*(7), 710–718.

Fekete, C., & Lechan, R. M. (2007). Negative feedback regulation of hypophysiotropic thyrotropin-releasing hormone (TRH) synthesizing neurons: Role of neuronal afferents and type 2 deiodinase. *Frontiers in Neuroendocrinology*, *28*(2–3), 97–114.

Gauthier, K., Chassande, O., Plateroti, M., Roux, J. P., Legrand, C., Pain, B., . . . Samarut J. (1999). Different functions for the thyroid hormone receptors TRalpha and TRbeta in the control of thyroid hormone production and post-natal development. *EMBO Journal*, *18*(3), 623–631.

Gerard, A. C., Poncin, S., Audinot, J. N., Denef, J. F., & Colin, I. M. (2009). Iodide deficiency-induced angiogenic stimulus in the thyroid occurs via HIF- and ROS-dependent VEGF-A secretion from thyrocytes. *American Journal of Physiology, Endocrinology and Metabolism*, *296*(6), E1414–1422.

Graham, C. E., Brocklehurst, K., Pickersgill, R. W., & Warren, M. J. (2006). Characterization of retinaldehyde dehydrogenase 3. *Biochemistry Journal*, *394*(Pt 1), 67–75.

Grün, F. (2010). Obesogens. *Current Opinion in Endocrinology, Diabetes, and Obesity*, *17*(5), 453–459.

Grün, F., & Blumberg, B. (2006). Environmental obesogens: Organotins and endocrine disruption via nuclear receptor signaling. *Endocrinology*, *147*(6 Suppl), S50–55.

Grün, F., & Blumberg, B. (2009). Minireview: The case for obesogens. *Molecular Endocrinology*, *23*(8), 1127–1134.

Guissouma, H., Dupré, S. M., Becker, N., Jeannin, E., Seugnet, I., Desvergne, B., & Demeneix, B. A. (2002). Feedback on hypothalamic TRH transcription is dependent on thyroid hormone receptor N terminus. *Molecular Endocrinology*, *16*(7), 1652–1666.

Guissouma, H., Froidevaux, M. S., Hassani, Z., & Demeneix, B. A. (2006). In vivo siRNA delivery to the mouse hypothalamus confirms distinct roles of TR beta isoforms in regulating TRH transcription. *Neuroscience Letters*, *406*(3), 240–243.

Guissouma, H., Ghorbel, M. T., Seugnet, I., Ouatas, T., & Demeneix, B. A. (1998). Physiological regulation of hypothalamic TRH transcription in vivo is T3 receptor isoform specific. *FASEB Journal*, *12*(15), 1755–1764.

Hadj-Sahraoui, N., Seugnet, I., Ghorbel, M. T., & Demeneix, B. (2000). Hypothyroidism prolongs mitotic activity in the post-natal mouse brain. *Neuroscience Letters*, *280*(2), 79–82.

Hamers, T., Kamstra, J. H., Sonneveld, E., Murk, A. J., Kester, M. H., Andersson, P. L., . . . Brouwer, A. (2006). In vitro profiling of the endocrine-disrupting potency of brominated flame retardants. *Toxicology Science*, *92*(1), 157–173.

Harris, K. B., & Pass, K. A. (2007). Increase in congenital hypothyroidism in New York State and in the United States. *Molecular Genetics and Metabolism*, *91*(3), 268–277.

Hollenberg, A. N. (2008). The role of the thyrotropin-releasing hormone (TRH) neuron as a metabolic sensor. *Thyroid*, *18*(2), 131–139.

Hood, A., Allen, M. L., Liu, Y., Liu, J., & Klaassen, C. D. (2003). Induction of T(4) UDP-GT activity, serum thyroid stimulating hormone, and thyroid follicular cell proliferation in mice treated with microsomal enzyme inducers. *Toxicology and Applied Pharmacology*, *188*(1), 6–13.

Howdeshell, K. L. (2002). A model of the development of the brain as a construct of the thyroid system. *Environmental Health Perspectives*, *110*(Suppl 3), 337–348.

Huszar, D., Lynch, C. A., Fairchild-Huntress, V., Dunmore, J. H., Fang, Q., Berkemeier,
 L. R., . . . Lee, F. (1997). Targeted disruption of the melanocortin-4 receptor results in
 obesity in mice. *Cell, 88*(1), 131–141.

Janesick, A., & Blumberg, B. (2011). Minireview: PPARgamma as the target of
 obesogens. *Journal of Steroid Biochemistry and Molecular Biology, 127*(1–2), 4–8.

Kaufman, S. C., Gross, T. P., & Kennedy, D. L. (1991). Thyroid hormone use: Trends in
 the United States from 1960 through 1988. *Thyroid, 1*(4), 285–291.

Köhrle, J. (2008). Environment and endocrinology: the case of thyroidology. *Annals of
 Endocrinology (Paris), 69*(2), 116–122.

Köhrle, J., Jakob, F., Contempré, B., & Dumont, J. E. (2005). Selenium, the thyroid, and
 the endocrine system. *Endocrine Reviews, 26*(7), 944–984.

Kouidhi, S., Seugnet, I., Decherf, S., Guissouma, H., Elgaaied, A. B., Demeneix,
 B., & Clerget-Froidevaux, M. S. (2010). Peroxisome proliferator-activated
 receptor-gamma (PPARgamma) modulates hypothalamic Trh regulation in vivo.
 *Molecular and Cellular Endocrinology, 317*(1–2), 44–52.

Lans, M. C., Klasson-Wehler, E., Willemsen, M., Meussen, E., Safe, S., &
 Brouwer, A. (1993). Structure-dependent, competitive interaction of
 hydroxy-polychlorobiphenyls, -dibenzo-p-dioxins and -dibenzofurans with human
 transthyretin. *Chemico-Biological Interactions, 88*(1), 7–21.

le Maire, A., Grimaldi, M., Roecklin, D., Dagnino, S., Vivat-Hannah, V., Balaguer,
 P., & Bourguet, W. (2009). Activation of RXR-PPAR heterodimers by organotin
 environmental endocrine disruptors. *EMBO Reports, 10*(4), 367–373.

Lezoualc'h, F., Hassan, A. H., Giraud, P., Loeffler, J. P., Lee, S. L., & Demeneix,
 B. A. (1992). Assignment of the beta-thyroid hormone receptor to 3,5,3'-triio
 dothyronine-dependent inhibition of transcription from the thyrotropin-releasing
 hormone promoter in chick hypothalamic neurons. *Molecular Endocrinology,
 6*(11), 1797–1804.

Logothetopoulos, J., & Scott, R. F. (1956). Active iodide transport across the placenta of
 the guinea-pig, rabbit and rat. *Journal of Physiology, 132*(2), 365–371.

Mathew, V., Misgar, R. A., Ghosh, S., Mukhopadhyay, P., Roychowdhury, P., Pandit,
 K., . . . Chowdhury, S. (2011). Myxedema coma: A new look into an old crisis.
 *Journal of Thyroid Research, 2011*, 493462.

Meerts, I. A., Assink, Y., Cenijn, P. H., Van Den Berg, J. H., Weijers, B. M., Bergman,
 A., & Brouwer, A. (2002). Placental transfer of a hydroxylated polychlorinated
 biphenyl and effects on fetal and maternal thyroid hormone homeostasis in the rat.
 *Toxicology Science, 68*(2), 361–371.

Mendel, C. M. (1989). The free hormone hypothesis: A physiologically based
 mathematical model. *Endocrine Reviews, 10*(3), 232–274.

Mendel, C. M., Weisiger, R. A., Jones, A. L., & Cavalieri, R. R. (1987). Thyroid
 hormone-binding proteins in plasma facilitate uniform distribution of thyroxine
 within tissues: A perfused rat liver study. *Endocrinology, 120*(5), 1742–1749.

Mishra, A., Zhu, X. G., Ge, K., & Cheng, S. Y. (2010). Adipogenesis is differentially
 impaired by thyroid hormone receptor mutant isoforms. *Journal of Molecular
 Endocrinology, 44*(4), 247–255.

Monaco, H. L. (2000). The transthyretin-retinol-binding protein complex. *Biochimica
 et Biophysica Acta, 1482*(1–2), 65–72.

Morgan, M. A., Dellovade, T. L., & Pfaff, D. W. (2000). Effect of thyroid hormone
 administration on estrogen-induced sex behavior in female mice. *Hormones and
 Behavior, 37*(1), 15–22.

Morse, D. C., Wehler, E. K., Wesseling, W., Koeman, J. H., & Brouwer, A. (1996). Alterations in rat brain thyroid hormone status following pre- and postnatal exposure to polychlorinated biphenyls (Aroclor 1254). *Toxicology and Applied Pharmacology, 136*(2), 269–279.

Mortimer, R. H., Landers, K. A., Balakrishnan, B., Li, H., Mitchell, M. D., Patel, J., & Richard, K. (2012). Secretion and transfer of the thyroid hormone binding protein transthyretin by human placenta. *Placenta, 33*(4), 252–256.

Nayak, B., & Burman, K. (2006). *Thyrotoxicosis and thyroid storm. Endocrinology and Metabolism Clinics of North America, 35*(4), 663–686, vii.

Newbold, R. R., Padilla-Banks, E., Snyder, R. J., & Jefferson, W. N. (2007). Perinatal exposure to environmental estrogens and the development of obesity. *Molecular Nutrition and Food Research, 51*(7), 912–917.

Osty, J., Rappaport, L., Samuel, J. L., & Lennon, A. M. (1988). Characterization of a cytosolic triiodothyronine binding protein in atrium and ventricle of rat heart with different sensitivity toward thyroid hormone levels. *Endocrinology, 122*(3), 1027–1033.

Pavelka, S. (2004). Metabolism of bromide and its interference with the metabolism of iodine. *Physiology Research, 53*(Suppl 1), S81–S90.

Pfaff, D. W., Vasudevan, N., Kia, H. K., Zhu, Y. S., Chan, J., Garey, J.,...Ogawa, S. (2000). Estrogens, brain and behavior: Studies in fundamental neurobiology and observations related to women's health. *Journal of Steroid Biochemistry and Molecular Biology, 74*(5), 365–373.

Piehl, S., Hoefig, C. S., Scanlan, T. S., & Köhrle, J. (2011). Thyronamines--past, present, and future. *Endocrine Reviews, 32*(1), 64–80.

Poncin, S., Gérard, A. C., Boucquey, M., Senou, M., Calderon, P. B., Knoops, B.,...Colin, I. M. (2008). Oxidative stress in the thyroid gland: From harmlessness to hazard depending on the iodine content. *Endocrinology, 149*(1), 424–433.

Richardson, S. J. (2007). Cell and molecular biology of transthyretin and thyroid hormones. *International Review of Cytology, 258*, 137–193.

Richardson, S. J. (2009). Evolutionary changes to transthyretin: Evolution of transthyretin biosynthesis. *FEBS Journal, 276*(19), 5342–5356.

Schreiber, G. (2002). The evolutionary and integrative roles of transthyretin in thyroid hormone homeostasis. *Journal of Endocrinology, 175*(1), 61–73.

Schreiber, G., Southwell, B. R., & Richardson, S. J. (1995). Hormone delivery systems to the brain-transthyretin. *Experimental and Clinical Endocrinology and Diabetes, 103*(2), 75–80.

Shepard, T. H. (1967). Onset of function in the human fetal thyroid: Biochemical and radioautographic studies from organ culture. *Journal of Clincial Endocrinology and Metablosim, 27*(7), 945–958.

Shepard, T. H. (1968). Development of the human fetal thyroid. *General and Comparative Endocrinology, 10*(2), 174–181.

Smith, T. J., Davis, F. B., Deziel, M. R., Davis, P. J., Ramsden, D. B., & Schoenl, M. (1994). Retinoic acid inhibition of thyroxine binding to human transthyretin. *Biochimica et Biophysica Acta, 1199*(1), 76–80.

Song, Y., Driessens, N., Costa, M., De Deken, X., Detours, V., Corvilain, B.,...Dumont, J. E. (2007). Roles of hydrogen peroxide in thyroid physiology and disease. *Journal of Clincial Endocrinology and Metablosim, 92*(10), 3764–3773.

Stagnaro-Green, A., & Pearce, E. N. (2013). Iodine and pregnancy: A call to action. *Lancet, 382*(9889), 292–293.

Taylor, T., Gyves, P., & Burgunder, J. M. (1990). Thyroid hormone regulation of TRH mRNA levels in rat paraventricular nucleus of the hypothalamus changes during ontogeny. *Neuroendocrinology*, *52*(3), 262–267.

van der Heide, D., Kastelijn, J., & Schroder-van der Elst, J. P. (2003). Flavonoids and thyroid disease. *Biofactors*, *19*(3–4), 113–119.

Vasudevan, N., Ogawa, S., & Pfaff, D. (2002). Estrogen and thyroid hormone receptor interactions: Physiological flexibility by molecular specificity. *Physiological Reviews*, *82*(4), 923–944.

Vilijn, F., & Carrasco, N. (1989). Expression of the thyroid sodium/iodide symporter in Xenopus laevis oocytes. *Journal of Biological Chemistry*, *264*(20), 11901–11903.

Visser, T. J., Kaptein, E., Gijzel, A. L., de Herder, W. W., Ebner, T., & Burchell, B. (1993). Glucuronidation of thyroid hormone by human bilirubin and phenol UDP-glucuronyltransferase isoenzymes. *FEBS Letters*, *324*(3), 358–360.

Vulsma, T., Gons, M. H., & de Vijlder, J. J. (1989). Maternal-fetal transfer of thyroxine in congenital hypothyroidism due to a total organification defect or thyroid agenesis. *New England Journal of Medicine*, *321*(1), 13–16.

Wardlaw, S. L. (2011). Hypothalamic proopiomelanocortin processing and the regulation of energy balance. *European Journal of Pharmacology*, *660*(1), 213–219.

Webster, B., Marine, D., & Cipra, A. (1931). The occurrence of seasonal variations in the goiter of rabbits produced by feeding cabbage. *Journal of Experimental Medicine*, *53*(1), 81–91.

Yamauchi, K., Nakajima, J., Hayashi, H., Horiuchi, R., & Tata, J. R. (1999). Xenopus cytosolic thyroid hormone-binding protein (xCTBP) is aldehyde dehydrogenase catalyzing the formation of retinoic acid. *Journal of Biological Chemistry*, *274*(13), 8460–8469.

Yoshida, D. (1996). Thyroid storm precipitated by trauma. *Journal of Emergency Medicine*, *14*(6), 697–701.

# Chapter 5

# Examples of Chemical Pollution Targeting Thyroid Hormone Action

## CHAPTER OUTLINE

Schematically, the structure of the thyroid hormones (THs), $T_4$ and $T_3$, can be likened to a pair of spectacles (Fig. 3.1). This similarity is due to the fact that iodothyronines are composed of a pair of phenyl rings. Different forms of TH have combinations of one or two iodine atoms on each ring. Chemists have always found the phenyl ring an extremely versatile base for synthesis, notably with other halogens besides iodine: chlorine, bromine, and fluorine. The result is that the environment is now heavily polluted by myriads of chemicals that structurally resemble TH. Examples include brominated flame retardants, polychlorinated biphenols, and fluorinated surfactants. Such chemicals can interfere with TH homeostasis by displacing TH from its physiological partners, thereby blocking, dampening, or even amplifying its action on target genes. Both inhibition and activation are concerns, as TH availability during development is timed to act within strict intervals and concentrations. Chemical competition with TH can occur at the level of distributor and transporter proteins, as well as with enzymes that metabolize the hormones. Few chemicals actually act directly at the level of the TH receptors, mainly because of the high selectivity of the ligand-binding pocket of the thyroid receptors (TRs). However, given the complex nature of TH synthesis, and the numerous mechanisms implicated in iodine uptake and organification, many chemicals with absolutely no homology with TH structure can interfere with TH production at the level of the thyroid gland. Further, given the number of processes in brain development influenced by TH, TH deficiency can exacerbate the effects of chemicals affecting other pathways and mechanisms. Both the synthesis of TH and the precise structure of $T_4$ and $T_3$ are conserved across vertebrates. Thus, the implications of interference with TH signaling go beyond human health and have long-ranging implications for biodiversity and ecology.

## BACKGROUND

First, a word of warning and an apology: The following presentation is not exhaustive and cannot cover all the different chemical classes that have already been described to have TH-disrupting properties, nor all of those that are suspected of such actions. The emphasis is placed on categories of chemicals for which there is either the most evidence or disquiet due to high production volumes and/or marked effects.

Conceptually, a discussion on the effects of chemicals on TH signaling could be structured in two ways. The first would be taking the different physiological levels implicated in TH synthesis, its control, action, and TH metabolism, as described in the previous chapter, and examining the evidence for the different chemicals that have been incriminated in disrupting these processes. The second is to consider environmentally relevant chemicals and describe current knowledge of their effects on TH homeostasis and, where known, their mode of action and impact. However, not only do certain chemicals affect TH signaling at more than one level, there are also chemicals that modify TSH, TH levels, or thyroid histology and for which there is, as yet, no insight into the mechanisms underlying their effects. Thus, given the gaps in knowledge on modes of action, it is this second approach, categories of relevant chemicals, that is chosen here.

Before entering this molecular stew, it should be emphasized that beyond the individual chemicals described here that modulate TH signaling at different levels, a second level of concern about the potential effects of compounds that do not in themselves affect TH signaling should be mentioned. This is the additive or synergistic effects of lower TH availability (due, for instance, to iodine deficiency) and the action of a chemical that might not itself modulate TH levels. The argument is that the combination of nutritional deficiency (iodine) and chemical exposure (whether affecting TH signaling directly or not) will have greater impact on brain development than either factor alone. An example might be the effects of certain pesticides, which are apparently without direct effect on TH production or signaling but whose effects, say, on synaptogenesis or synaptic function, would be aggravated in a hypothyroid environment or in a context where other chemicals were modulating TH action. And, as established for many situations, the earlier the effects, the more severe the outcome (Barouki, Gluckman, Grandjean, Hanson, & Heindel, 2012).

The list of chemicals affecting one or more levels of TH signaling is long, with several hundreds of suspects under investigation. A number of reviews have underscored the extent of the problem (Brucker-Davis, 1998; Howdeshell, 2002; Zoeller, 2007) and the potential for TH disruption to interfere with brain development (Colborn, 2004; Porterfield, 1994). Most substances can be grouped into categories of use (e.g., flame retardants or UV filters) or chemical families (e.g., perfluorinated compounds). Many of these chemicals are halogen-substituted biphenol rings. Halogens are a group of nonmetal elements that include iodine, bromine, fluorine, and chlorine. Chemists have regularly exploited the high reactivity of halogens, and many TH disruptors are organic molecules bearing different numbers of halogen atoms. Examples include the brominated flame retardants and polychlorinated biphenyls (PCBs). It is with this latter group, one of the most studied and one of the most environmentally ubiquitous, the PCBs, with which we start. For each category we deal first with a description of its structure and use, next with its environmental accumulation, and lastly, with its effects on TH signaling.

## Dioxin-like Chemicals: Dioxins and Polychlorinated Biphenyls

Polychlorinated biphenyls are a large group of industrially derived, highly persistent chemicals. Like THs, they are composed of a pair of phenyl rings, but instead of bearing iodine atoms on each ring, they have different numbers of atoms of another halogen, chlorine (Fig. 5.1). PCBs have strong structural similarity to the dioxins (see next subsection) that today are mainly produced during waste treatment (particularly incineration). These two large categories of chemicals, covering more than 400 biphenyl-based molecules, are often grouped together and studied in combination under the umbrella term *dioxin-like chemicals* (DLCs). For discussion, here we distinguish the PCBs that were chemicals designed and produced by the chemical industry from dioxins that are largely waste products. Many of these substances (notably the dioxins) bind directly to a transcription factor, the aryl hydrocarbon receptor (AhR; Barouki, Aggerbeck, Aggerbeck, & Coumoul, 2012). AhR is a member of the Helix-Loop-Helix-PAS (HLH-PAS) family of transcription factors, the mechanism of action of which resembles that of nuclear receptors, although there is no structural homology between the two families, and at times the term *nuclear receptor* is misleadingly used to refer to the AhR.

PCBs were first produced in the 1930s, with the rapid increase in manufacture and diversification of electrical equipment. Their high chemical stability and strong resistance to heat rapidly led to their wide usage in a range of components, including dielectric fluids (cooling fluids or lubricants) in capacitors and transformers, but also as ink solvents, plasticizers, and flame retardants. It is precisely their resistance to heat and high chemical stability that make them such persistent pollutants in the environment. Levels in the atmosphere are only now decreasing, and slowly, despite the bans on manufacturing more than 30–40 years ago. This persistence recalls the problems encountered with the accumulation of the pesticide DDT and its main metabolite, DDE. Moreover, given the amounts of PCBs still present in different forms (manufactured materials and stocks), reductions beyond a certain level are going to be difficult to attain (Diamond, Melymuk, Csiszar, & Robson, 2010). Half-lives in humans vary as a function of the PCB studied, age, and physiological status (breast-feeding or amounts of adipose tissue, PCBs being lipophilic), along with other factors such as smoking. According to the PCB analyzed, apparent

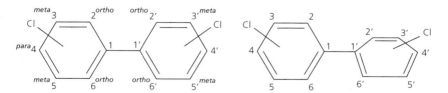

**Figure 5–1.** General structure of a coplanar (left) and a nonplanar polychlorinated biphenyl (PCB) (right).

half-lives of PCBs in the human body range from a matter of months to over 15 years (Milbrath et al., 2009).

PCBs exist in a variety of chemical forms or configurations (congeners). Two main categories can be distinguished, coplanar or nonplanar, according to the orientation of the phenyl rings with respect to each other. The total number of PCB congeners listed is 209 (McFarland & Clarke, 1989). Usually PCBs were commercialized as complex mixtures of coplanar and nonplanar congeners: Aroclors, with different trades names and numbers according to the mix (e.g., Aroclor 1254, etc.). New production of PCBs was banned in Europe and in North America in the 1970s. However, production continued elsewhere until 1993. They have been targeted for elimination by the UN-sponsored Stockholm Convention on protecting human health and the environment from persistent organic pollutants (POPs),[1] as a chemical class of particularly environmentally persistent chemicals. According to this organization, about 1.7 million tons of PCBs were manufactured between 1929 and 1989, with much of this still being in the environment, either in the forms of stocks requiring disposal or as electrical equipment that is still in use. A breakdown of production over the years is provided by Breivik et al. (2007). Their estimate of total PCB production is in the same order of magnitude as that calculated by the UN Stockholm Convention, with a global production from 1930 to 1993 of 1.3 million tons, of which nearly half (48%) was produced by Monsanto in the United States.

The Stockholm Convention has set a target of achieving environmentally sound management and disposal of PCBs by 2028. It was signed by 159 parties, but, as of 2010, only 35 had reported progress toward this goal (Diamond et al., 2010). Canada is one of those that has reported progress and has national legislation and a timetable for reductions in inventories. However, despite the ban, PCBs are not only still present in both the terrestrial and aquatic food chains, but also their levels are currently stable despite quite rapid declines in the first decade following legislation on production. It is impossible to review all the data on PCB levels and contamination in different geographical areas. It is well known that despite the widespread bans in the late 20th century, not only are stocks still massive but contamination through air, water, and food affects the whole of the globe.

One of the most emblematic examples is contamination of polar bears in the Arctic. Besides being the victims of climate change and glacial melt, polar bears are at the top of a predator food chain and thus accumulate contaminants, particularly POPs. In 2002, polar bears were found to have four times higher concentrations of PCB congeners in fat tissue (3.3 mg/g fat) than ringed seals (0.7 mg/g) on which they feed (Kucklick et al., 2002). To many in the general public the high levels of POPs in Arctic wildlife come as a surprise, notably, given their habitat at such distance from industrial sites, but the figures

---

1  Information on the Stockholm Convention on PCBs can be found at http://chm. pops.int/Implementation/PCBs/Overview/tabid/273

underline the extremely high general level of pollution of water and air by PCBs. PCBs can not only distribute through the food chain and water but also through the atmosphere, thus providing a means of transport on a global scale to the most remote areas (von Waldow, Macleod, Scheringer, & Hungerbühler, 2010). In fact, the capacity for long-range transport is one of the four screening criteria used by the Stockholm Convention when considering whether a substance should be added to this list of substances requiring international regulation. PCBs clearly fulfil this criterion.

Two urban examples of atmospheric distribution are detailed in papers on PCB stocks and atmospheric distribution of PCBs in Toronto (Diamond et al., 2010) and Chicago and Cleveland (Persoon, Peters, Kumar, & Hornbuckle, 2010). Diamond and colleagues provide historical data on PCB legislation, production, imports, and use in Canada. The estimated stocks of PCBs in the city of Toronto with about 2.5 million inhabitants are between 300 and 800 tons, excluding amounts in landfill or waste handling plants. The authors questioned whether current policies could reduce present daily emissions and air levels of five PCB congeners that they estimate to be, for just one set of PCB congeners, between 35 and 350 mg/person per year. Highest exposures were calculated to occur in commercially dense areas, such as those with skyscrapers that have high electricity usage. They note, not without a certain amount of irony, that the highest concentrations are in the business area of the city, which theoretically had the greatest financial capacity to take care of its removal. In the cases of Chicago and Cleveland (Persoon et al., 2010), the sum of 151 airborne PCB congeners or groups of congeners (Aroclor 1242 and 1254) were quantified using passive sampling. Values were compared for the same month (August 2008) and were found to be in the same range for each city, though significantly higher levels were found in Cleveland (1.73 ± 1.16 ng·m$^{-3}$) than in Chicago (1.13 ± 0.58 ng·m$^{-3}$). As for the Toronto study, "hot spots" of contamination were found, which the authors interpret as a reflection of highly localized emission sources. They also underline these atmospheric sources as contributing to the contamination of fish in the Great Lakes (Hanrahan et al., 1999; Humphrey et al., 2000).

There are many epidemiological,[2] environmental, and experimental studies that link PCB burdens to negative effects on thyroid function and action. Starting with the epidemiological evidence in humans, a number of reports show that PCB levels are associated with modified thyroid function (Langer et al., 2005; 2007), reduced circulating TH levels, and/or increased TSH concentrations (Hagmar, 2003; Langer et al., 2003). However, even though a number of reports show such correlations, others fail to show associations, and overall it is difficult to draw conclusions across different studies (Hagmar,

---

2  Here we discuss epidemiological data on individual chemicals and TH function. The epidemiological data on exposure to chemical mixtures and their associations with delay in neurological development will be discussed in Chapters 6 and 7.

2003). A number of reasons, mostly experimental approaches, PCBs measured, and cohort size and selection, contribute to this heterogeneity and will be discussed later. As the focus here is on environmental pollution and children's neurodevelopmental potential and behavior, focus is placed on epidemiological studies that include pregnant women, newborns, and children. However, it should be noted that in adults, epidemiological studies have shown negative correlations between PCB levels and $T_4$ levels with particularly strong correlations in women (Turyk, Anderson, & Persky, 2007). This result is the more disquieting as women are more prone than men to develop autoimmune thyroid disease, with the overall lifetime risk of developing a thyroid disorder at 1 in 8 for women.

Tasker and colleagues examined correlations of a number of environmental contaminants, including 14 different PCBs, with three measures of thyroid status, TSH, total $T_3$ ($TT_3$) and free $T_4$ ($FT_4$) in pregnant women and their babies' cord blood (Takser et al., 2005). The authors found negative correlations between certain PCBs in the mother and her $TT_3$. No correlations were found between *total* PCB levels and different TH parameters, underlining the fact that certain PCBs have greater TH-disrupting effects than others and that the large number of PCBs with different types of actions can mask individual effects of contaminants on TH levels and action. In this study no significant associations were found between cord blood PCB and TH levels. However, not only have many other studies found negative associations between placental PCB concentrations and cord blood $FT_4$ (Wang et al., 2005), or cord blood PCB and TH or TSH values (Chevrier, Eskenazi, Bradman, Fenster, & Barr, 2007; Chevrier, Eskenazi, Holland, Bradman, & Barr, 2008; Herbstman et al., 2008), others have found positive associations between PCBs and $FT_4$ (Otake et al., 2007), and certain authors, like Tasker and colleagues, only found associations with defined PCBs. Besides the problem of differential effects of the large number of PCB molecules and potential presence of other contaminants affecting TH levels, another confounding factor could be delivery method (Herbstman et al., 2008). Investigating associations between $TT_4$ measured in neonatal blood spots or cord blood and levels of PCBs or that of a flame retardant, polybrominated diphenyl ether (PBDE), Herbstman and colleagues found that PCBs were significantly associated with lower $TT_4$ and $FT_4$ in cord blood in infants born by spontaneous vaginal delivery. However, for babies born by nonelective caesarean section, no significant associations were revealed. The authors chose to compare results from infants born either by nonelective caesarean or natural birth as nonelective caesarean section can represent intrapartum stress that is known to alter levels of TH in cord blood. These factors, intrapartum stress and delivery methods, which are rarely taken into account in other studies, underline how such factors can mask effects in associative studies. Also, the spectrum of PCB congeners and different matrices (placental tissue or cord blood, maternal serum, plasma, or milk) could well contribute to the variability of the associations found in different studies. However, as in animal studies (see later), much epidemiological evidence shows maternal and fetal PCB load to reduce circulating THs.

Most animal studies on the effects of PCBs on thyroid status have used rodent models, mainly rats and to some extent mice. Such studies allow one to determine effects on TH status without the confounding conditions in human epidemiology. One of the earliest studies on PCB effects on thyroid homeostasis was that of Collins et al. in 1977. These authors examined the effects of a commercial mixture of PCBs Aroclor 1254 from Monsanto. They mixed it with the chow fed to adult rats at 50 and 500 parts/million (ppm) (controls were given chow and corn oil) for 12 weeks followed by up to 35 weeks on control diet. After 6 weeks the 500 ppm dosage had to be dropped to 250 ppm because of toxic effects and weight loss. Serum levels of $T_4$ and thyroid gland histology were studied during PCB treatment and during posttreatment. $T_4$ levels were reduced in all PCB-treated groups up to 12 weeks posttreatment, only returning to normal at 35 weeks recovery posttreatment. In both dose groups significant effects were seen at 4 weeks, values being decreased by about 30% and 70% in the lower and higher doses, respectively. After 12 weeks, the reduction was more severe, with reductions to about 25% of control values in both PCB-treated groups. Thyroid glands of PCB rats also displayed structural changes indicative of increased activity. At the higher dosage more severe ultrastructural lesions were observed at the end of treatment and some abnormalities remained even at 35 weeks posttreatment. Putting their results in the perspective of other results that had shown effects of PCB on hepatic metabolism, the authors concluded that PCB exposure induced a dose- and time-dependent decrease in circulating $T_4$ that resulted from a two-fold action, first, an enhanced peripheral metabolism and, second, degradation of TH that induced increase secretory activity by the thyroid, though this failed to compensate the lower circulating TH levels.

Since these pioneering studies, more work has been done on exposure during earlier stages of development, particularly intrauterine and the postnatal periods, as well as analyzing which PCBs present in the different mixtures were exerting the most detrimental effects on TH homeostasis and how they were affecting TH status. The leading groups in this field are those of Abraham Brower in the Netherlands and Tom Zoeller at the University of Massachusetts. In 1996, Brower's team showed that different doses (5 or 25 mg/kg) of PCBs in the form of Aroclor 1254 given to rats for 1 week in the middle of gestation reduced both fetal plasma and brain levels of $T_4$ at gestational day 20 (Morse, Wehler, Wesseling, Koeman, & Brouwer, 1996). In the cerebellum of pups from mothers given the highest dose, $T_4$ levels were reduced below the level of detection, and in those from dams with the lower dose they were half those of controls.

Zoeller's team also used Aroclor 1254 as a starting point and then selected congeners from this mixture. They have shown that PCB exposure affects gene expression in fetal brains directly, and this could be due to maternal hypothyroidism (Gauger et al., 2004). However, more recently they have also shown that certain PCBs can undergo metabolism in the liver to produce TRβ receptor agonists (Gauger et al., 2007). In this latter study, it was confirmed that PCB exposure strongly reduces circulating $TT_4$ in gestating rats, effects that were accompanied by increased activity of some liver enzymes, including CYP1A1. Using a pharmacological approach, they showed that certain PCBs act, not directly through a TR, but through the classical dioxin receptor, the AhR (see earlier). AhR then activated CYP1A1, producing metabolites that could activate a $T_3$/TRE- containing gene construct in a pituitary-derived cell line. Evidence for a more direct effect of certain PCBs on TR-dependent transcription came from a Japanese group (Miyazaki, Iwasaki, Takeshita, Tohyama, & Koibuchi, 2008). By studying TRβ1 effects on transcription from a TRE-containing construct in different cell culture systems, they established that certain nondioxin-like PCBs, and particularly one hydroxylated PCB, could interfere with TRβ1 interaction with a TRE, and that this interference required the presence of the DNA-binding domain of the TR.

This work of Zoeller's team, in particular, provided some of the first insights into the TH-disrupting mechanism of action of PCBs, other than through induction of hepatic enzymes that increase glucuronidation of iodothyronines, the UDP-glucuronosyltransferases. Many publications have reported PCB-induced increased activity of these enzymes that, with the deiodinases and the hepatic enzymes that sulfate THs, represent the major metabolic pathways for elimination of $T_4$ and $T_3$. However, a number of demonstrations (Kato et al., 2004), including using rats lacking a key UDP-glucuronosyltransferase (Richardson & Klaassen, 2010), indicate that this is not the only mechanism contributing to the decreases in circulating TH and the more general thyroid-disrupting effects of PCBs.

Dioxins

Dioxins, like PCBs, have a similar structure to THs (Fig. 5.2), and like PCBs, they constitute a large category of about 200 compounds. Collectively, the group covers two main types of molecules: the polychlorinated-$p$-dioxins (PCDDs) and their cousins, the polychlorinated dibenzofurans (PCDFs). The most studied and toxic is 2,3,7,8-tetrachlorodibenzo-$p$-dioxin (2378-TCDD, or commonly TCDD), which has one of the lowest recorded lethal doses ($LD_{50}$ or lethal dose to 50% of the population), being a mere 0.6 μg/kg body weight in guinea pigs (Hites, 2011). TCDD became infamous during the Vietnam War (mid-1950s to 1975) because of its presence, as a contaminant, in Agent Orange, a defoliating agent used by the US Army (Hites, 2011). As a consequence, the number of cancers (Beaulieu & Fessele, 2003) and thyroid disease (Spaulding, 2011) among US veterans is reportedly higher than in control populations. However, certain authorities still dispute the data (Young, Giesy, Jones, & Newton, 2004). The Institute of Medicine of the US National Academies provides regular updates and consensus reports on the health effects of Agent Orange exposure (http://www.iom.edu/Reports/), and Hites (2011) states that veterans can now claim up to 50% disability for certain health problems for which there is sufficient evidence of association. Similarly, the effects on the Vietnamese people are debated. Some Vietnamese groups unsuccessfully sued the US producers of Agent Orange, but the decision, delivered in 2005, was under appeal in 2012.

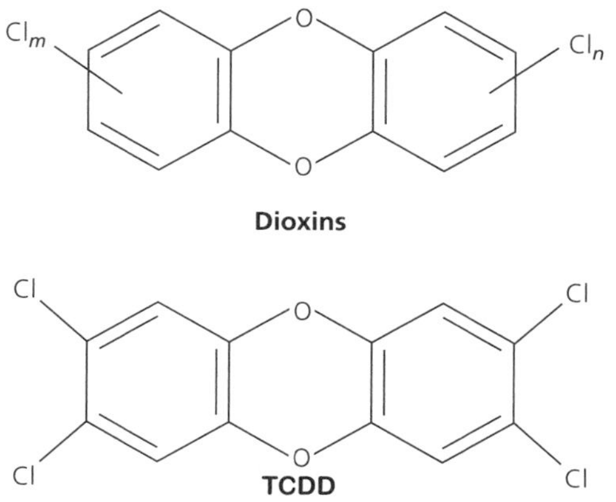

Figure 5–2. General structure of dioxins and of 2,3,7,8-tetrachlorodibenzo-*p*-dioxin (2378 TCDD)TCDD is the most toxic dioxin known.

Besides the Agent Orange scandals, there are a number of reasons for dioxin's notoriety with the general public in recent years. First, the Seveso[3] accident in Italy in 1976 and, second, the disfiguring poisoning in 2005 of the Ukrainian president Viktor Yushenko (Sterling & Hanke, 2005) (unfortunately, it has been noted with some irony, that he came to power after the "Orange Revolution"). Prior to these events, a series of accidents involving dioxin-contaminated animal feed or recycled industrial oil occurred in the United States, leading first, to the death of millions of chickens in the late 1950s and, then, to the deaths of a number of horses in 1971 and the evacuation of a whole town in Missouri between 1972 and 1976 (Hites, 2011; Powell, 1984).

Production of dioxins has two major sources: industrial production of chlorinated phenols and combustion. In the 1980s, following the Seveso incident (Bertazzi, Bernucci, Brambilla, Consonni, & Pesatori, 1998) and a number of TCDD-related accidents in the States, public opinion has regularly questioned authorities for information on dioxin levels. The overall result is that industrial production of chlorinated phenols has dropped, as have concentrations of TCDD in human tissue and serum (Fig. 5.3). As stated by Hites (2011), even though dioxins have not been the subject of extensive regulation, public concern about their action and toxicity has been a factor in driving regulation of many other environmentally relevant chemicals.

Many studies have examined associations between early dioxin exposure and TH levels, although here again conflicts of interest can color

3  The Seveso (Italy) cohort was exposed to high levels of TCDD following an industrial accident in 1976. The factory concerned was manufacturing pesticides and herbicides. A TCDD-containing vapor cloud was released from a reactor producing trichlorofenol.

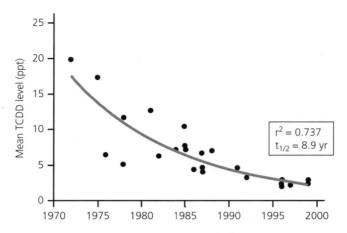

**Figure 5–3.** Concentrations of 2,3,7,8-tetrachlorodibenzo-*p*-dioxin (TCDD) in human samples have decreased nearly 10-fold over the 30 years. (Adapted from Hites, 2011.) TCDD concentrations in human tissue and plasma samples are plotted as a function of sampling time.

interpretation of data. Often concentrations of total dioxins (usually grouped as PCDD/PCDFs) are combined with PCB levels and chemical load calculated as toxic equivalents (Teqs[4]), making it difficult to separate out effects of different compounds. One of the most detailed recent studies in terms of spectrum of chemicals investigated is the Taiwanese study of Wang et al. (2005), already discussed for the data on PCBs. These authors measured PCDD/PCDFs and certain PCBs in placental tissue and TSH, $FT_4$, and $FT_3$ in cord serum from 118 mothers and their newborns. They analyzed the data for associations of TH parameters with either total chemical load or with PCDD/PCDFs versus PCBs. Besides the negative correlations of PCB levels with $FT_4$ already mentioned, their multivariate analyses showed that TSH levels were decreased as a function of PCDD/PCDF levels, with decreases being most significant in females. Also, they showed significant positive correlations between PCDD/PCDF levels and TBG levels (reflecting greater $TT_4$ binding capacity). These differential effects of PCBs and dioxins could be confounding factors in other studies that do not examine separate effects of the different categories of chemicals. In a follow-up study, the same group examined growth and thyroid status of 92 mother and child pairs when the children were 2 and 5 years old (Su, Chen, Chen, & Wang, 2010). A number of differences in TH-related levels were reported in both girls and boys

---

4  Toxic Equivalents (Teq) is calculated for each individual compound as the concentration in the sample scaled to the corresponding TCDD Toxicity Equivalent Factor for that compound. Then, all the Teq for all the compounds in the mixture are summed.

at 2 and 5 years, leading the authors to conclude that in utero exposure to PCDD/PCDFs affects growth and TH levels in preschool children.

This Taiwanese study is complementary to one carried out in the Netherlands in the mid-1990s by Koopman-Esseboom et al. (1994). These authors analyzed the levels of 4 nonplanar PCBs in maternal plasma at the end of gestation and 17 PCDD/PCDFs, 3 planar, and 23 nonplanar PCBs in human milk. These values were tested for associations for $T_4$, $T_3$, and TSH levels in mothers and infants at 2 weeks and 3 months of age. They reported higher levels of TSH in children with the highest levels of contaminants. Children with the highest chemical loads also showed lower plasma levels of $FT_4$ and $TT_4$. Similar negative correlations between circulating TH levels and TCDD toxic equivalents were found in a cohort of Japanese newborns (Nagayama et al., 1998).

Despite these reports from three different countries, a recent review of the literature by a privately owned consulting company managed to conclude their abstract by stating that "the absence of clear correlation between background exposures to dioxins and DLCs and thyroid function biomarkers during development is not consistent with the hypothesis that background exposures to these chemicals cause effect on thyroid function during development" (Goodman, Kerper, Boyce, Prueitt, & Rhomberg, 2010, p. 79) This emphasis on background exposures does not even allow mention, in the abstract, of the strong evidence from the accidental exposures such as at Seveso (Baccarelli et al., 2008) showing persistence of TCDD levels 20 years after the accident and significant correlations with increased neonatal TSH levels. In February 2012, the US Environmental Protection Agency (EPA) updated (available at http://www.epa.gov/dioxin/) their assessment of dioxin-related risks and used the TCDD exposure and TSH data of Baccarelli et al. (2008) to recalculate lowest observed adverse effect levels (LOAELs) for TCDD, underlining the validity of data sets that use only one TH parameter to analyze associations. Using the Seveso data, the EPA calculated an oral reference dose (http://www.epa.gov/iris. EPA's Reanalysis of Key Issues) for non-cancer link exposure (principally reproductive and thyroid risk) to aid in risk assessment. This figure, $7 \times 10^{-10}$ mg/kg per day, represents the upper limit for chronic exposure. People having continual exposures above this level are considered to be at risk.

To look more closely at the approach used by Goodman et al. (2010), a number of the reports they included in their survey showed statistically inverse relationships between TCDD levels and either increased TSH or lower $T_4$ but, probably due to individual variation, rarely both. The authors consider that because only one marker reaches significance (i.e., does not correlate with changes in another marker of thyroid function) that the study results are inconsistent or lack coherence. However, there are many epidemiological studies that show effects on one component of thyroid function that is not reflected in changes in others. This can be due to greater variation in one parameter or to changed set points. Moreover, as mentioned earlier in the discussion on PCBs, confounding factors in the cohorts comparing dioxin effects on TH status include different biological matrices and different combinations of DLCs and PCBs.

Moreover, other studies that have examined children's neurodevelopmental behavior have also revealed significant associations between dioxin and/or DLC levels. For instance, the Netherlands group (Huisman et al., 1995a, 1995b) compared breast-fed infants with formula-fed infants and noted that breast milk with the higher levels of PCBs and PCDD/PCDFs was associated with reduced neonatal neurological performance and even, at the higher levels of PCBs, with hypotonia (apathy). However, at 18 months of age, differences were no longer significant, with no relation between neurological status and dioxins or PCB levels in milk. However, as the authors could compare their data to that of Rogan et al. (1986), who looked at transplacental PCB transfer and neurological development, they concluded that transplacental transfer was more detrimental than breast milk transfer.

Studies on animal models support these epidemiological data and bolster the hypothesis that dioxins depress thyroid function and related physiological and neurological processes. For instance, in adult rodents many studies have shown depression of thyroid function following exposure to dioxins (see, for instance, Sewall et al., 1995), while others have shown neurological defects, such as demyelination and remyelination, following a single injection of TCDD (Fernandez et al., 2010). However, to the author's knowledge, only one experimental study has actually addressed experimentally effects on TCDD exposure throughout gestation or lactation on TH levels in both dams and pups. In this quite detailed study (Ahmed, 2011), the author used two doses of 2,3,7,8 TCDD (0.2 and 0.4 µg/kg per day by gastric intubation) from the first day of gestation until the end of lactation, postnatal day (PND) 30. Not only did the author follow maternal TSH, $T_3$, and $T_4$ during gestation (G) (days 16 and 18) and during lactation (PND 10, 20, and 30) but he also measured levels in fetal samples (umbilical cord blood at G 16 and 19) and in pups (PND 10, 20, and 30). Further, numerous biochemical assays were also run on cerebellar homogenates at the end of the experiment in brains from pups from control and TCDD-treated groups, at the same time points. A succinct conclusion would be that every parameter was significantly affected: Dose-dependent and time-dependent decreases in $T_3$ and $T_4$ and increases in TSH were seen in dams treated with TCDD compared to controls, and similar decreases, compared to controls, were seen in offspring.

As regards mechanism of action, current thinking holds that most actions of dioxins implicate direct interactions with the AhR receptor. Thus, it is probable that indirect effects on metabolism are responsible for inducing the decreases in circulating TH levels. However, in Hela cell cultures, TCDD can modify $T_3$-dependent transcription and increase the $T_3$-dependent expression of a panel of genes (Yamada-Okabe, Aono, Sakai, Kashima, & Yamada-Okabe, 2004). One of the $T_3$ target genes induced by TCDD was the AhR-inducible CYP1A1, a gene that was shown by Zoeller's team to be implicated in production of TR-active PCB metabolites (Gauger et al., 2007). Given that the Hela cell line used in these studies express the AhR receptor (Ruegg et al., 2008), the actions of TCDD on this cell line could well implicate either metabolites formed by CYP1A1 action or other indirect effects through AhR.

## Brominated Flame Retardants

Brominated flame retardants (BFRs) (sometimes referred to as polybrominated flame retardants [PFRs]) have been used for decades in various forms in electronic equipment, plastics, paints, and textiles such as foams and padding as well as curtains and carpets. In the 1990s their annual worldwide production was estimated at 150,000 tons. Succinctly put, their actions on TH signaling can be multiple, but two principal actions can be highlighted: first, interference of the BFRs with TH metabolism and action and, second, bromine inhibition of iodine uptake by the thyroid and, hence, reduction of TH synthesis. This latter action is exacerbated by iodine deficiency.

BFR classes include (in historical order of appearance) the polybrominated biphenyls (PBBs), the polybrominated diphenyl ethers (PBDEs), hexabromochlorodecane (HBCD, Fig. 5.4), and the more recently introduced tetra-bromo-bisphenol A (TBBPA, Fig. 5.5). Each of these categories of flame retardants has at least one bromine atom covalently bound to a carbon atom (in the phenyl ring). The bromine-carbon bond is easily broken by heat and the bromine atoms that are released slow-down fire progress. Their history is peppered with disquieting stories of precocious commercialization, ahead of testing, followed by delayed withdrawal. One such example is the case of a brominated organophosphate, tris(2,3-dibromo-propyl) phosphate, that was used in children's nightwear until 1977. When rat studies showed it to be a potent mutagen, it was replaced by its chlorinated analog, which too was shown, later, to give rise

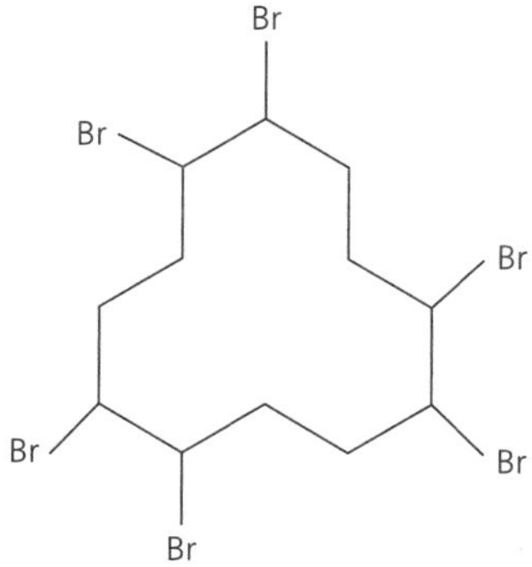

Figure 5–4. Structural formula of hexabromochlorodecane (HBCD). Shown is 1,2,5,6,9,10-HBCD. Bromination of cyclododeca-1,5,9-trienes theoretically results in 16 stereoisomers. Three, the α, β, and γ HBCD stereoisomers dominate in technical products. But the presence of different forms makes the study of their biodistribution and persistence particularly difficult.

to even more mutagenic metabolites (Hakk & Letcher, 2003). It is now used in furnishings!

In terms of thyroid disruption, despite the fact that the first report showing that a PBB, used as a flame retardant, affected thyroid function appeared in 1978 (Ringer, 1978), it was not until the early 2000s that the effects of BFRs on TH signaling received any significant research attention (Kitamura, Jinno, Ohta, Kuroki, & Fujimoto, 2002; McDonald, 2002). This low level of interest is even more surprising given the striking structural similarity between the two main categories of BFRs, the PBDEs and TBBPA, with their bromine-substituted biphenyl groups and THs, which are iodine-substituted (Fig. 5.5).

The PBDEs have been in use since the 1960s. Their production increased rapidly at the end of the 1970s with the phase-out of brominated additives in leaded petrol. Like the PCBs, many different variations on the basic structure exist and 209 congeners are known and marketed under different combinations to limit flammability of resins and polymers used in electronics and furnishings.

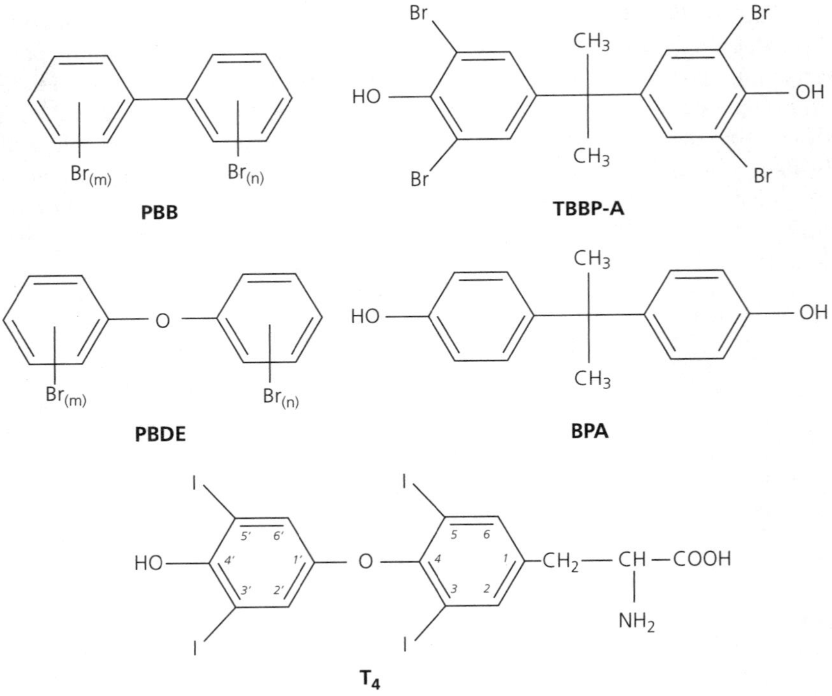

Figure 5–5. The polybrominated biphenyls (PBBs), polybrominated diphenyl ethers (PBDEs) and tetra-bromo-bisphenol A (TBBPA), and bisphenol A (BPA). Note all the compounds share strong structural homology with thyroid hormone (in this case $T_4$ is depicted). It is also pertinent to recall that TBBPA is broken down to BPA in the environment, increasing BPA load.

Most of the PBDE manufacturing destined for use in furniture (in the form of polyurethane foam) was based in the United States and Canada. Three principal mixtures were commercialized, classified according to the average number of bromine substitutions: 5 (penta-BDE), 8 (octa-BDE), or 10 (deca-BDE). In 2001, world production was about 66,000 tons (Birnbaum & Cohen Hubal, 2006). It was recognized in the early 2000s that PBDE were persistent and rapidly accumulating in the environment. This finding led to the penta and octa forms being banned in the European Union in 2004 and the deca-BDEs in 2008 (though it is registered, hence permitted, for specific applications). Some parts of the United States banned the penta and octa congeners around 2003 with a complete ban on US manufacturing in 2004, but as of 2008 deca-BDEs were still in production in the United States and it was not until the end of 2009 that a 3-year phase-out was agreed on. However, despite the bans, and because of their high bioaccumulative properties, PDBE congeners, and particularly the penta-BDE mixtures, are still found at high levels in human tissues, with particularly high levels in younger US populations. These higher levels appear to result from the greater exposure of young children to PBDE-contaminated house dust. In a recent report (Stapleton, Eagle, Sjödin, & Webster, 2012), significant levels of penta-BDEs were found in all North Carolina toddlers (12–36 months) tested, with average serum levels of 43.3 ng/g lipid. The principal source of contamination was thought to result from hand-to-mouth transfer from household dust, although breast-feeding also correlated with serum levels of one form of PBDE (congener BDE-153), which has a particularly long half-life.

Significant amounts of PDBEs are found universally in breast milk, with again the highest levels in the United States. In 2003 a US study reported total PDBE values of between 6.2 and 419 ng/g lipid with a mean of 74 ng/g (Schecter et al., 2003). Similar studies in European and Asian populations reveal mean levels of contamination of about an order of magnitude lower. For instance, levels in UK breast milk (Kalantzi et al., 2004) collected between 2001 and 2003 fell within a range of total PDBE from 0.3 to 69 ng/g lipid (mean 6.6 ng/g). In Japan, mean levels in maternal serum and milk were, respectively, 1.56 and 2.89 ng/g lipid (Inoue et al., 2006). Similar levels were found in urban Swedish mothers sampled in 2000/1 (Guvenius, Aronsson, Ekman-Ordeberg, Bergman, & Norén, 2003).

It is worth noting that generally these breast milk PBDE levels are one tenth of the values for PCBs, which were banned decades previously. But in the early years of the present century, levels of PBDEs in the particularly exposed younger generation were continually rising. The main source of contamination appears to be household dust with only a minor contribution from diet. For instance, in indigenous communities in northern Canada blood values increased with access to manufactured goods (Liberda et al., 2011).

Effects of Polybrominated Diphenyl Ethers on Thyroid Hormone Signaling

Both experimental and epidemiological studies show that PBDEs interfere with TH signaling at many levels. Even though the consistent co-contamination of blood samples with high levels of both PCBs and PBDEs makes it difficult to assess the contribution of PBDE effects to changes in circulating TH levels, certain correlations can be established. Examples include a recent study in low-income, nonsmoking pregnant Californian women, where high PBDE loads were found. Levels were clearly correlated with increased TSH levels (reflecting lower thyroid hormone availability; Zota et al., 2011). The authors suggest that the high PBDE levels could be related to California's stringent flammability standards for furniture.

Studies in animals consolidate these findings and show that acute exposure to PBDEs lowers TH levels, probably through effects on liver metabolism. The group of Kevin Crofton in the United States carried out pioneering work on PBDEs, treating weanling rats for just 4 days to different commercial mixtures and saw up to 80% reductions in circulating $T_4$ levels (Zhou, Ross, DeVito, & Crofton, 2001). The increased hepatic metabolism could be due to displacement of $T_4$ from its principal distributor proteins, transthyretin (TTR) and thyroxine-binding globulin (TBG), an interaction that has been shown to be strongest for hydroxylated PBDE metabolites (Meerts et al., 2000). Moreover, in the epidemiological data cited earlier (Zota et al., 2011), the most significant correlations for individual PBDEs were found for those that interact most strongly with TTR. Another antithyroid effect of these compounds might arise from bromine released during metabolism that could theoretically affect iodine uptake by the gland. Besides these effects on distribution and metabolism, PBDE metabolites also modulate the transcriptional effects of $T_3$ and TRs. Using different in vitro approaches, selective effects of individual PBDEs on $T_3$-dependent transcription and Purkinje cell differentiation were observed, with significant effects at doses as low as $10^{-11}$M for the deca-BDE, BDE 209 (Ibhazehiebo et al., 2011).

Given these numerous effects on TH signaling, from the level of the receptor to general metabolism, it is not surprising to find that PBDEs have direct and indirect neurotoxic effects. Many of the developmental processes affected by PBDEs are TH dependent, including neuronal proliferation, migration, Purkinje neuron differentiation, synaptogenesis, synaptic plasticity, and myelination. A recent review by Dingemans and colleagues (2011), which covers experimental data from in vitro and in vivo studies as well as epidemiological data, presents a disquieting scenario of the neurological consequences of PDBE-induced thyroid hormone disruption. The authors cite epidemiological data (Herbstman et al., 2010; Roze et al., 2009) that show strong associations between PBDE exposure during fetal and postnatal life on toddlers' psychomotor development and performance IQ at 2 and 3 years of age. Similarly, they review multiple sets of experimental data in rodents showing that exposure to various combinations of PBDEs in different dosage regimes (even a single oral dose given to neonates) can diminish performance in learning tasks and coordination while increasing locomotor activity (inducing hyperactivity). Effects on learning could be related to detrimental actions on hippocampal processes, as developmental exposure to BDE-47 or BDE-209 can impair hippocampal long-term potentiation (synaptic plasticity required for learning and memory). Since their review appeared more epidemiological evidence has accumulated showing in utero and childhood exposure to PBDEs to have adverse effects on neurodevelopment and IQ levels (Eskanazi, et al., 2013).

Hexabromochlorodecane

Hexabromochlorodecane (HBCD) has been marketed since the late 1960s. In 2008, nearly half a century later, Norway took the initiative of proposing that it should be classified as a POP. Thus, in late 2011, the UN committee on POPs published a report on the risk assessment of HBCD,[5] concluding that HBCD "is likely, as a result of long-range environmental transport, to lead to significant adverse effects on human health and/or the environment such that global action is warranted." The European Union had already listed it as a substance of very high concern (SVHC) as it is persistent, bioaccumulative, and toxic (a PBT substance). The report underlines that it appears to be particularly toxic to the aquatic environment and that HBCD levels in many regions are close to the adverse effect levels. As of 2015, it can no longer be used in the European Union without authorization. In the meantime, its continued use in insulation materials, electronic products, protective clothing, furnishings, and other textiles has led to significant levels accumulating in humans and in wildlife. Accumulation has been demonstrated despite the fact that the presence of different forms makes the study of their biodistribution and persistence particularly difficult (Law et al., 2005). HBCD concentrations of up to 260 ng/g lipid have been reported in liver of seals in the north Atlantic (Shaw, Berger, Weijs, & Covaci, 2012). A recent study measured numerous POPs in breast milk samples in Belgian and compared them to values taken 6 years earlier and to levels in breast milk in other EU countries (Croes et al., 2012). In 2009/10, HBCD values in the rural area of Belgium studied, Flanders, was 150% higher than the general level in Belgium mothers reported in 2005/6. The authors suggest that this increase might be due to HBCD being used as a replacement for most PBDEs that were banned in 2006. The values were in the range of 3.8 ng/g lipid, an order of magnitude lower than levels found in a Spanish study on breast milk (27 ng/g), but higher than in French, Swedish, or Norwegian samples taken 6 years previously.

Astonishingly, despite the well-researched effects of many other BFRs, few studies have addressed the effects of HBCD on thyroid function and neurodevelopment. One significant paper does, however, show inhibitory effects of low-dose ($10^{-10}$M) HBCD on $T_3$ transcriptional responses and development of Purkinje cell dendrites in cerebellar cultures (Ibhazehiebo, Iwasaki, Shimokawa, & Koibuchi, 2011).

Tetra-bromo-bisphenol A

As the PBDEs were taken off the market between 2004 and 2010, production of other flame retardants had to be found to fulfil stringent flame-resistant

5   See references given in http://saferinsulation.greensciencepolicy.org/wp-content/upl.

legislation for upholstery and for use in electronic equipment. The frontline candidate was tetra-bromo-bisphenol A (TBBPA), yet another BFR already used as a reactive for making polymers and used as an additive flame retardant. It rapidly became the most widely used BFR. Already by 2003, it was the BFR with the highest production volume, around 200,000 tons per year, a four-fold increase in 10 years. This was largely due to its apparently low toxicity. Starting from the late 1980s, initial tests showed it to be deceptively innocuous, displaying low mutagenicity in bacteria, both low teratogenicity and low toxicity in rodents and rabbits, though some tests indicated some renal impairment and some immunogenic effects (Darnerud, 2003). Up to 10 g/kg could be injected into rabbits with no acute toxicity seen. TBBPA caused little irritation in skin tests and appeared nonaccumulative in humans and rodents, displaying a short half-life in mammals. Studies (mainly in rats) showed it to be rapidly absorbed, but almost equally rapidly metabolized in the liver and the metabolites excreted through the bile into the feces. Moreover, a study carried out in workers exposed to TBBPA estimated the half-life in humans to be around 2 days, suggesting that it was rapidly flushed out of the system.

However, yet again history has taught that not all the spectrum of tests was run, and notably no complete endocrine disruption tests. In 2003, purely on the basis of a few tests, TBBPA was not considered to be an endocrine disruptor (Hakk & Letcher, 2003). This conclusion was reached despite the fact that in 2000, a first report had appeared showing that in in vitro tests, TBBPA, like some of the hydroxylated metabolites of PBDEs, displaced TH from the serum $T_4$ distributor protein, TTR (Meerts et al., 2000). At the same time numerous reports of high environmental contamination in sediments and wildlife were appearing along with data showing high levels of TBBPA in human samples, including umbilical cord blood (Kawashiro et al., 2008) and in babies born by caesarean section revealing placental transfer. Examining exposure in children and adults as a function of age, again, the highest concentrations were found in the youngest, 0- to 4-year-old, group (Thomsen, Lundanes, & Becher, 2002). These results contradicted the "rapidly flushed out" theory and the conclusion drawn, that despite the rapid clearance, environmental contamination was so high that wildlife, humans, and particularly unborn and young children, were continually exposed to significant amounts of TBBPA. As per usual, with the now standard regrettable delay, these findings are leading to the TH-disruptive and ensuing neurotoxic effects of TBBPA being revisited in greater detail. In this light it is worth noting that a major product of TBBPA degradation in the environment is the infamous oestrogenic plasticizer, bisphenol A (which will be discussed later).

Effects of TBBPA on Thyroid Hormone Signaling and Neurodevelopment

Compared to the literature on other BFRs, that on TBBPA is more limited, with no epidemiological studies on early-life exposure and neurobehavioral outcome. Similarly, there are few long-term studies covering early development. One rodent study using short exposure in neonatal rats showed TBBPA, unlike certain PBDEs, to have no effects on behavior. This negative result could be due to developmental stage studied or to length of exposure. As mentioned earlier, it is well established that TBBPA displaces $T_4$ from its distributor protein TTR, thereby increasing uptake and metabolism of $T_4$ by the liver, with the end result of reducing circulating $T_4$ levels, sometimes accompanied by increased $T_3$. These effects are seen in short and longer term experiments on rodents, including a one-generation study in rats that gave increasing doses of TBBPA to gestating and lactating dams and their offspring (Van der Ven et al., 2008). The authors estimate that this leaves a very small margin of exposure (about 2.6)[6] for certain human populations. Of course, in the everyday context of exposure to multiple chemicals, including other BFRs and residual PCBs, this margin of exposure is accordingly reduced, probably in some cases to insignificance. To examine TH effects on neurological development, the same group focused on hearing, as normal development of the cochlea requires tightly controlled TH levels within well-defined developmental windows. Detrimental dose-dependent effects on hearing were seen in both males and females (Lilienthal et al., 2008). Both of these studies were the targets of criticism by authors paid by the chemical industry (Banasik, Hardy, Harbison, Hsu, & Stedeford, 2009), criticisms to which the authors convincingly replied.

Other experimental demonstrations include inhibitory effects of TBBPA on $T_3$- dependent transcription, amphibian metamorphosis, and on $T_3$ signaling in a *Xenopus* embryonic reporter test system. These data also showed negative effects of TBBPA exposure on neuronal proliferation in the developing nervous system (Fini, Le Mével, et al., 2012) at concentrations that gave environmentally relevant exposure levels in tadpole tissues (Fini, Riu, et al., 2012). These experiments were carried out at a developmental stage equivalent to the first trimester of pregnancy in humans, a stage that is particularly important for TH effects on later brain development and neurobehavioral outcomes. Such findings argue for a need for epidemiological data on maternal TBBPA (and TH/iodine) levels in early pregnancy coupled with longitudinal studies on the neurodevelopmental characteristics and capacities of the children.

Perhaps it is due to the current, limited amount of experimental and epidemiological data that, according to the Bromine Science and Environment Forum (http://www.bsef.com/), no national or international authorities have yet limited the production and use of TBBPA.

Nonbrominated Flame Retardants and Replacement Flame Retardants

Not all flame retardants contain bromine; many contain another halogen, chlorine. One of the most used groups of compounds in this category, but understudied from the endocrine-disruption point of view, are organophosphates, including tris(1,3, dichloro-2 propyl) phosphate (TDCPP or "tris"). They are used in the manufacture of polyurethane foam, including that destined for

---

6  The margin of exposure is the ratio between estimated human intake and the lowest effective dose seen in experimental studies.

use in baby products. Interestingly, they have structural similarity to a common organophosphate pesticide, chrlorpyrifos, discussed in the section on "Pesticides." It is amazing to find that Tris has been allowed to be used so widely in furnishings given that it was one of the first flame retardants to be shown to be metabolized into a mutagen (Gold, Blum, & Ames, 1978). At that time it was used in children's sleepwear! In 2013 two reports simultaneously announced that this mutagen-generating substance, TDCPP, is now a virtually ubiquitous urban contaminant. In one study, TDCPP was found in 99% of office, vehicle, or house dust and that its main metabolite was present in 100% of urine samples (Carignan et al., 2013). The other found the metabolite in 91% of samples and levels correlated with those in house dust (Meeker, Cooper, Stapleton, & Hauser, 2013). Even though TDCPP is not brominated, it has been shown to interfere with TH signaling and TH action both with in vitro methods and in animal models (see, e.g., Farhat et al., 2013). Studies on human exposure also show associations with increased levels of TDCPP in house dust and reduced TH levels in men (Meeker & Stapleton, 2010).

Despite the recurrent thyroid-disrupting problems of different categories of bromine-containing flame retardants, the latest additions to the commercial mixtures seem equally troublesome. A new formulation of Firemaster 550 contains a replacement brominated compound, bis-(2-ethylhexyl) tetrabromophthalate (TBPH). Significant quantities are already found in dust from offices and houses. Yet again the product has TH-disrupting activities. In vitro tests showed a metabolite of TBPH to inhibit deiodinase 1 and activate adipogenesis, and exposing gestating rats for a mere 2 days caused maternal hypothyroidism with hepatotoxic effects (Springer et al., 2012).

As of March 2013, the EPA announced a list of 23 chemicals that were prioritized for assessment in 2014. Twenty of them are flame retardants, and TDCPP and TCPP are, belatedly, on this list. The list also includes some brominated phthalates as used in the Firemaster product. Given the TH-disrupting actions of phthalates on the one hand and brominated compounds, it will be important to test their activities on all levels of TH production and signaling.

Clearly, given the list of 20 flame retardants identified for closer risk assessment, first there is disquiet about the safety of those already in use and, second, there is a drive to find the least noxious substitutes for the most harmful.

## Bisphenol A

Bacterial activity in the environment degrades TBBPA to bisphenol A (BPA, Fig. 5.5), notorious for estrogen-disrupting effects, with links to reproductive cancers and obesity. First, tested in the 1930s for its estrogenic activities, it was sidelined into plastic production as diethylstilbestrol (DES) proved more potent (Vandenberg, Maffini, Sonnenschein, Rubin, & Soto, 2009). Recent estimates predict production of BPA to exceed 6.3 million tons in 2015 with about 100 tons released into the atmosphere during manufacture. Its uses include production of epoxy and polycarbonate (PC) resins. PC is required for manufacturing compact discs and DVDs, as a glass and metal substitute in the automobile industry, and of course for multiple uses in the food (packaging) industries, including in can liners and plastic bottles. Its use in the production of babies' bottles has only recently been legislated against in some countries, with Canada leading the way in 2010.

BPA has been mostly investigated for its estrogenic properties, but it also has TH-disrupting properties, although most demonstrations generally show effects at higher doses than for the estrogenic effects. For instance, in receptor-binding assays, BPA binds to both subtypes of estrogen receptors (ERα and ERβ) with an affinity of around 10,000-fold less (about $10^{-5}$M) than estrogen (17β estradiol). In contrast, the Ki for binding to the TRβ is $10^{-4}$M (Moriyama et al., 2002). Despite this weak affinity, in vitro reporter-based cell studies showed BPA to antagonize $T_3$/TR-dependent transcription at lower concentrations (i.e., $10^{-6}$M). Although these concentrations are not considered to be environmentally relevant in terms of serum levels observed in humans, one needs to take into account the effects of unremitting continual exposure that can to lead to high levels of BPA in tissues, including in humans, with higher accumulation in the placental and fetal compartments (Schonfelder et al., 2002).[7] Further, studies of BPA exposure in gestating rats showed alteration of TH-responsive genes in the brains of pups (Zoeller, Bansal, & Parris, 2005). Such factors are especially critical, given the ubiquitous nature of BPA contamination. Other points to be brought into the equation are, first, the combinatorial effects of BPA with other EDCs and the range of other potential targets for BPA, which can deepen the complexity of BPA effects. In this context it is already known that BPA can act through nongenomic ER-based mechanisms and on the closely related nuclear receptor, estrogen-related receptor (ERRγ), each of which could in turn cross talk with ER and TR signaling.

Surprisingly, only recently have epidemiological studies on human BPA exposure examined potential associations with thyroid function. One study published in 2013 shows significant negative associations between blood BPA levels and $FT_4$ levels in Thai men, but not in women (Sriphrapradang, Chailurkit, Aekplakorn, & Ongphiphadhanakul, 2013). No variations in TSH levels were seen. This finding echoes results from animal studies in which interesting thyroid signaling phenotypes resemble a clinical condition, thyroid resistance syndrome, in that circulating $T_4$ levels can be modified with no apparent effect on TSH levels. Given these effects, it is surprising that the first data on BPA and thyroid function and pregnancy are only now beginning to accumulate. A report from the Californian group working on chemical pollution in the Salinas Valley, the CHAMACOS study (Centre for the Health Assessment of Mothers and Children of Salinas), showed multiple, significant changes in

---

7  In this paper, the authors show BPA accumulating at higher concentrations in the serum of male fetuses when compared to females. This factor needs to be taken into consideration when discussing the higher frequency of autism spectrum disorders and neurodevelopmental disorders in boys.

maternal and fetal markers of thyroid function in association with maternal BPA exposure (Chevrier et al., 2013). Also, few studies to date have analyzed the potential links between maternal or fetal levels of BPA in relation to TH in the context of children's risk for neurodevelopmental disorders. One study (Miodovnik et al., 2011) examined third-trimester maternal phthalate and BPA levels (but not endocrine markers) in 400 mothers and then examined social impairment-related behaviors in the children 7–9 years later. Positive correlations of phthalate levels (see section on "Phthalates"), but not BPA, were found with social behavior impairment.

## Perfluorinated Compounds

Perfluorinated compounds (PFCs; Fig. 5.6) share a number of surfactant or surface protection properties that make them of industrial interest for literally thousands of industrial uses. They are found in stain- and oil-resistant coverings, including the coatings of cardboard packaging for fast foods, water- and stain-resistant materials, floor polishes, and fire-fighting foams. One of the widest uses is in production of fluoropolymers for nonstick cooking pans. Another notorious source is the lining of packaging for microwaved popcorn. Two main categories of long-chain PFCs, the perfluoroalkyl sulfonates (PFAS) and the perfluoroalkyl carboxylates (PFACs), are of particular concern as they are of high production rates and persistent. They bioaccumulate extensively in the environment. The two most intensely researched for their environmental levels and effects on biodiversity and human health are perfluorooctanic acid (PFOA) and perfluorooctane sulfonic acid (PFOS). Another frequently found form is perfluorononanoic acid (PFNA). In each case studies have to take into account not only the homologs of these substances but also precursor molecules, including fluorotelomer alcohols (FTOH) and acrylates (FTA), as well as derivatives. Both PFOA and PFOS have been reported worldwide in humans and in fauna at both North and South Poles (Dreyer, Weinberg, Temme, & Ebinghaus, 2009). PFCs, notably the more volatile precursors, enter the atmosphere during manufacturing, use, and disposal. Global distribution is through both atmospheric and water phases (rivers and oceans). Levels of PFCs were measured in gas and particle phases of samples in the Northern and Southern hemispheres (Dreyer et al., 2009) and found to vary from 4.5 to 335 pg per cubic meter of air ($pg/m^3$), with highest levels in European areas. In residential areas, indoor concentrations are higher than outdoor levels, with one report showing most elevated levels in shops selling outdoor equipment, furniture, or carpets (Langer, Dreyer, & Ebinghaus, 2010).

Human studies reveal significant levels of contamination. Studies on pregnant women in Denmark and Canada showed remarkably similar serum levels with, in one Danish cohort, mean PFOS and PFOA levels being 33 ng/ml and 5 ng/ml, respectively (Andersen et al., 2010). Some studies have looked at both maternal and umbilical cord blood levels and find, not only significant placental transfer, but also significant negative correlations between maternal

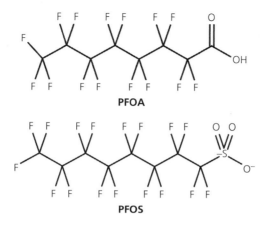

**PFOA**

**PFOS**

**Figure 5–6.** Chemical structure of the two most common perfluorinated compounds (PFCs): perfluorooctanic acid (PFOA) and perfluorooctane sulfonate (PFOS). Note that these thyroid hormone disruptors bear no structural similarity to the hormone itself.

PFC values and fetal $T_3$ levels (Kim et al., 2011). In a Swedish study (Karrman et al., 2007), total mean PFCs in lactating mothers were 32 ng/ml in serum with levels in breast milk being about 1% of serum levels. Studies in rodents also show placental and milk transfer, associated with adverse effects on fetal TH homeostasis (Yu et al., 2009). Despite these data, to date no studies have looked at associations of maternal PFC levels with their child's neurodevelopmental outcome. However, some studies have looked at PFC load and birth weight, but with contradictory results, no doubt due to confounding factors. The Danish study cited earlier showed maternal levels of PFOA and PFOS to be inversely associated with their children's weight over the first year of life, with most marked effects in boys.

Contamination continues after birth with levels accumulating with age. One extensive study examined thyroid function associations with perfluoroalkyl acid (PFAA) load in nearly 11,000 children living near Teflon production plants (Lopez-Espinosa, Mondal, Armstrong, Bloom, & Fletcher, 2012). Teflon is used for nonstick pans. Residents living near such plants in mid-Ohio and West Virginia had filed a class action suit against the manufacturers for contamination of drinking water with PFOA, and serum levels of the children near the mid-Ohio plant were nearly eight times national levels. There was an increased risk of hypothyroidism as a function of PFOA levels.

In adults, a study across a large population in Korea found measurable levels of 13 PFCs in all subjects examined, with higher levels in older men suggesting contamination with certain foodstuffs. One PFC in particular, perfluorotridecanoic acid (PFTrDA), was associated with decreased $T_4$ and increased TSH (Ji et al., 2012). Examination of PFCs in a population of US anglers has been investigated, as sport-fish consumption has been suggested to be a source of contamination. High levels of total PFCs were found, with means of PFOS reaching 19.6 ng/ml, but given the small sample size no significant correlations with TH levels were revealed (Bloom et al., 2010). However, a study on workers in a PFC manufacturing site showed levels were inversely correlated to $FT_4$ levels, and in another study higher levels in people living near such sites were associated with both modifications of thyroid function and increased probability of thyroid disease (references in Lopez-Espinosa et al., 2012). Data on exposure in the general population from the NHANES study also showed significant associations with PFOA and PFOS load and thyroid disease in women and for PFOS in men (Melzer et al., 2010). As to the mechanisms involved, in vivo and in vitro studies in animals showed effects on TH metabolism with increased glucuronidation in the liver (Yu, Liu, & Jin, 2009) and displacement of $T_4$ from TTR binding (Weiss et al., 2009), recalling the effects of PBDEs that also displace $T_4$ from TTR and increase hepatic TH clearance.

## Phthalates

Phthalates (different esters of 1,2-benzene-dicarboxylic acid, or phthalic acid) represent an exceedingly widely used group of chemicals. Over 25 esters of phthalic acid exist, and their broad spectrum of applications includes plasticizers for medical devices (especially single-use disposable items such as tubing and plastic bags), toys, personal care products (shampoo, soap, and cosmetics), some forms of food packaging including cardboard, production of polyvinyl chloride (PVC), and even the capsules of certain medications. PVC serves in a spectrum of industrial plastics for both the automobile and building industries, with examples of use including window frames and floor or wall coverings (e.g., paints). Phthalates are not chemically bound to the main components, and so they can leach from theses sources into the household environment, making them a common indoor pollutant, notably of household dust. The properties of phthalates vary as a function of their side chains and a core group of about nine have been repeatedly used as plasticizers by chemists to improve polymer flexibility, durability, and extensibility. These commonly used esters are di(2ethylhexyl) phthalate (DEHP, Fig. 5.7), di-isononyl phthalate (DINP), dibutyl phthalate (DBP), butylbenzyl phthalate (BBP), di-isododecyl phthalate (DIDP), di-n-octyl phthalate (DnOP), di-n-hexyl phthalate (DnHP), di-ethyl phthalate (DEP), and di-methyl phthalate (DMP).

Phthalate use in the plastics industry dates from the 1920s, when phthalate esters replaced the strongly smelling camphor as a plasticizer (Graham, 1973). In 2010, phthalates represented 70% of the US plasticizer market (Halden, 2010), with plastic production at that time being estimated at over 300 million tons and global production of the principal phthalate, DEHP, at between 1 and 4 million tons.[8]

8  http://www.cpsc.gov/about/cpsia/pthalexp.pdf and http://www.epa.gov/opptintr/existingchemicals/pubs/actionplans/phthalates.html

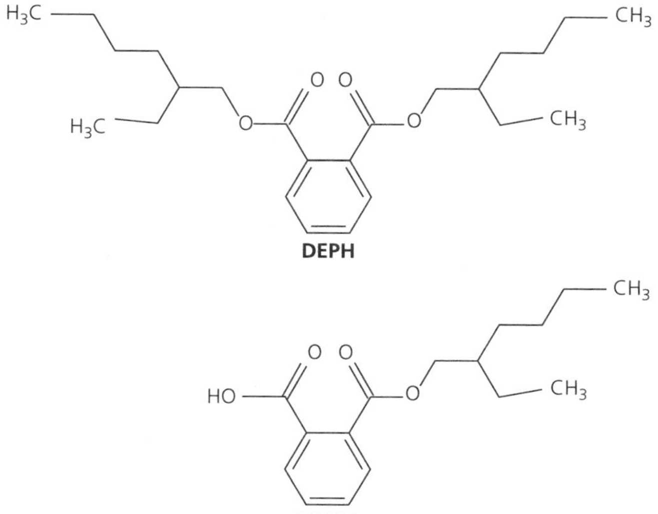

**Figure 5–7.** Chemical structure of di-(2ethylhexyl) phthalate (DEHP) and its primary metabolite mono-(2-ethyl hexyl) phthalate (MEHP).

Sources of contamination are numerous (Meeker, Sathyanarayana, & Swan, 2009) and the principal routes include ingestion (household dust, food), skin (personal care products), and inhalation from paints and other building materials. Vinyl products are particularly DEHP rich and thought to be a potential source of human contamination (Dodson et al., 2012). Most notably, disposal of PVC and other DEHP-containing materials by incineration and landfill leads to release of DEHP into the environment, notably into rivers, surface water, and drinking water. A series of studies on Chinese rivers showed systematic TH antagonist activities and that phthalates, notably dibutyl phthalate, represented the main source of this TH antagonist action that was not removed by drinking water treatment (Li et al., 2010). Furthermore, as detailed later, epidemiological studies show that phthalates cross the placenta and are found in breast milk and infant formula, raising the spectre of continued exposure through early development from conception onward. Given the fact that DEHP is not covalently bound to the PVC basis that is used for medical devices, it can leach out and thus become a common pollutant of blood products that are stocked in PVC-containing material or simply of air or liquids passing through PVC-based tubing. Such sources of contamination are of particular concern for infants undergoing intensive care.

As infants have a tendency to put their hands and toys into their mouths, their exposure levels are often higher than in other age groups. Obviously, the leaching of phthalates from children's toys is a major, preventable source of contamination that has led to recent legislative activity in the United States, Canada, and the European Union. The European Union first warned and recommended against use of phthalates in children's toys in 1998 and then introduced legislation in 2005 banning DEHP, DBP, and BBP, while maintaining warnings about DINP, DIDP, and DNOP. The US Consumer Protection Safety Improvement Act also provided similar provisions in 2009 (Section 108), banning DEHP, DBP, and BBP and giving temporary provision on the other three. In 2011, Canada limited the amounts of six major phthalate esters that could be used in toddlers' toys. Specifically, the permissible concentrations of DEHP, DBP, and BBP were limited to less than 1,000 mg/kg (0.1%) in the soft vinyl of all children's toys and child-care articles. What is more, the permitted amounts of DINP, DIDP, and DNOP were also restricted to the same amounts for use in any soft vinyl product that might be placed in the mouth of a toddler under the age of 4 years.

These restrictions have led to decreased production, but exposure levels are still high and ubiquitous. In 2004, publication of the US National Health and Nutrition Examination Survey (NHANES) provided insight into phthalate contamination levels across different groups from age 6 years upward. Seven monoester metabolites of commonly used phthalates were measured in 2,540 urine samples. As is often the case, the younger populations showed the highest levels of contamination of three of the seven phthalate metabolites measured (Silva et al., 2004), that is, monobutyl phthalate (MBP), mono-(2-ethyl hexyl) phthalate (MEHP, the first metabolite of DEHP produced),[9] and monobenzyl phthalate (MBzP). Mean values ranged from 5 to over 180 µg/L for MEHP and MEP, respectively. Levels of MEP an order of magnitude higher were reported for a group of non-occupationally exposed people in Germany (Koch, Rossbach, Drexler, & Angerer, 2003).

Given the concern about developmental effects of endocrine disruption, many recent studies have focused on exposure of pregnant and nursing women and their infants. Meeker and colleagues (2009) found different combinations of nine phthalate metabolites in the urine samples given by 242 women at prenatal and postnatal visits. Values were highest for mono-(2-ethyl-5-hydroxylhexyl) phthalate (MEHHP), MEHP, and mono-ethyl phthalate (MEP). The mean concentrations for these chemicals were MEP: 816 µg/L; MEHHP: 50 µg/L; and for MEHP: 15 µg/L. Similar levels have been reported for pregnant women in US and Taiwanese populations (Huang et al., 2007).

Phthalate contamination of the fetal environment is demonstrated by levels of metabolites in amniotic fluid and meconium. A recent study on Danish samples of amniotic fluid collected between 1980 and 1996 looked at both PFOS and certain phthalate metabolites. Levels of both categories of contaminants increased with gestational age and reached median levels in the 1 ng/ml (i.e., 1 µg/L) range for PFOS and 0.27 ng/ml for MEPP (Jensen et al., 2012). Meconium, the first stools that an infant produces after birth, is a very useful

---

9    MEHP is then metabolized to mono-(2-ethyl-5-hydroxylhexyl) phthalate (MEHHP) and mono-(2-ethyl-5-oxohexyl) phthalate MEOHP, among other oxidative products.

indicator of exposure because it is composed of materials swallowed by the fetus during gestation. Zhang and colleagues measured phthalate metabolites in meconium and cord serum from infants born in Shanghai between 2005 and 2006 (Zhang et al., 2009). Levels of MEHP and DBP in cord serum were in the 1–6 ng/ml range, and in meconium, values ranged from 1 to 6 mg/g for MBP and MEHP. The authors also found negative associations between phthalate exposure and birth weight, with infants of significantly lower birth weight having the higher phthalate levels. As infants of low birth weight (below 2.5 kg in EU and US studies) are at greater risk for developing obesity and metabolic disease in later life, the link between these different factors requires more research and closer evaluation.

As regards levels in breast milk and infant formula, successive studies have addressed this question in European, Asian, and American populations. Studying Danish and Finnish mothers in 2006, Main and colleagues (2006) reported median breast milk levels in 1- to 3-month postnatal samples to be in the 1 μg/L range for MEP and MBzP, 10 times higher for MEHP and MBP, and a disquieting 100-fold higher range for mono-isononyl phthalate (MINP). A study from the same group (Mortensen, Main, Andersson, Leffers, & Skakkebaek, 2005) also found measurable levels of certain metabolites in infant formula. In contrast, a more recent study on US women looked for four phthalate metabolites in urine, saliva, and breast milk (Hines, Calafat, Silva, Mendola, & Fenton, 2009). Metabolites were present in most urine samples but only in 10% of breast milk samples.

The immense majority of the work on developmental effects of phthalates has focused on the antiandrogenic effects in the context of the male reproductive system. Numerous excellent reviews have covered this area (see, for instance, Fisher, 2004; Hu, Lian, Ge, Hardy, & Li, 2009; Talsness, Andrade, Kuriyama, Taylor, & vom Saal, 2009). Key findings include the association of exposure with increased incidence of testicular dysgenesis syndrome that can include reduced anal genital distance and an increased risk of later development of testicular cancer (Jobling, Hutchison, van den Driesche, & Sharpe, 2011). Such findings have led to a ban on the use of specific phthalates in children's toys, as mentioned earlier. However, despite their universal usage, very few studies have examined effects of phthalates on TH signaling, and even fewer looked for associations between maternal phthalate levels during pregnancy and lactation on children's subsequent development and behavior.

Turning to the effects of phthalates on TH signaling, only a few studies have used in vitro methods to examine whether these chemicals can interfere with TH-dependent transcription or TH effects on cell proliferation. For instance, a series of phthalate esters were found to inhibit TH-dependent induction of proliferation in a cell line (Ghisari & Bonefeld-Jorgensen, 2009). As the primary phthalates and not their metabolites were tested in a system that has limited metabolic capacity (a pituitary cell line), the effects were seen at relatively high concentrations ($>10^{-6}$M), except for DINP, which was effective at $10^{-8}$M. Similar limitations, use of precursors and not the more biologically active metabolites, limit the relevance of these and other in vitro studies. By using cell lines that do not carry out the metabolic processes characteristic of liver cells, and that are found by definition in in vivo systems, most authors only see effects of phthalates such as DEHP at very high, nearly toxic, doses (see, for instance, Wenzel, Franz, Breous, & Loos, 2005). This limitation is also present in the experiments using a reporter gene assay where Hu and collaborators (2013) reported that phthalate-containing samples taken at different sites along the Yangtze River inhibited TR-dependent transcriptional responses, but again, at very high concentrations.

It is surprising that despite the large body of research into phthalates and reproduction, particularly in males, during development and in adults, few studies have used these animal models to examine whether and through what potential mechanisms phthalate exposure can affect other endocrine systems, notably thyroid status and TH action. Perhaps concern about the more readily observed effects on reproductive health has obscured the effects on brain development and behavior that require more detailed approaches to substantiate. This disparity is even more astonishing given that in one relatively early study (O'Connor, Frame, & Ladics, 2002) that examined effects in male rats of different potential antiandrogens, including vinclozolin and DBP, the authors wisely looked at other endocrine endpoints, including circulating TH levels. Significant effects of DBP on circulating $T_3$ levels were actually seen at levels half those required to see effects on circulating testosterone.

As it was noted early on that phthalates affect liver and lipid metabolism,[10] certain authors examined links between phthalate exposure, altered liver function, and thyroid status. For instance, Howarth and colleagues (2001) used histology to follow thyroid activity in rats and observed indications of increased thyroid activity subsequent to liver changes induced by DEHP and DNHP in the diet.

Intriguingly, although they provide no mechanistic insight, there are quite a few studies on phthalate exposure and its correlation to thyroid function in humans, and most of these studies show adverse effects of phthalate presence on thyroid function. For instance, in 208 adult men, significant inverse correlations between MEHP and circulating $FT_4$ and $FT_3$ levels were found. The same group carried out a more extensive study using the National Health and Nutrition Examination Survey (NHANES) data collected between 2007 and 2008 that included over 1,300 adults and 329 adolescents (Meeker & Ferguson, 2011). Again, they revealed significant inverse, dose-dependent correlations between levels of four oxidative DEHP metabolites, including MEHP, and total $T_4$ levels in adults. The smaller sample size of the adolescent group led to less significant relationships, but certain metabolites were correlated with decreased

10 It is now known that the PPAR receptors are targets of phthalate metabolites, notably MEHP. PPARs, like TRs, are examples of nuclear receptors that are tightly implicated in governing metabolism and, in the case of PPARγ, controlling adipogenesis.

$T_4$ and one with increased $T_3$. Similar results showing decreased circulating TH levels with increased phthalate exposure were found in Danish children aged between 4 and 9 years old. In this study (Boas et al., 2010) phthalate metabolites were found in all of the >800 urine samples collected and the most significant negative correlations were found for levels in girls.

One recent study from South Korea looked at mean urine levels of a number of phthalate metabolites in mothers' prenatal urine samples and examined correlations with their children's development at 6 months of age (Kim et al., 2011). Infant's Mental or Psychomotor Developmental Indices were inversely associated with certain metabolites present in maternal prenatal urine samples, including MEHHP and MEOHP (mono(2-ethyl-5oxohexyl) phthalate). The authors suggest that prenatal exposure to phthalates can adversely affect neurodevelopmental outcome, particularly in boys. As other studies have shown negative associations between maternal phthalate contamination (notably the DBP metabolite, MBP) and their TH levels (Huang et al., 2007), it is plausible that, given the importance of maternal TH levels for early fetal brain development (see Chapter 3) that the adverse effects of maternal phthalate exposure and later infant development implicate the TH axis.

### Perchlorate and Other Thyroid-Inhibiting Anions

The antithyroid effects of perchlorate are well established. Perchlorate acts by inhibiting the sodium-iodide symporter thus blocking iodine uptake by the thyroid gland. Perchlorate and related substances are used clinically to treat hyperthyroidism by blocking TH production. Given this clear antithyroid effect and the generalized exposure at least in the United States (see later), the urgent question is not whether it is active but how severe is human exposure, particularly in children and pregnant women, and whether perchlorate contamination is another potential contributor to the rise in autism spectrum disorders and neurodevelopmental disorders. Most drinking water is contaminated with both perchlorate and nitrate, and urinary levels of these chemicals are among the highest of all chemical contaminants (see Chapter 6, section on "CDC 2013 Data on Exposure to Environmental Chemicals in the United States").

Perchlorate is a strong oxidant used in rocket propellants, ammunition, road flares, fireworks, and airbag deployment. Because of its prevalence of use and extreme stability, it has become a widespread contaminant in water used for irrigation and drinking and, thus, in food. Exposure data show perchlorate contamination to be generalized in the US population (Blount, Valentin-Blasini, Osterloh, Mauldin, & Pirkle, 2007). In the study cited, urinary perchlorate levels were measured in children aged 6 years or more and adults. Perchlorate was found in all samples, with highest levels in children. Urinary concentrations showed means around 3.6 µg/L (with values up to 14 µg/L) from which the authors estimated the daily intake across the population to approximate 0.23 µg/kg per day. This value is below the current EPA reference dose (0.7 µg/kg per day). The higher urinary levels (mean 5.4 µg/L) in children aged 6 or over would be closer to the EPA daily intake limit and could reflect higher intake to body weight factors; this underlines the importance of identifying the source of contamination. Some studies have shown that even these low exposures adversely affect TH levels in women, particularly if their iodine intake is insufficient (Blount et al., 2006). Interestingly in this study urinary perchlorate was associated with increased TSH whatever their iodine status, and also with both TSH and $T_4$ levels if urinary iodine was below 100 µg/L. Thus, the universal contamination of water supplies combined with frequent iodine lack in susceptible populations is a clear risk factor for adversely affecting TH signaling in women and, of greatest concern, in those of child-bearing age.

Given that the most vulnerable windows of development are during early pregnancy and the perinatal period, more measures of perchlorate in pregnant mothers' serum and urine, in breast milk, and infant formula are needed. Such data are particularly relevant as not only does perchlorate pass the placental barrier, it also can block iodide uptake in the breast, which like the thyroid expresses the sodium iodide symporter. Thus, most well-designed studies on perchlorate levels also examine iodine content in these fluids, as clearly, iodine lack will exacerbate the effects of perchlorate. Studies often include measures of thiocyanate of another oxidant found in cigarette smoke. Thiocyanate also inhibits (but to a lesser extent than perchlorate) the sodium iodide symporter.

Studies have been reported on cohorts of pregnant women in the United States, Europe, and Asia. In Greece (Pearce et al., 2012), measurable perchlorate and thiocyanate levels were found in all 134 women examined, with some associations with TH or TSH levels, but no simple overall correlation was found with thyroid function, and this despite a general slight iodine lack. Similarly, in a study of women in the Boston area, most of whom used iodized salt or iodide-containing multivitamins, there was no correlation between perchlorate and breast milk iodide, but thyroid status was not evaluated (Pearce et al., 2007). Perchlorate, because it is a universal contaminant, is present in infant formula. However, a recent study (Valentin-Blasini et al., 2011) of perchlorate and related substance in infant's urine, found highest levels in breast-fed (mean 9 µg/L) versus formula-fed infants, with 9% of infants receiving daily levels above the reference level. Levels reported for cow's milk and formula in Japan and South Korea are in similar or higher ranges (mean values of 7.8 µg/g for formula and 4.6 µg/L for dairy milk). However, as will be emphasized again, the multiple benefits of breast-feeding outweigh the slightly higher amounts in some breast-milk samples versus formula.

Nitrate and Thiocyanate

Nitrate is another thyroid-inhibiting anionic pollutant that is found as a common water contaminant in agricultural areas (Fig. 5.8), nitrate being a major component of fertilizer. The latest CDC data set shows urinary nitrate values in

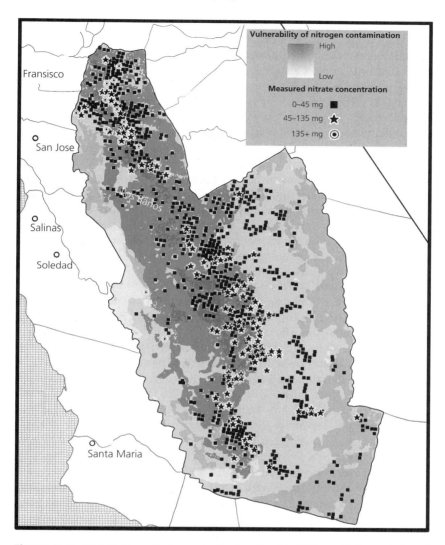

**Figure 5–8.** Distribution of nitrates in the San Joachin Valley, California (adapted from Stanford University library sources). The Californian Central Valley is one of the most important sites of intense agricultural activity worldwide; it covers the Sacramento and San Joachin Valleys. Various levels of pollutants are found throughout the area, including arsenic, nitrates, and different categories of pesticides. Here the distribution of nitrates is shown in three levels of contamination, 0–45 mg/L, 45–135 mg/L, and greater than 135 mg/ml.

the general population of about 48 mg/L urine. Nitrate acts by inhibiting thyroidal iodine uptake by the sodium–iodide symporter. Thiocyanate also inhibits iodine uptake, and at higher concentrations it also interferes with iodine organification. Certain vegetables, such as those in the cabbage (Brassicaceae) family, are sources of thiocyanates, though consumption of such vegetables (cabbage, brussels sprouts, cauliflower, kale, bok chow, and broccoli) has to be excessive (over 1 kg per day on a regular basis) to reach physiological levels that will inhibit thyroid function. In contrast, cassava consumption in certain parts of Africa has been documented as being linked to goiter and cretinism (Thilly et al., 1993). Another source of thiocyanate is cigarette smoke.

It has been calculated, on the basis of a broad bibliographic study, that given their prevalence in water and food, nitrate and thiocyanate will have greater effects on limiting iodide uptake by the thyroid than perchlorate (De Groef, Decallonne, Van der Geyten, Darras, & Bouillon, 2006). Such effects will occur, despite the fact that the relative potencies of nitrate and thiocyanate to inhibit the sodium-iodide symporter are, respectively, 240 and 15 times less than that of perchlorate. Given that nitrate is present in urinary samples at around 50 mg/L and perchlorate at 5 µg/L means that the thyroid-inhibiting capacity of nitrate exceeds that of perchlorate by a factor of 40. As general perchlorate intake is about one third to half the US EPA reference dose, the high nitrate exposure confounds the safety margin.

Perchlorate and nitrate contamination of surface water supplies is universal. Removing these anions from drinking water is costly and often incomplete. In France many of the main tap water supplies have levels of nitrate over 20 mg/L (WWF report on French Drinking Water, 2011, in French). No data are available for perchlorate, neither in France nor many of the EU member states, as perchlorate is not currently regulated in surface or drinking water.

Moreover, surface water levels of perchlorate can be particularly high in areas of past military activity, such as around battle sites (perchlorate contamination is still found in some sites of World War I, a century ago). However, most contemporary contamination comes from aerospace activity. This is the case in the United States, where data show California to use one third of all perchlorate used in the United States and mostly for the aerospace industry. Moreover, within a given country or state, quite limited geographical areas reveal social disparities in perchlorate and/or nitrate contamination of drinking water. Such was the case in a study of the San Joaquin Valley in California, where higher nitrate levels were found in water systems serving communities with larger Latino populations, potentially related to the closer proximity of these communities to agricultural sources (Balazs, Morello-Frosch, Hubbard, & Ray, 2011).

Nitrate content of tap water has been associated with higher TSH levels and increased thyroid volume in humans (van Maanen et al., 1994; i.e., with inhibition of the thyroid axis and consequent thyroid hypertrophy as seen in iodide deficiency provoked goitre). Yet the antithyroid effects of nitrate and thiocyanate (and their possible interactions with other pollutants) are rarely taken into account in epidemiological studies. One notable exception is the study of Cao et al. (2010), who examined correlations of each of these goitrogenic anions with TSH. They found that children with higher levels of nitrate and thiocyanate had higher TSH levels. Perchlorate was only associated with higher TSH when there was concomitant iodide lack.

## Pesticides

The term "pesticides" covers insecticides (used to limit insect pest populations), fungicides (chemicals directed against mycoses or fungi), and rodent poisons. The term "biocides" includes pesticides and the broadly used herbicides or weed-killers. Pesticides account for 33 of the 47 substances covered by the UN Rotterdam convention on hazardous chemicals, adopted in 1998 by 152 parties and enforced in 2004. Chemical pesticides can be broadly grouped into four categories: organophosphates and carbamates that target the evolutionary conserved neurotransmitter acetylcholine found throughout the animal kingdom; organochlorines such as DDT; and chlordane and pyrethroids, which can be neurotoxic. Current research includes development of transgenic plants that are genetically engineered to express proteins or interference RNA targeting a particular pest, or specific metabolites, such as pyrethroid, originally found in chrysanthemums.

Since the publication of Rachel Carson's prescient work in 1962, efforts have been made to reduce and restrict the use of pesticides by many nations. Most significant perhaps was the ban on the general use of dichloro-diphenyl-trichloroethane (DDT) by the US EPA in 1972 and across the European Union in the 1980s. However, DDT is still used (mainly) for indoor spraying to control malaria-carrying mosquitos in areas of high malaria risk. The EPA estimates that in the time since its large-scale introduction during World War II and the general restriction on use, more than $1.3 \times 10^9$ pounds of DDT were used in the United States. Besides domestic use, large amounts were produced and exported. Despite the restrained use of DDT today, both DDT and its main metabolite dichloro-diphenyl-dichloroethylene (DDE) are still found in significant amounts in the environment, including human fluids such as blood but also ovarian follicle fluid and amniotic fluid (Petro et al., 2012).

During the debate on DDT use, it began to be replaced by many other insecticides. The drive to find alternatives was not only due to increasing concern and regulatory procedures but also due to its decreasing effectiveness, as many insects developed resistance. Currently, the EPA estimates that about 1.2 billion pounds (over half a million metric tons) of pesticides are used in the United States annually. And yet many arguments can be given to rationalize and reduce use of all types of pesticides. In Sweden a 63% reduction in pesticide use has been estimated to confer important reductions in public health costs. Others have reviewed 286 interventions designed to increase sustainability in 57 countries. Of those with data on pesticide use, overall use was reduced by 71% and yields increased by 42% (Pretty et al., 2006). In Indonesia, data show that a similar level of pesticide reduction (65%) in rice production was associated with increased yields and reduced production costs. Similarly, in Vietnam reductions in pesticide usage (sometimes even complete cessation) has increased rice yields (Normile, 2013).

Given the numbers of different categories of pesticides, and their widespread use, it is impossible to cover all potentially thyroid-active pesticides and mixtures.[11] However, many halogenated-phenol (organochlorine [OC])-based pesticides, including DDT and DDE, hexachlorobenzene (HCB), Chlordane, and Lindane, have been shown to have TH-disrupting capacities, as have certain organophosphate (OP) pesticides. It is worth noting that both of the two main categories of pesticides, the OCs and the OPs, have been liked to autism spectrum disorders through epidemiologic studies (Eskenazi et al., 2008; London et al., 2012) as well as animal experiments. The links between pesticide exposure and neurodevelopment have been reviewed by Theo Colborn (2004). In terms of TH effects of pesticides, Brucker-Davis reviewed the situation in 1998. Other more recent reviews have included some data on pesticides and TH signaling (Boas, Feldt-Rasmussen, & Main, 2012), but the field is vast and difficult to navigate in detail. One factor, already encountered in the discussion of PCBs, is that epidemiological studies will reveal a spectrum of different chemicals in the samples. Thus, separating out and determining contributions of individual pesticides is difficult and analyses rarely go beyond associations.

Taking the OC chemicals first, a point of entry into this mix is that with the longest history of use: DDT. As mentioned earlier, despite its increasingly restricted use since the 1970s, the main metabolite is still found universally 40 years later in human tissues, and its presence has been repeatedly associated with detrimental effects of neurodevelopment and behavior in children. As regards effects on TH signaling, studies in two Spanish cohorts of pregnant women carried out between 2004 and 2006 showed that DDE was present in virtually all samples examined and that levels showed a negative association with $T_3$ (Alvarez-Pedrerol et al., 2009). However, stronger significant effects on TH levels were found for a series of PCBs and most significantly for another OC pesticide, HCB, despite the fact that it was present in lower amounts than DDE. However, high levels of DDE exposure during the first trimester of pregnancy have been associated with a significant reduction in infants' psychomotor neurodevelopment (Torres-Sanchez et al., 2007).

In a Japanese study, breast milk samples were taken as indicators of previous contamination that could be related to congenital hypothyroidism and cretinism. Four major categories of chemicals in breast milk showed significant associations with thyroid dysfunction in the newborns (Nagayama et al., 2007). The strongest associations were for dioxin-like compounds, followed by PCBs, and the pesticides DDT and HCB. A Spanish study also showed a significant association between umbilical cord blood of HCB and increased levels of TSH

11 In 2013 the European Food Safety Authority reported that of 287 pesticides screened, 103 affected thyroid signaling at different levels (EFSA Journal 2013, 11(7) 3293–3414).

(reflecting lower TH availability) in male newborns (Alvarez-Pedrerol et al., 2008). Some studies have addressed the mechanism of action of HCB. HCB acts like dioxins, binding to the AhR, and therefore its effects on TH levels are probably similar to dioxins, indirectly increasing TH metabolism and thereby reducing circulating levels.

Another OC is the herbicide Nitrofen (or NIT), 2, 4- dichlorophenyl-p-nitrophenyl ether, that was used worldwide until 1996 when it was banned in the European Union and the United States because of its carcinogenic properties. However, the chemical also exerts strong antithyroidal effects (Manson, Brown, & Baldwin, 1984). Many of the strongest associations between OC exposure and modified thyroid status come from studies on OC levels in agricultural workers in both Europe and in the United States (see, for instance, Goldner et al., 2010). In this light it can be recalled that populations living near intense agricultural zones can also be exposed to increased nitrate levels as well (see section on "Perchlorate and Other Thyroid-Inhibiting Anions"), potentially amplifying the effects of the pesticides on TH signaling and further compromising children's neurodevelopment.

As DDT and different OCs were shown to lose their effectiveness on insect populations and/or have detrimental effects on health or biodiversity, alternatives were sought, notably the OP class. Two recent papers linking prenatal pesticide exposure and autism or IQ loss to pesticides provide data on pesticide usage. Accordingly, OP usage represented about 20% of pesticide US usage in 1964 but rose to nearly 90% in 2000 (Shelton, Hertz-Picciotto, & Pessah, 2012). More specifically, about 27 OP chemicals are used in hundreds of different pesticide formulations in the United States with 1.6 million kg (1,600 metric tons) of OP pesticides used in California alone in 2008 and 10 times that figure used in the United States the previous year (see data cited in Bouchard et al., 2011). Yet OPs only represent 36% of insecticides used (Bouchard et al., 2011) and, in turn, insecticides represent less than one tenth of the volume of pesticides used annually (EPA market estimates, 1998–2007).

Many OPs act through inhibition of acetylcholinesterase (AChE), an enzyme that metabolizes the neurotransmitter acetylcholine (ACh). Given the role of Ach in neurotransmission during development and in many brain functions at all ages (e.g., learning, attention, and memory), it is not surprising that this class of pesticides has been suspected of contributing to increased incidence of autism spectrum disorders and attention-deficit/hyperactivity disorder. Disorders of cholinergic signaling have been correlated with autism spectrum disorder symptoms (Shelton et al., 2012). However, many animal studies have shown that OPs can exert neurotoxic effects at levels below those required for AChE inhibition.

One such study used prenatal and postnatal administration of chlorpyrifos, the most frequently used OP (Fortenberry, Hu, Turyk, Barr, & Meeker, 2012), with nearly 5 million kilos used in the United States per annum. For example, despite the fact that its main site of action is AChE inhibition, developmental exposure of mice to levels of chlorpyrifos that had no effect on AChE activity in mice adversely affected TH levels (De Angelis et al., 2009). Although in this study the levels of chlorpyrifos administered were above daily estimated intake from dietary sources in children, the authors argue that continued exposure could also lead to accumulation in humans. Another exposure factor could be airborne exposure (including dust). Three different groups have shown chlorpyrifos to affect TH signaling in animal models (see citations in Fortenberry et al., 2012). Moreover, the NHANES group data (Fortenberry et al., 2012) was used to examine the relationships between urinary levels of a chlorpyrifos metabolite and TH parameters. The authors found gender-specific significant associations with $T_4$ and TSH levels. TSH was positively associated with chlopyrifos exposure in women while a negative association was seen in men. In an other study, imaging was used to examine structures of different brain regions in children exposed in utero to chlorpyrifos. The children came from a community cohort where umbilical cord blood had been sampled 6–12 years previously. Those with the highest exposure showed enlargement of some structures, thinner frontal cortical layers, and modification of certain sex-specific brain structures (Rauh et al., 2012). Previous work on this cohort had revealed negative effects of exposure on cognition, notably working memory (Rauh et al., 2011). As the 2013 paper made reference to animal studies on chlorpyrifos that used higher levels than found in the exposure data, a representative of one company producing the pesticide thought it opportune to criticize this (Juberg, 2012). However, it is interesting to note that according to the EPA site,[12] in 2000 companies producing or using chlorpyrifos agreed with authorities to remove it from formulations of household pesticides (except ant and cockroach baits in "childproof" packaging). The reasons for this agreement are not clear but could well involve demonstrations of or disquiet concerning toxic effects on neurodevelopment and/or thyroid signaling. At the time of writing, the EU authorities are re-evaluating chlorpyrifos usage, one of the first cases in which an approved pesticide is being reviewed.

Other studies showing significant effects of OP concentrations on TH signaling bring into the equation an enzyme involved in metabolizing OPs, the paraoxanose 1 enzyme (PON1). In people with lower activities of PON1, and therefore lesser capacity to metabolize the pesticides, the effects of OPs on TH function were greater (Lacasana et al., 2010). Given these links between OP levels and TH signaling, it is relevant to note that a recent large-scale study showed that the most marked correlations of OP levels and children's intellectual development were seen with prenatal maternal urine levels as opposed to children's own postnatal urine levels (Bouchard et al., 2011). This finding yet again underlines the prenatal period of neurodevelopment as a particularly vulnerable window for chemical exposure.

## Ultraviolet Filters

Besides the most obvious uses in sunscreens, ultraviolet (UV) filters are also used in food to delay color loss. Although four UV filters show TH-disrupting effects in animal studies, there are as yet no epidemiological studies on whether these

12 http://www.epa.gov/oppsrrd1/REDs/factsheets/chlorpyrifos_fs.htm

chemicals affect TH signaling in humans. The absence of epidemiological data is all the more surprising given the high amounts that can be found in sunscreens (up to 10% wt) combined. Most have been investigated for their estrogenic properties, but three filters so far have been shown to have thyroid-modulating properties, Benzophenone 2 (BP2), 4-methylbeneylidene-camphor (4MBC) and octyl-methoxycinnimate (OMC), with the most marked effects for BP2 and OMC (Klammer et al., 2007; Schmutzler et al., 2004).

BP2 has been banned for use in sunscreens in Europe, but it is still used in a myriad of personal care products in the United States (http://household-products.nlm.nih.gov/cgi-bin/household/brands?tbl=chem&id=488), notably in perfumes, after shave lotions, and balms. In detailed in vitro and in vivo studies, Josef Köhrle's team in Berlin investigated the effects of four UV screens on the efficiency of human TPO activity and on circulating TH levels in rats (Schmutzler et al., 2007). Only BP2 inhibited human TPO activity, but in the absence of iodine, it did so with an efficiency one or two orders of magnitude greater that two well-known inhibitors of TPO, methimazole (MMI) and propylthiouracil (PTU). Not surprisingly, given the strength of the inhibitory response in vitro, the in vivo work showed that BP2 exposure dose-dependently reduced $T_4$, but not $T_3$ levels, and increased TSH values.

As yet no prospective associative studies on UV usage and TH status have been carried out in humans, although many studies have examined exposure levels. Janjua and collaborators (Janjua et al., 2004), studying transdermal exposure of sunscreens in human volunteers, showed that a 5-day usage of a 10% mixture of OMC, BP3, and 4-MBC (i.e., within the allowable limits established by European authorities) results in serum levels of 200 ng/ml BP3 and 20 and 10 ng/ml for 4-MBC and OMC, respectively. OMC has been shown in multiple animal studies to affect TH signaling at many levels, including dose-dependent decreases in circulating TH levels and increased expression of the TSH receptor in the thyroid within a 5-day exposure in rats (Klammer et al., 2007).

## Examples of Other Classes of Chemicals With Thyroid Hormone–Disrupting Actions: The Antimicrobials Triclosan and the Parabens

The generalized use of antimicrobial compounds in personal care products, soaps, deodorants, toothpaste, mouth washes, face and body creams, and cosmetics means that most human populations are widely exposed to parabens and/or triclosan on a regular basis. First introduced in the 1970s, they have gained in usage. It is difficult to find data on paraben production, but individual companies boast annual production capacities of over 2,500 tons. EU triclosan production today has been estimated to be around 1,000 tons and is thought to be a major contributing factor to the growing concern of antimicrobial resistance (http://ec.europa.eu/health/scientific_committees/consumer_safety/docs/sccs_o_023.pdf).

Kevin Crofton and collaborators were among the first to suggest and test whether triclosan (5-chloro-2-(2,4-dichlorophenoxy)phenol) might have

TH-disrupting properties on the basis of its structural similarity to TH (Crofton, Paul, Devito, & Hedge, 2007) (Fig. 5.9). At the same time, others were beginning to suspect similar actions of parabens (Janjua et al., 2007), prior to which there had been virtually no investigations of possible interactions, despite the fact that over 30 years ago there were isolated reports using in vitro methods that demonstrated antithyroid effects, for instance, that of one paraben, the methyl derivative (Rousset, 1981).

Parabens, alkyl esters of p-hydroxybenzoic acid, are not only found in skin care products but are also used in food to extend shelf life, as well as in certain pharmaceuticals. Human exposure can be through ingestion or inhalation, but skin care products are the main usage and probable principal exposure route. The length of the alkyl chain modifies water and oil solubility. Four different parabens are commonly used and can be found in human urine: ethyl paraben (EP), methyl paraben (MP), propyl paraben (PP), and butyl paraben (BP). According to the National Biomonitoring Program of the US Center for Disease Control and Prevention (CDC), the regulated limit for their inclusion in cosmetics or food products (jams, preserves, baked goods, etc.) is 0.8% for a paraben mixture and 0.4% for a single paraben. Most studies on parabens have examined effects on reproductive parameters, as animal studies have shown decreased testosterone levels and sperm counts following prenatal or perinatal exposure (Janjua et al., 2007). But parabens have also been suspected of TH-disrupting effects, and many animal studies have shown effects on thyroid

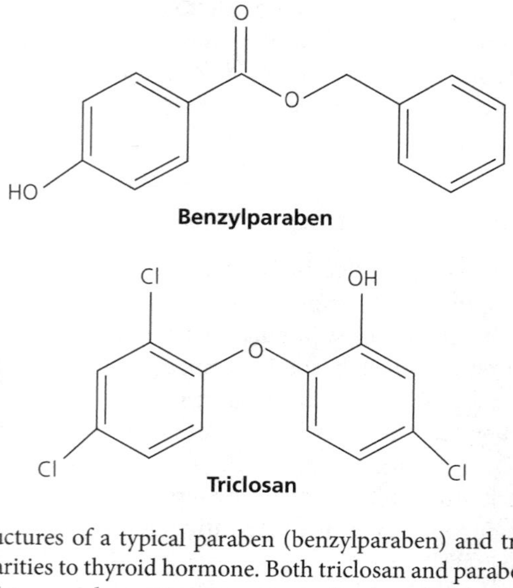

**Figure 5–9.** Structures of a typical paraben (benzylparaben) and triclosan, showing their overall similarities to thyroid hormone. Both triclosan and parabens are found in a variety of personal care products most at concentrations varying from 0.3% to up to 2%, as shown in the labels of toothpaste and deodorant.

gland function (Vo, Yoo, Choi, & Jeung, 2010), even if most of the research focus has been, and still is, on the effects on reproductive endocrinology.

A large population base involving both sexes and addressing thyroid function was used in a recent epidemiological study on antimicrobial levels in urine from the US National Health and Nutrition Examination Survey (NHANES). This study focused on thyroid parameters and associations with both paraben and triclosan concentrations in urine samples of 1,831 people aged 12 years or over (Koeppe, Ferguson, Colacino, & Meeker, 2013). Their analysis revealed that higher levels of both categories of chemicals were present in higher levels in girls and women, no doubt due to the greater feminine use of cosmetics and personal care products. In men and women, adolescents and adults, the highest values were for the parabens MP and PP, with mean values of MP in urine from women being six times that of men.

Triclosan values did not differ as much between groups. Lowest mean triclosan values were found in adolescent boys, where they were 12 μg/g creatine (a urinary marker used for standardisation), but one boy in the group had a level of over 500 μg/g creatine and the maximum level found in an adolescent girl was twice that at over 1,112 μg/g (1.1 mg/g) creatine. In adults, maximal levels were even higher at over 2 mg/g creatine for both men and women, mean levels being 13.5 and 19.9 μg/g in men and women, respectively. As to the parabens, highest concentrations were found for MP, mean levels being 26.9 and 151.4 μg/g creatine for men and women, respectively. PP levels were about an order of magnitude lower. In terms of effects on TH signaling, interestingly the data revealed a positive association of triclosan levels with $T_3$ values in adolescents, and negative associations with paraben products in adults, especially women (Koeppe et al., 2013). These results therefore bolster the data from animal studies, mostly amphibians and rodents, showing thyroid-disrupting effects of triclosan (Crofton et al., 2007; Helbing, Propper, & Veldhoen, 2011; Rodriguez & Sanchez, 2010), effects that are due (at least in rats) to increased hepatic metabolism of TH. However, a major research lack clearly remains: that of the insufficient data on parabens and TH function, especially as significant levels of parabens and UV filters are found alongside many other pollutants in human breast milk and that women are the primary users of cosmetics.

A final point is that these substances may be present in "alternative" cosmetics that do not even list them among the ingredients (Dodson et al., 2012), underlining a need for better regulations on product composition.

## Mercury

The history and epidemiology of mercury neurotoxicity were described in Chapter 1 and the main mechanisms by which it interferes with TH signaling, through inhibition of deiodinases in target tissues and glutathione peroxidases in the thyroid and other organs, in Chapter 3. The story of mercury contamination in Minamata provided yet another chilling example of how long it can take between demonstrations of developmental neurotoxicity and the inclusion of such data in risk analyses. To recapitulate briefly, mercury is found in three main forms in the environment: methyl mercury from industrial sources that accumulates in the food chain, notably through fish consumption; ethyl mercury that was used in certain vaccine formulations; and lastly, mercury amalgams used for dental fillings. Effects of mercury vapor from dental amalgam, either on dentists or on patients, have been a matter of vigorous debated for decades (Clarkson, 2002), but there is little evidence to suggest that maternal dental mercury can affect the developing brain of the fetus. The greater concern is methyl mercury contamination from food sources, most significantly marine fish.

The full extent of cellular and subcellular neurodevelopmental processes affected by mercury or methylmercury is not known. However, a recent review paper underlines the disquietingly numerous parallels between the effects of mercury on neuronal development and function and certain features of autism (Kern et al., 2012). The authors list and discuss the evidence showing no fewer than 20 processes to be affected or induced in both mercury exposure and autism, from microtubule degeneration, oxidative stress, and activation of inflammatory pathways through a variety of mechanisms.

Given the scope of TH actions on brain development, it is not surprising that most of these mechanisms are candidates for synergistic negative actions of TH disruption and mercury poisoning. Many epidemiological studies show general, TH-lowering effects of mercury exposure. One study examined associations of blood levels of PCBs, chlorinated pesticides, and mercury with circulating TH levels in pregnant women and in cord blood samples (Takser et al., 2005). All three categories showed independent and significant negative associations with maternal total $T_3$ levels, but it was only inorganic mercury levels that showed a negative association with levels of total $T_4$ in cord blood. As to effects of mercury on cellular actions of TH, suffice it to reiterate here that one of the main actions of mercury, at environmentally relevant doses (which despite the extensive nature of their review is not cited by Kern et al., 2012), is through its avid interaction with selenium and selenocysteine in the deiodinase enzymes. Mercury exposure in animal models has been shown to inhibit D3 activity in the fetal brain, potentially disrupting TH levels and interfering with sensitive windows of development and to inhibit D2 activity in cultured neuronal cell lines (Mori et al., 2006a, 2006b). Thus, mercury can affect not only production of TH but also its activation in target tissues. This fact alone places TH signaling at the center of considerations for analyzing the effects of (methyl)mercury neurotoxicity and its relationship with neurodevelopmental disorders such as autism and attention-deficit/hyperactivity disorder.

## Examples of Chemicals Interfering With the Thyroid Receptor Heterodimeric Partner, RXR: The Case of Tributyltin

Despite the fact that few chemicals actually bind to the small and selective ligand-binding pocket of the TRs, the heterodimeric partners of TRs, the RXRs have larger and more flexible ligand-binding domains that allow binding of a variety of molecules. One such molecule is the antifouling agent Tributyltin (TBT; le Maire et al., 2009). This organotin and some similar molecules have been used as paint additives in the marine environment since the 1960s to limit the growth of different organisms, such as barnacles, mussels, and algae on hulls of boats, fishing nets, and buoys. Hundreds of scientific papers have documented the off-target effects of TBT on the marine environment during the last 20 years. It was primarily because of its actions in causing imposex (changes of sex and hermaphrodism) in marine mollusks such as oysters that alerted authorities and users to its deleterious effects. In some coastal areas concentrations increased 100-fold between 1960 and 1980 and it is thought that steadily increasing levels of this contaminant were responsible for the collapse of the oyster industry in Arcachon, near Bordeaux, France (Ruiz, Bachelet, Caumette, & Donard, 1996), between 1977 and 1981. Its use was restricted gradually, with France banning its application on small boats as early as 1982, after the collapse of the oyster industry. Finally, the International Marine Organisation (IMO) requested a general ban that came into full effect in 2008 (Antizar-Ladislao, 2008). However, even if this ruling led to a significant decrease in the amounts of TBT accumulating in the environment, its use, or that of related molecules, continues in different guises, including in the paper and brewing industries (Antizar-Ladislao, 2008). Furthermore, given the facts, first, that the half-life in the environment can range from months in fresh water but can reach decades in sediments and, second, that it is rapidly taken up by plankton, where it enters the food chain and undergoes bioaccumulation, it is easy to appreciate consequences on the environment and human health.

Recent evidence has shown that through its actions on binding to RXR, TBT can affect PPARγ signaling, an initiating event in adipogenesis, the formation of fat tissue. It is for this reason that Bruce Blumberg applied the term "obesogen" (for its obesogen-promoting actions) to TBT (Kirchner, Kieu, Chow, Casey, & Blumberg, 2010). More disquieting, most recent work from Blumberg's team has shown that if mice are exposed to nM quantities of TBT throughout gestation, then the next three generations of mice show significantly increased amounts of white fat deposits as compared to control mice (Chamorro-Garcia et al., 2013). The European Food Safety Authority considers the tolerable daily intake (TDI) to be 0.1 µg/kg body weight if calculated on the base of tin or 0.27 µg/kg body weight if on the base of TBT salt. These values are in turn based on the published no observable adverse effect level (NOAEL) of 25 µg/kg body weight. The exposure regime used by Blumberg's group was between 2- and 50-fold lower than the NOAEL, and the lowest doses were in the same range as the TDI. One is prompted to question whether similar transgenerational effects are occurring in humans. If so, then the obesity epidemic and the fight against fat will be with us for some time yet.

TBT many not only be acting on adipogenesis through PPAR actions in the tissue itself; other mechanisms could implicate more general effects on metabolic control and set points established during development. Experiments in animal models have shown that TBT can also affect TH homeostasis. For instance, Adeeko et al. administered the organotin, TBT, to gestating mice and reported significantly reduced TH levels in the dams. The authors suggest that these reduced maternal TH levels could be related to marked effects of TBT exposure on pups' growth, with pups in the highest exposure group being 25% smaller that the controls (Adeeko et al., 2003). Notably, low birth weight (<2.5 kg) in humans has been related to a number of metabolic diseases, including obesity (Casey et al., 2012) and autism spectrum disorders (Lampi et al., 2012).

Other obesity-promoting mechanisms that affect TH signaling could implicate the fact that TBT binds to both to PPARγ and RXR, its heterodimeric partner (le Maire et al., 2009). In fact, TBT binds to PPARγ and RXR with high affinity, respectively, 20 and 5 nM, well superior to the affinity of natural ligands for the PPARγ receptor. Moreover, even though TBT does not bind to TRs, RXR isotypes are the heterodimeric partners for TRs, and significant molecular and physiological crosstalk takes place between PPARγ and TR signaling, both in the periphery and in the hypothalamus. Thus, the regulations co-governed by PPARγ and TR can be targets of TBT disruption. One example is newborn mice treated acutely with TBT that show altered $T_3$-dependent set points of hypothalamic *Trh*, the central controller of TH levels and general metabolism (Decherf & Demeneix, 2011; Decherf et al., 2010). Such obesogenic effects of TBT in the hypothalamus will exacerbate peripheral effects at the level of adipose tissue and could be implicated in the lower birth weight of pups born to TBT-exposed mothers.

Surprisingly, to date there are very few data on TBT exposure in human populations and, at the time of writing, no published analyses of associations with TH function in any age group, nor on neurodevelopmental outcome of children as a function of maternal exposure to organotins.

## Last but Not Least, Is a Natural Product, the Phytoestrogen Genistein, a Particular Risk for Soy-Fed Infants?

As already remarked in the section on "Perchlorate and Other Thyroid-Inhibiting Anions" on vegetables containing thiocyanates, not all thyroid-disrupting compounds are products of the chemical industry. Another plant product that interferes with TH production is the phytoestrogen genistein. Genistein has two well-documented thyroid-disrupting activities: TPO inhibition (Schmutzler et al., 2007) and displacement of TH from TTR (Radovic, Mentrup, & Köhrle, 2006). $T_4$ availability is consequently reduced by two mechanisms, decreased production and increased hepatic TH metabolism as a consequence of displacement from TTR.

Genistein is an isoflavone or flavonoid, belonging to the largest group of polyphenols that also includes resveratrol, which is found in red wine and much researched for its potential antiaging properties. Genistein and another isoflavone, daidzein, are referred to as phytoestrogens because of their estrogenic activity on vertebrate estrogen receptors. The evolution of phytoestrogen production is fascinating and is found notably in the nitrate fixing leguminous plants, such soy and red clover. The production of flavones by these plants and their associated bacteria, many of which possess some activity on estrogen receptors, must have conferred an evolutionary advantage to the plants to be so conserved. John McLachlan has published a well-argued discussion of the complex symbiotic mechanisms underlying their production and potential benefit to the plant (McLachlan, 2001) and of the potential epigenetic effects of estrogenic molecules on vertebrate organisms.

Most of the phytoestrogen activity of genistein and daidzein appears to be exerted through binding to the $ER\beta$ receptor. It is for this reason that phytoestrogen products are sold in different guises with marketing overwhelmingly directed at perimenopausal and postmenopausal women but also as a preventive measure for prostate and breast cancer and osteoporosis. Products are also publicized as a means of reducing intake of either cholesterol or lactose. In terms of TTR-TH-disrupting activity, daidzein is much less potent that genistein (Radovic et al., 2006), but in a study of iodine-sufficient rats, both compounds, given at 10 mg/kg body weight, were equipotent, significantly reducing circulating total $T_4$ levels by about 20% (Sosic-Jurjevic et al., 2010). Effects on total $T_3$ were lesser but still reached significance. TSH levels increased significantly with both isoflavones. Interestingly, the effects on TSH secretion were greatest in the rats receiving diadzein. These results, showing antithyroid effects of two common isoflavones, are in accordance with observations on human studies. Doerge and Sheehan (2002) in their discussion of the goitrogenic effects of genistein cite a series of cases where soy intake in humans was associated with either goiter or reductions in circulating TH levels.

Phytoestrogens are present in significant amounts in all soy products, as the raw soybean contains on average 60–80 g/100 g of each isoflavone, and a total isoflavone content of about 150 mg/100 g (US Department of Agriculture, USDA, 2008, http://www.ars.usda.gov/). Genistein is usually the main component of the isoflavones present. The amounts of isoflavones in sprouted beans are somewhat less, around 12 mg/100 g of each isoflavone, diadzein and genistein. Extracts of another plant, red clover, are also often sold as over-the-counter treatments for menopausal symptoms. Like soy, red clover contains equal proportions of diadzein and genistein, with 100 g of product totaling 20 mg of phytoestrogens.

Needless to say, soy products—whether soy milk, soy infant formula, or soy-derived products, such as tofu—contain high amounts of these phytoestrogens. Most pertinent to the subject discussed here are foodstuffs that will be fed to babies and children. The USDA tables provide data on genistein and daidzein content of three groups of infant formula, with the values for the powder and the reconstituted "ready to feed" mix. In all cases the content of genistein, the most potent TH disruptor, is double that of daidzein, with genistein values in formula and "ready to feed" being in the order of 12–14 mg/100 g and 1.5–2.5 mg/100 g, respectively. Soy milk contains between 2 and 5 mg/100g.

Many people in the general public think that there is no risk in feeding soy milk to babies and children because they consider that children from Asian countries where soy consumption is high (e.g., Japan) must be exposed through the mother's breast milk, and no adverse effects have been reported. However, this concept is unfounded. Breast milk of mothers eating soy contains far less phytoestrogen content than soy formula (Franke, Custer, & Tanaka, 1998). Setchell and collaborators compared the levels of isoflavones in human milk and soy formula. In accordance with the USDA data sets, they found soy formula to contain up to 47 mg/L, whereas levels in human breast milk were over 1,000-fold less, at 5 µg/L (Setchell, Zimmer-Nechemias, Cai, & Heubi, 1998). They and others have calculated that the amounts of genistein and daidzein consumed by infants on soy formula is between four and six times greater (on a body weight basis) than for an adult who is a regular consumer of soy products, especially given that infants show higher bioavailability of isoflavones (Franke et al., 1998; Setchell et al., 1998). Setchell and colleagues conclude their abstract by emphasizing that in infants fed on soy, the circulating levels of isoflavones are tens of thousands times higher than endogenous estrogens at the same developmental period. They then state that these levels "may have long-term health benefits for hormone dependent diseases." The explanation for this outrageously unfounded statement probably comes from the fact that Wyeth Laboratories, one of the producers of soy formula (USDA data), funded the research. And this is not by any means the only example. Despite this type of data and those on the goitrogenic effects of soy, many authors consider that the fact that between 20% and 25% of infant formula sold in the United States is soy based presents no health risk (see, for example, Badger et al., 2009). The paper cited refers to a 5-year study comparing growth statistics in children in Arkansas fed initially either breast milk, milk-based formula, or soy formula. However, the paper provides no actual data on children but provides data on piglets. It makes no mention of the risks to either thyroid function or to the need for iodine supplementation in the diet if fed soy. The fact that one of the authors on this paper is a member of the Scientific Advisory Board of the Soy Nutrition Institute may again help to explain why the abstract concludes with the ambiguous and unfounded statement that soy formula "*may* be even advantageous for bone growth."

Such irresponsible reporting of data may well be contributing to the increased used of soy-based infant formula, the long-term effects of which have yet to be established on general health and more particularly on reproductive health, TH status, and the overall consequences on behavior and/or mental health.

Take-Home Messages and Future Research Needs

- Given the large number of chemical categories with the capacity to disrupt thyroid signaling (Fig. 5.10) and the exposure of the general population to mixtures of these chemicals, it is urgent to obtain epidemiological data on chemical load and association with congenital

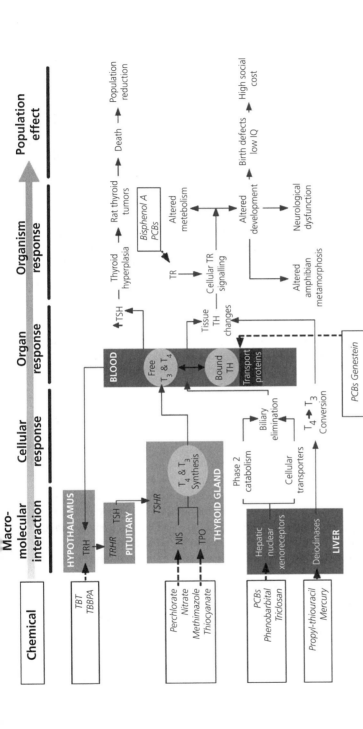

Figure 5–10. Major thyroid disruption pathways with a few examples of chemicals that can affect thyroid hormone (TH) signaling in humans and wildlife. (Modified from Crofton, 2008 and Perkins et al., 2013.) The numbers of chemicals that can affect each pathway are far greater than those indicated here and give some indication of disruption. In the center is placed the blood compartment. Blood levels of THs are often measured, as they are easy to obtain and give some indication of disruption. Major regulatory systems are indicated in shaded boxes and include hypothalamus, pituitary, liver, and blood, in which interactions between pollutants and molecules implicated in governing TH availability can occur (macro-molecular interactions). Note that deiodinases are also expressed in *all* target tissues, not only in the liver. Thus, effects of mercury on deiodinase activity will affect all tissues, including the brain. PCBs, polychlorinated biphenyls; TBT, Tributyl Tin; TBBPA, tetra-bromo-bisphenol A; TRH, TSH releasing hormone; TSH, thyroid-stimulating hormone.

hypothyroidism and neurodevelopmental outcome. Similarly, animal models need to be optimized to characterize the effects of mixtures and combinations of these chemicals on TH signaling and brain development.

- Few rigorous studies have addressed the effects of dioxin exposure during fetal or postnatal life on TH homeostasis and neurodevelopmental outcome. This lack of data could be well be related to the highly toxic nature of TCDD and the exposure risks that some experiments entail. Given the contention around the epidemiological data, and the persistence of TCDD in the environment, governments enable well-equipped laboratories to investigate these questions, not only for TCDD but also, as argued earlier, for other emergent and underevaluated TH-disrupting compounds.

- Despite the ban on manufacturing of PCBs in the last decades of the 20th century, and the ban on most PDBEs between 2004 and 2010, significant levels of both chemical categories are still found in the environment, echoing the continuing presence of DDT and its metabolite DDE. Many studies show that PCBs decrease circulating TH in humans during development and in adults. This effect can involve direct action on the thyroid gland and/or indirect action through hepatic metabolism, either increasing degradation and excretion of THs and/or production of TR active metabolites. The same is true of the PBDEs, and it is likely to be the case for so many of these halogen-substituted phenyls that are designed to be heat resistant without any concern for biodegradability and are brought onto the market with only limited data on their potential endocrine-disrupting properties.

- International efforts are required to investigate, in a standardized manner (same matrices, developmental stages, and chemicals studied) in longitudinal studies, the associations between EDC burden and TH status in mothers and newborns and the neurodevelopmental outcome of the children. In particular, more data are needed on the recently introduced BFRs, such as TBBPA, as well as on high-production pesticides. The principal chemical culprits need to be removed from the market and replaced with validated, biodegradable alternatives. In the case of flame retardants, the requirements for stringent flammability controls need to be revisited in a "risk-benefit" analysis. Many authors have argued that the ever-increasing use of BFRs, and their chlorinated equivalents, is causing adverse health effects with potentially enormous adverse socioeconomic impacts that are largely outweighing the advantages.

- One area that shows a most surprising lack of basic research and mechanistic investigation is the effect of phthalates on TH production, metabolism, and action. It seems the intense focus on phthalates on male reproductive health has almost totally eclipsed potential effects in girls and women and effects on thyroid hormone and neurodevelopment and behavior.

## Postscript

Currently, 84,000 chemicals are on the US EPA Toxic Substances Control Act (TSCA) inventory. This list covers substances authorized for manufacture or import in the United States at levels above 10 tons. This TSCA list does not include substances covered by other legislations, such as pesticides, foodstuffs, and food additives and cosmetics. One can wonder how so many compounds that have later proven to persist in the environment and/or to be detrimental to wildlife and human health have been ratified for widespread use. Next are summarized the procedures for marketing or importing chemicals in the United States or in the European Union. Simply put, in the United States one can put a substance on the market in 3 months, and it can take more than 30 years to take it off, as many examples in this chapter sadly illustrate.

### Getting a Chemical on the Market in the United States

The procedure for marketing a new chemical in the United States is described on the EPA's Web site (http://www.epa.gov/How Are Chemicals Added to the TSCA Inventory). Succinctly, in the United States, a first step for a company to manufacture or import a new chemical is to address a premanufacturing notice (PMN) to the EPA. The EPA has to review the PMN and reply to the company within 90 days. To cite the EPA Web site:[13] "Because many PMNs include little or no toxicity or fate data, the program uses several risk screening approaches to facilitate assessment in the absence of specific data. This enables rapid evaluation of potential risks and making risk-management decisions for the new chemicals within the 90-day time frame prescribed by TSCA".

If the EPA considers that there is a risk to health or the environment, or insufficient information to ascertain risk to health or the environment, they will issue a special order to prohibit or limit production. Over 90% of PMNs are accepted without modification, that is, without suggestion of restriction or regulation. The EPA receives about 1,000 PMNs per annum, so about 900 new chemicals are ratified for production or import each year. If the chemical is only to be produced or imported at low volume, less than 10,000 kg (10 metric tons) per year, then it is exempt from the registration process.

After obtaining a favorable response to the PMN, the company has 30 days from the start of manufacture or import to inform the EPA of commencement with a "Notification of Commencement of Manufacture or Import."

13 Last consulted in September 2013.

Getting a Chemical on the Market in the European Union

The European Union brought in the Registration, Evaluation, Authorisation and Restriction of Chemicals (REACH) regulations in 2007.[14] The European Chemical Agency is responsible for registration, which is currently undergoing a staggered process: companies had until November 2010 to register substances manufactured or imported at amounts equal to or above 1,000 tons per year. This limit was lowered to 1 ton per year for any substance that was carcinogenic, mutagenic, or toxic to reproduction. For substances known to be dangerous to aquatic organisms or the environment, the limit for exclusion from the need for registration was set at 100 tons per year.

As of May 2013, all substances manufactured or imported within the range of 100–1,000 tons per year need to be registered, and by May 2018 those within the 1–100 tons per year range must also be included.

The REACH procedure is more stringent than that of the EPA, and submission requires information on substance identity, physicochemical properties, mammalian toxicity, ecotoxicity, environmental fate (including abiotic and biotic degradation), and details of manufacture process and uses. Finally, risk management measures should be described.

A number of interested parties and stakeholders have criticized the REACH program. Certain governments said it would hamper trade while persons concerned with animal rights said that it would engender overuse of animal experimentation. Not surprisingly, some representatives of the chemical industry said it would be too costly and blunt their competitive edge. However, the European Union asked an independent accounting firm to estimate the cost to the Chemical Industry of applying REACH. They calculated that over 11 years the cost would be in the range of 2.3 billion €, actually less than 0.05% of the total turnover of the Chemical Industry for the same period.[15] In contrast, the estimated prospective savings in health care for the European Union were 50 billion € over 30 years.

## REFERENCES

Adeeko, A., Li, D., Forsyth, D. S., Casey, V., Cooke, G. M., Barthelemy, J.,...Hales, B. F. (2003). Effects of in utero tributyltin chloride exposure in the rat on pregnancy outcome. *Toxicological Sciences, 74*(2), 407–415.
Ahmed, R. G. (2011). Perinatal TCDD exposure alters developmental neuroendocrine system. *Food Chemical Toxicology, 49*(6), 1276–1284.
Alvarez-Pedrerol, M., Guxens, M., Ibarluzea, J., Rebagliato, M., Rodriguez, A., Espada, M.,...Sunyer, J. (2009). Organochlorine compounds, iodine intake, and thyroid

14 http://ec.europa.eu/enterprise/sectors/chemicals/reach/index_en.htm.
15 According to the French financial newspaper *Les Echos* in 2005, the EU Chemical Industry (grouped under CEFIC) had a total turnover of 615 billion €.

hormone levels during pregnancy. *Environmental Science and Technology, 43*(20), 7909–7915.

Alvarez-Pedrerol, M., Ribas-Fitó, N., Torrent, M., Carrizo, D., Garcia-Esteban, R., Grimalt, J. O., & Sunyer, J. (2008). Thyroid disruption at birth due to prenatal exposure to beta-hexachlorocyclohexane. *Environment International, 34*(6), 737–740.

Andersen, C. S., Fei, C., Gamborg, M., Nohr, E. A., Sørensen, T. I., & Olsen, J. (2010). Prenatal exposures to perfluorinated chemicals and anthropometric measures in infancy. *American Journal of Epidemiology, 172*(11), 1230–1237.

Antizar-Ladislao, B. (2008). Environmental levels, toxicity and human exposure to tributyltin (TBT)-contaminated marine environment. A review. *Environment International, 34*(2), 292–308.

Baccarelli, A., Giacomini, S. M., Corbetta, C., Landi, M. T., Bonzini, M., Consonni, D., ... Bertazzi, P. A. (2008). Neonatal thyroid function in Seveso 25 years after maternal exposure to dioxin. *PLoS Medicine, 5*(7), e161.

Badger, T. M., Gilchrist, J. M., Pivik, R. T., Andres, A., Shankar, K., Chen, J. R., & Ronis, M. J. (2009). The health implications of soy infant formula. *American Journal of Clinical Nutrition, 89*(5), 1668S–1672S.

Balazs, C., Morello-Frosch, R., Hubbard, A., & Ray, I. (2011). Social disparities in nitrate contaminated drinking water in California's San Joaquin Valley. *Environmental Health Perspectives*, ePub ahead of print.

Banasik, M., Hardy, M., Harbison, R. D., Hsu, C. H., & Stedeford, T. (2009). Tetrabromobisphenol A and model-derived risks for reproductive toxicity. *Toxicology, 260*(1–3), 150–152; author reply 153–154.

Barouki, R., Aggerbeck, M., Aggerbeck, L., & Coumoul, X. (2012). The aryl hydrocarbon receptor system. *Drug Metabolism and Drug Interactions, 27*(1), 3–8.

Barouki, R., Gluckman, P. D., Grandjean, P., Hanson, M., & Heindel, J. J. (2012). Developmental origins of non-communicable disease: Implications for research and public health. *Environmental Health, 11*, 42.

Beaulieu, A., & Fessele, K. (2003). Agent Orange: Management of patients exposed in Vietnam. *Clinical Journal of Oncology Nursing, 7*(3), 320–323.

Bertazzi, P. A., Bernucci, I., Brambilla, G., Consonni, D., & Pesatori, A. C. (1998). The Seveso studies on early and long-term effects of dioxin exposure: A review. *Environmental Health Perspectives, 106*(Suppl 2), 625–633.

Birnbaum, L. S., & Cohen Hubal, E. A. (2006). Polybrominated diphenyl ethers: A case study for using biomonitoring data to address risk assessment questions. *Environmental Health Perspectives, 114*(11), 1770–1775.

Bloom, M. S., Kannan, K., Spliethoff, H. M., Tao, L., Aldous, K. M., & Vena, J. E. (2010). Exploratory assessment of perfluorinated compounds and human thyroid function. *Physiology and Behavior, 99*(2), 240–245.

Blount, B. C., Pirkle, J. L., Osterloh, J. D., Valentin-Blasini, L., & Caldwell, K. L. (2006). Urinary perchlorate and thyroid hormone levels in adolescent and adult men and women living in the United States. *Environmental Health Perspectives, 114*(12), 1865–1871.

Blount, B. C., Valentin-Blasini, L., Osterloh, J. D., Mauldin, J. P., & Pirkle, J. L. (2007). Perchlorate exposure of the US Population, 2001–2002. *Journal of Exposure Science and Environmental Epidemiology, 17*(4), 400–407.

Boas, M., Feldt-Rasmussen, U., & Main, K. M. (2012). Thyroid effects of endocrine disrupting chemicals. *Molecular and Cellular Endocrinology, 355*(2), 240–248.

Boas, M., Frederiksen, H., Feldt-Rasmussen, U., Skakkebæk, N. E., Hegedüs, L., Hilsted, L., . . . Main, K. M. (2010). Childhood exposure to phthalates: Associations with thyroid function, insulin-like growth factor I, and growth. *Environmental Health Perspectives, 118*(10), 1458–1464.

Bouchard, M. F., Chevrier, J., Harley, K. G., Kogut, K., Vedar, M., Calderon, N., . . . Eskenazi, B. (2011). Prenatal exposure to organophosphate pesticides and IQ in 7-year-old children. *Environmental Health Perspectives, 119*(8), 1189–1195.

Breivik, K., Sweetman, A., Pacyna, J. M., & Jones, K. C. (2007). Towards a global historical emission inventory for selected PCB congeners--a mass balance approach 3. An update. *Science of the Total Environment, 377*(2–3), 296–307.

Brucker-Davis, F. (1998). Effects of environmental synthetic chemicals on thyroid function. *Thyroid, 8*(9), 827–856.

Cao, Y., Blount, B. C., Valentin-Blasini, L., Bernbaum, J. C., Phillips, T. M., & Rogan, W. J. (2010). Goitrogenic anions, thyroid-stimulating hormone, and thyroid hormone in infants. *Environmental Health Perspectives, 118*(9), 1332–1337.

Carignan, C. C., McClean, M. D., Cooper, E. M., Watkins, D. J., Fraser, A. J., Heiger-Bernays, W., . . . Webster, T. F. (2013). Predictors of tris(1,3-dichloro-2-propyl) phosphate metabolite in the urine of office workers. *Environment International, 55*, 56–61.

Carson, R. (1962). *Silent spring.* New York, NY: Houghton Mifflin.

Casey, P. H., Bradley, R. H., Whiteside-Mansell, L., Barrett, K., Gossett, J. M., & Simpson, P. M. (2012). Evolution of obesity in a low birth weight cohort. *Journal of Perinatology, 32*(2), 91–96.

Chamorro-Garcia, R., Sahu, M., Abbey, R. J., Laude, J., Pham, N., & Blumberg, B. (2013). Transgenerational inheritance of increased fat depot size, stem cell reprogramming, and hepatic steatosis elicited by prenatal exposure to the obesogen tributyltin in mice. *Environmental Health Perspectives, 121*(3), 359–366.

Chevrier, J., Eskenazi, B., Bradman, A., Fenster, L., & Barr, D. B. (2007). Associations between prenatal exposure to polychlorinated biphenyls and neonatal thyroid-stimulating hormone levels in a Mexican-American population, Salinas Valley, California. *Environmental Health Perspectives, 115*(10), 1490–1496.

Chevrier, J., Eskenazi, B., Holland, N., Bradman, A., & Barr, D. B. (2008). Effects of exposure to polychlorinated biphenyls and organochlorine pesticides on thyroid function during pregnancy. *American Journal of Epidemiology, 168*(3), 298–310.

Chevrier, J., Gunier, R. B., Bradman, A., Holland, N. T., Calafat, A. M., Eskenazi, B., & Harley, K. G. (2013). Maternal urinary bisphenol a during pregnancy and maternal and neonatal thyroid function in the CHAMACOS study. *Environmental Health Perspectives, 121*(1), 138–144.

Clarkson, T. W. (2002). The three modern faces of mercury. *Environmental Health Perspectives, 110*(Suppl 1), 11–23.

Colborn, T. (2004). Neurodevelopment and endocrine disruption. *Environmental Health Perspectives, 112*(9), 944–949.

Collins, W. T., Jr., Capen, C. C., Kasza, L., Carter, C., & Dailey, R. E. (1977). Effect of polychlorinated biphenyl (PCB) on the thyroid gland of rats. Ultrastructural and biochemical investigations. *American Journal of Pathology, 89*(1), 119–136.

Croes, K., Colles, A., Koppen, G., Govarts, E., Bruckers, L., Van de Mieroop, E., . . . Baeyens, W. (2012). Persistent organic pollutants (POPs) in human milk: A biomonitoring study in rural areas of Flanders (Belgium). *Chemosphere, 89*(8), 988–994.

Crofton, K. M. (2008). Thyroid disrupting chemicals: mechanisms and mixtures. *International Journal of Andrology, 31*(2), 209–223.

Crofton, K. M., Paul, K. B., Devito, M. J., & Hedge, J. M. (2007). Short-term in vivo exposure to the water contaminant triclosan: Evidence for disruption of thyroxine. *Environmental Toxicology and Pharmacology, 24*(2), 194–197.

Darnerud, P. O. (2003). Toxic effects of brominated flame retardants in man and in wildlife. *Environment International, 29*(6), 841–853.

De Angelis, S., Tassinari, R., Maranghi, F., Eusepi, A., Di Virgilio, A., Chiarotti, F., . . . Mantovani, A. (2009). Developmental exposure to chlorpyrifos induces alterations in thyroid and thyroid hormone levels without other toxicity signs in CD-1 mice. *Toxicological Sciences, 108*(2), 311–319.

De Groef, B., Decallonne, B. R., Van der Geyten, S., Darras, V. M., & Bouillon, R. (2006). Perchlorate versus other environmental sodium/iodide symporter inhibitors: Potential thyroid-related health effects. *European Journal of Endocrinology, 155*(1), 17–25.

Decherf, S., & Demeneix, B. A. (2011). The obesogen hypothesis: A shift of focus from the periphery to the hypothalamus. *Journal of Toxicology and Environmental Health B: Critical Reviews, 14*(5–7), 423–448.

Decherf, S., Seugnet, I., Fini, J. B., Clerget-Froidevaux, M. S., & Demeneix, B. A. (2010). Disruption of thyroid hormone-dependent hypothalamic set-points by environmental contaminants. *Molecular and Cellular Endocrinology, 323*(2), 172–182.

Diamond, M. L., Melymuk, L., Csiszar, S. A., & Robson, M. (2010). Estimation of PCB stocks, emissions, and urban fate: Will our policies reduce concentrations and exposure? *Environmental Science and Technology, 44*(8), 2777–2783.

Dingemans, M. M., van den Berg, M., & Westerink, R. H. (2011). Neurotoxicity of brominated flame retardants: (In)direct effects of parent and hydroxylated polybrominated diphenyl ethers on the (developing) nervous system. *Environmental Health Perspectives, 119*(7), 900–907.

Dodson, R. E., Nishioka, M., Standley, L. J., Perovich, L. J., Brody, J. G., & Rudel, R. A. (2012). Endocrine disruptors and asthma-associated chemicals in consumer products. *Environmental Health Perspectives, 120*(7), 935–943.

Doerge, D. R., & Sheehan, D. M. (2002). Goitrogenic and estrogenic activity of soy isoflavones. *Environmental Health Perspectives, 110*(Suppl 3), 349–353.

Dreyer, A., Weinberg, I., Temme, C., & Ebinghaus, R. (2009). Polyfluorinated compounds in the atmosphere of the Atlantic and Southern Oceans: Evidence for a global distribution. *Environmental Science and Technology, 43*(17), 6507–6514.

Eskenazi, B., Rosas, L. G., Marks, A. R., Bradman, A., Harley, K., Holland, N., . . . Barr, D. B. (2008). Pesticide toxicity and the developing brain. *Basic and Clinical Pharmacology and Toxicology, 102*(2), 228–236.

Eskenazi, B., Chevrier, J., Rauch, S. A., Kogut, K. Harley, K. G. Johnson, C., . . . Bradman, A. (2013) In utero and childhood polybrominated diphenyl ether (PBDE) exposures and neurodevelopment in the CHAMACOS study. *Environ Health Perspect, 121*(2), 257–262.

Farhat, A., Crump, D., Chiu, S., Williams, K. L., Letcher, R. J., Gauthier, L. T., & Kennedy, S. W. (2013). In ovo effects of two organophosphate flame retardants, TCPP and TDCPP, on pipping success, development, mRNA expression and thyroid hormone levels in chicken embryos. *Toxicological Sciences, 134*(1), 92–102.

Fernandez, M., Paradisi, M., D'Intino, G., Del Vecchio, G., Sivilia, S., Giardino, L., & Calzà, L. (2010). A single prenatal exposure to the endocrine disruptor 2,3,7,8-tet rachlorodibenzo-p-dioxin alters developmental myelination and remyelination potential in the rat brain. *Journal of Neurochemistry, 115*(4), 897–909.

Fini, J. B., Le Mével, S., Palmier, K., Darras, V. M., Punzon, I., Richardson, S. J.,...Demeneix, B. A. (2012). Thyroid hormone signaling in the Xenopus laevis embryo is functional and susceptible to endocrine disruption. *Endocrinology, 153*(10), 5068–5081.

Fini, J. B., Riu, A., Debrauwer, L., Hillenweck, A., Le Mével, S., Chevolleau, S.,...Zalko, D. (2012). Parallel biotransformation of tetrabromobisphenol A in Xenopus laevis and mammals: Xenopus as a model for endocrine perturbation studies. *Toxicological Sciences, 125*(2), 359–367.

Fisher, J. S. (2004). Environmental anti-androgens and male reproductive health: Focus on phthalates and testicular dysgenesis syndrome. *Reproduction, 127*(3), 305–315.

Fortenberry, G. Z., Hu, H., Turyk, M., Barr, D. B., & Meeker, J. D. (2012). Association between urinary 3, 5, 6-trichloro-2-pyridinol, a metabolite of chlorpyrifos and chlorpyrifos-methyl, and serum T4 and TSH in NHANES 1999–2002. *Science of the Total Environment, 424*, 351–355.

Franke, A. A., Custer, L. J., & Tanaka, Y. (1998). Isoflavones in human breast milk and other biological fluids. *American Journal of Clinical Nutrition, 68*(6 Suppl), 1466S–1473S.

Gauger, K. J., Giera, S., Sharlin, D. S., Bansal, R., Iannacone, E., & Zoeller, R. T. (2007). Polychlorinated biphenyls 105 and 118 form thyroid hormone receptor agonists after cytochrome P4501A1 activation in rat pituitary GH3 cells. *Environmental Health Perspectives, 115*(11), 1623–1630.

Gauger, K. J., Kato, Y., Haraguchi, K., Lehmler, H. J., Robertson, L. W., Bansal, R., & Zoeller, R. T. (2004). Polychlorinated biphenyls (PCBs) exert thyroid hormone-like effects in the fetal rat brain but do not bind to thyroid hormone receptors. *Environmental Health Perspectives, 112*(5), 516–523.

Ghisari, M., & Bonefeld-Jorgensen, E. C. (2009). Effects of plasticizers and their mixtures on estrogen receptor and thyroid hormone functions. *Toxicology Letters, 189*(1), 67–77.

Gold, M. D., Blum, A., & Ames, B. N. (1978). Another flame retardant, tris-(1,3-dic hloro-2-propyl)-phosphate, and its expected metabolites are mutagens. *Science, 200*(4343), 785–787.

Goldner, W. S., Sandler, D. P., Yu, F., Hoppin, J. A., Kamel, F., & Levan, T. D. (2010). Pesticide use and thyroid disease among women in the Agricultural Health Study. *American Journal of Epidemiology, 171*(4), 455–464.

Goodman, J. E., Kerper, L. E., Boyce, C. P., Prueitt, R. L., & Rhomberg, L. R. (2010). Weight-of-evidence analysis of human exposures to dioxins and dioxin-like compounds and associations with thyroid hormone levels during early development. *Regulatory Toxicology and Pharmacology, 58*(1), 79–99.

Graham, P. R. (1973). Phthalate ester plasticizers--why and how they are used. *Environmental Health Perspectives, 3*, 3–12.

Guvenius, D. M., Aronsson, A., Ekman-Ordeberg, G., Bergman, A., & Norén, K. (2003). Human prenatal and postnatal exposure to polybrominated diphenyl ethers, polychlorinated biphenyls, polychlorobiphenylols, and pentachlorophenol. *Environmental Health Perspectives, 111*(9), 1235–1241.

Hagmar, L. (2003). Polychlorinated biphenyls and thyroid status in humans: A review. *Thyroid, 13*(11), 1021–1028.

Hakk, H., & Letcher, R. J. (2003). Metabolism in the toxicokinetics and fate of brominated flame retardants--a review. *Environment International, 29*(6), 801–828.

Halden, R. U. (2010). Plastics and health risks. *Annual Review of Public Health, 31,* 179–194.

Hanrahan, L. P., Falk, C., Anderson, H. A., Draheim, L., Kanarek, M. S., & Olson, J. (1999). Serum PCB and DDE levels of frequent Great Lakes sport fish consumers-a first look. The Great Lakes Consortium. *Environmental Research, 80*(2 Pt 2), S26–S37.

Helbing, C. C., Propper, C. R., & Veldhoen, N. (2011). Triclosan affects the thyroid axis of amphibians. *Toxicological Sciences, 123*(2), 601–2; author reply 603–605.

Herbstman, J. B., Sjödin, A., Apelberg, B. J., Witter, F. R., Halden, R. U., Patterson, D. G.,...Goldman, L. R. (2008). Birth delivery mode modifies the associations between prenatal polychlorinated biphenyl (PCB) and polybrominated diphenyl ether (PBDE) and neonatal thyroid hormone levels. *Environmental Health Perspectives, 116*(10), 1376–1382.

Herbstman, J. B., Sjödin, A., Kurzon, M., Lederman, S. A., Jones, R. S., Rauh, V.,...Perera, F. (2010). Prenatal exposure to PBDEs and neurodevelopment. *Environmental Health Perspectives, 118*(5), 712–719.

Hines, E. P., Calafat, A. M., Silva, M. J., Mendola, P., & Fenton, S. E. (2009). Concentrations of phthalate metabolites in milk, urine, saliva, and serum of lactating North Carolina women. *Environmental Health Perspectives, 117*(1), 86–92.

Hites, R. A. (2011). Dioxins: An overview and history. *Environmental Science and Technology, 45*(1), 16–20.

Howarth, J. A., Price, S. C., Dobrota, M., Kentish, P. A., & Hinton, R. H. (2001). Effects on male rats of di-(2-ethylhexyl) phthalate and di-n-hexylphthalate administered alone or in combination. *Toxicology Letters, 121*(1), 35–43.

Howdeshell, K. L. (2002). A model of the development of the brain as a construct of the thyroid system. *Environmental Health Perspectives, 110*(Suppl 3), 337–348.

Hu, G. X., Lian, Q. Q., Ge, R. S., Hardy, D. O., & Li, X. K. (2009). Phthalate-induced testicular dysgenesis syndrome: Leydig cell influence. *Trends in Endocrinology and Metabolism, 20*(3), 139–145.

Hu, X., Shi, W., Zhang, F., Cao, F., Hu, G., Hao, Y.,...Yu, H. (2013). In vitro assessment of thyroid hormone disrupting activities in drinking water sources along the Yangtze River. *Environmental Pollution, 173,* 210–215.

Huang, P. C., Kuo, P. L., Guo, Y. L., Liao, P. C., & Lee, C. C. (2007). Associations between urinary phthalate monoesters and thyroid hormones in pregnant women. *Human Reproduction, 22*(10), 2715–2722.

Huisman, M., Koopman-Esseboom, C., Fidler, V., Hadders-Algra, M., van der Paauw, C. G., Tuinstra, L. G.,...Boersma, E. R. (1995a). Perinatal exposure to polychlorinated biphenyls and dioxins and its effect on neonatal neurological development. *Early Human Development, 41*(2), 111–127.

Huisman, M., Koopman-Esseboom, C., Lanting, C. I., van der Paauw, C. G., Tuinstra, L. G., Fidler, V.,...Touwen, B. C. (1995b). Neurological condition in 18-month-old children perinatally exposed to polychlorinated biphenyls and dioxins. *Early Human Development, 43*(2), 165–176.

Humphrey, H. E., Gardiner, J. C., Pandya, J. R., Sweeney, A. M., Gasior, D. M., McCaffrey, R. J., & Schantz, S. L. (2000). PCB congener profile in the serum of humans consuming Great Lakes fish. *Environmental Health Perspectives*, *108*(2), 167–172.

Ibhazehiebo, K., Iwasaki, T., Kimura-Kuroda, J., Miyazaki, W., Shimokawa, N., & Koibuchi, N. (2011). Disruption of thyroid hormone receptor-mediated transcription and thyroid hormone-induced Purkinje cell dendrite arborization by polybrominated diphenyl ethers. *Environmental Health Perspectives*, *119*(2), 168–175.

Ibhazehiebo, K., Iwasaki, T., Shimokawa, N., & Koibuchi, N. (2011). 1,2,5,6,9,10-alph aHexabromocyclododecane (HBCD) impairs thyroid hormone-induced dendrite arborization of Purkinje cells and suppresses thyroid hormone receptor-mediated transcription. *Cerebellum*, *10*(1), 22–31.

Inoue, K., Harada, K., Takenaka, K., Uehara, S., Kono, M., Shimizu, T., . . . Koizumi, A. (2006). Levels and concentration ratios of polychlorinated biphenyls and polybrominated diphenyl ethers in serum and breast milk in Japanese mothers. *Environmental Health Perspectives*, *114*(8), 1179–1185.

Janjua, N. R., Mogensen, B., Andersson, A. M., Petersen, J. H., Henriksen, M., Skakkebaek, N. E., & Wulf, H. C. (2004). Systemic absorption of the sunscreens benzophenone-3, octyl-methoxycinnamate, and 3-(4-methyl-benzylidene) camphor after whole-body topical application and reproductive hormone levels in humans. *Journal of Investigative Dermatology*, *123*(1), 57–61.

Janjua, N. R., Mortensen, G. K., Andersson, A. M., Kongshoj, B., Skakkebaek, N. E., & Wulf, H. C. (2007). Systemic uptake of diethyl phthalate, dibutyl phthalate, and butyl paraben following whole-body topical application and reproductive and thyroid hormone levels in humans. *Environmental Science and Technology*, *41*(15), 5564–5570.

Jensen, M. S., Nørgaard-Pedersen, B., Toft, G., Hougaard, D. M., Bonde, J. P., Cohen, A., . . . Jönsson, B. A. (2012). Phthalates and perfluorooctanesulfonic acid in human amniotic fluid: Temporal trends and timing of amniocentesis in pregnancy. *Environmental Health Perspectives*, *120*(6), 897–903.

Ji, K., Kim, S., Kho, Y., Paek, D., Sakong, J., Ha, J., . . . Choi, K. (2012). Serum concentrations of major perfluorinated compounds among the general population in Korea: Dietary sources and potential impact on thyroid hormones. *Environment International*, *45*, 78–85.

Jobling, M. S., Hutchison, G. R., van den Driesche, S., & Sharpe, R. M. (2011). Effects of di(n-butyl) phthalate exposure on foetal rat germ-cell number and differentiation: Identification of age-specific windows of vulnerability. *International Journal of Andrology*, *34*(5 Pt 2), e386–e396.

Juberg, D. R. (2012). Differentiating experimental animal doses from human exposures to chlorpyrifos. *Proceedings of the National Academy of Science USA*, *109*(33), E2195; author reply E2196.

Kalantzi, O. I., Martin, F. L., Thomas, G. O., Alcock, R. E., Tang, H. R., Drury, S. C., . . . Jones, K. C. (2004). Different levels of polybrominated diphenyl ethers (PBDEs) and chlorinated compounds in breast milk from two U.K. Regions. *Environmental Health Perspectives*, *112*(10), 1085–1091.

Karrman, A., Ericson, I., van Bavel, B., Darnerud, P. O., Aune, M., Glynn, A., . . . Lindström, G. (2007). Exposure of perfluorinated chemicals through lactation: Levels of matched human milk and serum and a temporal trend, 1996–2004, in Sweden. *Environmental Health Perspectives*, *115*(2), 226–230.

Kato, Y., Ikushiro, S., Haraguchi, K., Yamazaki, T., Ito, Y., Suzuki, H., & Degawa, M. (2004). A possible mechanism for decrease in serum thyroxine level by polychlorinated biphenyls in Wistar and Gunn rats. *Toxicological Sciences, 81*(2), 309–315.

Kawashiro, Y., Fukata, H., Omori-Inoue, M., Kubonoya, K., Jotaki, T., Takigami, H.,...Mori, C. (2008). Perinatal exposure to brominated flame retardants and polychlorinated biphenyls in Japan. *Endocrine Journal, 55*(6), 1071–1084.

Kern, J. K., Geier, D. A., Audhya, T., King, P. G., Sykes, L. K., & Geier, M. R. (2012). Evidence of parallels between mercury intoxication and the brain pathology in autism. *Acta Neurobiologica Experia (Wars), 72*(2), 113–153.

Kim, S., Choi, K., Ji, K., Seo, J., Kho, Y., Park, J.,...Giesy, J. P. (2011). Trans-placental transfer of thirteen perfluorinated compounds and relations with fetal thyroid hormones. *Environmental Science and Technology, 45*(17), 7465–7472.

Kim, Y., Ha, E. H., Kim, E. J., Park, H., Ha, M., Kim, J. H.,...Kim, B. N. (2011). Prenatal exposure to phthalates and infant development at 6 months: Prospective Mothers and Children's Environmental Health (MOCEH) study. *Environmental Health Perspectives, 119*(10), 1495–1500.

Kirchner, S., Kieu, T., Chow, C., Casey, S., & Blumberg, B. (2010). Prenatal exposure to the environmental obesogen tributyltin predisposes multipotent stem cells to become adipocytes. *Molecular Endocrinology, 24*(3), 526–539.

Kitamura, S., Jinno, N., Ohta, S., Kuroki, H., & Fujimoto, N. (2002). Thyroid hormonal activity of the flame retardants tetrabromobisphenol A and tetrachlorobisphenol A. *Biochemical and Biophysical Research Communications, 293*(1), 554–559.

Klammer, H., Schlecht, C., Wuttke, W., Schmutzler, C., Gotthardt, I., Köhrle, J., & Jarry, H. (2007). Effects of a 5-day treatment with the UV-filter octyl-methoxycinnamate (OMC) on the function of the hypothalamo-pituitary-thyroid function in rats. *Toxicology, 238*(2–3), 192–199.

Koch, H. M., Rossbach, B., Drexler, H., & Angerer, J. (2003). Internal exposure of the general population to DEHP and other phthalates--determination of secondary and primary phthalate monoester metabolites in urine. *Environmental Research, 93*(2), 177–185.

Koeppe, E. S., Ferguson, K. K., Colacino, J. A., & Meeker, J. D. (2013). Relationship between urinary triclosan and paraben concentrations and serum thyroid measures in NHANES 2007–2008. *Science of the Total Environment, 445–446,* 299–305.

Koopman-Esseboom, C., Morse, D. C., Weisglas-Kuperus, N., Lutkeschipholt, I. J., Van der Paauw, C. G., Tuinstra, L. G.,...Sauer, P. J. (1994). Effects of dioxins and polychlorinated biphenyls on thyroid hormone status of pregnant women and their infants. *Pediatric Research, 36*(4), 468–473.

Kucklick, J. R., Struntz, W. D., Becker, P. R., York, G. W., O'Hara, T. M., & Bohonowych, J. E. (2002). Persistent organochlorine pollutants in ringed seals and polar bears collected from northern Alaska. *Science of the Total Environment, 287*(1–2), 45–59.

Lacasana, M., López-Flores, I., Rodríguez-Barranco, M., Aguilar-Garduño, C., Blanco-Muñoz, J., Pérez-Méndez, O.,...Cebrian, M. E. (2010). Interaction between organophosphate pesticide exposure and PON1 activity on thyroid function. *Toxicology and Applied Pharmacology, 249*(1), 16–24.

Lampi, K. M., Lehtonen, L., Tran, P. L., Suominen, A., Lehti, V., Banerjee, P. N.,...Sourander, A. (2012). Risk of autism spectrum disorders in low birth weight and small for gestational age infants. *Journal of Pediatrics, 161*(5), 830–836.

Langer, P., Kocan, A., Tajtáková, M., Petrík, J., Chovancová, J., Drobná, B., ... Klimes, I. (2003). Possible effects of polychlorinated biphenyls and organochlorinated pesticides on the thyroid after long-term exposure to heavy environmental pollution. *Journal of Occupational and Environmental Medicine, 45*(5), 526–532.

Langer, P., Kocan, A., Tajtakova, M., Petrik, J., Chovancova, J., Drobna, B., ... Klimes, I. (2005). Human thyroid in the population exposed to high environmental pollution by organochlorinated pollutants for several decades. *Endocrine Regulations, 39*(1), 13–20.

Langer, P., Tajtáková, M., Kocan, A., Petrík, J., Koska, J., Ksinantová, L., ... Klimes, I. (2007). Thyroid ultrasound volume, structure and function after long-term high exposure of large population to polychlorinated biphenyls, pesticides and dioxin. *Chemosphere, 69*(1), 118–127.

Langer, V., Dreyer, A., & Ebinghaus, R. (2010). Polyfluorinated compounds in residential and nonresidential indoor air. *Environmental Science and Technology, 44*(21), 8075–8081.

Law, R. J., Kohler, M., Heeb, N. V., Gerecke, A. C., Schmid, P., Voorspoels, S., ... Thomsen, C. (2005). Hexabromocyclododecane challenges scientists and regulators. *Environmental Science and Technology, 39*(13), 281A–287A.

le Maire, A., Grimaldi, M., Roecklin, D., Dagnino, S., Vivat-Hannah, V., Balaguer, P., & Bourguet, W. (2009). Activation of RXR-PPAR heterodimers by organotin environmental endocrine disruptors. *EMBO Reports, 10*(4), 367–373.

Li, N., Wang, D., Zhou, Y., Ma, M., Li, J., & Wang, Z. (2010). Dibutyl phthalate contributes to the thyroid receptor antagonistic activity in drinking water processes. *Environmental Science and Technology, 44*(17), 6863–6868.

Liberda, E. N., Wainman, B. C., Leblanc, A., Dumas, P., Martin, I., & Tsuji, L. J. (2011). Dietary exposure of PBDEs resulting from a subsistence diet in three First Nation communities in the James Bay Region of Canada. *Environment International, 37*(3), 631–636.

Lilienthal, H., Verwer, C. M., van der Ven, L. T., Piersma, A. H., & Vos, J. G. (2008). Exposure to tetrabromobisphenol A (TBBPA) in Wistar rats: Neurobehavioral effects in offspring from a one-generation reproduction study. *Toxicology, 246*(1), 45–54.

London, L., Beseler, C., Bouchard, M. F., Bellinger, D. C., Colosio, C., Grandjean, P., ... Stallones, L. (2012). Neurobehavioral and neurodevelopmental effects of pesticide exposures. *Neurotoxicology, 33*(4), 887–896.

Lopez-Espinosa, M. J., Mondal, D., Armstrong, B., Bloom, M. S., & Fletcher, T. (2012). Thyroid function and perfluoroalkyl acids in children living near a chemical plant. *Environmental Health Perspectives, 120*(7), 1036–1041.

Main, K. M., Mortensen, G. K., Kaleva, M. M., Boisen, K. A., Damgaard, I. N., Chellakooty, M., ... Skakkebaek, N. E. (2006). Human breast milk contamination with phthalates and alterations of endogenous reproductive hormones in infants three months of age. *Environmental Health Perspectives, 114*(2), 270–276.

Manson, J. M., Brown, T., & Baldwin, D. M. (1984). Teratogenicity of nitrofen (2,4-dichloro-4'-nitrodiphenyl ether) and its effects on thyroid function in the rat. *Toxicology and Applied Pharmacology, 73*(2), 323–335.

McLachlan, J. A. (2001). Environmental signaling: What embryos and evolution teach us about endocrine disrupting chemicals. *Endocrine Reviews, 22*(3), 319–341.

McDonald, T. A. (2002). A perspective on the potential health risks of PBDEs. *Chemosphere, 46*(5), 745–755.

McFarland, V. A., & Clarke, J. U. (1989). Environmental occurrence, abundance, and potential toxicity of polychlorinated biphenyl congeners: Considerations for a congener-specific analysis. *Environmental Health Perspectives, 81*, 225–239.

Meeker, J. D., Cooper, E. M., Stapleton, H. M., & Hauser, R. (2013). Urinary metabolites of organophosphate flame retardants: Temporal variability and correlations with house dust concentrations. *Environmental Health Perspectives, 121*(5), 580–585.

Meeker, J. D., & Ferguson, K. K. (2011). Relationship between urinary phthalate and bisphenol A concentrations and serum thyroid measures in U.S. adults and adolescents from the National Health and Nutrition Examination Survey (NHANES) 2007–2008. *Environmental Health Perspectives, 119*(10), 1396–1402.

Meeker, J. D., Sathyanarayana, S., & Swan, S. H. (2009). Phthalates and other additives in plastics: human exposure and associated health outcomes. *Philosophical Transactions of the Royal Society of London B: Biological Sciences, 364*(1526), 2097–2113.

Meeker, J. D., & Stapleton, H. M. (2010). House dust concentrations of organophosphate flame retardants in relation to hormone levels and semen quality parameters. *Environmental Health Perspectives, 118*(3), 318–323.

Meerts, I. A., van Zanden, J. J., Luijks, E. A., van Leeuwen-Bol, I., Marsh, G., Jakobsson, E., ... Brouwer, A. (2000). Potent competitive interactions of some brominated flame retardants and related compounds with human transthyretin in vitro. *Toxicological Sciences, 56*(1), 95–104.

Melzer, D., Rice, N., Depledge, M. H., Henley, W. E., & Galloway, T. S. (2010). Association between serum perfluorooctanoic acid (PFOA) and thyroid disease in the U.S. National Health and Nutrition Examination Survey. *Environmental Health Perspectives, 118*(5), 686–692.

Milbrath, M. O., Wenger, Y., Chang, C. W., Emond, C., Garabrant, D., Gillespie, B. W., & Jolliet O. (2009). Apparent half-lives of dioxins, furans, and polychlorinated biphenyls as a function of age, body fat, smoking status, and breast-feeding. *Environmental Health Perspectives, 117*(3), 417–425.

Miodovnik, A., Engel, S. M., Zhu, C., Ye, X., Soorya, L. V., Silva, M. J., ... Wolff, M. S. (2011). Endocrine disruptors and childhood social impairment. *Neurotoxicology, 32*(2), 261–267.

Miyazaki, W., Iwasaki, T., Takeshita, A., Tohyama, C., & Koibuchi, N. (2008). Identification of the functional domain of thyroid hormone receptor responsible for polychlorinated biphenyl-mediated suppression of its action in vitro. *Environmental Health Perspectives, 116*(9), 1231–1236.

Mori, K., Yoshida, K., Hoshikawa, S., Ito, S., Yoshida, M., Satoh, M., & Watanabe, C. (2006a). Effects of perinatal exposure to low doses of cadmium or methylmercury on thyroid hormone metabolism in metallothionein-deficient mouse neonates. *Toxicology, 228*(1), 77–84.

Mori, K., Yoshida, K., Tani, J., Hoshikawa, S., Ito, S., & Watanabe, C. (2006b). Methylmercury inhibits type II 5'-deiodinase activity in NB41A3 neuroblastoma cells. *Toxicology Letters, 161*(2), 96–101.

Moriyama, K., Tagami, T., Akamizu, T., Usui, T., Saijo, M., Kanamoto, N., ... Nakao, K. (2002). Thyroid hormone action is disrupted by bisphenol A as an antagonist. *Journal of Clinical Endocrinology and Metabolism, 87*(11), 5185–5190.

Morse, D. C., Wehler, E. K., Wesseling, W., Koeman, J. H., & Brouwer, A. (1996). Alterations in rat brain thyroid hormone status following pre- and postnatal exposure to polychlorinated biphenyls (Aroclor 1254). *Toxicology and Applied Pharmacology, 136*(2), 269–279.

Mortensen, G. K., Main, K. M., Andersson, A. M., Leffers, H., & Skakkebaek, N. E. (2005). Determination of phthalate monoesters in human milk, consumer milk, and infant formula by tandem mass spectrometry (LC-MS-MS). *Analytical and Bioanalytical Chemistry, 382*(4), 1084–1092.

Nagayama, J., Kohno, H., Kunisue, T., Kataoka, K., Shimomura, H., Tanabe, S., & Konishi, S. (2007). Concentrations of organochlorine pollutants in mothers who gave birth to neonates with congenital hypothyroidism. *Chemosphere, 68*(5), 972–976.

Nagayama, J., Okamura, K., Iida, T., Hirakawa, H., Matsueda, T., Tsuji, H.,... Watanabe, T. (1998). Postnatal exposure to chlorinated dioxins and related chemicals on thyroid hormone status in Japanese breast-fed infants. *Chemosphere, 37*(9–12), 1789–1793.

Normile, D. (2013). Vietnam turns back a "tsunami of pesticides." *Science, 341*(6147), 737–738.

O'Connor, J. C., Frame, S. R., & Ladics, G. S. (2002). Evaluation of a 15-day screening assay using intact male rats for identifying antiandrogens. *Toxicological Sciences, 69*(1), 92–108.

Otake, T., Yoshinaga, J., Enomoto, T., Matsuda, M., Wakimoto, T., Ikegami, M.,... Kato, N. (2007). Thyroid hormone status of newborns in relation to in utero exposure to PCBs and hydroxylated PCB metabolites. *Environmental Research, 105*(2), 240–246.

Pearce, E. N., Alexiou, M., Koukkou, E., Braverman, L. E., He, X., Ilias, I.,... Markou, K. B. (2012). Perchlorate and thiocyanate exposure and thyroid function in first-trimester pregnant women from Greece. *Clinical Endocrinology (Oxford), 77*(3), 471–474.

Pearce, E. N., Leung, A. M., Blount, B. C., Bazrafshan, H. R., He, X., Pino, S.,... Braverman, L. E. (2007). Breast milk iodine and perchlorate concentrations in lactating Boston-area women. *Journal of Clinical Endocrinology and Metabolism, 92*(5), 1673–1677.

Petro, E. M., Leroy, J. L., Covaci, A., Fransen, E., De Neubourg, D., Dirtu, A. C.,... Bols, P. E. (2012). Endocrine-disrupting chemicals in human follicular fluid impair in vitro oocyte developmental competence. *Human Reproduction, 27*(4), 1025–1033.

Perkins, E. J., Ankley, G. T., Crofton, K. M., Garcia-Reyero, N., LaLone, C. A., Johnson, M. S.,... Villeneuve, D. L. (2013). Current perspectives on the use of alternative species in human health and ecological hazard assessments. *Environmental Health Perspectives, 121*(9), 1002–1010.

Persoon, C., Peters, T. M., Kumar, N., & Hornbuckle, K. C. (2010). Spatial distribution of airborne polychlorinated biphenyls in Cleveland, Ohio and Chicago, Illinois. *Environmental Science and Technology, 44*(8), 2797–2802.

Porterfield, S. P. (1994). Vulnerability of the developing brain to thyroid abnormalities: Environmental insults to the thyroid system. *Environmental Health Perspectives, 102*(Suppl 2), 125–130.

Powell, R. L. (1984). Dioxin in Missouri: 1971–1983. *Bulletin of Environmental Contamination and Toxicology, 33*(6), 648–654.

Pretty, J. N., Noble, A. D., Bossio, D., Dixon, J., Hine, R. E., Penning De Vries, F. W., & Morison, J. I. (2006). Resource-conserving agriculture increases yields in developing countries. *Environmental Science and Technology, 40*(4), 1114–1119.

Radovic, B., Mentrup, B., & Köhrle, J. (2006). Genistein and other soya isoflavones are potent ligands for transthyretin in serum and cerebrospinal fluid. *British Journal of Nutrition, 95*(6), 1171–1176.

Rauh, V., Arunajadai, S., Horton, M., Perera, F., Hoepner, L., Barr, D. B., & Whyatt, R. (2011). Seven-year neurodevelopmental scores and prenatal exposure to chlorpyrifos, a common agricultural pesticide. *Environmental Health Perspectives, 119*(8), 1196–1201.

Rauh, V. A., Perera, F. P., Horton, M. K., Whyatt, R. M., Bansal, R., Hao, X.,...Peterson, B. S. (2012). Brain anomalies in children exposed prenatally to a common organophosphate pesticide. *Proceedings of the National Academy of Science USA, 109*(20), 7871–7876.

Richardson, T. A., & Klaassen, C. D. (2010). Disruption of thyroid hormone homeostasis in Ugt1a-deficient Gunn rats by microsomal enzyme inducers is not due to enhanced thyroxine glucuronidation. *Toxicology and Applied Pharmacology, 248*(1), 38–44.

Ringer, R. K. (1978). PBB fed to immature chickens: Its effect on organ weights and function and on the cardiovascular system. *Environmental Health Perspectives, 23*, 247–255.

Rodriguez, P. E., & Sanchez, M. S. (2010). Maternal exposure to triclosan impairs thyroid homeostasis and female pubertal development in Wistar rat offspring. *Journal of Toxicology and Environmental Health A, 73*(24), 1678–88.

Rogan, W. J., Gladen, B. C., McKinney, J. D., Carreras, N., Hardy, P., Thullen, J.,...Tully, M. (1986). Neonatal effects of transplacental exposure to PCBs and DDE. *Journal of Pediatrics, 109*(2), 335–341.

Rousset, B. (1981). Antithyroid effect of a food or drug preservative: 4-hydroxybenzoic acid methyl ester. *Experientia, 37*(2), 177–178.

Roze, E., Meijer, L., Bakker, A., Van Braeckel, K. N., Sauer, P. J., & Bos, A. F. (2009). Prenatal exposure to organohalogens, including brominated flame retardants, influences motor, cognitive, and behavioral performance at school age. *Environmental Health Perspectives, 117*(12), 1953–1958.

Ruegg, J., Swedenborg, E., Wahlström, D., Escande, A., Balaguer, P., Pettersson, K., & Pongratz, I. (2008). The transcription factor aryl hydrocarbon receptor nuclear translocator functions as an estrogen receptor beta-selective coactivator, and its recruitment to alternative pathways mediates antiestrogenic effects of dioxin. *Molecular Endocrinology, 22*(2), 304–316.

Ruiz, J. M., Bachelet, G., Caumette, P., & Donard, O. F. (1996). Three decades of tributyltin in the coastal environment with emphasis on Arcachon Bay, France. *Environmental Pollution, 93*(2), 195–203.

Schecter, A., Pavuk, M., Päpke, O., Ryan, J. J., Birnbaum, L., & Rosen, R. (2003). Polybrominated diphenyl ethers (PBDEs) in U.S. mothers' milk. *Environmental Health Perspectives, 111*(14), 1723–1729.

Schmutzler, C., Bacinski, A., Gotthardt, I., Huhne, K., Ambrugger, P., Klammer, H.,...Köhrle, J. (2007). The ultraviolet filter benzophenone 2 interferes with the thyroid hormone axis in rats and is a potent in vitro inhibitor of human recombinant thyroid peroxidase. *Endocrinology, 148*(6), 2835–2844.

Schmutzler, C., Hamann, I., Hofmann, P. J., Kovacs, G., Stemmler, L., Mentrup, B., ... Köhrle, J. (2004). Endocrine active compounds affect thyrotropin and thyroid hormone levels in serum as well as endpoints of thyroid hormone action in liver, heart and kidney. *Toxicology, 205*(1–2), 95–102.

Schonfelder, G., Wittfoht, W., Hopp, H., Talsness, C. E., Paul, M., & Chahoud, I. (2002). Parent bisphenol A accumulation in the human maternal-fetal-placental unit. *Environmental Health Perspectives, 110*(11), A703–707.

Setchell, K. D., Zimmer-Nechemias, L., Cai, J., & Heubi, J. E. (1998). Isoflavone content of infant formulas and the metabolic fate of these phytoestrogens in early life. *American Journal of Clinical Nutrition, 68*(6 Suppl), 1453S–1461S.

Sewall, C. H., Flagler, N., Vanden Heuvel, J. P., Clark, G. C., Tritscher, A. M., Maronpot, R. M., & Lucier, G. W. (1995). Alterations in thyroid function in female Sprague-Dawley rats following chronic treatment with 2,3,7,8-tet rachlorodibenzo-p-dioxin. *Toxicology and Applied Pharmacology, 132*(2), 237–244.

Shaw, S. D., Berger, M. L., Weijs, L., & Covaci, A. (2012). Tissue-specific accumulation of polybrominated diphenyl ethers (PBDEs) including Deca-BDE and hexabromocyclododecanes (HBCDs) in harbor seals from the northwest Atlantic. *Environment International, 44*, 1–6.

Shelton, J. F., Hertz-Picciotto, I., & Pessah, I. N. (2012). Tipping the balance of autism risk: Potential mechanisms linking pesticides and autism. *Environmental Health Perspectives, 120*(7), 944–951.

Silva, M. J., Barr, D. B., Reidy, J. A., Malek, N. A., Hodge, C. C., Caudill, S. P., ... Calafat, A. M. (2004). Urinary levels of seven phthalate metabolites in the U.S. population from the National Health and Nutrition Examination Survey (NHANES) 1999–2000. *Environmental Health Perspectives, 112*(3), 331–338.

Sosic-Jurjevic, B., Filipović, B., Ajdzanović, V., Savin, S., Nestorović, N., Milosević, V., & Sekulić, M. (2010). Suppressive effects of genistein and daidzein on pituitary-thyroid axis in orchidectomized middle-aged rats. *Experimental Biology and Medicine (Maywood), 235*(5), 590–598.

Spaulding, S. W. (2011). The possible roles of environmental factors and the aryl hydrocarbon receptor in the prevalence of thyroid diseases in Vietnam era veterans. *Current Opinion in Endocrinology, Diabetes and Obesity, 18*(5), 315–320.

Springer, C., Dere, E., Hall, S. J., McDonnell, E. V., Roberts, S. C., Butt, C. M., ... Boekelheide, K. (2012). Rodent thyroid, liver, and fetal testis toxicity of the monoester metabolite of bis-(2-ethylhexyl) tetrabromophthalate (TBPH), a novel brominated flame retardant present in indoor dust. *Environmental Health Perspectives, 120*(12), 1711–1719.

Sriphrapradang, C., Chailurkit, L. O., Aekplakorn, W., & Ongphiphadhanakul, B. (2013). Association between bisphenol A and abnormal free thyroxine level in men. *Endocrine, 44*(2), 441–447.

Stapleton, H. M., Eagle, S., Sjödin, A., & Webster, T. F. (2012). Serum PBDEs in a North Carolina toddler cohort: Associations with handwipes, house dust, and socioeconomic variables. *Environmental Health Perspectives, 120*(7), 1049–1054.

Sterling, J. B., & Hanke, C. W. (2005). Dioxin toxicity and chloracne in the Ukraine. *Journal of Drugs in Dermatology, 4*(2), 148–150.

Su, P. H., Chen, J. Y., Chen, J. W., & Wang, S. L. (2010). Growth and thyroid function in children with in utero exposure to dioxin: A 5-year follow-up study. *Pediatric Research, 67*(2), 205–210.

Takser, L., Mergler, D., Baldwin, M., de Grosbois, S., Smargiassi, A., & Lafond, J. (2005). Thyroid hormones in pregnancy in relation to environmental exposure to organochlorine compounds and mercury. *Environmental Health Perspectives, 113*(8), 1039–1045.

Talsness, C. E., Andrade, A. J., Kuriyama, S. N., Taylor, J. A., & vom Saal, F. S. (2009). Components of plastic: Experimental studies in animals and relevance for human health. *Philosophical Transactions of the Royal Society of London B: Biological Sciences, 364*(1526), 2079–2096.

Thilly, C. H., Swennen, B., Bourdoux, P., Ntambue, K., Moreno-Reyes, R., Gillies, J., & Vanderpas, J. B. (1993). The epidemiology of iodine-deficiency disorders in relation to goitrogenic factors and thyroid-stimulating-hormone regulation. *American Journal of Clinical Nutrition, 57*(2 Suppl), 267S–270S.

Thomsen, C., Lundanes, E., & Becher, G. (2002). Brominated flame retardants in archived serum samples from Norway: A study on temporal trends and the role of age. *Environmental Science and Technology, 36*(7), 1414–1418.

Torres-Sanchez, L., Rothenberg, S. J., Schnaas, L., Cebrian, M. E., Osorio, E., Del Carmen Hernandez, M.,... Lopez-Carrillo, L. (2007). In utero p,p'-DDE exposure and infant neurodevelopment: a perinatal cohort in Mexico *Environmental Health Perspectives, 115*(3), 435–438.

Turyk, M. E., Anderson, H. A., & Persky, V. W. (2007). Relationships of thyroid hormones with polychlorinated biphenyls, dioxins, furans, and DDE in adults. *Environmental Health Perspectives, 115*(8), 1197–1203.

US Department of Agriculture, USDA (2008). USDA Database for the Isoflavone Content of Selected Foods Release 2.0. Consulted April 2014.

Valentin-Blasini, L., Blount, B. C., Otero-Santos, S., Cao, Y., Bernbaum, J. C., & Rogan, W. J. (2011). Perchlorate exposure and dose estimates in infants. *Environmental Science and Technology, 45*(9), 4127–4132.

Vandenberg, L. N., Maffini, M. V., Sonnenschein, C., Rubin, B. S., & Soto, A. M. (2009). Bisphenol-A and the great divide: A review of controversies in the field of endocrine disruption. *Endocrine Reviews, 30*(1), 75–95.

Van der Ven, L. T., Van de Kuil, T., Verhoef, A., Verwer, C. M., Lilienthal, H., Leonards, P. E.,... Piersma, A. H. (2008). Endocrine effects of tetrabromobisphenol-A (TBBPA) in Wistar rats as tested in a one-generation reproduction study and a subacute toxicity study. *Toxicology, 245*(1–2), 76–89.

van Maanen, J. M., van Dijk, A., Mulder, K., de Baets, M. H., Menheere, P. C., van der Heide, D.,... Kleinjans, J. C. (1994). Consumption of drinking water with high nitrate levels causes hypertrophy of the thyroid. *Toxicology Letters, 72*(1–3), 365–374.

Vo, T. T., Yoo, Y. M., Choi, K. C., & Jeung, E. B. (2010). Potential estrogenic effect(s) of parabens at the prepubertal stage of a postnatal female rat model. *Reproductive Toxicology, 29*(3), 306–316.

von Waldow, H., Macleod, M., Scheringer, M., & Hungerbühler, K. (2010). Quantifying remoteness from emission sources of persistent organic pollutants on a global scale. *Environmental Science and Technology, 44*(8), 2791–2796.

Wang, S. L., Su, P. H., Jong, S. B., Guo, Y. L., Chou, W. L., & Päpke, O. (2005). In utero exposure to dioxins and polychlorinated biphenyls and its relations to thyroid function and growth hormone in newborns. *Environmental Health Perspectives, 113*(11), 1645–1650.

Weiss, J. M., Andersson, P. L., Lamoree, M. H., Leonards, P. E., van Leeuwen, S. P., & Hamers, T. (2009). Competitive binding of poly- and perfluorinated compounds to the thyroid hormone transport protein transthyretin. *Toxicological Sciences, 109*(2), 206–216.

Wenzel, A., Franz, C., Breous, E., & Loos, U. (2005). Modulation of iodide uptake by dialkyl phthalate plasticisers in FRTL-5 rat thyroid follicular cells. *Molecular and Cellular Endocrinology, 244*(1–2), 63–71.

World Wildlife Fund International (2011) Eau de Boisson:Analyses comparées de l'eau du robinet et de l'eau en bouteille. WWF France, Paris.

Yamada-Okabe, T., Aono, T., Sakai, H., Kashima, Y., & Yamada-Okabe, H. (2004). 2,3,7,8-tetrachlorodibenzo-p-dioxin augments the modulation of gene expression mediated by the thyroid hormone receptor. *Toxicology and Applied Pharmacology, 194*(3), 201–210.

Young, A. L., Giesy, J. P., Jones, P. D., & Newton, M. (2004). Environmental fate and bioavailability of Agent Orange and its associated dioxin during the Vietnam War. *Environmental Science and Pollution Research International, 11*(6), 359–370.

Yu, W. G., Liu, W., & Jin, Y. H. (2009). Effects of perfluorooctane sulfonate on rat thyroid hormone biosynthesis and metabolism. *Environmental Toxicology and Chemistry, 28*(5), 990–996.

Yu, W. G., Liu, W., Jin, Y. H., Liu, X. H., Wang, F. Q., Liu, L., & Nakayama, S. F. (2009). Prenatal and postnatal impact of perfluorooctane sulfonate (PFOS) on rat development: A cross-foster study on chemical burden and thyroid hormone system. *Environmental Science and Technology, 43*(21), 8416–8422.

Zhang, Y., Lin, L., Cao, Y., Chen, B., Zheng, L., & Ge, R. S. (2009). Phthalate levels and low birth weight: A nested case-control study of Chinese newborns. *Journal of Pediatrics, 155*(4), 500–504.

Zhou, T., Ross, D. G., DeVito, M. J., & Crofton, K. M. (2001). Effects of short-term in vivo exposure to polybrominated diphenyl ethers on thyroid hormones and hepatic enzyme activities in weanling rats. *Toxicological Sciences, 61*(1), 76–82.

Zoeller, R. T., (2007). Environmental chemicals impacting the thyroid: targets and consequences. *Thyroid, 17*(9), 811–817.

Zoeller, R. T., Bansal, R., & Parris, C. (2005). Bisphenol-A, an environmental contaminant that acts as a thyroid hormone receptor antagonist in vitro, increases serum thyroxine, and alters RC3/neurogranin expression in the developing rat brain. *Endocrinology, 146*(2), 607–612.

Zota, A. R., Park, J. S., Wang, Y., Petreas, M., Zoeller, R. T., & Woodruff, T. J. (2011). Polybrominated diphenyl ethers, hydroxylated polybrominated diphenyl ethers, and measures of thyroid function in second trimester pregnant women in California. *Environmental Science and Technology, 45*(18), 7896–7905.

# Chapter 6

## Mixtures and Low Doses

### The Complexity of Risk Assessment

CHAPTER OUTLINE

The current US Environmental Protection Agency (EPA) Toxic Substance Control Act (TSCA) inventory lists over 84,000 chemicals manufactured in or imported into the United States in quantities above 10 tons. This list does not include substances covered by other legislation, such as pesticides, foodstuffs, food additives, and cosmetics. Given that many substances are released into the environment, it is hardly surprising to find that each one of us is contaminated with dozens of them. In the early 2000s, before the debate on REACH, the World Wildlife Fund (WWF) carried out two studies, one measuring about 100 common chemicals in three generations of women, the other in Members of the European Parliament (MEPs). Over 70 of the chemicals analyzed were found, with numbers of chemicals per individual ranging from 18 to 54. Even more disquieting are the numerous reports showing that amniotic fluid, umbilical cord blood, and breast milk are also cocktails of contaminants. Thus, the most vulnerable periods of life are played out in an unprecedented mixture of chemical compounds of industrial origin. Many of these substances are present at low doses, although the "low dose" definition is continually discussed. Another point debated by policy makers and scientists of different backgrounds is how to assess responses that may not be simple linear relationships, despite the fact that the concept of nonlinear responses has always been recognized by endocrinologists. Most hormones exert their maximal effects at nanomolar (nM) concentrations, with higher doses inducing lesser, or even inhibitory effects. There are very little data on the full extent of chemical load in different body compartments, nor on the effects of these multiple low-dose mixtures on developmental and physiological processes. Determining the main players in the adverse health effects documented over the last 30 years, and notably in the pervasive epidemic of mental disorders, is a matter of urgency no government or international body can afford to ignore.

BACKGROUND

The number of chemicals manufactured and destined for industrial, agricultural, or personal use has increased steadily over the last century. Production of plasticizers such as bisphenol A (BPA) and polychlorinated biphenyls (PCBs) and the pesticide DDT was increased from the 1950s onward. It is estimated that since then about a thousand new chemicals are introduced each year, such that well over 84,000 chemicals are currently on the EPA register, many for which no toxicology data have been obtained (see end of Chapter 5). As outlined by Theo Colborn in 2004, the first generations to undergo significant postnatal exposure to a variety of compounds were those born in the 1940s and 1950s. Children born between the late 1950s and 1970s were probably the first to be exposed in utero to mixtures, and they began to start families 20–30 years later, producing a second generation of children exposed prenatally, but now to an even greater spectrum of chemicals. Even though it is rarely possible to relate current health problems to exposure of previous generations, many governments are endeavoring to obtain population-wide data on the levels of contemporary exposure. One of the most comprehensive databases is that of the US Center for Disease Control and Prevention (CDC), which provides regular updates on their reports documenting population-wide exposure to environmental chemicals (http://www.cdc.gov/exposurereport/). It is with this data that we start.

## CDC 2013 Data on Exposure to Environmental Chemicals in the United States

The CDC datasets cover urinary and/or serum measurements of chemicals in a wide population base with the aim of providing a representative, and regularly updated, picture of the general level of exposure. Samples are taken from men and women, boys and girls in different age groups and from different ethnic backgrounds. The adult samples will usually total about 2,000 people. In 2009, the report covered over 200 chemicals and the latest update, in early 2013, provided new data on 117 of them and on 34 newly introduced substances. The chemicals chosen for updates, and the list of new chemicals, make interesting reading. The new list includes metabolites of two fungicides that are thiourea derivatives, which, like nitrate and thiocyanate also on the "new list," have the potential to interfere with thyroid hormone (TH) synthesis (see Chapter 5). Also added are no fewer than 17 sulfonylurea herbicides, 4 new paraben metabolites, 2 phthalate metabolites, and 4 new organophosphate (OP) pesticide metabolites. Again, all fall within chemical classes that include known TH disruptors. The inclusion of so many potential TH disruptors may be coincidental or simply reflect the fact that, as argued in Chapter 4, the structure of the hormone along with the complexity of TH synthesis, distribution, and signaling makes it vulnerable to more classes of chemicals than any other endocrine system. Alternatively, it could be seen as indicating that selection prioritized substances that could interfere with TH signaling, although the absence of any brominated or chlorinated flame retardants argues against this interpretation. Many other potential TH disruptors are also selected for updates, including BPA, a suite of perfluorinated compounds, and a number of phytoestrogens with their metabolites. As it happens, all of the sulfonylurea herbicides and the thioureas came out below the detection level in all of the samples tested. This was not the case for nitrate, which averaged 46.7 mg/g creatine (creatine being the marker used to normalize urinary values across samples). Perchlorate and thiocyanate reached 4.0 and 1.39 mg/g creatine across groups, respectively, making these three thyroid-inhibiting anions the chemical class with the highest concentrations, no other compounds showing levels in the mg/g creatine range. All population sections were positive for at least some paraben metabolites, with every sample coming out positive for methyl and n-propyl paraben, which together averaged 67 µg/g of creatine. In comparison, BPA values averaged 2 µg/g; genistein, 31.4 µg/g; perfluorooctane sulfonic acid (PFOS), 9.3 µg/g; triclosan, 15.1 µg/g; dimethyl thiophosphate (DMTP), a metabolite of a number of OPs, 2.34 µg/g. Total mercury values over the last 8 years have averaged 0.5 µg/g creatine in urine and 0.86 µg/L in blood. Thus, just taking the chemicals included in the updates shows the average person is exposed to significant levels of a spectrum of thyroid hormone-disrupting chemicals. These chemicals can be acting at the level of thyroid by inhibiting iodide uptake (perchlorate, nitrate, and thiocyanate) or iodine organification (genistein), with production of active hormone in target tissues (mercury) or at the levels of interference with hormone distribution in the blood (genistein again) and increased metabolism, and therefore reduced levels, of natural hormones (triclosan, PFOS, and probably parabens and BPA).

Arsenic, although not discussed in Chapter 5, can also interfere with TR signaling in some systems, and total urinary values averaged 9.9 µg/g, the source most often being drinking water. Also cobalt, which is known to interfere with iodide uptake, averaged 0.3 µg/g. Lead was in the same range (0.5 µg/g). Other substances, not associated with specific effects on TH, that showed levels in the µg/g creatine ranges included chloroform (a disinfection by-product); 2,5-dichlorophenol used in mothballs, insect repellents, and deodorizers; and barium (1.5 µg/g), cadmium (0.2 µg/g), and cesium (4.4 µg/g). Neither the updates, nor the 2009 tables, provide information on any class of flame retardants besides the polybrominated diphenyl ethers (PBDEs; which were measured in 2009). At that time, according to the report, PBDEs accounted for 25% of flame retardant production, with the other 75% of this chemical class not covered by the survey.

Despite the absence of certain chemical categories, from these measures on urinary and in some cases blood samples, one can deduce that multiple exposure is overwhelmingly the rule and not the exception.

## European Examples: Blood Sampling in Adults and Across Generations

Two of the most interesting European reports are the WWF studies: the three-generation analysis published in early 2005[1] and the study on MEPs in 2004.[2] These studies appeared in the period before the REACH debate in the

1  http://wwf.panda.org/what_we_do/how_we_work/policy/wwf_europe_ environment/news/?uNewsID=23635
2  http://wwf.panda.org/what_we_do/how_we_work/policy/wwf_europe_ environment/news/?uNewsID=12622

European parliament in late 2005. The EU parliamentary study managed to obtain blood samples from 47 volunteers (including 39 MEPs) from 17 different countries. The blood samples were screened for 101 chemicals that could be grouped into five major categories: OC pesticides, including the banned DDT and lindane, 21 PBDE flame retardants along with TBBPA and HBCD, 45 PCBs, 8 phthalates, and 13 perfluorinated compounds. The highest number of chemicals found in any one sample was 54. Over a dozen chemicals were found in all samples, including the pesticide hexachloro-benzene (HCB) and the DDT derivative DDE, one PBDE, two PCBs, seven of the perfluorinated substances, and one phthalate. The median number of chemicals found was 41. DDE, a metabolite of DDT banned 30 years previously, showed the highest median levels at over 1 ng/g serum. The chemical with the highest concentration in any single sample was a flame retardant, polybrominated diphenyl ether (PDBE), that registered 18 ng/g serum. Seven of the ten chemicals with highest median concentrations were PCBs. In the study comparing grandmothers, mothers, and children, blood samples were taken from members of 13 families from 12 EU countries and examined for up to 107 chemicals. Many were the same as those analyzed in the MEP study but also included were triclosan and BPA. Key observations included the fact that every person was carrying a chemical cocktail of at least 18 substances, with the levels of certain compounds, the PDBE flame retardants and BPA, displaying the highest levels in the younger generation. One substance found in all samples (but not examined in the MEP study) was galaxolide (or HHCB), an artificial musk added to cosmetics and household cleaning products (yes, both) as a fragrance. According to an assessment report disseminated for comment by the EPA in December 2012, over 90% of the HHCB produced ends up in the environment, where it is considered to show moderate persistence and bioaccumulation. As yet no reports have been published on potential thyroid disruption by this chemical. Again, the three-generation study detected over 70 chemicals, with banned chemicals such as PCBs and DDT derivatives being found ubiquitously, thus again reiterating the universally applicable, multiple exposure scenarios.

Each of these population studies cited addresses levels in children and adults, but one of the main concerns in trying to understand the epidemic of autism spectrum disorders, attention-deficit/hyperactivity disorder, and congenital hypothyroidism is exposure of unborn children, particularly during early pregnancy. Assessing exposure during these time windows is obviously more difficult than in adults, and one can only rely on association studies examining maternal levels and samples taken at birth as indicators of prior contamination. Experimentally addressing effects of chemicals on organ formation in this period of early development is also difficult and best addressed in nonmammalian models such as tadpoles and fish embryos. These alternative vertebrate models have many advantages, including the facts that, due to evolutionary conservation, TH and the mechanisms implicated in its production and metabolism are exactly the same as in mammals.

Furthermore, TH actions on early neurogenesis are also conserved across vertebrates, and the fact that these molecular and cellular processes can be studied and visualized in these "free-living" (i.e., developing outside the mother) embryos (Fini, Le Mével, et al., 2012; Fini, Riu, et al., 2012) is an additional advantage.

## Indicators of Fetal and Postnatal Mixture Exposure

To apprehend the level of prenatal contamination, a number of studies have examined chemical load in different physiological fluids either sampled at birth or during pregnancy. Five main physiological compartments can be assessed to obtain information on in utero exposure. During pregnancy two indicators can be used: maternal serum and amniotic fluid. At delivery three sources can be exploited: umbilical cord blood, the placental tissue, and meconium. In terms of chemical load, and associations with children's cognitive and neurobehavioral development, many studies focus on pesticides, PCBs, BPA, and more recently PDBEs. However, very few studies address the full possibilities of exposure to complex mixtures during gestation. The US NHANES[3] group carried out one of the broadest approaches on serum and urine from pregnant women. Levels of up to 163 chemicals from 12 chemical classes, including the usual trio of OC pesticides, PFCs, and PBDEs but also perchlorate, polycyclic aromatic hydrocarbons (PAHs), polyfluorinated compounds (PFCs), phenols and phthalates, among others, were compared in pregnant and nonpregnant women (Woodruff, Zota, & Schwartz, 2011). Pregnancy did not seem to affect exposure levels. Nearly all women (over 99%) had measurable serum or urine levels of seven chemical classes: perchlorate, phthalates, PFCs, PAHs, PBDEs, OC pesticides, and PCBs. Mercury was found in 90% of women, lead in over 95%, and cadmium in 66% of the pregnant women. Most women had about 30–40 different chemicals in their serum. Median levels of the most common categories are shown in Table 6.1.

One other study is chosen for discussion here, the most recent to date from the CHAMACOS[4] group, published in early 2013 (Eskenazi et al., 2013). Here the focus was on just one category of chemical in prenatal maternal serum among the seven common ones, namely the PCBE class of flame retardants. Among the many studies on mixtures in maternal serum that could be cited, this one is highlighted here because it provides information on associations between prenatal exposure, judged from maternal serum, and on development 7 years later. It also includes data on postnatal exposure in the children. The analysis showed, first, that four PBDE types were found in virtually all samples (97%), with total PBDEs averaging 28 ng/g lipid (maximum levels reached 1.3 µg/g) and, second, that the levels of these PBDE mixtures were associated with impaired attention and decrements in IQ measures at age 7.

---

3   National Health and Nutritional Examination Survey.
4   Center for Health Assessment of Mothers and Children of Salinas.

Table 6–1. Median Concentrations of Major Chemical Classes in Serum of Pregnant Women

| Chemical | Blood | Serum | Urine |
|---|---|---|---|
| BPA (μg/L)* | | | 1.63 |
| Triclosan (μg/L)* | | | 23.81 |
| Benzophenone 3 (μg/L) | | | 38.09 |
| Mercury (total)* | 0.71 | | |
| Lead (μg/dL) | 0.80 | | |
| Cadmium (μg/L)* | 0.27 | | |
| Organochlorine pesticides (ng/g lipid)* | | 198.34 (DDE) 13.74 (HCB) | |
| Organophosphate insecticide metabolites (μg/L) | | | 4.39 |
| Perchlorate (μg/L)* | | | 3.35 |
| Phthalates (μg/L)* | | >40 | |
| PBDEs (ng/g lipid)* | | >250 | |
| PCBs and other dioxin-like chemicals (ng/g lipid)* | | >28 | |
| 2-Napthol (μg/L)* | | | 3 |
| Perfluorinated compounds (PFOS)* | | 12.81 | |

*Notes*: Data are from the NHANES study (Woodruff et al., 2011). Values are given for examples of the major chemical groups discussed in Chapter 5. The high levels of DDE, the major metabolite of DDT, illustrate its omnipresence despite the ban for use in the United States over 40 years ago.

*Denote substances known to interfere with thyroid hormone signaling

PFOS: perfluorooctane sulfonic acid

## Amniotic Fluid

Amniocentesis, a procedure that obtains a sample of amniotic fluid and some fetal cells, may be carried out between 15 and 20 weeks of pregnancy. As it represents a risk for the fetus, the method cannot be used routinely and is only used if there are concerns about chromosomal abnormalities (for instance, trisomy 21 or Down syndrome) or infection. Amniotic fluid is produced by the fetus and represents mainly fetal urine, but this fluid is swallowed by the child and so is continually being recycled. Measuring levels in amniotic fluid therefore gives a reasonable vision of the diversity and quantities of chemicals to which the fetus is exposed. The first use of amniotic fluid to investigate chemical contamination with a view to assessing potential endocrine disruption was reported in 2000 (Foster, Chan, Platt, & Hughes, 2000). This study looked for and found PCB and OC pesticides in about one in three samples, using detection levels of 0.01 and 0.1 ng/ml, respectively. Since then other researchers have used amniocentesis samples that were to be discarded to examine, mainly, levels of pesticides.

Bradman and colleagues (2003) examined 100 samples from women from the Joaquin Valley in California, an agricultural area, but with a number of urban centers. This study looked for organophosphate, carbamate, and other pesticides and their metabolites. Their detection levels were the same as in the previous study, but this time higher rates of contamination were found, with 70% of samples having at least one pesticide present and often many other metabolites of consumer products such as naphthalene (used in mothballs). A more recent study focused on mixtures of PBDEs. The authors report high levels of different PBDEs, with total amounts reaching ng/ml concentrations. Certain PBDEs were found in all samples (Miller, Chernyak, Domino, Batterman, & Loch-Caruso, 2012). This study could not compare amniotic fluid levels with maternal fluids. Often levels in amniotic fluid are lower than in those in urine or maternal serum, or other fluids from the fetal compartment taken at birth, such as meconium or umbilical cord blood (see later). Given that cord blood samples frequently show higher levels of flame retardants than maternal serum at birth (Chen et al., 2013) and equivalent levels of pesticides (Dewan, Jain, Gupta, & Banerjee, 2013) and that meconium shows higher levels of most contaminants than cord blood (see later), one wonders if the relatively low levels of contaminants in amniotic fluid is representative of exposure, or reflects a different physiological handling of xenobiotics by the fetus with lesser amounts being excreted through the immature kidneys into the urine. Animal studies support this possibility of partitioning of certain chemicals by the fetus and clearly show that the placenta does not act as a barrier and that half-lives of chemicals can be longer in the fetus than in the mother (Takahashi & Oishi, 2000).

Meconium

In some senses meconium, the first stools formed after birth, is one of the best markers of prenatal exposure as it represents the accumulation of material eliminated by the fetal liver and digestive system during gestation. As meconium starts to form from the 12th week of gestation onward, it does not give an indication of exposure in the critical first trimester but reflects exposure in the latter two thirds. Principally, methods for meconium analysis were developed to assess prenatal exposure of infants to alcohol and drugs such as cocaine in order to implement appropriate care for vulnerable children (Ostrea et al., 2006). However, more recently the value of meconium analysis as an indicator of exposure to pesticides and other endocrine disruptors has been assessed (Li et al., 2013; Ostrea et al., 2008). Meconium appears to be a better indicator than infant hair or even cord blood (Ostrea et al., 2008), and given the ease of obtaining samples in suitable amounts for analysis, its use could well provide better indications of exposure than other matrices currently employed. However, despite the current limited amount of data, in one study cited the authors found seven pesticides in meconium samples but only one of them was found at measurable levels in cord blood (Ostrea et al., 2008). Furthermore, in a later study, the same team again found that meconium was a better indicator of exposure than maternal serum or cord blood. They also found that the levels of one of the pesticides noted in the first study, propoxur, an insecticide used against cockroaches, was found in more than one in five samples in the second, and levels were negatively associated with children's neurodevelopmental outcome by the age of 2 years (Ostrea et al., 2012).

Thus, using meconium samples, an easily obtained source of information on exposure, could provide better data than that provided by cord blood analyses. Cord samples, even when made with and allowing comparisons with maternal levels, still only present a snapshot of immediate exposure and provide little indication of earlier exposure.

Umbilical Cord Blood as Compared to Maternal Blood Samples

Most studies on cord blood focus on different categories of chemicals, and thus it is impossible to estimate the full spectrum of chemical exposure, other than by extrapolation from data such as the CDC source cited earlier. Numerous studies have addressed pesticide mixtures, one of the most recent being that of Wickerham and colleagues (2012), who looked at 20 pesticides in 112 samples of cord blood from babies born at term in a rural part of China. Between 5 and 10 different pesticides were found per sample, and as is often the case, the greater the number of chemicals, the lower the birth weight of the child. Other studies have examined brominate-flame retardants or PCB load. A French study in 2009 showed about 20 different PBDEs (brominate-flame retardants) in cord blood, with PBDEs levels being three times higher in cord blood than in maternal serum (Antignac et al., 2009). Mean total PBDEs were 13.6 and 48.9 ng/g lipid in maternal and cord blood, respectively. The same team also examined levels of another brominate-flame retardant, TBBPA, in these samples (Cariou et al., 2008) and found that mean TBBPA levels were five times higher in cord blood (>100 ng/g lipid) than in maternal blood (just under 20 ng/g lipid). These two studies on the same samples show not only multiple exposure but also accumulation within the fetal tissues, with higher levels of contaminants in cord blood than in the maternal compartment. In contrast, a recent report (Zhang, Sun, & Kannan, 2013) that followed partitioning of BPA between maternal and fetal compartments by measuring the levels of BPA in maternal and umbilical cord blood at delivery found only 10% of maternal levels in cord blood. However, the authors noted particularly high levels of BPA in pregnant women and particularly high levels in women who received intravenous medication during delivery.

Breast Milk

The French group from Toulouse (Antignac et al., 2009; Cariou et al., 2008) also measured mean levels of TBBPA and PBDEs in maternal milk, finding mean TBBPA and PDBEs levels of 4 and 3.8 ng/g lipid, respectively. Interestingly, these levels are at least an order of magnitude lower than the levels to which the unborn child is potentially exposed, if one judges by cord blood levels, again emphasizing the greater risk of in utero exposure rather than breast-feeding. Researchers in many countries have addressed the question of different categories of chemicals, notably mixtures of pesticides,

PBDEs, and PCBs in human milk. A recent Tunisian study measured nine PBDEs, eight PCBs, and seven pesticides or their metabolites in breast milk samples collected in 2010 from women who had given birth in a provincial hospital. Total PDBEs averaged 10.5 ng/g lipid, about two to three times those in Toulouse, but one third of the values in California. The Tunisian results show disquietingly high levels of total DDT or DDT metabolites, in the microgram per gram lipid range, though levels have decreased about three-fold since an earlier study in the same region 8 years before, indicative of reduced exposure (Hassine, Ameur, Gandoura, & Driss, 2012). Total DDT/DDT metabolite values were also twice as high in women feeding their first child than in multiparous women. No such differences were seen in levels of other pesticides, nor in PCBs or PPBDEs, suggesting continuing exposure to these chemicals. The authors compared their results with published data on pesticides and PCBs in breast milk from a series of countries. According to their summary table, the highest levels of DDT metabolites in human milk in the last decade were found in South Africa, where values averaged 6 µg/g lipid. The Tunisian study also reported relatively high levels of another pesticide, HCB, and total PCBs (both in the 300 ng/g lipid range). As regards PCBs, the highest levels by far (1.8 µg/g lipid) were found in samples taken from women in the Faroe Islands, a region of high consumption of whale meat.

Cosmetics and ultraviolet (UV) screens are not often included in breast milk analyses. However, Schlumpf and colleagues (2010) measured a series of these chemicals along with OC pesticides, PBDEs, and PCBs in an extensive screen of milk samples from Swiss women in Basel, between 7 and 10 days after having given birth. Fifty-four samples were obtained over 3 years in summer or winter. All but one woman filled in a detailed questionnaire on cosmetic use and nutritional habits. Nearly 80% of the women used cosmetics and/or sunscreens. Milk was analyzed for 8 UV filters (out of the 29 permitted for use in Switzerland), 16 synthetic musks, 30 pesticides, 7 PCBs, and 6 PBDEs. UV filters were found in 85% of milk samples. In contrast to data on wildlife where contamination is widespread, differences in milk content of these chemicals were associated with individual use of sunscreens and cosmetics (that also contain these filters) and little seasonal variation was found. As to the pesticides, PCBs, and PBDEs, levels were similar to those reported in other EU studies but suggested daily intakes for infants were close to or above current EPA recommended levels. This was the case for the phthalate metabolite MEPH, for which average intake was calculated at 5,158 ng/kg bw/day with maximal levels reaching over 20,000 ng/kg bw/day, nearly four times over the recommended limit of 5,800 ng/kg bw/day. Intake, through breast milk, of the three most common UV filters found was calculated to range between 130 and 200 ng/kg bw/day.

One of the broadest analyses of breast milk published is a Japanese study that examined associations between maternal chemical load as judged from milk contamination and the three-fold increase in incidence of congenital hypothyroidism (CH) in Japan over the last 30 years (Nagayama et al.,

2007). The authors had already reported on the negative associations between infants' TH levels and pre- or perinatal exposure to either PCBs and dioxins or pesticides. Here they examined simultaneous exposure to a suite of dioxin-like substances and organochlorine pesticides in children with CH or cretin-ism, high levels of TSH, and normal controls. The total PCDD, PCDFs, and dioxin-like PCB load was associated with cretinism and decreased thyroid function. Highest levels of contaminants, 0.62 toxic equivalents per gram of breast milk, were found in cretins. Levels reached 0.42 in the high TSH group and were only 0.26 in the controls. Similarly, the total pesticide load reached 0.34 ng/g milk in the group classified as cretins and 0.24 and 0.15 ng/g in the high TSH and normal groups, respectively. Thus, the severe CH group (referred to as cretins by the authors) had three and two times higher dioxin-like and pesticide exposure, respectively, than controls. Two points can be usefully underlined here. First, that a mere two-fold increase in chemical load can cause major effects on thyroid signaling (and hence neurodevelopmental outcome) and, second, that given that the children were born with CH, the breast milk analysis was carried out as an indication of the levels of exposure to which the children could have been exposed in utero.

Again, as for the cord blood analyses, no doubt because of the cost and perhaps the difficulty of obtaining sufficient samples, there are no exhaustive analyses of the spectrum of mixtures of components comprising contamination in breast milk. However, it must be reiterated here that it is not only human breast milk which contains pesticides and flame retardants; infant formula and cow's milk are also contaminated to similar extents (see Chapter 5). Most authorities consider that the multiple benefits of breast-feeding, notably on immune function, largely outweigh the risk of endocrine disruption, which would also be encountered by formula feeding. In fact, in the early studies on PCB contamination in the Lake Michigan study, the Jacobsons' data showed that, despite the extra load transferred by breast-feeding, most of the damage was correlated with prenatal development and placental transfer in utero (Jacobson & Jacobson, 1996). Moreover, no doubt due to the multiple benefits of breast-feeding, the breast-fed children actually came out better on neurodevelopmental scores than their formula-fed peers (Jacobson & Jacobson, 2002). However, it seems reasonable to suggest that, given the high transfer of some chemicals, women who are breast-feeding should reduce their use of cosmetics and sunscreens.

## Young Children, and Flame-Retardant Mixtures in House Dust

Much emphasis in previous chapters has been placed on the recently recognized role of TH in early prenatal brain development. However, it should be recalled that TH actions on neurogenesis were first described in animal studies addressing the perinatal and the postnatal period (Eayrs, 1953), where TH plays particularly important roles. Interestingly, the first studies in the late 19th century on correction of cretinism in humans identified the early years of life as the time window during which the effects of TH lack on intellect and growth could be corrected by administering thyroid extract, with supplementation in adolescence or later life only producing adverse effects. Clearly, beyond intra-uterine and early postnatal exposure, it is vital to identify sources of contamination that could be affecting brain growth in the first years of life as the child gains independence. The main sources identified are food, air, and house dust.

Toddlers and babies that are starting to crawl are acutely exposed to house dust as they move around on the floor or close to the floor, and quite naturally place their fingers in their mouths. House dust is one of the most complex and highest sources of contamination of both pesticides and flame retardants. Clearly the proportion of each category will be higher in different countries, areas, and socioeconomic sectors. Pesticides, notably insecticides such as those used against mosquitos and cockroaches, will override flame retardants in tropical countries, whereas the inverse, or equal contributions, will be found in developed countries. Brenda Eskanazi's team at the University of Berkeley has done a series of detailed investigations on both rural and urban areas in the Salina Valley of California (Quiros-Alcala et al., 2011a, 2011b). This region shows high levels of both flame retardants and pesticides in house dust. Here, as in many agriculturally dense situations, with farmers and their families living in substandard housing, the pesticides can be either of domestic or agricultural origin. Overall it seems that although house dust is an important source of pesticides, food remains the most significant source of pesticide exposure in urban and rural communities in these areas. However, in rural areas proximity to agricultural pesticide usage is determinant in increasing exposure, potentially through a number of routes whether airborne, or products brought home on clothing, or food and house dust itself. This increased exposure has been a driving factor for proposals to consider children of farm workers as a particularly vulnerable population (Bradman et al., 2011).

Returning to the specific problem of house dust and flame retardants, the mixture effect is again routinely emphasized. Flame retardants will accumulate in house dust from multiple sources, including furnishings (curtains, carpets, and other floor coverings), furniture (particularly soft parts of foam-based couches and cushions), building and insulating materials, computers, and electronic devices such as flat screen televisions. PDBEs are of particular concern in this context because they are partially volatile and thus can be released into the indoor environment and settle with dust. As described in Chapter 5, the main flame retardants used in the last 50 years have been in the category of brominated flame retardants (BFRs), such as the PBDEs and HBCD. PBDEs, introduced in the 1960s, were largely phased out between 2004 and 2009 in the European Union and the United States. Not surprisingly, given their most stringent flammability standards for furniture, California holds the world record for house-dust contamination with flame retardants (Dodson et al., 2012). The detailed study by Dodson and colleagues compared levels of 62 flame retardants and other halogenated organic compounds in dust collected from 16 homes at a 5-year interval, covering the phasing out of pentaBDE and OctaBDE. Fifty-five of the 62 chemicals investigated were found in at least one of the samples. PentaBDE was still found in 2011 but at significantly lower levels than in 2006, mean levels decreasing from about 5,000 ng/g house dust to around 1,000 ng/g. In contrast, levels of chemicals used in a commercial flame retardant mixture, Firemaster 550, increased as expected, given its use as a pentaBDE replacement. Levels doubled from around 50 to 100 ng/g over the 5 years. TBBPA levels were not different, averaging about 200 ng/g in 2011. Amazingly, a mutagenic chemical (TDBPP), commonly referred to as brominated Tris, which had been banned in children's sleepwear in the 1970s because of the dangers of skin absorption (Blum et al., 1978), was found in 75% of samples. However, levels had decreased since 2006 and in 2011 median levels were below the detection level. Levels of banned OC pesticides such as DDT and its metabolites decreased slightly, by factors of two or three. PBDEs still found at median levels over 1,000 ng/g in the 2011 samples included BDE 47 (a tetraBDE), BDE 99 (pentaBDE), and BDE 209 (decaBDE). Currently, decaBDE is the only PBDE registered in Europe, but its use is continually under reevaluation. Other flame retardants at high levels included triphenyl phosphate (a Firemaster 550 component) and three chlorinated organophosphates each found at over 2,000 ng/g (2 μg/g), including one chlorinated organophosphate flame retardant (TCEP), a registered carcinogen in California!

There are many questions and unknowns about the chemistry of potential flame retardant replacements. As mentioned in Chapter 5, it is significant that of the 23 chemicals listed by the EPA for close assessment in 2014, 20 are flame retardants. Chemical structures are not given for four on the list, so an independent laboratory cannot test their effects. Secrecy also shrouds many flame-retardant mixtures currently on the market after the PDBE phase-out, such as Firemaster 550, for which the full composition is not known (Dodson et al., 2012).

Many authorities consider that flame-retardant use today is excessive and that the risks have long outweighed the benefits. One of the pioneers in this field is Arlene Blum. In 1977/1978 she coauthored three high-visibility papers on the mutagenic effects of flame retardant used in children's pyjamas, one tellingly entitled "Another Flame Retardant...and Its Expected Metabolites Are Mutagens" (Gold, Blum, & Ames, 1978). Having trained as a chemist, she left science for a while to concentrate on her other passion, mountaineering, leading an all-women team (also the first American team) to the summit of Annapurna. She has since returned to environmental science and in 2008 founded the Green Science Policy Institute (http://greensciencepolicy.org/about-us). This action was spurred by her having realized that the same chemical she had identified as a mutagen 30 years previously in children's sleepware had been reintroduced in furnishings. The institute's current focus is the reduction of unnecessary use of flame retardants. In 2010, she, Theo Colborn, and Brenda Eskanazi along with many other scientists and policy makers signed the "San Antonio statement" advocating increased responsibility and control of the use of brominated and chlorinated flame retardants globally

(DiGangi et al., 2010). This point will be rediscussed in Chapter 8, but suffice it to say here that children are significantly exposed to complex mixtures of multiple chemical classes at all stages of development, from fertilization on. Of course, exposure does not end with the toddler phase, and children and adolescents are continually exposed to mixtures of flame retardants. A Belgian study reported not only significant correlations of BFR load with decreased FT3 and increased TSH levels in 515 adolescents but also found that small increases in total PBDE levels correlated with decreased motor coordination (Kicinski et al., 2012).

Given that many, but by no means all, of these chemicals are present at what is commonly termed "low doses," we move into this area—another scene of intense debate.

## The Questions of Low Doses and Nonmonotonic Dose–Response Curves

Assessment of the effects of low doses of chemicals and placing nonmonotonic dose–response curves (NMDRCs) in a physiological context is relevant to the whole of the endocrine-disrupting chemical (EDC) debate and its importance extends to many fields beyond the scope of this book. However, some succinct background to these thorny questions is provided because, especially with regard to mixtures, they are relevant not only to scientists and policy makers but also to laypeople seeking to understand the problems posed by EDCs. Vanderberg and 11 other scientists reviewed these questions in detail in 2012. They adopted a definition of "low dose" previously used by the US National Toxicology Program: "those (doses) that are found in the range of human exposure…and doses below those used for traditional toxicology studies" (Vandenberg et al., 2012, p. 379).

BPA can be used as a paradigm for both questions (Vandenberg, Maffini, Sonnenschein, Rubin, & Soto, 2009). First, BPA has been at the center of the low-dose stage for many years, and, second, in many systems, as can be expected for a factor with estrogen-like properties, it displays NMDRC responses. As mentioned in the previous chapter, BPA was first investigated in the 1930s for its potential estrogenic activities. These properties were considered insufficient for using BPA in a clinical setting, and DES was selected for marketing instead, with the disastrous multigenerational effects now documented. However, the use of BPA as a plasticizer has amplified unabated since then.

Humans, wildlife, soil, and surface water (Flint, Markle, Thompson, & Wallace, 2012) are universally contaminated with low levels of BPA. Its presence has been associated with numerous reproductive cancers and sterility problems. As detailed earlier, the CDC data, based on a representative US population, showed mean urinary BPA values of 2 μg/g creatine (just under 2 μg/L urine), three to four orders of magnitude lower that the mg/g quantities of all three thyroid-inhibiting anions, perchlorate, nitrates, and thiocyanate in urine. These urinary BPA values represent daily intakes of 0.4–5 μg/kg per day (Vandenberg et al., 2012). The lowest observed adverse effect level (LOAEL) has been reported to be 50 mg/kg per day, 10,000 times higher, while

administering about 400 µg/kg per day to rodents results in blood levels equivalent to those seen in human populations. Despite this LOAEL of 50 mg/kg per
day, innumerable animal studies examining physiological and developmental
effects have documented BPA effects at levels similar to those found in humans.
In 2012, Vandenberg and colleagues reviewed the literature on low-dose effects
and NMDRCs of natural hormones and EDCs, bringing into their discussion
data from no fewer than 845 scientific papers, covering the main endocrine
systems. They underline the need to go beyond the erroneous vision of biological responses as simply linear, based on the simple-minded concept that
lower doses must necessarily be less effective or harmful than higher doses.
They provide details and explain the different dose responses that can be found
regularly in endocrinology (Fig. 6.1), arguing that these physiological examples
of NMDRCs should be taken into account in toxicological studies.

Vandenberg et al. (2012) also explain the biochemistry of ligand–receptor
interaction and the important concept of how lower doses of one substance can
modulate action of another at a different dose. Unfortunately, these basic and
vital concepts are rarely taken into consideration by many toxicologists and
policy makers, who no doubt find it easier to deal with and make decisions on
straightforward linear responses.

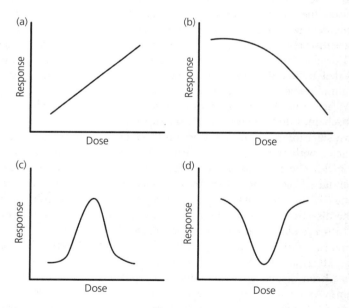

Figure 6–1. Linear, monotonic, and nonmonotonic dose–response curves. A linear
response (a) is compared to (b) a monotonic response (no change in sign or direction of
response). In (c) and (d) "U" and inverse "U" (left) dose responses are shown, responses
that can be found with some hormones and endocrine-disrupting chemicals (EDCs) in
physiological systems. In these cases, studying effects at high doses does not allow one
to extrapolate or deduce effects at lower doses.

BPA is the most discussed example, but many others could be mentioned. One of the most dramatic examples of low doses having detrimental effects on brain development in defined windows of time is that derived from the PCB studies around Lake Michigan. Here it was shown that despite the higher levels of PCBs in milk rather than maternal serum, prenatal exposure to lower levels had the greater impact on intelligence (Jacobson & Jacobson, 1996) and that small increases in exposure could have significant detrimental effects on neurodevelopmental outcome. The pernicious effects of low doses can again be seen when looking at lead exposure data, and the lessons learned there could be usefully transferred to legislation and restriction of other substances. As related by Markowitz and Rosner (2013) nonfatal, but continuous, low-dose exposures have transformed our understanding of toxicology and what we can consider as "safe levels." Public health-related methods and decision-making processes established as a function of infectious diseases prevalent in the first half of the 20th century need to be revised in response to the chronic disease patterns that have emerged in the latter part of that century. Not only do experimental and assessment methods need to be rethought but also the power balance between industrial lobbies and governments as well as other social forces, including economic inequality, need to be factored into the equations.

Take-Home Messages and Future Research Needs

- It is surprising that despite the evidence for multiple exposure, and the particularly high levels of flame retardants in cord blood, no studies have attempted to assess the full extent of mixture constituents in cord blood, meconium, or breast milk. Such information will be critical in assessing the most deleterious elements and combinations that show associations with children's postnatal TH levels and/or later neurodevelopmental and behavioral progress.
- Newly identified ubiquitous contaminants need to be thoroughly assessed for their endocrine-disrupting properties, both in isolation and in mixtures.
- Given the seven common categories of chemicals found in maternal serum—perchlorate, PAHs, phthalates, PFCs, PBDEs, OC pesticides, and PCBs—the effect of gestational exposure to representative combinations should be carried out in animal studies to assess neurobehavioral effects in offspring.
- The inclusion of representative heavy metal loads would also provide important information.
- Pregnant and breast-feeding mothers would do well to reduce their use of cosmetics and sunscreens and to follow recently published advice (http://www.rcog.org.uk/files/rcog-corp/5.6.13ChemicalExpo sures.pdf).
- More data are needed on the effects of long-term multiple exposures to low- (and high-) dose mixtures, and appropriate analytical methods

applied for their risk assessment in terms of brain and behavioral development.

- More cost–benefit analyses need to be carried out on the use of flame retardants, and their replacements should be closely analyzed for toxicity and endocrine disruptive properties. The reduction in smoking, notably inside houses, has contributed to reducing the number and severity of house fires; however, at the same time the accumulation of flame retardants in urban environments is increasing.

## REFERENCES

Antignac, J. P., Cariou, R., Zalko, D., Berrebi, A., Cravedi, J. P., Maume, D., . . . Le Bizec, B. (2009). Exposure assessment of French women and their newborn to brominated flame retardants: Determination of tri- to deca- polybromodiphenylethers (PBDE) in maternal adipose tissue, serum, breast milk and cord serum. *Environment and Pollution*, *157*(1), 164–173.

Blum, A., Gold, M. D., Ames, B. N., Jones, F. R., Hett, E. A., Dougherty, R. C., . . . Thenot, J. P. (1978). Children absorb tris-BP flame retardant from sleepwear: Urine contains the mutagenic metabolite, 2,3-dibromopropanol. *Science*, *201*(4360), 1020–1023.

Bradman, A., Barr, D. B., Claus Henn, B. G., Drumheller, T., Curry, C., & Eskenazi, B. (2003). Measurement of pesticides and other toxicants in amniotic fluid as a potential biomarker of prenatal exposure: A validation study. *Environmental Health Perspectives*, *111*(14), 1779–1782.

Bradman, A., Castorina, R., Barr, D. B., Chevrier, J., Harnly, M. E., Eisen, E. A., . . . Eskenazi, B. (2011). Determinants of organophosphorus pesticide urinary metabolite levels in young children living in an agricultural community. *International Journal of Environmental Research and Public Health*, *8*(4), 1061–1083.

Cariou, R., Antignac, J. P., Zalko, D., Berrebi, A., Cravedi, J. P., Maume, D., . . . Le Bizec, B. (2008). Exposure assessment of French women and their newborns to tetrabromobisphenol-A: Occurrence measurements in maternal adipose tissue, serum, breast milk and cord serum. *Chemosphere*, *73*(7), 1036–1041.

Chen, A., Park, J. S., Linderholm, L., Rhee, A., Petreas, M., DeFranco, E. A., . . . Ho, S. M. (2013). Hydroxylated polybrominated diphenyl ethers in paired maternal and cord sera. *Environmental Science and Technology*, *47*(8), 3902–3908.

Colborn, T. (2004). Neurodevelopment and endocrine disruption. *Environmental Health Perspectives*, *112*(9), 944–949.

Dewan, P., Jain, V., Gupta, P., & Banerjee, B. D. (2013). Organochlorine pesticide residues in maternal blood, cord blood, placenta, and breastmilk and their relation to birth size. *Chemosphere*, *90*(5), 1704–1710.

DiGangi, J., Blum, A., Bergman, A., de Wit, C. A., Lucas, D., Mortimer, D., . . . Webster, T. F. (2010). San Antonio Statement on brominated and chlorinated flame retardants. *Environmental Health Perspectives*, *118*(12), A516–518.

Dodson, R. E., Perovich, L. J., Covaci, A., Van den Eede, N., Ionas, A. C., Dirtu, A. C., . . . Rudel, R. A. (2012). After the PBDE phase-out: A broad suite of flame retardants in repeat house dust samples from California. *Environmental Science and Technology*, *46*(24), 13056–13066.

Eayrs, J. T. (1953). Thyroid hypofunction and the development of the central nervous system. *Nature, 172*(4374), 403–404.

Eskenazi, B., Chevrier, J., Rauch, S. A., Kogut, K., Harley, K. G., Johnson, C.,...Bradman, A. (2013). In utero and childhood polybrominated diphenyl ether (PBDE) exposures and neurodevelopment in the CHAMACOS study. *Environmental Health Perspectives, 121*(2), 257–262.

Fini, J. B., Le Mével, S., Palmier, K., Darras, V. M., Punzon, I., Richardson, S. J.,...Demeneix, B. A. (2012). Thyroid hormone signaling in the Xenopus laevis embryo is functional and susceptible to endocrine disruption. *Endocrinology, 153*(10), 5068–5081.

Fini, J. B., Riu, A., Debrauwer, L., Hillenweck, A., Le Mével, S., Chevolleau, S.,...Zalko, D. (2012). Parallel biotransformation of tetrabromobisphenol A in Xenopus laevis and mammals: Xenopus as a model for endocrine perturbation studies. *Toxicological Sciences, 125*(2), 359–367.

Flint, S., Markle, T., Thompson, S., & Wallace, E. (2012). Bisphenol A exposure, effects, and policy: A wildlife perspective. *Journal of Environmental Management, 104*, 19–34.

Foster, W., Chan, S., Platt, L., & Hughes, C. (2000). Detection of endocrine disrupting chemicals in samples of second trimester human amniotic fluid. *Journal of Clinical Endocrinology and Metabolism, 85*(8), 2954–2957.

Gold, M. D., Blum, A., & Ames, B. N. (1978). Another flame retardant, tris-(1,3-dic hloro-2-propyl)-phosphate, and its expected metabolites are mutagens. *Science, 200*(4343), 785–787.

Hassine, S. B., Ameur, W. B., Gandoura, N., & Driss, M. R. (2012). Determination of chlorinated pesticides, polychlorinated biphenyls, and polybrominated diphenyl ethers in human milk from Bizerte (Tunisia) in 2010. *Chemosphere, 89*(4), 369–377.

Jacobson, J. L., & Jacobson, S. W. (1996). Intellectual impairment in children exposed to polychlorinated biphenyls in utero. *New England Journal of Medicine, 335*(11), 783–789.

Jacobson, J. L., & Jacobson, S. W. (2002). Association of prenatal exposure to an environmental contaminant with intellectual function in childhood. *Journal of Toxicology and Clinical Toxicology, 40*(4), 467–475.

Kicinski, M., Viaene, M. K., Den Hond, E., Schoeters, G., Covaci, A., Dirtu, A. C.,...Nawrot, T. S. (2012). Neurobehavioral function and low-level exposure to brominated flame retardants in adolescents: A cross-sectional study. *Environmental Health, 11*, 86.

Li, L. X., Chen, L., Meng, X. Z., Chen, B. H., Chen, S. Q., Zhao, Y.,...Zhang, Y. H. (2013). Exposure levels of environmental endocrine disruptors in mother-newborn pairs in China and their placental transfer characteristics. *PLoS One, 8*(5), e62526.

Markowitz, G. E., Rosner, D., & Milbank Memorial Fund. (2013). *Lead wars: the politics of science and the fate of America's children*. Berkeley: University of California Press.

Miller, M. F., Chernyak, S. M., Domino, S. E., Batterman, S. A., & Loch-Caruso, R. (2012). Concentrations and speciation of polybrominated diphenyl ethers in human amniotic fluid. *Science of the Total Environment, 417–418*, 294–298.

Nagayama, J., Kohno, H., Kunisue, T., Kataoka, K., Shimomura, H., Tanabe, S., & Konishi, S. (2007). Concentrations of organochlorine pollutants in mothers who gave birth to neonates with congenital hypothyroidism. *Chemosphere, 68*(5), 972–976.

Ostrea, E. M., Jr., Bielawski, D. M., Posecion, N. C., Jr., Corrion, M., Villanueva-Uy, E., Jin, Y.,... Ager, J. W. (2008). A comparison of infant hair, cord blood and meconium analysis to detect fetal exposure to environmental pesticides. *Environmental Research*, *106*(2), 277–283.

Ostrea, E. M., Jr., Hernandez, J. D., Bielawski, D. M., Kan, J. M., Leonardo, G. M., Abela, M. B.,... Sokol, R. J. (2006). Fatty acid ethyl esters in meconium: Are they biomarkers of fetal alcohol exposure and effect? *Alcoholism: Clinical and Experimental Research*, *30*(7), 1152–1159.

Ostrea, E. M., Jr., Reyes, A., Villanueva-Uy, E., Pacifico, R., Benitez, B., Ramos, E.,... Ager, J. W. (2012). Fetal exposure to propoxur and abnormal child neurodevelopment at 2 years of age. *Neurotoxicology*, *33*(4), 669–675.

Quiros-Alcala, L., Bradman, A., Nishioka, M., Harnly, M. E., Hubbard, A., McKone, T. E., & Eskenazi, B. (2011a). Concentrations and loadings of polybrominated diphenyl ethers in dust from low-income households in California. *Environment International*, *37*(3), 592–596.

Quiros-Alcala, L., Bradman, A., Nishioka, M., Harnly, M. E., Hubbard, A., McKone, T. E.,... Eskenazi, B. (2011b). Pesticides in house dust from urban and farmworker households in California: An observational measurement study. *Environmental Health*, *10*, 19.

Schlumpf, M., Kypke, K., Wittassek, M., Angerer, J., Mascher, H., Mascher, D.,... Lichtensteiger, W. (2010). Exposure patterns of UV filters, fragrances, parabens, phthalates, organochlor pesticides, PBDEs, and PCBs in human milk: Correlation of UV filters with use of cosmetics. *Chemosphere*, *81*(10), 1171–1183.

Takahashi, O., & Oishi, S. (2000). Disposition of orally administered 2,2-Bis(4-hydroxyphenyl)propane (Bisphenol A) in pregnant rats and the placental transfer to fetuses. *Environmental Health Perspectives*, *108*(10), 931–935.

Vandenberg, L. N., Colborn, T., Hayes, T. B., Heindel, J. J., Jacobs, D. R., Jr., Lee, D. H.,... Myers, J. P. (2012). Hormones and endocrine-disrupting chemicals: Low-dose effects and nonmonotonic dose responses. *Endocrine Review*, *33*(3), 378–455.

Vandenberg, L. N., Maffini, M. V., Sonnenschein, C., Rubin, B. S., & Soto, A. M. (2009). Bisphenol-A and the great divide: A review of controversies in the field of endocrine disruption. *Endocrine Review*, *30*(1), 75–95.

Wickerham, E. L., Lozoff, B., Shao, J., Kaciroti, N., Xia, Y., & Meeker, J. D. (2012). Reduced birth weight in relation to pesticide mixtures detected in cord blood of full-term infants. *Environment International*, *47*, 80–85.

Woodruff, T. J., Zota, A. R., & Schwartz, J. M. (2011). Environmental chemicals in pregnant women in the United States: NHANES 2003-2004. *Environmental Health Perspectives*, *119*(6), 878–885.

Zhang, T., Sun, H., & Kannan, K. (2013). Blood and urinary bisphenol A concentrations in children, adults, and pregnant women from China: Partitioning between blood and urine and maternal and fetal cord blood. *Environmental Science and Technology*, *47*(9), 4686–4694.

# Chapter 7

## Autism Spectrum Disorders, Attention-Deficit/Hyperactivity Disorder, and Congenital Hypothyroidism

*The Case for Gene × Environment Interactions*

CHAPTER OUTLINE

In the 70 years since Kanner's prescient observation that "autism" was "probably more frequent" than his studies showed, diagnoses of autism spectrum disorders (ASD) have risen dramatically from 1 in 5,000 in 1975 to over 1 in 88 in 2009 in some areas (see Fig. 7.1). Incidence of attention-deficit/hyperactivity disorder (ADHD) has also increased, affecting 8% of US children in 2011. Diagnostic change and greater social awareness account for less than 40% of the ASD increase. As the gene pool has not changed, environmental causes must be implicated. Despite vastly improved genetic sequencing methods and large amounts of funds invested, only a few genetic variations in DNA sequence have been linked to ASD. Clearly there is a need to focus more on environmental factors, particularly the impact of environmental factors on cellular responses and gene expression (gene × environment interactions) occurring during early development. Studies on associations of exposure with disease incidence should examine critical developmental windows, notably early pregnancy. The numbers of children born with congenital hypothyroidism is also increasing in certain areas and, like ASD and ADHD, the rise cannot be explained by genetic causes. When congenital hypothyroidism is identified after birth, TH deficiency can be corrected in the early perinatal period and continued if necessary. TH disruption during fetal growth is potentially more problematic. As TH modulates expression of numerous neurodevelopmental gene networks, TH signaling can be seen as a highway linking the environment to gene expression. Deficiency and disruption of TH signaling by environmental chemicals can thus be considered front-line candidates contributing to the increasing incidence of ASD and ADHD. Given that determining environmental causes offers the most scope to staunch the ASD epidemic, it is argued that precautionary principles should be applied while more research is directed to identifying the principal culprits and determining replacement strategies.

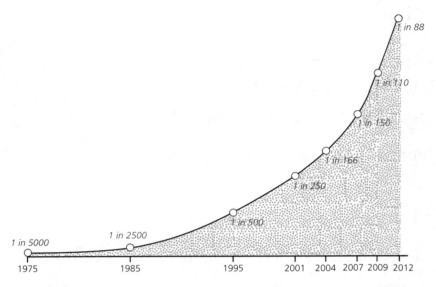

**Figure 7–1.** The increasing incidence of autism spectrum disorders in the United States. (Modified and adapted from Wientraub, 2011.) The time line of autism diagnosis incidence in US studies reveals that the slope of the curve over the last 10 years has steepened dramatically. Note that the same diagnostic criteria were applied in the studies published in 2009 and 2012. Also, with an incidence of 1 in 88 children, the incidence in boys reaches 1 in 54. Data from 2014 show rates of 1 in 68 children, 1 in 42 boys.

## History of Autism Spectrum Disorder, Asperger's Syndrome, and Attention-Deficit/Hyperactivity Disorder Classification and Diagnosis

### Autism

In 1943, Leo Kanner published his seminal paper describing a new syndrome that he established based on a series of observations of 11 children sharing an "*inability to relate themselves*[1]. . . . to people and situations from the beginning of life." He concluded (p. 250) by stating that these cases represented "examples of *inborn disturbances of affective contact*." The original paper was republished in 1968 (Kanner, 1968). A number of factors in these detailed observations discussed by Kanner remain highly pertinent today. Not the least is that he predicted the condition to have a higher incidence than suggested on his small sample size. Figures published in 2012 on diagnoses of ASD from the US Center for Disease Control and Prevention (Anonymous, 2012) fully support his prediction. Analyzing data collected in 2008, the Autism and Developmental Disabilities Monitoring (ADDM) group show the estimated incidence to have reached 1 in 88 children, with 11.3 cases per 1,000 children aged 8 years old.

---

1   Italics were used in the original text.

A second point is the three common traits identified by Kanner—problems with communication, repetitive behavior, and lack of social interaction—have provided the core of ASD diagnosis for over half a century. Lack of social interaction, or as Kanner phrased it "social awareness" or " extreme autistic aloneness," is probably the basis for the term *autism*, from the Greek "autos" or self and "ismos" or state, apparently introduced into the medical literature by the 19th-century Swiss psychiatrist Paul Bleuler. In 2013, the main English language manual for psychiatric disease, the *Diagnostic and Statistical Manual of Mental Disorders* (DSM) came to the end of a 14-year revision of its fourth version, *DSM-IV*. The fifth edition (*DSM-5*), which replaced *DSM-IV-TR*,[2] can be consulted on http://www.dsm5.org. A central idea is that ASD diagnosis is based on two main criteria of impairment, communication/interaction on the one hand and restricted or repetitive behavior on the other. This "two-category" grouping differs from that elaborated under *DSM-IV* guidelines that were operative up until 2012/2013, where the classification into one of these four different categories of autistic-type disorders was based on the three original domains of impairment (i.e., social interaction, communication, and restricted or stereotyped behavior; Fig. 7.2). ASD incorporates four main disease categories namely, autistic disorder, Asperger's disorder, childhood disintegrative disorder (CDD), and pervasive developmental disorder/not otherwise specified (PDD/NOS).

Returning to Kanner's paper, a third point to be highlighted is his insistence on the "inborn" nature of the condition, that is, the fact that it is present at birth and not a result of inappropriate parenting. Unfortunately, despite the insistence on the fact that he thought the children had an *innate* incapacity to interact affectively with their parents, following Kanner's publication many parents, particularly mothers, were made to feel that their children's autistic behavior was a result of their own failure to interact sufficiently with them. The concept was later enshrined in the notion of the cold or "refrigerator" mother (Amaral, 2011). It was no doubt related to the fact that within the 1943 text Kanner does make the observation that in the group there were "very few really warmhearted fathers and mothers." This idea was taken up by many leading psychologists and psychoanalysts as a causative factor in the etiology of the disease, and it recalls the old dichotomy of nature versus nurture with, in this interpretation, the parents' nurturing overriding nature. Perhaps this unfounded attribution of guilt to the parents' incapacity to care for the child correctly has contributed to the overriding current emphasis on intrinsic, genetic causes and the reluctance to consider environmental factors. However, many other arguments can be raised to explain this emphasis on genetics rather than environment. First, there is the deterministic mindset that prioritizes genetic causes rather than considering development as a continual interplay between environment and genes and second, the greater facility that exists today for carrying out large-scale genetic analyses. We will return to this point in the discussion of gene × environment

2  *DSM-IV*-Text Revised.

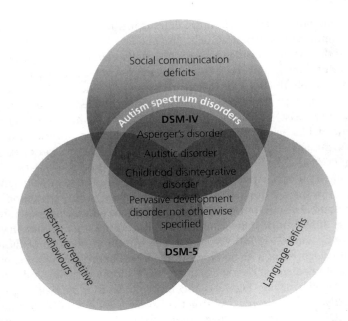

**Figure 7–2.** Modulation of autism phenotypic classification between two editions of the *Diagnostic and Statistical Manual of Mental Disorders, DSM-IV* and *DSM-5.* (Adapted from Devlin, 2012.) Note that in *DSM-5* the domains of impairment are grouped under the single category of autism spectrum disorders (ASD). See text for more details.

interactions in the section on "Epigenetic Contributions to Gene × Environment Interactions in Autism Spectrum Disorders, Attention-Deficit/Hyperactivity Disorder, and Congenital Hypothyroidism."

The fourth factor drawn from his observations that still holds with the hindsight of today's statistics and knowledge is the ratio of affected boys to affected girls. Eight out of the 11 children in Kanner's group were boys and, interestingly, they were all brought to Kanner for diagnosis and treatment at a much earlier age than each of the three girls. The average age of the boys was just under 4 years (age range: 2–6 years), while that of the girls was 9 years old (respectively: 7, 8, and 11). As will be regularly emphasized and discussed, boys are diagnosed with autistic characteristics about four to five times more frequently than girls. The question of why girls are less frequently diagnosed with ASD and ADHD is discussed in at the end of the section on "Inherited Genetic Risk Factors for Autism Spectrum Disorders and Attention-Deficit/ Hyperactivity Disorder."

Another aspect of Kanner's commentary that still has significant resonance today is that many of the symptoms could have led, and sometimes did, to a diagnosis of childhood schizophrenia. Both disorders cover large spectra of symptoms and phenotypes. Autism, like schizophrenia, is often called an umbrella disease because of its wide range of possible forms, with ASD covering a range of behavioral disorders and intellectual abilities. A number of current areas of research are showing overlap between ASD and schizophrenia, notably in terms of genetic susceptibility, similar neurological deficits, treatments (King & Lord, 2011), and to underlying problems with TH signaling. The use of hypothyroid animals as a model for autism has been reviewed (Roman, 2007), as have the multiple links between modified TH signaling and schizophrenia (Santos et al., 2012). An important common idea is the link between TH and environmental influence. As emphasized by Palha and Goodman (2006), not only are a number of genes implicated in TH signaling positional or functional candidates associated with schizophrenia but also TH pathways could serve as a mediator of gene × environment interactions in the pathology.

A final point is that the parents who consulted Kanner were all described as "highly intelligent," with most of the fathers having academic, research, or legal backgrounds and with nine of the eleven mothers having a college education. This feature is often highlighted today with the higher rate of ASD in children of engineers and geeks almost being expected. However, appraising the data from Kanner's observations should take into account the cost of consulting a highly reputed psychiatrist in the United States in the late 1930s/early 1940s, which would certainly be prohibitive for parents with lower incomes.

## Asperger's Syndrome

At the same time that Kanner, working in the Johns Hopkins Hospital in Baltimore, Maryland, was bringing together his ideas on the common characteristics of autism, Hans Asperger was working in Vienna with children displaying certain similar characteristics. He published his work on four boys in German in 1944. As many authors have underlined, the main difference between the children studied by Kanner and those studied by Asperger was that the Viennese boys all had normal intelligence and use of language, though they had a tendency to speak in monologues (Cox, 1991). In contrast, three of Kanner's cases were so withdrawn that they did not speak. This difference in language skills, potentially reflecting higher intellectual capacity, with shared repetitive behavior and lack of social communication skills, has led to the concept that Asperger's syndrome represents a "high-functioning" end of the autism spectrum. Apparently, in England, this concept was first suggested by Lorna Wing (Pearce, 2005).

## Rett's Syndrome

Rett's syndrome is another neurodevelopmental disorder that is classified as an ASD in the *DSM-IV-TR*. This disease affects primarily girls, as the gene affected in most cases, *MEPC2*, is located on the X-chromosome and mutations in boys are usually lethal during early development. *MECP2* encodes the methyl-CpG-binding protein 2, which is a nuclear transcriptional regulator that binds to methylated CpG dinucleotides in DNA. Recognition of CpG methylation is central to control of gene transcription, and MECP2 is a key protein in recognizing the methylated dinucleotides and repressing or activating gene transcription and thus to epigenetic regulations (see section on "Epigenetic Contributions...").

Rett's syndrome has a number of distinctive features, notably in the early stages of the disease a repetitive handwringing caused by loss of controlled hand movements. It was this feature that was spotted by the Viennese pediatrician, Dr. Andreas Rett, in the mid-1950s and described in a group of patients in a German publication in 1966. However, the English-speaking community only became fully aware of the syndrome in 1983 when a Swedish physician reported the condition in 35 girls (Hagberg, Aicardi, Dias, & Ramos, 1983). Even though the *Mecp2* gene is expressed in all cells, neurons and glial cells are the most affected, leading to the symptoms of intellectual disability and loss of purposeful movements and speech. One of the most distressing characteristics of the disease for parents of affected children is that the girls show apparently normal development for the first year of life, but then their development stagnates before a slow deterioration sets in over the next 20 years, with death ensuing due to respiratory failure. Rett's syndrome has different degrees of manifestation, according to the effect of the precise mutation in the *Mecp2* gene and how, as a consequence, it affects the function of the MECP2 protein. The disease falls under the umbrella of ASD as autistic features, including withdrawal and eye gaze avoidance, are diagnostic features included in the *DSM-IV-TR* criteria of PDD-NOS. Fortunately, the incidence of Rett's syndrome is low, less than 1 in 10,000 live births (in females); thus, it represents a small fraction of ASD.

## Attention-Deficit/Hyperactivity Disorder

According to the *DSM-IV-TR*, ADHD was defined as a "pattern of inattention and/or hyperactivity-impulsivity symptoms that persist for at least six months to a degree that is maladaptive and inconsistent with developmental level." Within each category, inattention or hyperactivity/impulsivity, six common symptoms are listed, including difficulty sustaining attention or organizing tasks, fidgeting, or talking excessively. To be conclusive, such patterns need to be observed in at least two settings, usually home and school. Like the first descriptions of ASD, clinical reports with features of ADHD also appeared at the beginning of the 20th century. Many authors addressing the history of ADHD diagnosis attribute the first description to the founder of the discipline of pediatrics, Sir George F. Still, not an insignificant name for the person who classifies pathological hyperactivity as "a defect of moral control"! However, more comprehensive historical accounts (Lange, Reichl, Lange, Tucha, & Tucha, 2010) document earlier descriptions of children displaying many symptoms in common with those used to diagnose ADHD today. Most notable in Lange and colleagues' fascinating history of ADHD diagnosis (Lange et al., 2010) is that of the work of an Edinburgh practitioner Sir Alexander Crichton, who worked at the end of the 18th century. According to these authors, in 1798 Crichton wrote a three-book treatise on mental illness. Crichton had studied medicine in Leiden and practiced in three different European cities. Two of those cities have particular resonance for their schools of psychiatry and psychoanalysis, Paris and Vienna. One chapter of the second volume of the treatise describes his observations on children with one of the main symptoms of what today would be classified as ADHD, that is, the incapacity to attend with constancy to any one object and frequently changing the object of their attentions. Crichton presciently reflected that the condition could be inborn or may develop later, was due to nervous hypersensitivity, and made education difficult. He also observed that symptoms generally lessened with age. The idea that the symptoms of ADHD attenuate with age was generally accepted until recently. However, numerous studies are showing its persistence in late adolescents and adults, with adverse effects on work capacity (Ebejer et al., 2012; Kooij et al., 2010).

Lange and coauthors also cite the perceptive studies of a 19th-century German physician, Heinrich Hoffmann. Like Crichton, Hoffmann traveled through Europe (Heidelberg, Halle, and Paris) for his medical studies. His observations are cited for their reports on the "fidgety" nature of the behavior patterns and their persistence, two symptoms again listed in *DSM-IV*.

Returning to Still's 1902 description of moral control defects, it is perhaps the resemblance of the symptoms he described to modern definitions of ADHD that have led to his work as most often being cited as the forerunner of the field, in the same way that Kanner is seen as the founder of autism studies. Although the descriptions in his clinical reports in 1902 do not fully match the diagnostic determinants in use over a century later, three key problem areas, cited by Lange et al. (2010), are particularly pertinent. These "three psychical factors" are problems with "a cognitive relation to environment, moral consciousness, and volition," but "without impairment of intellect." The problems with cognitive relation to the environment and moral consciousness are later described as being characterized by a requirement for self-gratification, incapacity for sustained attention, inattention, and impulsivity, each recalling modern classifications of ADHD symptoms. Furthermore, the fact that Still underlines that the 20 children he observed had no intellectual incapacity and that it was more their failure to act in a "moral" manner was inappropriate for their age again resonates with current ADHD diagnosis. Two final points of convergence are, first, that of the 20 cases that formed the basis of his description, 15 were boys and only 5 girls, a fact than he notes as not being fortuitous but significant; and second, that the problems had developed before the children reached the age of 7 years. Current statistics show a predominance of three boys diagnosed for each girl with ADHD and guidelines recognize that some of the symptoms that cause impairment are observed before 7 years of age. Despite these strong parallels, Lange et al. (2010) underline that many other symptoms described by Still do not actually fall under current ADHD diagnostic guidelines, particularly the concept of "moral defect," but were broader descriptions of unacceptable social behaviors.

Historically, the next significant contributions to the field came in 1932 from two German doctors, Kramer and Pollnow (as cited in Lange et al., 2010), who described "hyperkinetic" behaviors that could not be attributed to previous infections, such as encephalitis already known to induce similar behavioral problems. These physicians highlighted the excessive need of the children studied to be in constant movement and their inability to focus and concentrate. The first feature clearly recalls the line in the ADHD diagnosis hyperactivity section where children are described as being often "on the go" or act as if "driven by a motor," and the second feature recalls the guideline's underscoring of "difficulty in sustaining attention." Other parallels include lack of perseverance and mood changes and a key determinant in current diagnosis, problems with the scholastic environment.

A fast-forward to the latter part of the 20th century shows a shift of emphasis in diagnostic practice to impulsivity and deficits in attention rather than hyperactivity (Lange et al., 2010). This shift of focus was reflected in the third *DSM* edited in 1980 that refers to attention-deficit disorder (ADD) with or without hyperactivity, and it is not until its revision in 1987 that the term "attention-deficit/hyperactivity disorder (ADHD)" was coined and hyperactivity reincorporated into the set of diagnostic criteria. This terminology was maintained in the *DSM-IV-TR* used up until mid-2013 and its revised form and through to *DSM-5*.

## The Exponential Increase in Autism Spectrum Disorders: Not Only a Matter of Increased Diagnosis

### Prevalence of Autism Spectrum Disorders

In March 2012, the US Centers for Disease Control and Prevention (CDC) published their latest analysis of ASD prevalence, drawing on statistics generated by the Austism and Developmental Disabilities Network Monitoring (ADDM) Network. This network obtains and reanalyzes data on all 8-year-olds in 14 states. A child is recorded as a positive ASD case if he or she met the *DSM-IV-TR* diagnosis criteria, which in 2008, the year of the last survey, included within the ASD spectrum, autism disorder, PDD-NOS (including atypical autism), or Asperger's disorder. The methodology for diagnosis used was exactly the same as applied in previous ADDM assessments for 2002 and 2006 and therefore allowed a comparison of incidence rates over time. The network also obtains data on racial and ethnic origin as well as, in about 70% of cases, on IQ. Because only 14 states are in the network, the authors of the report (Anonymous, 2012) underline that the data cannot be seen as representative of the United States as a whole. However, it should be noted that some of the states not included, such as California, also have high, if not higher incidence in certain areas.

The most striking statistic to come out of this study is that, despite use of constant diagnostic criteria, ASD incidence in 2008 had increased by 23% over the previous 2 years and by an astounding 73% in the 6 years between 2002 and 2008. In the data from 2008, the incidence, according to state, ranged from around 4 to over 20 per 1,000 children, with an average rate of 11.3 per 1,000, representing more that one child in 88. The ratio of boys affected to girls remained the same as before, with five times more boys (1 in 54) diagnosed than girls (1 in 252). Moreover, the percentage of girls diagnosed with ASD who also had intellectual disability (IQ < 70) was higher than for boys, being respectively 46% for girls and only 37% for boys. This result means that nearly half of the girls diagnosed with ASD are actually intellectually disabled, and if there is a significant increase in this category, then given current thinking that there is a female–specific protective genetic component to ASD (Werling & Geschwind, 2013), then the arguments for intensifying the search for environmental factors affecting gene expression are significantly strengthened.

The overall rise in incidence in the US data is represented in Figure 7.1. However, despite the high figures in the latest reports, some authors consider that they could be underestimates. For instance, Weintraub (2011) emphasizes that the US data are based on children in the school system and on symptoms that are sufficiently marked to get a clear diagnosis. Given that ASD is usually recognized before the age of 3 years, one can predict that the rise in numbers of 8-year-olds with ASD in 2008 should be the tip of an underlying larger increase in the younger population. Whether or not the data on 8-year-olds are underestimates of their age group, this type of increase, nearly two-fold in 6 years, is not restricted to the United States. Recent data from Australia support this concept, as the incidence shows similar trends with the most marked increases being in the latest periods of analysis. Comparing data from Australian general practitioners in the BEACH[3] study for the periods 2000/2001 and 2008/2009 revealed a more than two-fold increase of the percentage of psychological problems general practitioners dealt with that were due to autism, rising from 4.9% to 11% (Charles, Harrison, & Britt, 2011). According to Australian national statistics, autism prevalence increased two-fold between 2003 and 2009.[4] One of the highest incidences has been reported in South Korea, with rates reaching 2.64% of children aged between 7 and 12 years old (Kim et al., 2011).

Obviously, a number of theories have been put forward to explain the increased incidence. Before dealing with the current genetic and environment hypotheses, which are discussed later in this chapter, it is important to consider the contributions of changing diagnosis and social awareness of the disease.

As for many diseases that are on the increase, including breast and prostate cancer and other childhood diseases besides ASD, an essential factor to take into account is the change in diagnostic practice or diagnostic substitution. For certain diseases, such as type I diabetes, an actual rise in incidence cannot be confounded by change in diagnosis. However, for reproductive cancers more regular screening can contribute, but again not account for the full extent of the rise, particularly not in younger patients (Aben et al., 2012). That changes in diagnostic practice are in some way contributing to the increased prevalence of ASD is generally accepted. For instance, in the United States children with an IQ under 70, who previously would have been diagnosed as mentally retarded, or

3   Bettering the Evaluation and Care of Health.
4   http://www.abs.gov.au/ausstats/

intellectually disabled to use the terminology redefined in 2010, are often now being classified as autistic (King & Bearman, 2009). In this case, the diagnostic change can be related to the fact that insurance coverage for an autistic child is better than for a child diagnosed as intellectually disabled or mentally retarded. The CDC data from the ADDM network show that about 40% of the children with ASD to have intellectually disability (IQ < 70). However, even the authors who have closely documented and analyzed these changes in medical classification consider that diagnosis substitution can only account for about 25% of the increase in California between 1992 and 2005 (Kim et al., 2011). Most important, as stated previously, one of the strengths of the latest ADDM data is that the diagnostic criteria were constant for comparisons made between 2002 and 2008. Thus, the most significant, latest increases cannot be accounted for by diagnostic change. Another frequently cited social factor is greater awareness among parents, educators, and the general public. Such increased knowledge has notably been put forward to explain geographical hotspots of higher incidence, though clearly many other factors, notably environmental, could be affecting geographical groupings or clustering.

A final, but very important, point before leaving the question of increased incidence is to deal with the fallacy of the association between autism incidence and vaccination. Besides being a disgraceful example of editorial irresponsibility and criminal scientific behavior, the story that follows also illustrates the public's need to attribute a cause to the startling increase in ASD incidence. The main, supposedly "scientific," evidence for the vaccine-autism legend was the irresponsible publication in 1998 by the respected British medical journal, the *Lancet*, of a paper linking cases of chronic enterocolitis and regressive developmental disorder in 12 children with the triple vaccine Measles, Mumps, and Rubella (MMR). The paper reported that 8 of the 12 sets of parents attributed the loss of language skills and the developmental regression to the MMR vaccine. Twelve years later the *Lancet* retracted the paper after the senior author, Dr. Wakefield, was found guilty of unethical conduct, of selecting the children, some of whose parents were trying to sue the vaccine manufacturers, and of accepting money for his research from lawyers acting on behalf of the parents who obviously had an interest in positive associations being published (Eggerston, 2010). Since the original publication, besides the loss of public trust in vaccinations, money has been wasted in studies carried out that disproved the findings, and one also has to take into account the public health cost of the renewed incidence of measles in some areas, cases of which can be fatal.

Prevalence of Attention-Deficit/Hyperactivity Disorder

ADHD is often classified as ADHD with, or ADHD without, learning disability. In the United States, statistics from the CDC (http://www.cdc.gov) that cover the period 2004–2006 showed 8.4% of children aged between 4 and 17 years old to be diagnosed with one form of ADHD. The CDC site states that on the basis of parents' reporting, the incidence reaches 9.5%, a figure that adds up to a staggering 5.4 million American children. The site also provides information on changes in prevalence and states that the US incidence of ADHD increased by 22% between 2003 and 2007 (about 5.5% per year), whereas between 1997 and 2006 the increase averaged 3% (most probably independent of any major changes in diagnostic methods). Thus, even if the increase in incidence is not as large as that of ASD over the same period, in absolute numbers of children affected, the ADHD rise far exceeds the rise in ASD. In contrast, current estimates of the incidence of this class of disorders place worldwide prevalence at around 5%, with no major differences in incidence between Europe and North America, but with greater differences between data from North America compared to Africa and the Middle East (Polanczyk et al., 2007). The authors attribute these differences to methodological differences in diagnosis between the continents.

## Attention-Deficit/Hyperactivity Disorder and Thyroid Hormone Disorders

A flurry of discussion occurred in the mid-1990s (Hauser et al., 1994) on the possible link between thyroid hormone (TH) levels and the symptoms of ADHD. The discussion followed the publication of a paper associating ADHD to another disease, resistance to thyroid hormone (RTH), a congenital disease that results from a mutated TRβ, which does not bind $T_3$ (Hauser et al., 1993). The symptoms and severity of RTH vary according to the mutation, but they most often result in high circulating $T_3$ levels due to the absence of the vital role of TRβ isoforms in $T_3$ feedback on *Trh* and *Tsh* transcription. Modified TH is often accompanied by behavioral changes that can be reminiscent of ADHD (Pearl, Weiss, & Stein, 2001). The findings that RHT was associated in 70% of the children and 50% of the adults with AHDH symptoms led many authors to examine cohorts of ADHD subjects for altered TH levels, most often reporting mild but not major associations (Spencer, Biederman, Wilens, Guite, & Harding, 1995). Two reasons can be proposed for this absence of obvious associations. First, the sample sizes of populations without RHT would show a typically wide range of TH levels that would have insufficient power to determine associations with ADHD. Second and more important, they were probably looking for associations in the wrong time frame. If ADHD is linked to TH levels, it is most probably associated with maternal TH levels during pregnancy and brain development. Thus, examining TH levels in children is not predicted to show associations, rather like shutting the stable door after the horse has gone! Indeed, the one longitudinal study that did examine ADHD rates in children with indicators of maternal thyroid function at different points in pregnancy did reveal significant findings. Vermiglio and colleagues (2004) compared ADHD rates in areas of moderate iodine insufficiency (Area A) with an area that was marginally iodine sufficient (Area B). They found a significant increase in the numbers of children with ADHD born to mothers in the area with slight iodine lack. In this area 11 of the 16 children were diagnosed with ADHD while none were found in the other area. This increase correlated with an 18-point decrease in mean IQ scores in area A (92.1 ± 7.8) versus area B (110 ± 10). ADHD children in Area A had the lowest IQ scores (88 ± 6.9).

These differences in IQ and ADHD occurred despite the fact that the mothers' circulating $T_3$ and $T_4$ levels were apparently within normal ranges. However, their TSH levels were much higher than the mothers of normal children, indicating a state of mild hypothyroidism. The authors suggest that ADHD in RHT patients might have a similar etiology to that seen with their studies on ADHD, iodine lack and maternal hypothyroidism in early pregnancy (i.e., a lack of $T_3$ availability to the developing fetal brain).

## Increased Incidence of Congenital Hypothyroidism

Abnormalities in thyroid gland formation, or congenital hypothyroidism (CH), are the most common endocrine disorders seen in newborn children. Failure to correct CH is the leading cause of *preventable* intellectual disability, which is why screening of thyroid-stimulating hormone (TSH) levels in all newborns was instigated in the 1970s. One of the indirect advantages of universal TSH screening for CH was that it provided data on prevalence of the condition, which was surprisingly constant worldwide, being 1 in 3,500 births in the 1980s. Overall, the historical expected rate of CH is around 1 in 3,000 to 4,000 births, with a two-fold higher rate in girls than boys. This increased prevalence in girls has no obvious attributable cause.

As introduced in Chapter 2, a number of countries are reporting unexplained increases in incidence of children born with CH (i.e., either born without a correctly formed thyroid, referred to as thyroid dysgenesis or with significant problems in production of TH, known as thyroid dyshormonogenesis). CH is usually permanent and most often due to thyroid dysgenesis. Some cases can be transient due to maternal factors (antithyroid medication or antibodies) or due to preterm birth that can be associated with delayed maturation of the thyroid axis. Although epidemiology is far from complete, the increases in CH appear to be worldwide, including in the United States and Mexico, certain parts of Europe, Japan, and Australasia (see Chapter 2). Many authorities are attempting to find the cause of these surges and are examining contributions of changed diagnosis, iodine availability, and, sometimes, chemical exposure.

One can cite data from New York State, where compulsory neonatal screening for thyroid function was begun in 1978. Comparing incidence between 1978 and 2005 revealed an increase in CH of 138% (Harris & Pass, 2007). Similar increases have been found in other US states, with an overall annual rate of increase of 3% in the 9 years between 1991 and 2000 (Hinton et al., 2010). Changes in screening methods have been proposed to contribute to the rise in some states (Mitchell, Hsu, & Sahai, 2011), but even when such factors are taken into account, the increase in incidence is confirmed nationwide (Hertzberg, Mei, & Therrell, 2010). In the study on data from New York State, the authors (Harris & Pass, 2007) also ruled out any contribution of changes in laboratory methods but questioned the potential involvement of either excess or lack or iodine. However, data suggest that a decline in urinary iodine concentrations seen in pregnant American women between the early 1970s and

1990s had stabilized and even slightly reversed 10 years later, thus potentially precluding this as a contributor to the increase in CH seen between 1991 and 2000 (Olney, Grosse, & Vogt, 2010). In this light, it is interesting to turn to a Turkish study that investigated precisely this question, that is, the incidence of iodine deficiency in patients with CH (Evliyaoglu, Kutlu, Kara, & Atavci, 2008). The study is also pertinent as Turkey is located in an area of mild to moderate iodine deficiency. Although the sample size was relatively small (only 25 cases), the analysis was very comprehensive, with thyroid function tests, thyroid scintigraphy, and ultrasonography being compared to the babies' (average age 12 days) and maternal urine iodine content. Incidence of iodine deficiency reached 36% in babies (median, 110 µg/L) and 88% in the mothers (median, 40 µg/L). However, despite this high incidence of iodine lack,[5] all the babies with thyroid agenesis or hypoplasia had normal iodine levels, suggesting other causes notably maternal iodine lack. Here again it should be noted that genetic causes have only been associated with 2% of the cases of thyroid dysgenesis (Harris & Pass, 2007), leaving the great majority of cases with unknown etiology, and opening the debate to environmental causes.

Factors that do associate with incidence of CH include preterm birth, sex, and race/ethnicity. The increased incidence in preterm babies may be related to diagnosis of transient hypothyroidism that, in turn, could be related to not only the immature state of the thyroid but also the stressful events around early birth and associated medication. As mentioned earlier, the overall rate is usually twice as high in girls. However, the data on incidence in the United States are showing changes in this ratio. For instance, in Texas, which had a historical rate of 2 girls to 1 boy, the ratio since 2001 has shifted to 1.5 (Hinton et al., 2010), indicating more male children born with CH. In terms of racial groups or ethnicity, the highest rates in the United States are found in the Hispanic populations. The authors suggest that genetic or environmental factors could be contributing to higher, and increasing, incidence of thyroid dysgenesis in this group.

Other countries with increasing rates of CH include New Zealand and Japan. In New Zealand the increase has been attributed to changing demographics, with an increase in the number of children born to parents from the Pacific Islands that have a higher general incidence of thyroid dyshormonogenesis. In contrast, in the case of Japan increased incidence is clearly related to environmental factors. In Japan, three-fold increases have been reported since screening began in 1979, and one study shows a clear positive association of severity with increased maternal levels of organochlorine pollutants (Nagayama et al., 2007). In this case a mere two-fold increase in pesticide contamination and three-fold increase in dioxin-like contamination over controls were found in cases of severe CH that had been classed as cretins. Unfortunately, no similar

---

5  This lack occurs despite a national salt iodization program in Turkey, emphasizing the need for other forms of iodine supplementation in some cases.

studies on extent of maternal pollution burden and incidence of CH are available in other countries.

As mentioned previously, increased incidence of CH is also associated with preterm birth, in which case it may be transient, but not always. Given that twins and other multiple pregnancies are frequently born early, the incidence of CH is higher in these groups. In Italy, the group of Antonella Olivieri has been following the incidence and characteristics of CH for a number of years (Cassio et al., 2013) within the national surveillance strategy. Her data show that in the Italian population there are three times more twins in the CH group than in the general population (Olivieri et al., 2007). The Italian database has been exploited to assess genetic and environmental causes on the basis of concordance rates. The authors of the paper cited (Olivieri et al., 2007) consider that although genetic factors cannot be ruled out, the contributions of environmental factors exacerbating genetic predisposition is a plausible explanation. Such factors could be acting by inducing epigenetic changes in gene expression or inducing early mutations affecting the development of the gland.

Until more data are available on the incidence of CH in other countries and the potential association with chemical exposure investigated, the enigma of the increased incidence will remain unsolved. Suffice it to say that if there is an increase in pathological cases of CH, then more subtle disorders of thyroid function might be occurring during development and could be missed by pediatricians and health workers. Along with the increased numbers of confirmed CH, such mild thyroid disorders could also be contributing to the increased incidence of ASD and ADHD.

## Neuroanatomical Studies on Autism Spectrum Disorders

As the numbers of children with autism increased, and prior to the large-scale searches for genetic causes, neurobiological and/or neuropathological features were sought to explain the more common traits such as disorders in social interaction and language development and repetitive behavior patterns. As ASD phenotypes cover various broad cognitive and behavioral brain functions, many neuroanatomical structures were examined. In some early studies some gross pathophysiological morphological trends were noted, including a larger head circumference, although imaging studies on brain structures could not explain the increased circumference (Davidovitch, Patterson, & Gartside, 1996). Later, longitudinal imaging studies investigating brain structures in larger numbers of autistic children examined relationships of head circumference to increased volumes of certain structures (Hazlett et al., 2005). However, it should be emphasized that large variations in overall size of brain structures exist and the interpretation of such data is difficult and often subject to controversy. These inherent variations are compounded by the limited sample size frequently found in imaging studies. Thus, current studies tend to exploit the increasing power of imaging techniques by focusing more on functional connections between structures, often in the context of task-related functions where children's brain function is imaged during performance of a standardized assignment (Minshew & Keller, 2010). Moreover, such task-orientated studies will also provide information on the relative size on specific brain components.

Another approach to understanding brain pathology in ASD is autopsy. In 1997, the data on autopsy specimens were limited to fewer than 20 subjects compared to a dozen controls (Courchesne, 1997), but they already revealed problems in development of a number of structures, notably the cerebellum.

Courchesne (1997) reviewed data on postmortem studies of the cerebellum from 12 autistic patients, with all 12 showing cerebellar abnormalities. At the microscopic level, the most reproducible finding was reduced numbers and size of the Purkinje cell population in the cerebellum (Courchesne, 1997; Fatemi et al., 2002; Ritvo et al., 1986). Although they are not the only neuronal population affected in the autistic cerebellum (Yip, Soghomonian, & Blatt, 2009), the postmortem studies showed Purkinje neuron numbers to be reduced by 35%–50% on average. It was deduced that the problems arose before birth because other neuronal populations were not affected. A number of mouse models of ASD display modified cerebellar development and often modified Purkinje cell morphology. For instance, the *Tsc1* mutant mouse model of autistic-like behavior was engineered for loss of the TSC1 protein specifically in Purkinje cells (Tsai et al., 2012). This model has reduced Purkinje cell numbers, a feature frequently associated with ASD, but increased dendritic arborization. Similarly, significant cerebellar hypoplasia is a distinctive characteristic of the Reeler mouse that has a mutated *Reelin* gene (Fatemi, 2001).

As emphasized by Strick and colleagues (2009), the cerebellum is not only a control center for motor behavior but also for nonmotor responses, notably through its dense interconnections with the cerebral cortex. The authors underline that recent imaging studies show that the cerebellum has more influence on the activity of the cerebral cortex than previously thought, reaching many cortical areas controlling nonmotor activities. Thus, problems with cerebellar development can have widespread consequences on cognition, attention, and affective behavior, all hallmarks of ASD.

As explained in Chapter 3, not only is the Purkinje cell the integrating hub of the cerebellum with all output from this complex structure passing through these cells (Strick, Dum, & Fiez, 2009), the Purkinje cell population is an exceedingly TH-sensitive cell population. Both TH and TRs are essential to regulate expression of numerous genes implicated in early development and differentiation of these remarkable cells (see Fig. 7.3).

In a more recent analysis, Courchesne's team analyzed another set of postmortem brains from young autistic or control male children between the ages of 2 and 16 years (Courchesne et al., 2011). As to be expected for a study based on autopsies, the sample size was small, only seven ASD cases and six controls. Despite this limitation, the study revealed a number of important findings, notably increased numbers of neurons (67% increase) in the prefrontal cortex as compared to control brains. These higher neuron numbers were attributed to prenatal and/or perinatal modifications in the numbers of neurons produced or surviving. (During neurogenesis more neurons are produced than are

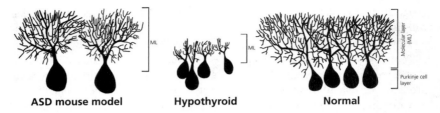

**ASD mouse model**        **Hypothyroid**              **Normal**

**Figure 7–3.** Schematic comparison of Purkinje cell morphology in different mouse models. One mouse model of autism spectrum disorders (ASD) (left) is compared with that of Purkinje cells in hypothyroid brain (middle panel) and a normal brain (right). The mouse model of autistic-like behavior illustrated is that of a Tsc1 mutant (Tsai et al., 2012). This model has reduced Purkinje cell numbers, a feature frequently associated with ASD, but increased dendritic arborization. Few studies have actually addressed Purkinje cell morphology in ASD. One study that did address this question found significantly decreased Purkinje cell size as well as decreased numbers (Fatemi et al., 2003), recalling the phenotypes seen in hypothyroidism and in the *Reelin* mutant mouse (see Fig. 7.6). (Middle panel adapted from J. Bernal: http://www.thyroidmanager.org/chapter/thyroid-hormones-in-brain-development-and-function/)

needed and the excess numbers are pruned back by apoptosis, active cell death, processes known since the 1950s to be directly affected by TH [Eayrs, 1953].)

Other morphological and imaging studies have reported abnormalities in numerous different brain areas, including limbic structures (notably hippo-campus and amygdala), the brainstem, and the superior olive (Courchesne, 1997; Kulesza, Lukose, & Stevens, 2011), a structure implicated in hearing. Di Martino and colleagues surveyed brain-imaging data from 39 studies ana-lyzing social (such as perception of facial features) and nonsocial (for instance, working memory) functions comparing ASD subjects to controls (Di Martino et al., 2009). ASD subjects showed reduced activity in areas implicated in social signals (including notably the amygdala and regions of the frontal cortex) but variable responses in structures participating in nonsocial, executive task processing.

However, as mentioned earlier, the focus in many brain-imaging studies is placed more on connectivity and network activity rather than structural varia-tion per se. In the light of both improved imaging techniques and the increased incidence of the disease, in the next few years one can expect rapid progression in the understanding of how changes in connectivity and circuitry in ASD can be related to underlying structural changes and developmental mechanisms. The combination of increased knowledge in the fields of genetics and imaging, along with more understanding of the contribution of environmental effects, will be determinant in understanding the heterogeneity of ASD phenotypes. In fact, current technologies allow the combination of genetic information with functional brain studies in the same individual, a mode of analysis referred to as "genetic imaging." When applied together to a given patient or animal model, the combination of the two approaches provides better understanding of how genetic changes relate to function as appraised by imaging. Already many of the connectivity changes observed across different ASD phenotypes, notably those affecting synaptic structure or function, have been associated with genetic factors, and it is these factors that constitute the next part of the puzzle addressed.

## Inherited Genetic Risk Factors for Autism Spectrum Disorders and Attention-Deficit/Hyperactivity Disorder

Until the advent of next-generation sequencing, most of the genetic studies on ASD and/or ADHD were based on more classical approaches to identify genetic links and associations. These approaches included studies on monozygotic (MZ, or identical from early division of one zygote or fertilization event) and dizygotic (DZ, or nonidentical from two different fertilization events) twin studies, chromosomal abnormalities, whole-genome linkage studies, and candidate gene approaches (Folstein & Rosen-Sheidley, 2001). Despite the strong heritability revealed in many studies, particularly the first twin studies, it rapidly became evident that none of the most common ASD phenotypes displayed standard Mendelian inheritance patterns[6] with identifiable mutations affecting genes with strong penetrance and effects (Fig. 7.4). Even different genetic disorders in which affected individuals have increased incidence of ASD, such as Fragile X disorder that is related to mutations in the *FMR1* gene, only 25% of boys and 6% of girls display ASD features, ruling out strong penetrance and arguing for a role of the gene as a modulator of disease risk. This concept can be strengthened by tackling the problem the other way round, that is, by examining the number of ASD cases that can be accounted for by the presence of mutations in *FMR1* gene. In this case one finds only 1% or 2% of ASD cases harbor *FMR1* mutations (Abrahams & Geschwind, 2008). This example, along with many others, has led to the cornerstone concept that ASD phenotypes present an extremely heterogenic genetic basis. This idea means that, on the one hand, multiple individual or combined mutations can contribute as risk factors to the spectrum, and inversely, on the other hand, that a given genetic mutation shown to be implicated in ASD can also be involved in multiple disorders other than ASD (such as in the example given of the *FMR1* gene in either Fragile X syndrome and/or ASD). Another way of looking at the problem of the large heterogeneity of disease phenotypes is provided by Eva Jablonka and Marion Lamb (2005), who wryly coined the term "genetic astrology" to describe efforts to seek genetic explanations and determination for complex phenotypes.

This concept also applies to other mental diseases showing a spectrum of phenotypes, such as schizophrenia, where it has aptly and succinctly been described by Sebat and colleagues (2009) in the title of a review as "one disorder, multiple mutations; one mutation, multiple disorders." In fact, at the time of writing, despite the enormous investment in genetic research into the

---

6  Mendelian syndromes or disorders involve dominant or recessive, usually single gene, mutations that show standard patterns of inheritance.

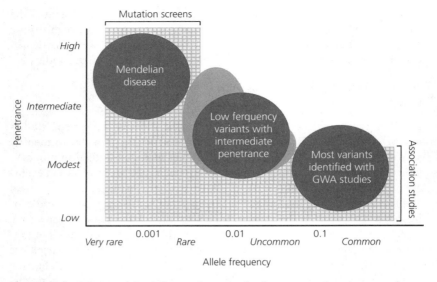

**Figure 7–4.** Schema of the difference between the frequency and penetrance of common versus rare genetic variants and the propensity for their identification by genetic methods. (Adapted from Geschwind, 2011and McCarthy, 2008).

causes of ASD, the current consensus is that only between 5% and 15% of ASD patients have an identifiable chromosomal rearrangement or single gene disorder (for instance, linked to another known pathology), and the genomes of another only 5%–10% of patients harbor one or more inherited or de novo modifications that confer increased risk to develop the disorder. The hundreds of common or rare de novo modifications uncovered and the brain processes affected are discussed in the section on "De Novo Genetic Mutations in Autism Spectrum Disorders."

The search for rare inherited genetic links has been difficult. However, one recent report succeeded in identifying a few inheritable ASD-linked genes by analyzing consanguineous families, with many cases of marriage between first cousins, many of which had more than one child with autistic features (Yu et al., 2013). The approach exploited was exome sequencing. This methodology focuses the sequencing effort on coding sequences of the genome and the untranslated regions (UTRs) immediately next to them. DNA coding sequences that make RNA (and in most cases, proteins) represent approximately 1% of the human genome, about 180,000 exons. Much of the rest of the genome represents regulatory regions that contribute to controlling where, when, and at what level a gene is expressed. Variations, both gain or loss, in these regulatory regions can have high evolutionary significance in terms of morphological change, notably affecting brain structure and higher functions accounting for major differences between primates such as chimpanzees and humans (McLean et al., 2011). No doubt as whole genome sequencing becomes more generally available and accessible, sequencing of whole genomes, covering regulatory regions as well as exomes, will reveal more potential links between both inherited and de novo mutations associated with ASD.

Returning to exome sequencing, the approach identified inherited mutations in coding sequences in just three consanguineous families. In one family four of the five children were diagnosed with ASD. In this case, the parents were actually double first cousins; that is, the husband and wife had the same four grandparents[7] (Yu et al., 2013). The mutation was tracked to the *SYNE* gene, a gene that codes for a protein that had already been implicated by gene sequencing approaches as a rare variant in one other patient with ASD and in another with bipolar disorder. Total lack of *SYNE* causes another neuronal disorder, cerebellar ataxia.

This case and the other genes identified in the study illustrate the point that variations in one gene can be implicated in multiple neuronal phenotypes and leads to the question of how context, whether genomic or environmental, determines type and severity of phenotype. Gender regularly shows up as a factor affecting expression of genotype. Current research suggests that the markedly reduced incidence of ASD in girls is due to a protective effect, as the numbers of de novo risk mutations seem similar between genders and girls can carry a significantly higher risk load before developing ASD traits (Werling & Geschwind, 2013). These findings do not exclude the possibility of male-specific factors such as testosterone entering into the equation, or environmental factors such as the as-yet-unexplained greater intrauterine uptake of bisphenol A by male fetuses (see Chapter 5).

### Twin Studies in Autism Spectrum Disorders and Attention-Deficit/ Hyperactivity Disorder: Consensus and Controversy

As in other disorders with strong, but unidentified, genetic origins, the contributions of twin studies have been seminal to unraveling the relative contributions of nature and nurture, and as we will see later, potential interactions between them. Before the first twin studies were carried out, evidence for hereditary components came, first, from observations that some genetic disorders displayed increased ASD frequency and, second, from data showing higher risk for close relatives of affected families. However, with family studies the question is raised of shared (and nonshared) environment, and in twin studies this includes shared, but not absolutely identical, interuterine environment. Over the last decade twin studies have significantly consolidated the concept of genetic contributions. One of the first twin studies to demonstrate unequivocally strong genetic contributions to ASD was that of Folstein and Rutter (1977), who analyzed 21 pairs of same-sexed twins. The authors compared ASD rates

---

7   As opposed to "standard" first cousins, where only one set of grandparents is shared. In most societies marriage between first cousins is rarely allowed or recommended because of the risk of increasing adverse gene dosage.

in MZ and DZ twins of the same sex to avoid the sex bias inherent in the disorder. The greater significance of concordance in the MZ twins, with basically identical genome sequences, than in the DZ group (only sharing 50% of their genomes, as for other siblings) consolidated the observations that ASD had a strong genetic component. This small set showed 36% concordance in MZ twins. Concordance is not the same as heritability. Heritability is calculated at the part of the variation that is attributable to genetics, excluding other factors such as environment. Thus, in this study, only about one in three of the twins of an affected child actually had autism, hence the concordance rate of 36% (just over one third). Other twin studies, often with different recruitment methods, including advertising, began to show higher concordance, reaching over 92%. But as Folstein herself mentions in a review (Folstein & Rosen-Sheidley, 2001), advertising can skew the recruitment toward concordant twins as their parents are more likely to join.

Despite these differences in concordance rates, Folstein and Rutter's early findings have been confirmed in a number of other twin studies (Fig. 7.5), though some have raised some intriguing contrasts. As Ronald and Hoekstra emphasize in their excellent review of twin studies in ASD, ADHD, and related disorders (Ronald & Hoekstra, 2011), these analyses, besides confirming the hereditary component and reducing the guilt pressure on parents, also fueled the intense financial and human effort directed to identifying causative genes. Ronald and Hoekstra distinguish three phases in ASD/twin research. An initial phase focused on strict autism and ASD, a second on separate autistic traits across wide populations, and a third on using the genetic data from twins to understand etiology (causes) and the relationship of ASD to intellectual and language disabilities in general, as well as to ADHD. They are also careful to note the degree of intellectual disability in the twin studies. For instance, in the first study 48% of patients were severely affected (IQ < 50). In the twin studies that focus on ASD, seven studies are cited, and six of them concur on overall concordance rates in MZ twins of between 75% and 86%, according to whether the definition of ASD was strict or broad. However, this level was not reached in the last study cited. This analysis of a Swedish cohort appeared in 2010 and was one of the largest studies carried out until then (Lichtenstein, Carlstrom, Rastam, Gillberg, & Anckarsater, 2010), including 117 twin pairs. It received attention because it reported concordance rates in MZ male twins of below 50%. This lower concordance rate still supported a heritability factor of 80% with the remaining 20% variation being attributed to environment. A year later a similar, relatively low, concordance rate was reported in a Californian study on 192 twins in 2011 (Hallmayer et al., 2011), the authors finding a rate of 59% for male MZ twins. To cite the conclusion of these authors: "Susceptibility to ASD has moderate genetic hereditability and a substantial shared twin environmental component." The authors do not place any onus on parental behavior but instead underline the importance of shared prenatal and perinatal factors that could act as modulators during the critical windows of early development. Many of the factors discussed have been associated with ASD and other

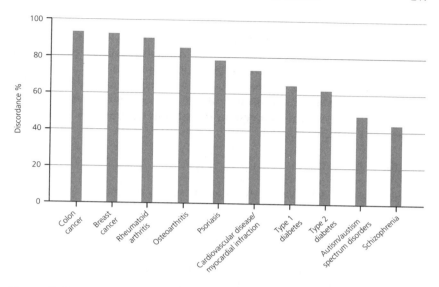

**Figure 7–5.** Studies on monozygotic twins show lower discordance rates for autism spectrum disorders (ASD). (Adapted from Bell & Specter, 2012.) ASD shows lower discordance rates as compared, for example, to breast cancer or diabetes type 1 or type 2, indicating stronger genetic associations. The stronger genetic associations do not rule out contributions of environmental factors.

developmental problems, including low birth weight, parental age, maternal infections, and multiple births. However, the potential contribution of chemical pollution is not introduced into the discussion, despite the fact that the cohort is located in California, one of the states with the highest usages of both brominated flame retardants and halogen-substituted pesticides.

Turning to twin studies in the context of ADHD, the Swedish study published in 2010 (Lichtenstein et al., 2010) also examined heritability scores for ADHD and other related neuropsychiatric disorders. A strong overlap was reported, with half of the children with ASD also fulfilling ADHD criteria. Also, if one MZ twin had ASD, then the probability that the other twin had ADHD reached 44%, whereas it was 15% for DZs. Few studies have examined the relative contributions of environment and heredity to the onset and progression of ADHD. When examining potential genetic versus environmental contributions to ADHD, there is a need to distinguish between adult ADHD (aADHD) that persists through adolescence into maturity, and forms that show gradual remission with development, that is, childhood ADHD (cADHD). Logically, one would expect the persistent form, aADHD, to have the greater (Franke et al., 2012), but not necessarily exclusive, genetic component. Reviewing current literature, aADHD was found to have moderate heritability, around 30%–40%, clearly lower than ASD. Ronald and Hoekstra analysed four twin studies of children with ADHD and one with 18- to 33-year-olds (Ronald & Hoekstra, 2011).

Their aim was to identify comorbidity (the presence of symptoms of both disorders), as studies on the general population had already shown an overlap in symptoms and diagnosis. They found strong genetic correlations between behavioral traits found in ADHD and those identified in ASD.

Twin studies can also reveal how changes in DNA methylation may contribute to epigenetic modifications and modulate gene expression without mutation of a genome sequence, a question to which we return in the section on "Epigenetic Contributions...".

## De Novo Genetic Mutations in Autism Spectrum Disorders

De novo mutations generating two main categories of genetic variation have been associated with cases of ASD. The first identified were those generating copy number variations (CNVs). CNVs represent insertions or deletions of relatively large sequences of nucleotides (>50 kb) from the DNA sequence. The second type of de novo mutations associated with ASD covered smaller variations, called "indels," often implicating insertions or deletions of single nucleotides. These differences in the nucleotide sequence of the DNA are the most common form of variation in the human genome. De novo mutations causing indel changes or CNVs are new sequence changes in the genetic information that are not present in the parents' somatic (cells in the main body) genome but arise in the germline (the cells that produce the gametes or reproductive cells; i.e., the sperm or the eggs). These new mutations or variations arise during division of the germ cells and are therefore present in the sperm or the egg prior to fertilization and so introduce the genetic variation into the genome of the offspring. Such modifications are often without effect, but those shown to be associated in different ways with ASD are often related to production of missense or nonsense coding sequences or changes in the way the RNA produced by the gene is edited (splice variants).

In general, new mutations that occur in the germline and that cause sporadic genetic disease can be more harmful than inherited mutations, as they have not been subjected to evolutionary control. In other terms, inherited mutations that pass down generations are usually less deleterious, as they permit development and reproduction, though there are cases of highly deleterious genes that can resist evolutionary selection, such as X-linked hemophilia. Furthermore, as mentioned earlier, some mutated genes, notably certain X-linked genes, have been associated with ASD in a few cohorts. Most of the studies on new mutations and ASD date from the last 6 or 7 years, as new techniques in genome analysis, notably whole-exome sequencing, came on the scene. To date, those studies that do find associations (and many do not) confirm the roles of rare de novo mutations in genes with high rates of mutability as opposed to inherited mutations (Michaelson et al., 2012).

The first report on association of CNVs with ASD appeared in 2007 (Sebat et al., 2007). The authors used microarray analysis to compare CNVs in coding DNA from 99 control families and from 264 families with at least one child affected with well-defined autism, that is, excluding children having autistic syndrome with severe intellectual disability (IQ below 70) or congenital malformations. In all, 17 de novo CNVs were found in 16 of the subjects, 14 autism patients and 2 controls. Interestingly, higher rates of de novo CNVs were found in cases of sporadic autism (10% of patients) as opposed to children with a close affected relative (3%). Significantly fewer de novo CNV occurrences were found in children from control families (1%). Most CNV represented large deletions. The authors concluded that as the incidence of CNV was three times higher in the ASD patients as compared to controls, and notably in the sporadic cases, it could argue for a causal effect of CNV on ASD. As to the functions of the genes included in the deletions, one significant deletion in an Asperger's patient involved a 1.1 Mb sequence in chromosome 20 (20p13), a region covering the oxytocin gene. This gene product, oxytocin, is increasingly implicated in many forms of social behavior in both humans and rodents. Aberrant oxytocin signaling has also been associated with ASD (Gregory et al., 2009). However, yet again links to TH signaling are evident as TH modulates oxytocin signaling at many levels (see, for instance, Dellovade, Kia, Zhu, & Pfaff, 1999). Another deletion was found in the chromosomal region covering the SHANK3 gene, a site previously shown to be associated with recurrent deletions in severe forms of autism (Durand et al., 2007). SHANK3 is a scaffolding protein, a protein that provides structural connections allowing organization of many other proteins into multimolecular complexes at synaptic connections.

Five deletions causing de novo CNVs affected a single gene, and all of them were situated within the largest human genes. Large genes are often associated with less stable chromosome regions and spontaneous genetic disorders such as Duchenne's muscular dystrophy. The explanation is that random genome reorganization events will have a greater probability of hitting large genes. The affected genes included SLC4A4, which encodes a putative ion transporter, and ataxin2 binding protein 1 (A2BP1). Mutations of either of these genes are associated with intellectual disability. A final point raised by this study is that each deletion was only usually observed once, and rarely twice. This finding underlines that deletions at many different sites can contribute to ASD, and it explains the difficulty in finding common genetic causes for the pathology without taking environmental factors into account.

The more recent studies on de novo mutations leading to missense or nonsense sequences or modified RNA editing (splice site modifications) were made possible by the increased power of sequencing techniques and the decision to apply the power to whole-exome sequencing. This approach allowed the identification of much smaller variations than CNV studies. In 2012, a group of publications virtually simultaneously reported associations of such mutations with ASD and one more looked for rare recessive mutations (Chahrour et al., 2012; Iossifov et al., 2012; Muers, 2012; Neale et al., 2012; O'Roak et al., 2012a, 2012b; Sanders et al., 2012). The de novo mutation studies focused on family trios, parents and an affected child; or quads, parents with one affected and one nonaffected child. The rates of de novo mutation were similar in each study, around $2 \times 10^{-8}$ per base pair per generation, but interestingly, the rates were not different among patients and controls. However, more mutations had paternal origin, as opposed to maternal origin, and the frequency increased most significantly with paternal age. Many of the shared affected genes identified were brain-expressed genes that had often been associated with neurodevelopmental disorders. Despite the large range of the studies, the total number of mutations identified as causing gene disruption was only 127 and only six were found in more than one affected subject (Muers, 2012). Together, these reports stress yet again that alone, de novo mutations play limited roles in ASD and that loss of function of one gene will rarely increase risk significantly. Such findings re-emphasize the importance of considering environmental context to explain increased incidence. Thus, taken together these studies underline that despite finding several hundred genes that can be associated to different degrees with ASD, not only is there no common genetic cause for the syndrome, but that the syndrome is polygenic and that like CNV modifications, the de novo mutations need to be combined with other risk factors, such as environmental contaminants, to cause disease.

To take these observations further, one group involved in the initial exome sequencing (O'Roak et al., 2012a) took a reverse approach. Instead of looking at all the exomes of a restricted number of patients, they took a set of "candidate" genes and looked for mutations in these genes in thousands of ASD patients. Succinctly, they chose 44 of the genes identified by either exome sequencing, or the CNV approaches or other associative studies and looked for mutations in these genes in DNA samples from 2,446 ASD cases. Six of the 44 genes showed recurrent de novo mutations. The genes identified were centered on chromosome remodeling, cell proliferation/cycling, and neuronal conduction. Given this relatively modest success, the authors estimate that only 1% of sporadic ASD cases will implicate mutations in these six genes, leaving a great majority of ASD cases with unexplained causes.

Turning to ADHD, to date despite the higher frequency of the disorder, as yet insufficient de novo variant searches have been carried out to begin to provide a genetic basis for the immense heterogeneity of the disorder. It has been estimated that 12,000 genomes will have to be sequenced (controls and patients) in order to obtain significant results on gene associations from this approach (Franke et al., 2012). However, linkage analyses and studying candidate genes polymorphisms in cohorts of either adult or child ADHD has revealed a limited number of associations with a handful of genes, notably two dopamine receptors, a serotonin transporter, a dopamine transporter, and a synaptosome associated protein, SNAP-25. However, more often than not the findings of a significant association in one cohort are rarely duplicated in a second, reflecting yet again the immense heterogeneity of the disorder. Intriguingly, one enzyme that frequently comes up in candidate gene studies on ADHD is monoamine oxidase (MAO; Liu et al., 2011). MAO metabolizes three major neurotransmitters: dopamine, serotonin, and noradrenaline. Multiple anatomical and neuropharmacological mechanisms link TH signaling and each of these pathways, dopamine, noradrenaline, and serotonin, all of which are implicated in numerous psychiatric disorders (for review, see for instance Santos et al., 2012). A rarely cited, yet experimentally very solid paper, showed that slight maternal hypothyroidism, induced by removal of half the thyroid gland, in rats significantly reduced MAO activity in fetal brains both at day 16 and 19 of gestation (Evans et al., 1999). The authors underlined the importance of neurotrophic roles for the different neurotransmitters that would be modified by these changed levels and the link to neurodevelopmental disorders.

### The Common Ground: Neurodevelopmental Processes and Genes Associated With Autism Spectrum Disorders, Attention-Deficit/Hyperactivity Disorder, and Untreated Congenital Hypothyroidism

Different avenues of research, whether at the anatomical or genetic level, have converged on certain key neurodevelopmental processes as being affected in ASD and to a lesser extent in ADHD. The processes and genes identified are often implicated in generation and survival of neurons, cell migration, and synaptogenesis. That TH affects each of these developmental processes in the brain is well established (see Chapter 3).

In fact, the problem can be taken from some more general starting points. First, maternal hypothyroidism is associated in both animal models and in humans with lower birth weight infants, and very low (<1,500g) or moderate (<2,500g) (Lampi et al., 2012) birth weight is a risk factor for ASD. In turn, low birth weight is a risk factor for hypothyroidism in the child. Second, maternal hypothyroidism and uncorrected CH are associated with impaired intellectual development. Even in treated CH there can be no realistic assessment of the effects of the uncorrected lack experienced prenatally; however, there are clear dose- and time-dependent effects of $T_4$ treatment in CH. IQ is significantly higher in CH children treated before 21 days after birth and with a minimum of 6 µg/$T_4$ per day (Boileau, Bain, Rives, & Toublanc, 2004). The studies on maternal TH levels during early pregnancy and iodine supply clearly show not only a strong correlation with the child's neurodevelopmental progression but also that even moderate iodine lack is correlated with ADHD incidence (Vermiglio et al., 2004). Furthermore, impaired intellectual development (IQ < 70) is found in about half the cases of ASD under current diagnostic terms (Anonymous, 2012). Third, animal models that have been used to study either ASD or ADHD have often exploited either hypothyroid situations or altered TR signaling. In a comprehensive review Roman (2007) has drawn parallels between, even short term, maternal hypothyroidism during early pregnancy and autism and placed these findings in the context of chemical pollution. The link between RTH and ADHD has also been studied in the context of a mouse model bearing a RTH mutation and displaying many of the features of the disease (McDonald et al., 1998). More recently, an Egyptian study (Hamza, Hewedi, & Sallam, 2013) showed a clear link between ASD and iodine deficiency.

Determining to what extent TH signaling and its modulation during development affects the expression of the genes that have been associated to different degrees with ASD and ADHD pathology depends critically on expanding clinical and basic research. Increased knowledge is required on multiple fronts: better understanding of the gene targets regulated by TH in different regions of the brain within specific developmental windows; further genome-wide studies on patients, notably in the ADHD cases; modeling of gene interactions within different contexts; and information on the degree of epigenetic regulation of target genes and their sensitivities to environmental factors. Quite an agenda.

To illustrate the point, we take just two genes that different screens highlight in ASD and ADHD, examining the data on their connections and control by TH. We then go on to discuss how these factors could be targets of epigenetic regulations and gene × environment interactions.

The *Reelin* gene (refered to as "*RELN*" in humans and either "*Reln*" or "*Reelin*" in mice) encodes large extracellular matrix protein. It was one of the first ASD candidates as linkage studies and the phenotype of a mutant, *reeler*, mouse, studied for over 50 years, converged on this locus. The protein, Reelin, is an extracellular matrix protein and has major roles in neuronal migration and correct cell positioning and formation of cortical layers during brain development. During development, *Reelin* is expressed in the forebrain and the cerebellum (Fig. 7.6). Its expression continues in the adult brain, albeit at lower levels than during development. In adults it is thought to play a role in maintaining synaptic function. Postmortem brains from ASD patients show lower levels of RELN mRNA and protein. The gene is highly polymorphic with numerous variations found in the general population (see Fatemi, 2002), which can contribute to the fact that not all association studies showed positive results in ASD cohorts; however, many did, not only in ASD but also in schizophrenia. Furthermore, as for any gene candidate, it is important to keep in mind that when autopsy studies show a modification in gene or protein levels, that the modification could be due to a number of modulatory factors impinging on expression of the gene or the stability of the protein.

*Reelin* is a direct target of MECP2, the Rett's syndrome culprit, and also of the growth factor, BDNF. Inversely, Reelin is implicated in modulating BDNF expression. Furthermore, both BDNF and Reelin are targets of TH signaling. Expression of Reelin is reduced by 60% in the brains of hypothyroid newborn mice (Alvarez-Dolado et al., 1999). Maternal TH deficiency during gestation also affects neuronal migration in the rat cerebral cortex during prenatal development (Pathak, Sinha, Mohan, Mitra, & Godbole, 2011). In this paper the authors confirm previous results showing fetal hypothyroidism to significantly modify migration of newly formed neurons, but they go further and show that is related to decreased *Reelin* mRNA and protein through a direct action of TR/$T_3$ on the *Reelin* promoter. They also find that fetal hypothyroidism significantly reduces *Bdnf* mRNA, and this is most marked at the earliest stage examined, 14 days gestation. The conclusion is that TH deficiency impacts first *reelin* expression and then a number of events implicated in neuronal migration.

Brain-derived neurotrophic factor (BDNF) has been linked in numerous gene associations studies with ASD and ADHD, as well as a number of other psychiatric disorders (Balaratnasingam & Janca, 2012). Like RELN, BDNF is

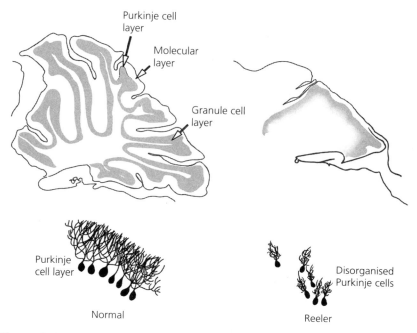

**Figure 7–6.** Comparison of cerebellar structure and Purkinje cell morphology in a normal mouse and the *Reelin* mutant mouse. Note that the *Reelin* mutation affects not only the Purkinje cell morphology but also the general anatomy of the cerebellum.

also found in plasma and modifications of circulating levels have been associated with disease, including ASD (Abdallah et al., 2012). The BDNF gene has a complex structure with numerous polymorphisms that, as for RELN, have provided contradictory studies on the relative importance of different polymorphisms in disease etiology. Although the overall implication of the gene in many cases of ASD and ADHD is generally accepted, as for RELN, no genome-wide screens have as yet identified any de novo mutations in the gene. However, protein–protein interaction screens link RELN (and hence, indirectly, BDNF) to other de novo mutations identified by genome-wide approaches (Neale et al., 2012). BDNF is one of the three principal neurotrophic factors (NGF, BDNF, and NT3) expressed in both the developing and adult brain. Literature dating from the time of discovery of these factors has shown that TH administration in mammals modulates the expression of all three factors in development and in the mature brain. Even mild maternal hypothyroidism affects expression of BDNF in the postnatal rat brain (Chakraborty et al., 2012; Liu et al., 2010). Given the high levels of expression of both BDNF and RELN in the cerebellum, the principal brain structure repeatedly implicated in ASD, the probability that even subtle modification of these genes by endocrine-disrupting chemicals (EDCs) interfering with TH signaling provides a serious working hypothesis for further studies. Furthermore, the BDNF gene is subject to epigenetic regulation through modulation of DNA methylation (Balaratnasingam & Janca, 2012) discussed in the next section.

## Epigenetic Contributions to Gene × Environment Interactions in Autism Spectrum Disorders, Attention-Deficit/Hyperactivity Disorder, and Congenital Hypothyroidism

Clearly, the fact that genetic etiology alone, even with changing diagnostics, cannot account for more than 25% of the increase in ASDs means that effects of the environment on cellular processes and gene expression have to be taken into account (Weintraub, 2011). ASD is not the only group of pathologies with this striking increase. Over the last three or four decades, the incidence of a series of major human diseases, such as cancers, reproductive disorders, and metabolic disease, is increasing at rates that cannot be explained neither by changes in the genetic structure of populations nor by changes in diagnostic practice. These increases, particularly in younger patients (Johnson, Chien, & Bleyer, 2013), have led many authors to speculate on the potential implications of environmental effects that could modify expression of genes implicated in these pathologies. As discussed earlier, the last decades have witnessed enormous technological strides in genome sequencing and conceptual advances in understanding the molecular mechanisms underlying regulation of gene expression. The technological improvements that have underpinned the expansion of genome-wide association studies have advanced analysis of the genetic basis of disease and provided the rapid sequencing methods that permit identification of genetic variation and de novo mutations cited earlier. However, despite this progress and the undisputable contribution of genetic factors, mutations, or copy number variants, whether inherited or de novo occurrences, no single gene can account for more than a few percentage of cases (Landrigan, Lambertini, & Birnbaum, 2012).

It is fascinating to note that, somewhat serendipitously, in parallel to the increased occurrence of so many noncommunicable diseases, there has been a simultaneous explosion of scientific research into understanding the mechanisms controlling gene expression. One of the major conceptual advances has been to relate modifications of chromatin structure to gene activity. One way of thinking about these changes is to think of chromatin like an accordion that opens up and allows transcription to occur, producing RNA, or alternatively being squeezed and compressed shut, with no transcription occurring. The molecular mechanisms underlying chromatin remodeling can result in short-term changes or can induce changes that last a lifetime, with information on closed or open states even being transmitted from one generation to another. Generally speaking, when remodeling events leave marks that are maintained through cell division and over long periods of development and growth, the changes are referred to as epigenetic.

Numerous examples are known of environmental effects inducing long-term, transgenerational epigenetic changes. As yet there are few associations of epigenetic factors affecting ASD incidence in the clinical arena and only a small number of animal models where epigenetic modulation of genes associated

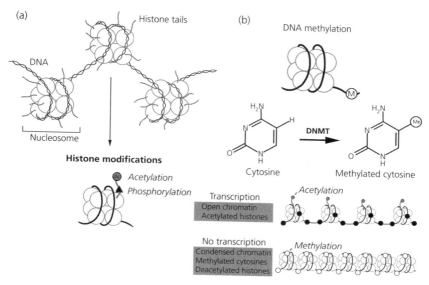

**Figure 7–7.** Simplified schema of some molecular determinants of chromatin accessibility and DNA methylation. (*a*) The histone code. DNA sequences of genes are packed into chromosomes with histone proteins. Histones are positively charged and so complex avidly with the negatively charged DNA. Together they are the principal components of the chromatin material in the nucleus. Chromatin is organized like beads on a string, the beads being the nucleosomes. The tails of the histones stick out of the nucleosomes, making them available to be labeled by enzymes that write the histone code. The transcriptional machinery can then read these labels that determine whether a gene is to be transcribed. (*b*) DNA methylation status also contributes to controlling transcriptional activity. DNA can be methylated on the cytosine bases. The enzymes that carry out methylation of cytosine, producing 5-methylcytosine, are the DNA methyltransferases (DNMTs). In many (but by no means all) cases, DNA methylation and histone deacetylation are associated with closed chromatin and repressed transcription.

with ASD has shown transmission through generations. However, before dealing with these ASD-related examples, it is important to examine the biology underlying epigenetic mechanisms, as there is a strong probability that gene × environment interactions involving epigenetic regulations could well be implicated in ASD and in many other noncommunicable diseases, such as Type-2 diabetes and cancer showing marked increases.

As mentioned in Chapter 2, and succinctly put, epigenetic mechanisms produce long-term modifications of gene expression by modifying the structure of the chromatin around the gene and determining whether it is accessible to and read by the transcriptional machinery to produce RNA. These epigenetic mechanisms that govern transcription include methylation of the DNA sequence in the gene itself and/or modification of the histone proteins that pack the DNA into nucleosomes within the chromosome (Fig. 7.7). A number of signals can be added to the histone tails that protrude from the nucleosomes. These signals

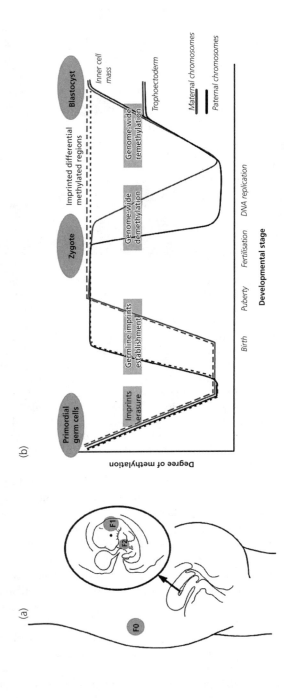

**Figure 7–8.** Exposure of a pregnant woman to chemicals that cause epigenetic modifications affects three generations. (Part B adapted from Ishida and Moore, 2013.) (*a*) In the fetus the germ cells that will produce the eggs or sperm of the third generation are forming. Thus, when the mother (generation F0) is exposed, so is the child (F1) and the germ cells that will participate in the child's future progeny (F2). (*b*) The developing germ cells undergo successive waves of DNA methylation, demethylation, and methylation.

are written down by enzymes that label different amino acids, mostly lysines, in the tails with markers such as acetylation and methylation. Lysine residues can be marked with one, two, or three methyl groups. According to the location of the lysine, on which histone protein and at which position in the tail, the marks can be read as repressive (no transcription), permissive (transcription is activated), or paused (transcription ready to go but halted). Acetylation is also carried out on lysine residues. Acetylation removes a positive charge, thereby reducing the interaction of the histone protein with the negatively charged DNA. Acetylation of histones therefore allows the chromatin to open up, rather like an accordion unfolding. Deacetylation restores DNA–histone interactions and closes the accordion, blocking access to the chromatin by the transcriptional machinery. Specific enzymes carry out histone acetylation and deacetylation: the histone acetylases (HACs) and histone deacetylases (HDACs).

There are many demonstrated links between epigenetic control of gene function and the environment. In this context, "environment" can be taken as the immediate environment around the gene, or given a wider sense. The environmental context can be thought of like a series of Russian dolls, going from local chromatin configuration and the overall localization of the gene within heterochromatin or euchromatin; through to the energetic state of the mitochondria, cell, or tissue; or in the largest sense, that of external environment, nutrition, atmospheric contamination, and so on; and in the case of neurobiology, even social interactions. Well-documented examples of each of the levels of interaction have accumulated over the last 10 to 15 years with the most striking examples related to environmental effects in early stages of development. This is to be expected: The earlier an adverse event occurs, the more likely it is that its effects will be amplified as the developmental program unfolds, simply because disturbing an initial element in a series will by necessity have a domino effect on the next steps in an amplifying cascade.

Some of the most interesting cases relate to nutrition and particularly parents' diet. For a number of years the focus in this domain was the maternal diet, and many illustrations of how food availability and composition affect the child's early development and later propensity to disease have accumulated. To cite but a few, the cases of the Dutch famine in 1944/1945 (Roseboom et al., 2001), the importance of folic acid supplementation (Roth et al., 2011), and not the least interesting in terms of brain development and function, iodine supplementation, are all examples of how early diet affects physiology in the adult. In many of these cases the effects can be directly related to gene expression, and often through epigenetic mechanisms that can cause long-term, and potentially heritable, changes in gene expression. The earlier these changes occur during development, then the greater the probability of wider and more deleterious effects. These concepts have become the cornerstone of the "developmental origins of adult disease" hypothesis, often referred to as the Barker hypothesis, after David Barker, who is often cited as one of the first to formulate these ideas (Barker, 2003), though the concept far predates his papers (see references and discussion in Gluckman et al., 2009).

That maternal exposure to a chemical during gestation can affect the next generation is easily understood. However, what is less frequently realized is that when a pregnant woman is exposed to a substance affecting gene expression, then three generations are simultaneously affected, not only the mother and child but also the next generation. The explanation lies in the fact that in the fetus the germ cells are forming (Fig. 7.8a). These germ cells are the cells that will go on to produce the eggs if the child is a girl or the sperm if it is a boy. Furthermore, during the formation of the germ cells, complex waves of DNA demethylation and remethylation occur, making this period a window of extreme vulnerability to endocrine disruption (Fig. 7.8b).

In terms of transgenerational endocrine disruption, one of the most cited examples is that of maternal exposure during early pregnancy to a synthetic estrogen, diethylstilbestrol (DES). In the United States, DES was prescribed to prevent miscarriage from 1938 until 1971 when the increased incidence of vaginal cancer in girls born to mothers who had taken the drug alerted authorities

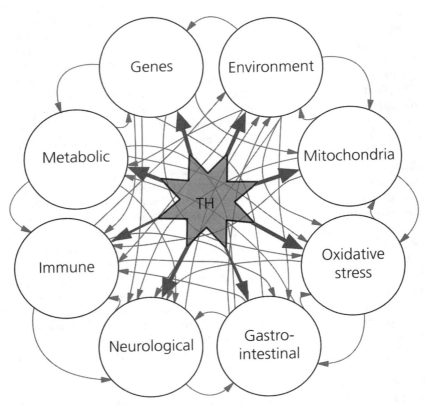

**Figure 7–9.** Potential interactions between thyroid hormone (TH) signaling and physiological systems associated with autism spectrum disorders (ASD).

to the dangers. Since then epidemiology shows that mothers also have a heightened increase of breast cancer and male children are at increased risk of reproductive disorders and/or cancers (Giusti, Iwamoto, & Hatch, 1995). Effects on grandchildren are still undergoing analysis.

One of the first studies to investigate transgenerational transmission in animal models revealed reduced sperm quality and quantity in up to three generations of male rats born to a mother or grandmother that had been exposed during gestation to the fungicide vinclozilin (Anway & Skinner, 2006). Work from Blumberg's team also demonstrates transgenerational epigenetic effects of chemical exposure (Chamorro-Garcia et al., 2013), but the most disquieting observation in this study was that three generations of males and females post-exposure were similarly affected, including the last generation that had had no direct exposure. Gestating mice were exposed to nM quantities of the organotin TBT throughout gestation and pups were bred to nonexposed animals. The next three generations of male and female mice showed significantly increased amounts of white fat deposits and increased hepatic lipid accumulation, similar to nonalcoholic liver disease (Chamorro-Garcia et al., 2013). TBT exposure affected lipid stores through changes in expression of genes implicated in adipose tissue development and lipid metabolism, and the magnitude of the effect on gene expression in the third generation of nonexposed animals was as great as in the first generation. Clearly it is urgent to take these findings into account in understanding the easily measurable increase in obesity and metabolic disease. TBT activates PPARγ, a gene also expressed in the brain, where it can interfere with TH signaling by modifying hypothalamic gene signaling. Whether TBT affects neurogenesis and behavioral outcomes needs to be addressed.

However, it is not only maternal diet and exposure that influence the child's development outcome and disease risk profile. Paternal life history, including prenatal stress, diet and lifestyle habits, and paternal age, affects fetal development and growth. Epidemiological studies in human populations have shown an increased risk for autism as function of paternal age, though current thinking holds that the risk is mostly associated with increased accumulations of mutations in either the sperm or the testes affecting sperm production and status. Most of the work in this field has come from studies on disease with clear associations with increased paternal age, such as Apert's disease, which is due to a mutation in a fibroblast growth factor receptor (FGFR) gene (Goriely & Wilkie, 2012). The mutated genes appear to confer a selection advantage to the sperm during their maturation, leading to increased numbers of sperm produced bearing the mutation. At the moment, given the fact that there is no statistical increase in the number of de novo mutations in cohorts of ASD patients as compared to controls (O'Roak et al., 2012b; Sanders et al., 2012), it seems more likely that the contribution of paternal age to the increased incidence of ASD could implicate other mechanisms, such as epigenetic and/or environmental causes.

One approach that is attracting much interest to identifying epigenetic regulations is the comparison of twins' genomes. Twin studies, particularly

MZ twins that are discordant for a disease phenotype, are very informative for understanding factors that influence and maintain epigenetic regulation in disease, as MZ twins conform for most genetic information and share most environmental influences (Bell & Spector, 2012). Recently, epigenome-wide studies that examine epigenetic changes across the genome, particularly methylome studies that analyze DNA methylation throughout the genome, have been applied to a series of diseases, including ASD (Nguyen, Rauch, Pfeifer, & Hu, 2010; Wong et al., 2013). However, given that these approaches are only applicable at the moment to fresh tissues, they cannot be carried out on human cells affected by ASD (i.e., brain tissue, neurons, and glia). Many studies use easily accessible cells, such as some blood cells. This experimental approach is seriously limited, as DNA methylation is a cell- and tissue-specific process (Bell & Spector, 2012). Despite this drawback, studies are beginning to examine DNA methylation status on blood cells from MZ twins discordant for ASD. One of the earliest studies (Nguyen, Rauch, Pfeifer, & Hu, 2010) examined three sets of twins and isolated a number of differentially methylated promoters, two of which were confirmed by closer examination, RORα and BCL2. RORα has major roles in cerebellar development and is also a TH-regulated gene (Koibuchi & Chin, 1998). BCL2 is an antiapoptotic gene, essential for controlling cell death and survival.

As only a little over a hundred candidate genes have been associated with ASD and/or ADHD,[8] it should be feasible today to examine the methylation status of these genes in control and affected populations. One candidate gene for which there is already a rich literature on its epigenetic regulation is BDNF (see also section on "The Common Ground"). Epigenetic regulation of BDNF gene expression has been reported in physiological and pathological situations such as early life stress and psychiatric disease (Boulle et al., 2012).

Implication of Endocrine-Disrupting Chemical Alteration of Thyroid Hormone Signaling and Increased Incidence of Autism Spectrum Disorder, Attention-Deficit/Hyperactivity Disorder, Congenital Hypothyroidism, and Reduced IQ: The Case for Gene × Environment Interactions

Any consideration of gene × environment interactions as related to neurodevelopmental disorders falls under the shadow of David Rall's disquieting question posed in the early 1960s about the potentially invisible effects of certain drugs on general intelligence across populations as compared to the distressing, immediately obvious, physical deformities seen on individuals born following thalidomide exposure (Weiss, 2009, cited fully in Chapter 1). As emphasized by Weintraub (2011), over the last 10 years the US government has directed 250 times more funds into genetic research than into environmental causes

8   Given the low attribution of specific genetic causes to CH, it is difficult to analyze any specific gene × environment contribution at the moment.

---

**Box 7–1. The Socioeconomic Costs of IQ Loss, Autism Spectrum Disorders, and Attention-Deficit/Hyperactivity Disorder**

---

IQ loss: Even a few points IQ loss across populations can have major socioeconomic consequences. In 2001 Muir and Zegarac (2001) calculated that a 5-point loss in IQ through childhood neurodevelopmental disorders and hypothyroidism, much of which had environmental causes, cost the United States up to 326 billion US dollars per annum.

ADHD: As the symptoms of ADHD do not necessarily diminish with age but can persist in adults, the costs per individual are around 15 to 17,000 US dollars per year, which over a lifetime translates to around a million dollars. The CDC site puts the annual societal cost of ADHD disease at up to 52 billion US dollars, based on a prevalence of 5%. However, the most recent data presented show almost twice that incidence (nearly 10% of US children) and given the lifetime cost cited previously, one could calculate an upper estimate that would be over 100 billion US dollars.

ASD: The lifetime cost of a child with ASD can reach 3.5 million US dollars. Thus, as a function of increasing incidence, costs at national levels are continually rising. For instance, in 2009 it was calculated that the UK costs were £25 billion per annum (Knapp, Romeo, & Beecham, 2009), but the latest figures put the cost at £34 billion in the United Kingdom and 126 billion US dollars in the states (http://www.autismspeaks.org),[9] Moreover, the lifetime cost of caring for an autistic child with intellectual disability is far greater than for a child without (about 2.4 million US dollars with ID versus 1.4 million US dollars without intellectual disability).

The "Autism Speaks" site provides a report on an economic analysis showing that in the United States alone the cost of caring for autistic patients is greater that the gross domestic product (GDP) of 139 countries.

Putting together the cost of ASD (126 billion US dollars) and the cost of ADHD care, one reaches a range of 176 and 226 billion US dollars per annum in the United States.

Despite these increasing figures, reflecting increased incidence on a background of a stable gene pool, research into the environmental causes of ASD and ADHD are almost entirely focused on genetic factors.

---

(1 billion versus 4 million US dollars). This discrepancy ignores the data on societal cost of ASD and the arguments for environmental cause (see, respectively, Boxes 7.1 and 7.2).

Finding the causes and preventing an environmental exacerbation of genetic predisposition is vital to the individual, to families, and to society in general. As can be deduced from the previous discussion, there are probably few or no common causes or environmental contaminant × gene combinations to

---

9  http://www.autismspeaks.org/about-us/press-releases/annual-cost-of-autism-triples

---

**Box 7–2. The Genes Versus Environment Debate and Its Consequences for Research Funding**

---

Funding into genetic causes of ASD over the last decade has exceeded that of research into environmental causes by 250 times (Weintraub, 2011). This disparity is surprising given the fact that the gene pool is not evolving and genetic change cannot account for the enormous increase in ASD and ADHD incidence.

Six principal factors contribute to the emphasis on genes rather than environment:

1. The demonstration of heritability in ASD.
2. The technological advances that have facilitated and reduced the cost of sequencing and genome analysis.
3. Genetic causes are somewhat easier to tackle conceptually and experimentally, especially as patients can be studied individually at any age.
4. Comprehensive environmental studies require large-scale longitudinal approaches to determine associations of maternal chemical burden with developmental outcome.
5. Genetic causes are perhaps more acceptable politically and easier to argue than the concept that environmental pollution for which governments are ultimately responsible is affecting our children's, and potentially their children's, mental health and intellectual capacity.
6. The prevailing genetic determinism frame of mind in both the research and the policy maker communities.

---

account for all the neurodevelopmental disorders discussed. It is far more probable that each class of disorders has multiple genetic and environmental causes and therefore even greater combinatorial aggravating gene × environment scenarios. Similarly, a single cause, whether genetic or environmental, can be implicated in multiple disorders according to the genetic and environmental context. To date, a nonexhaustive list of factors that have been regularly associated with increased ASD or ADHD risk include parental age (both mother and father independently), low birth weight, maternal infection, prenatal and perinatal stress, and zinc deficiency. Obviously, other authors have already raised the possibilities of environmental factors such as chemical pollution being implicated in neurodevelopmental disorders, including ASD, and cited potential mechanisms, including modification of the methylome (LaSalle, 2011). A recent essay suggested that a systems biology approach exploiting mining of extensive data sets and modeling of interactions was needed to begin to unravel crosstalk and identify important nodes (Randolph-Gips & Srinivasan, 2012; Fig. 7.9). Furthermore, such approaches could be applied within categories. Given that TH signaling has reciprocal interactions and controls with

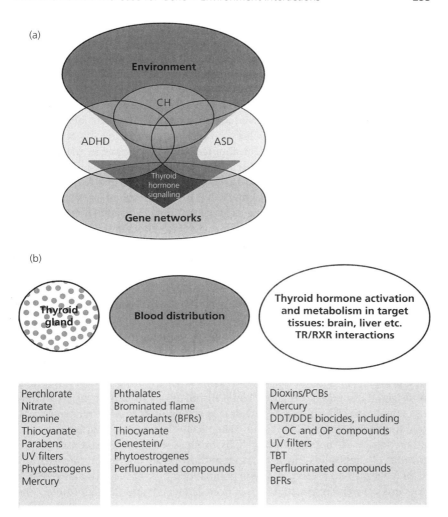

**Figure 7–10.** A scenario for combinatorial effects of environmental pollutants on thyroid hormone (TH) production, distribution, and action. (*a*) Schema for potential interactions of mild to severe congenital hypothyroidism (CH) as an aggravating factor for autism spectrum disorders (ASD) or attention-deficit/hyperactivity disorder (ADHD). CH can be due to failure for the gland to form correctly or to problems with hormone synthesis (for instance, iodine deficiency). Transient or permanent modulations of TH availability will affect cellular processes and gene networks determining brain development. Increased severity of TH lack will exacerbate effects of other environmental pollutants that affect brain development. TH signaling thus forms a bridge between environment, cellular responses, and gene programs. (*b*) Simplified list of chemical classes that affect TH availability, showing three main levels: thyroid gland, blood, and metabolism in target tissues. Resulting modulation of TH production, distribution, and availability at each level will amplify interference with TH-dependent genetic programs controlling brain development.

each of the components identified, such an approach could be applied with TH (Fig. 7.9) or any other major signaling pathway as a starting point.

As between 40 and 50% of ASD cases in the United States concern patients with IQ <70, there is a need to determine whether the overall increase in ASD incidence is accentuated or lessened in this part of the ASD spectrum. If there is a greater increase in ASD cases with IQs <70, then this would be a very compelling argument for a set of environmental factors exerting detrimental effects on vulnerable genotypes, particularly on TH production and/or action during sensitive windows of brain development. It is important to reiterate that the main cellular processes for which gene variants have been highlighted in ASD (chromatin remodeling, mitochondrial function, synapse formation and function, neurite growth and Purkinje cell differentiation) are all key processes affected by TH signaling. Given the tight controls that evolved to determine TH availability in target tissues during each stage of development, combinations of factors that affect successively iodine uptake and TH production (e.g., bromine, perchlorate nitrate), distribution (e.g., BFRs, PBCs, phthalates, pesticides), and action (e.g., mercury) will have combinatorial negative effects on brain development (Fig. 7.10a). A second consideration is that, schematically, one could see the effects of mild to serious CH as exacerbating genetic predisposition to either ASD or ADHD (Fig. 7.10b). Furthermore, many of TH effects during development are increasingly understood as being dependent on epigenetic modifications and thus potentially even more susceptible to environmental disturbance.

Strong arguments for more research into environmental causes of autism were provided in an editorial for *Environmental Health Perspectives* by Philip Landrigan, Luca Lambertini, and Linda Birnbaum in 2012. They listed a number of factors for which studies had already shown links to ASD behavior traits, including many of the TH-disrupting chemicals discussed in Chapter 5, such as certain pesticides, methylmercury, PCBs, brominated flame retardants, and perfluorinated compounds. However, as yet authorities are not responding with any major legislation to protect or advise populations. Nor have any major research programs into environmental causes been launched, and certainly not at the scale of those into genetic causes (Weintraub, 2011) or into potential therapies (Murphy & Spooren, 2012) that can, at best, attempt to alleviate the difficulties of the patients and their caregivers but never redress the harm caused.

Take-Home Messages and Perspectives for Future Research

- The one central take-home message is that neither genetics nor change in diagnostic and screening practice can explain the escalating incidence in developmental disorders ranging from CH to intellectual disability, ASD, and ADHD.
- The most urgent need is the identification of and legislation covering the major environmental factors implicated in the ASD and ADHD increases, on the one hand, and the CH increase, on the other.
- Longitudinal studies on maternal pollution burden and incidence of ASD, ADHD, and CH in children are required. As incidence of

pathological CH is rising, closer investigation of mild, or transitory, thyroid dysfunction during early development is needed to decipher whether such cases could be contributing to the increase in ASD and ADHD. Such studies should include data on maternal chemical load.

- Given the current emphasis on epigenetic influences on gene expression and transgenerational effects, it is opportune to direct funds into increasing knowledge on gene × environment interactions in each of the disorders and the possibility of transmission across generations.
- The old adage "prevention is better than cure" is more pertinent than ever as there are no cures. Still, the limited, but potentially palliative therapeutic opportunities of reversing some of the epigenetic markers affecting behavior, memory, and intellectual achievement should be addressed.
- The protective effect seen in girls, or the greater susceptibility of boys, needs to be better understood from genomic and environmental perspectives.

## REFERENCES

Abdallah, M. W., Mortensen, E. L., Greaves-Lord, K., Larsen, N., Bonefeld-Jørgensen, E. C., Nørgaard-Pedersen, B.,...Grove, J. (2012). Neonatal levels of neurotrophic factors and risk of autism spectrum disorders. *Acta Psychiatrica Scandinavica, 128*(1), 61–69.

Aben, K. K., van Gaal, C., van Gils, N. A., van der Graaf, W. T., & Zielhuis, G. A. (2012). Cancer in adolescents and young adults (15–29 years), a population-based study in the Netherlands 1989–2009. *Acta Oncologica, 51*(7), 922–933.

Abrahams, B. S., & Geschwind, D. H. (2008). Advances in autism genetics: On the threshold of a new neurobiology. *Nature Reviews Genetics, 9*(5), 341–355.

Alvarez-Dolado, M., Ruiz, M., Del Río, J. A., Alcántara, S., Burgaya, F., Sheldon, M.,...Muñoz, A. (1999). Thyroid hormone regulates reelin and dab1 expression during brain development. *Journal of Neuroscience, 19*(16), 6979–6993.

Amaral, D. G. (2011). The promise and the pitfalls of autism research: An introductory note for new autism researchers. *Brain Research, 1380*, 3–9.

Anonymous. (2012). Prevalence of autism spectrum disorders--Autism and Developmental Disabilities Monitoring Network, 14 sites, United States, 2008. *Morbidity and Mortality Weekly Report Surveillance Summaries, 61*(3), 1–19.

Anway, M. D., & Skinner, M. K. (2006). Epigenetic transgenerational actions of endocrine disruptors. *Endocrinology, 147*(6 Suppl), S43–49.

Balaratnasingam, S., & Janca, A. (2012). Brain derived neurotrophic factor: A novel neurotrophin involved in psychiatric and neurological disorders. *Pharmacology and Therapeutics, 134*(1), 116–124.

Barker, D. J. (2003). The developmental origins of adult disease. *European Journal of Epidemiology, 18*(8), 733–736.

Bell, J. T., & Spector, T. D. (2012). DNA methylation studies using twins: What are they telling us? *Genome Biology, 13*(10), 172.

Boileau, P., Bain, P., Rives, S., & Toublanc, J. E. (2004). Earlier onset of treatment or increment in LT4 dose in screened congenital hypothyroidism: Which as the more important factor for IQ at 7 years? *Hormone Research, 61*(5), 228–233.

Boulle, F., van den Hove, D. L., Jakob, S. B., Rutten, B. P., Hamon, M., van Os, J.,...Kenis, G. (2012). Epigenetic regulation of the BDNF gene: Implications for psychiatric disorders. *Molecular Psychiatry, 17*(6), 584–596.

Cassio, A., Corbetta, C., Antonozzi, I., Calaciura, F., Caruso, U., Cesaretti, G.,...Olivieri, A. (2013). The Italian screening program for primary congenital hypothyroidism: Actions to improve screening, diagnosis, follow-up, and surveillance. *Journal of Endocrinological Investigation, 36*(3), 195–203.

Chahrour, M. H., Yu, T. W., Lim, E. T., Ataman, B., Coulter, M. E., Hill, R. S.,... Walsh, C. A. (2012). Whole-exome sequencing and homozygosity analysis implicate depolarization-regulated neuronal genes in autism. *PLoS Genetics, 8*(4), e1002635.

Chakraborty, G., Magagna-Poveda, A., Parratt, C., Umans, J. G., MacLusky, N. J., & Scharfman, H. E. (2012). Reduced hippocampal brain-derived neurotrophic factor (BDNF) in neonatal rats after prenatal exposure to propylthiouracil (PTU). *Endocrinology, 153*(3), 1311–1316.

Chamorro-Garcia, R., Sahu, M., Abbey, R. J., Laude, J., Pham, N., & Blumberg, B. (2013). Transgenerational inheritance of increased fat depot size, stem cell reprogramming, and hepatic steatosis elicited by prenatal exposure to the obesogen tributyltin in mice. *Environmental Health Perspectives, 121*(3), 359–366.

Charles, J., Harrison, C. M., & Britt, H. (2011). Management of children's psychological problems in general practice 1970–1971, 1990–1991 and 2008–2009. *Australian and New Zealand Journal of Psychiatry, 45*(11), 976–984.

Courchesne, E. (1997). Brainstem, cerebellar and limbic neuroanatomical abnormalities in autism. *Current Opinion in Neurobiology, 7*(2), 269–278.

Courchesne, E., Mouton, P. R., Calhoun, M. E., Semendeferi, K., Ahrens-Barbeau, C., Hallet, M. J.,...Pierce, K. (2011). Neuron number and size in prefrontal cortex of children with autism. *Journal of the American Medical Association, 306*(18), 2001–2010.

Cox, A. D. (1991). Is Asperger's syndrome a useful diagnosis? *Archives of Disease in Childhood, 66*(2), 259–262.

Davidovitch, M., Patterson, B., & Gartside, P. (1996). Head circumference measurements in children with autism. *Journal of Child Neurology, 11*(5), 389–393.

Dellovade, T. L., Kia, H. K., Zhu, Y. S., & Pfaff, D. W. (1999). Thyroid hormone coadministration inhibits the estrogen-stimulated elevation of preproenkephalin mRNA in female rat hypothalamic neurons. *Neuroendocrinology, 70*(3), 168–174.

Devlin, B., & Scherer, S. W. (2012). Genetic architecture in autism spectrum disorder. *Current Opinion in Genetic Development 22*(3), 229–237.

Di Martino, A., Ross, K., Uddin, L. Q., Sklar, A. B., Castellanos, F. X., & Milham, M. P. (2009). Functional brain correlates of social and nonsocial processes in autism spectrum disorders: A activation likelihood estimation meta-analysis. *Biological Psychiatry, 65*(1), 63–74.

Durand, C. M., Betancur, C., Boeckers, T. M., Bockmann, J., Chaste, P., Fauchereau, F.,...Bourgeron, T. (2007). Mutations in the gene encoding the synaptic scaffolding protein SHANK3 are associated with autism spectrum disorders. *Nature Genetics, 39*(1), 25–27.

Eayrs, J. T. (1953). Thyroid hypofunction and the development of the central nervous system. *Nature, 172*(4374), 403–404.

Ebejer, J. L., Medland, S. E., van der Werf, J., Gondro, C., Henders, A. K., Lynskey, M., ... Duffy, D. L. (2012). Attention deficit hyperactivity disorder in Australian adults: Prevalence, persistence, conduct problems and disadvantage. *PLoS One*, *7*(10), e47404.

Eggertson, L. (2010). Lancet retracts 12-year-old article linking autism to MMR vaccines. *Canadian Medical Association Journal*, *182*(4), E199–200.

Evans, I. M., Sinha, A. K., Pickard, M. R., Edwards, P. R., Leonard, A. J., & Ekins, R. P. (1999). Maternal hypothyroxinemia disrupts neurotransmitter metabolic enzymes in developing brain. *Journal of Endocrinology*, *161*(2), 273–279.

Evliyaoglu, O., Kutlu, A., Kara, C., & Atavci, S. G. (2008). Incidence of iodine deficiency in Turkish patients with congenital hypothyroidism. *Pediatrics International*, *50*(3), 276–280.

Fatemi, S. H. (2001). Reelin mutations in mouse and man: From reeler mouse to schizophrenia, mood disorders, autism and lissencephaly. *Molecular Psychiatry*, *6*(2), 129–133.

Fatemi, S. H. (2002). The role of Reelin in pathology of autism. *Molecular Psychiatry*, *7*(9), 919–920.

Fatemi, S. H., Halt, A. R., Realmuto, G., Earle, J., Kist, D. A., Thuras, P., & Merz, A. (2002). Purkinje cell size is reduced in cerebellum of patients with autism. *Cellular and Molecular Neurobiology*, *22*(2), 171–175.

Folstein, S., & Rutter, M. (1977). Infantile autism: A genetic study of 21 twin pairs. *Journal of Child Psychology and Psychiatry*, *18*(4), 297–321.

Folstein, S. E., & Rosen-Sheidley, B. (2001). Genetics of autism: Complex aetiology for a heterogeneous disorder. *Nature Reviews Genetics*, *2*(12), 943–955.

Franke, B., Faraone, S. V., Asherson, P., Buitelaar, J., Bau, C. H., Ramos-Quiroga, J. A., ... Reif, A. (2012). The genetics of attention deficit/hyperactivity disorder in adults, a review. *Molecular Psychiatry*, *17*(10), 960–987.

Geschwind, D. H. (2011). Genetics of autism spectrum disorders. *Trends in Cognitive Science*, *15*(9), 409–416.

Giusti, R. M., Iwamoto, K., & Hatch, E. E. (1995). Diethylstilbestrol revisited: A review of the long-term health effects. *Annals of Internal Medicine*, *122*(10), 778–788.

Gluckman, P. D., Hanson, M. A., Bateson, P., Beedle, A. S., Law, C. M., Bhutta, Z. A., ... West-Eberhard, M. J. (2009). Towards a new developmental synthesis: adaptive developmental plasticity and human disease. *Lancet*, *373*(9675), 1654–1657.

Goriely, A., & Wilkie, A. O. (2012). Paternal age effect mutations and selfish spermatogonial selection: Causes and consequences for human disease. *American Journal of Human Genetics*, *90*(2), 175–200.

Gregory, S. G., Connelly, J. J., Towers, A. J., Johnson, J., Biscocho, D., Markunas, C. A., ... Pericak-Vance, M. A. (2009). Genomic and epigenetic evidence for oxytocin receptor deficiency in autism. *BMC Medicine*, *7*, 62.

Hagberg, B., Aicardi, J., Dias, K., & Ramos, O. (1983). A progressive syndrome of autism, dementia, ataxia, and loss of purposeful hand use in girls: Rett's syndrome: Report of 35 cases. *Annals of Neurology*, *14*(4), 471–479.

Hallmayer, J., Cleveland, S., Torres, A., Phillips, J., Cohen, B., Torigoe, T., ... Risch, N. (2011). Genetic heritability and shared environmental factors among twin pairs with autism. *Archives of General Psychiatry*, *68*(11), 1095–1102.

Hamza, R. T., Hewedi, D. H., & Sallam, M. T. (2013). Iodine deficiency in Egyptian autistic children and their mothers: Relation to disease severity. *Archives of Medical Research*, *44*(7), 555–561.

Harris, K. B., & Pass, K. A. (2007). Increase in congenital hypothyroidism in New York State and in the United States. *Molecular and Genetic Metabolism, 91*(3), 268–277.

Hauser, P., Zametkin, A. J., Martinez, P., Vitiello, B., Matochik, J. A., Mixson, A. J., & Weintraub, B. D. (1993). Attention deficit-hyperactivity disorder in people with generalized resistance to thyroid hormone. *New England Journal of Medicine, 328*(14), 997–1001.

Hauser, P., Zametkin, A. J., Martinez, P., Vitiello, B., Matochik, J. A., Mixson, A. J., & Weintraub, B. D. (1994). ADHD and the thyroid controversy. *Journal of the American Academy of Child and Adolescent Psychiatry, 33*(5), 756–758.

Hazlett, H. C., Poe, M., Gerig, G., Smith, R. G., Provenzale, J., Ross, A., . . . Piven, J. (2005). Magnetic resonance imaging and head circumference study of brain size in autism: Birth through age 2 years. *Archives of General Psychiatry, 62*(12), 1366–1376.

Hertzberg, V., Mei, J., & Therrell, B. L. (2010). Effect of laboratory practices on the incidence rate of congenital hypothyroidism. *Pediatrics, 125*(Suppl 2), S48–S53.

Hinton, C. F., Harris, K. B., Borgfeld, L., Drummond-Borg, M., Eaton, R., Lorey, F., . . . Pass, K. A. (2010). Trends in incidence rates of congenital hypothyroidism related to select demographic factors: Data from the United States, California, Massachusetts, New York, and Texas. *Pediatrics, 125*(Suppl 2), S37–S47.

Iossifov, I., Ronemus, M., Levy, D., Wang, Z., Hakker, I., Rosenbaum, J., . . . Wigler, M. (2012). De novo gene disruptions in children on the autistic spectrum. *Neuron, 74*(2), 285–299.

Ishida, M., & Moore, G. E. (2013). The role of imprinted genes in humans. *Molecular Aspects of Medicine, 34*(4), 826–840.

Jablonka, E., & Lamb, M. J. (2005). *Evolution in four dimensions: Genetic, epigenetic, behavioral, and symbolic variation in the history of life.* Cambridge, MA: MIT Press.

Johnson, R. H., Chien, F. L., & Bleyer, A. (2013). Incidence of breast cancer with distant involvement among women in the United States, 1976 to 2009. *Journal of the American Medical Association, 309*(8), 800–805.

Kanner, L. (1968). Autistic disturbances of affective contact. *Acta Paedopsychiatrica, 35*(4), 100–136.

Kim, Y. S., Leventhal, B. L., Koh, Y. J., Fombonne, E., Laska, E., Lim, E. C., . . . Grinker, R. R. (2011). Prevalence of autism spectrum disorders in a total population sample. *American Journal of Psychiatry, 168*(9), 904–912.

King, B. H., & Lord, C. (2011). Is schizophrenia on the autism spectrum? *Brain Research, 1380,* 34–41.

King, M., & Bearman, P. (2009). Diagnostic change and the increased prevalence of autism. *International Journal of Epidemiology, 38*(5), 1224–1234.

Knapp, M., Romeo, R., & Beecham, J. (2009). Economic cost of autism in the UK. *Autismm, 13*(3), 317–336.

Koibuchi, N., & Chin, W. W. (1998). ROR alpha gene expression in the perinatal rat cerebellum: Ontogeny and thyroid hormone regulation. *Endocrinology, 139*(5), 2335–2341.

Kooij, S. J., Bejerot, S., Blackwell, A., Caci, H., Casas-Brugué, M., Carpentier, P. J., . . . Asherson, P. (2010). European consensus statement on diagnosis and treatment of adult ADHD: The European Network Adult ADHD. *BMC Psychiatry, 10,* 67.

Kulesza, R. J., Jr., Lukose, R., & Stevens, L. V. (2011). Malformation of the human superior olive in autistic spectrum disorders. *Brain Research, 1367,* 360–371.

Landrigan, P. J., Lambertini, L., & Birnbaum, L. S. (2012). A research strategy to discover the environmental causes of autism and neurodevelopmental disabilities. *Environmental Health Perspectives, 120*(7), a258–260.

Lampi, K. M., Lehtonen, L., Tran, P. L., Suominen, A., Lehti, V., Banerjee, P. N.,... Sourander, A. (2012). Risk of autism spectrum disorders in low birth weight and small for gestational age infants. *Journal of Pediatrics, 161*(5), 830–836.

Lange, K. W., Reichl, S., Lange, K. M., Tucha, L., & Tucha, O. (2010). The history of attention deficit hyperactivity disorder. *Attention Deficit and Hyperactivity Disorders, 2*(4), 241–255.

LaSalle, J. M. (2011). A genomic point-of-view on environmental factors influencing the human brain methylome. *Epigenetics, 6*(7), 862–869.

Lichtenstein, P., Carlstrom, E., Rastam, M., Gillberg, C., & Anckarsater, H. (2010). The genetics of autism spectrum disorders and related neuropsychiatric disorders in childhood. *American Journal of Psychiatry, 167*(11), 1357–1363.

Liu, L., Guan, L. L., Chen, Y., Ji, N., Li, H. M., Li, Z. H.,... Wang, Y. F. (2011). Association analyses of MAOA in Chinese Han subjects with attention-deficit/ hyperactivity disorder: Family-based association test, case-control study, and quantitative traits of impulsivity. *American Journal of Medical Genetics B: Neuropsychiatric Genetics, 156B*(6), 737–748.

Liu, D., Teng, W., Shan, Z., Yu, X., Gao, Y., Wang, S.,... Zhang, H. (2010). The effect of maternal subclinical hypothyroidism during pregnancy on brain development in rat offspring. *Thyroid, 20*(8), 909–915.

McCarthy, M. I., Abecasis, G. R., Cardon, L. R., Goldstein, D. B., Little, J., Ioannidis, J. P., & Hirschhorn, J. N. (2008). Genome-wide association studies for complex traits: Consensus, uncertainty and challenges. *Nature Reviews Genetics, 9*(5), 356–369.

McDonald, M. P., Wong, R., Goldstein, G., Weintraub, B., Cheng, S. Y., & Crawley, J. N. (1998). Hyperactivity and learning deficits in transgenic mice bearing a human mutant thyroid hormone beta1 receptor gene. *Learning and Memory, 5*(4–5), 289–301.

McLean, C. Y., Reno, P. L., Pollen, A. A., Bassan, A. I., Capellini, T. D., Guenther, C.,... Kingsley, D. M. (2011). Human-specific loss of regulatory DNA and the evolution of human-specific traits. *Nature, 471*(7337), 216–219.

Michaelson, J. J., Shi, Y., Gujral, M., Zheng, H., Malhotra, D., Jin, X.,... Sebat, J. (2012). Whole-genome sequencing in autism identifies hot spots for de novo germline mutation. *Cell, 151*(7), 1431–1442.

Minshew, N. J., & Keller, T. A. (2010). The nature of brain dysfunction in autism: Functional brain imaging studies. *Current Opinion in Neurology, 23*(2), 124–130.

Mitchell, M. L., Hsu, H. W., & Sahai, I. (2011). The increased incidence of congenital hypothyroidism: Fact or fancy? *Clinical Endocrinology (Oxford), 75*(6), 806–810.

Muers, M. (2012). Human genetics: Fruits of exome sequencing for autism. *Nature Reviews Genetics, 13*(6), 377.

Muir, T., & Zegarac, M. (2001). Societal costs of exposure to toxic substances: Economic and health costs of four case studies that are candidates for environmental causation. *Environmental Health Perspectives, 109*(Suppl 6), 885–903.

Murphy, D., & Spooren, W. (2012). EU-AIMS: A boost to autism research. *Nature Revies Drug Discoveries, 11*(11), 815–816.

Nagayama, J., Kohno, H., Kunisue, T., Kataoka, K., Shimomura, H., Tanabe, S., & Konishi, S. (2007). Concentrations of organochlorine pollutants in mothers who gave birth to neonates with congenital hypothyroidism. *Chemosphere, 68*(5), 972–976.

Neale, B. M., Kou, Y., Liu, L., Ma'ayan, A., Samocha, K. E., Sabo, A., … Daly, M. J. (2012). Patterns and rates of exonic de novo mutations in autism spectrum disorders. *Nature, 485*(7397), 242–245.

Nguyen, A., Rauch, T. A., Pfeifer, G. P., & Hu, V. W. (2010). Global methylation profiling of lymphoblastoid cell lines reveals epigenetic contributions to autism spectrum disorders and a novel autism candidate gene, RORA, whose protein product is reduced in autistic brain. *FASEB Journal, 24*(8), 3036–3051.

Olivieri, A., Medda, E., De Angelis, S., Valensise, H., De Felice, M., Fazzini, C., … Stazi, M. A. (2007). High risk of congenital hypothyroidism in multiple pregnancies. *Journal of Clinical Endocrinology and Metabolism, 92*(8), 3141–3147.

Olney, R. S., Grosse, S. D., & Vogt, R. F., Jr. (2010). Prevalence of congenital hypothyroidism--current trends and future directions: Workshop summary. *Pediatrics, 125*(Suppl 2), S31–S36.

O'Roak, B. J., Vives, L., Fu, W., Egertson, J. D., Stanaway, I. B., Phelps, I. G., … Shendure, J. (2012a). Multiplex targeted sequencing identifies recurrently mutated genes in autism spectrum disorders. *Science, 338*(6114), 1619–1622.

O'Roak, B. J., Vives, L., Girirajan, S., Karakoc, E., Krumm, N., Coe, B. P., … Eichler, E. E. (2012b). Sporadic autism exomes reveal a highly interconnected protein network of de novo mutations. *Nature, 485*(7397), 246–250.

Palha, J. A., & Goodman, A. B. (2006). Thyroid hormones and retinoids: A possible link between genes and environment in schizophrenia. *Brain Research Reviews, 51*(1), 61–71.

Pathak, A., Sinha, R. A., Mohan, V., Mitra, K., & Godbole, M. M. (2011). Maternal thyroid hormone before the onset of fetal thyroid function regulates reelin and downstream signaling cascade affecting neocortical neuronal migration. *Cerebral Cortex, 21*(1), 11–21.

Pearce, J. M. (2005). Kanner's infantile autism and Asperger's syndrome. *Journal of Neurology, Neurosurgery and Psychiatry, 76*(2), 205.

Pearl, P. L., Weiss, R. E., & Stein, M. A. (2001). Medical mimics. Medical and neurological conditions simulating ADHD. *Annals of the New York Academy of Sciences, 931*, 97–112.

Polanczyk, G., de Lima, M. S., Horta, B. L., Biederman, J., & Rohde, L. A. (2007). The worldwide prevalence of ADHD: A systematic review and metaregression analysis. *American Journal of Psychiatry, 164*(6), 942–948.

Randolph-Gips, M., & Srinivasan, P. (2012). Modeling autism: A systems biology approach. *Journal of Clinical Bioinformatics, 2*(1), 17.

Ritvo, E. R., Freeman, B. J., Scheibel, A. B., Duong, T., Robinson, H., Guthrie, D., & Ritvo, A. (1986). Lower Purkinje cell counts in the cerebella of four autistic subjects: Initial findings of the UCLA-NSAC Autopsy Research Report. *American Journal of Psychiatry, 143*(7), 862–866.

Roman, G. C. (2007). Autism: Transient in utero hypothyroxinemia related to maternal flavonoid ingestion during pregnancy and to other environmental antithyroid agents. *Journal of Neurological Sciences, 262*(1–2), 15–26.

Ronald, A., & Hoekstra, R. A. (2011). Autism spectrum disorders and autistic traits: A decade of new twin studies. *American Journal of Medical Genetics B: Neuropsychiatric Genetics, 156B*(3), 255–274.

Roseboom, T. J., van der Meulen, J. H., Ravelli, A. C., Osmond, C., Barker, D. J., & Bleker, O. P. (2001). Effects of prenatal exposure to the Dutch famine on adult disease in later life: An overview. *Molecular and Cellular Endocrinology, 185*(1–2), 93–98.

Roth, C., Magnus, P., Schjølberg, S., Stoltenberg, C., Surén, P., McKeague, I. W.,...Susser, E. (2011). Folic acid supplements in pregnancy and severe language delay in children. *Journal of the American Medical Association, 306*(14), 1566–1573.

Sanders, S. J., Murtha, M. T., Gupta, A. R., Murdoch, J. D., Raubeson, M. J., Willsey, A. J.,...State, M. W. (2012). De novo mutations revealed by whole-exome sequencing are strongly associated with autism. *Nature, 485*(7397), 237–241.

Santos, N. C., Costa, P., Ruano, D., Macedo, A., Soares, M. J., Valente, J.,...Palha, J. A. (2012). Revisiting thyroid hormones in schizophrenia. *Journal of Thyroid Research, 2012,* 569147.

Sebat, J., Lakshmi, B., Malhotra, D., Troge, J., Lese-Martin, C., Walsh, T.,...Wigler, M. (2007). Strong association of de novo copy number mutations with autism. *Science, 316*(5823), 445–449.

Sebat, J., Levy, D. L., & McCarthy, S. E. (2009). Rare structural variants in schizophrenia: One disorder, multiple mutations; one mutation, multiple disorders. *Trends in Genetics, 25*(12), 528–535.

Spencer, T., Biederman, J., Wilens, T., Guite, J., & Harding, M. (1995). ADHD and thyroid abnormalities: A research note. *Journal of Child Psychology and Psychiatry, 36*(5), 879–885.

Strick, P. L., Dum, R. P., & Fiez, J. A. (2009). Cerebellum and nonmotor function. *Annual Review of Neuroscience, 32,* 413–434.

Tsai, P. T., Hull, C., Chu, Y., Greene-Colozzi, E., Sadowski, A. R., Leech, J. M.,...Sahin, M. (2012). Autistic-like behaviour and cerebellar dysfunction in Purkinje cell Tsc1 mutant mice. *Nature, 488*(7413), 647–651.

Vermiglio, F., Lo Presti, V. P., Moleti, M., Sidoti, M., Tortorella, G., Scaffidi, G.,...Trimarchi, F. (2004). Attention deficit and hyperactivity disorders in the offspring of mothers exposed to mild-moderate iodine deficiency: A possible novel iodine deficiency disorder in developed countries. *Journal of Clinical Endocrinology and Metabolism, 89*(12), 6054–6060.

Weintraub, K. (2011). The prevalence puzzle: Autism counts. *Nature, 479*(7371), 22–24.

Weiss, B. (2009). The first 83 and the next 83: Perspectives on neurotoxicology. *Neurotoxicology, 30*(5), 832–850.

Werling, D. M., & Geschwind, D. H. (2013). Understanding sex bias in autism spectrum disorder. *Proceedings of the National Academy of Science USA, 110*(13), 4868–4869.

Wong, C. C., Meaburn, E. L., Ronald, A., Price, T. S., Jeffries, A. R., Schalkwyk, L. C.,...Mill, J. (2013). Methylomic analysis of monozygotic twins discordant for autism spectrum disorder and related behavioural traits. *Molecular Psychiatry,* doi: 10.1038/mp.2013.41. Epub ahead of print.

Yip, J., Soghomonian, J. J., & Blatt, G. J. (2009). Decreased GAD65 mRNA levels in select subpopulations of neurons in the cerebellar dentate nuclei in autism: An in situ hybridization study. *Autism Research, 2*(1), 50–59.

Yu, T. W., Chahrour, M. H., Coulter, M. E., Jiralerspong, S., Okamura-Ikeda, K., Ataman, B.,...Walsh, C. A. (2013). Using whole-exome sequencing to identify inherited causes of autism. *Neuron, 77*(2), 259–273.

# Chapter 8

# What Can Be Done by Individuals, Associations, and Governments

*Time to End the Pied Piper Scenario*

CHAPTER OUTLINE

The tale of the Pied Piper of Hamelin is well known for its final imagery of a town losing its children as they are led away by a musician clad in multicolored clothes. What is less often recalled is that the cause was the council's attempts to save money. In effect, the children were sacrificed for financial gain—a disquieting metaphor. This final chapter argues that actions by individuals in their daily lives, but also within associations and as electors, can be significant and worthwhile. Despite the depressing situation that may seem to have gone beyond the point of no return, there is an urgent need for collective action to counteract inertia by elected representatives and legislators, and collusion by industrial lobbies. Furthermore, individual action and lifestyle choices can, to some extent, limit exposure to certain chemical categories. Clearly, pregnant women and nursing mothers need to be informed of potential risks so they can take precautionary action, and the medical profession needs to be trained to help. Ensuring that women do not enter pregnancy in a state of even mild iodine lack is a first inexpensive requirement with immense cost-benefit. Other lifestyle choices, notably in diet, avoidance of alcohol during pregnancy and reduced use of certain consumer products, can bolster protection against exposure to and the action of some pollutants. As is often the case, legislation can be more effective than individual action. But given the time frame, both are recommended. Efforts to modify legislation are most effective through collective action. I provide examples of associations that are raising awareness of chemical pollution in general and of specific categories of chemicals, such as pesticides or flame retardants.

BACKGROUND

In the debate on the adoption of precautionary principles as opposed to waiting for proof of damage, many arguments are presented in defense of nonaction. Apart from the standard arguments that the industries concerned create jobs, and that without the chemicals industry we would return to the Stone Age, many authorities and individuals consider that things cannot be that bad, as after all we are living longer than ever before. The observation that longevity has been increasing in many (though not all) countries up until recently is often thought to be related to the adaptive capacity of physiological mechanisms that humans and biodiversity in general possess. In the context of endocrinology, some argue that the thyroid hormone (TH) axis has evolved to compensate for changes in hormone use and degradation, and that the multiple rheostat mechanisms, or yin-yang of forward stimulation and feedback control, will override transient disruption.

Both of these arguments—increased longevity and capacity of physiological mechanisms to adapt—are inappropriately applied in this context. The current increase in longevity is based, by definition, on data from populations that were born in the 1920s and early 1930s. These birth cohorts were among the first to benefit from improvements in perinatal care and reduction in early infant mortality, better sanitation, vaccinations, and antibiotics, together reducing the incidence of infectious disease and associated childhood mortality. But these cohorts were also born just before the main waves of introduction of plastics, DDT, leaded petrol, and many of the other substances listed in Chapter 5. So none of the healthy seniors currently playing golf and dancing into their late nineties underwent the in utero exposure of the next generations. Furthermore, recent data from the United States show that decreases in longevity are now being seen. Most striking are the recent 4-year decreases in longevity seen in less educated White women (http://www.cdc.gov/nchs/). In this light it is interesting to note that there is an overall correlation between longevity and intelligence (Deary, 2008). Thus, given the premises of this book, one can wonder whether the causes underlying such declines in longevity are actually related to the rise in behavioral and neurodevelopmental problems that have been creeping up since the mid-1970s. The logic would be that children with such behavioral problems would be the most likely to fail in the education system.

In some countries, such as Russia, declines in longevity have been evident for many years.[1] To this one can add that in all developed countries the gap between life span and healthy life span is widening, meaning we spend more time in ill health. This increasing gap means that the toll of noninfectious (noncommunicable) diseases such as neurodegenerative disorders, cancer, cardiovascular disease, and metabolic disease is constantly eroding healthy life span, while the burden of care is further amplified with increasing longevity. In other words, we are keeping sick people alive longer with noncommunicable diseases, many of which have been repeatedly associated with environmental factors. To these statistics one should add the increased incidence of cancers in children and young adults (Aben et al., 2012).

As to the argument that our physiology is built to adjust continually to environmental challenge and to changes in TH availability, four counterarguments can be given. The first is that during critical windows of development a slight change in TH availability can have major, irreversible effects, notably

---

1  At the time of writing the media is resonating with the 5.5-year decrease in life expectancy reported in certain areas of China, a decrease directly related to air pollution.

on early brain development, before the regulatory compensation mechanisms can come into play. The second is that during development, even as the regulatory mechanisms appear, they may be less able to respond. The third is that given the continual exposure to multiple chemicals, even a mature system can be overridden. Finally, increasing evidence, including epidemiological studies in humans, shows that compensatory adjustments made during development most often induce detrimental effects in the longer term. Examples include the increased occurrence of adult metabolic disorders in lower birth weight babies that "catch up" too rapidly to normal growth curves and data from UK and Dutch populations showing that fetuses that had been exposed to restricted nutritional supplies during or after World War II displayed increased risk of cardiovascular and diabetes in middle age. Moreover, even without this knowledge, many people are tempted to shrug their shoulders and say that things have gone so far that there is nothing we can do other than make the best of a bad situation. Here we argue the contrary, that individuals can make a difference to their own and their children's lives, both immediately and by collective action in the longer term.

Individual Choices

Although the levels of contaminants found in Arctic and Antarctic fauna might make one think that any attempt to reduce individual exposure is a lost cause, facts show that it is worth the effort, as small changes in behavior can have significant effects on certain forms of chemical load. As detailed later in this chapter, this is particularly true for choices of organic versus classic produce and paying attention to the way food and drink are packed and prepared. Originally, this chapter was separated into sections of advice for the general public, on the one hand, and for women who were thinking of becoming pregnant, or who are already pregnant or breast-feeding, on the other. This thinking was based on the idea that fetal and postnatal life, especially the first 3 months of pregnancy, appear to be the most critical in terms of early exposure and late effects on neurodevelopment and behavior. But seen another way, it seems not only justifiable to focus on this group but also to explain the scientific reasons underlying the precautionary advice currently available for pregnant women, so that others in the general population can understand and choose whether to apply the arguments themselves. If they do, they will probably be adopting habits that will ultimately be better for their own health.

Many lifestyle choices can affect personal exposure levels. The recommendations from the Royal College of Obstetricians and Gynecologists (RCOG) (http://www.rcog.org.uk/files/rcog-corp/5.6.13ChemicalExposures.pdf) for pregnant and nursing mothers make a good starting point for discussion. The report emphasizes awareness of food choices, personal care and household products, and pharmaceuticals available without prescription, including herbal treatments. As the title of their 2013 report underlines, many of the associations between chemicals and adverse effects on children's health are as yet unproven, but potentially damaging. Thus, applying a precautionary approach is not scaremongering, as some have suggested, but simply applying the rule that most mothers would want, that is, doing one's best to provide the most favorable start to your child's life. Many authors have drawn parallels between personal choices and actions that can lead to reduction of chemical exposure with the early recommendations such as wearing of seat belts in cars or not smoking, two examples that started off as advisory and later led to legislative action.

To simplify the presentation, we will organize individual actions into categories around awareness of sources and packaging of food and water, on the one hand, and furnishings, household, and electronic equipment on the other. Given its importance and the disquiet many women have when hearing about the levels of chemical exposure to which we are subjected, the arguments in favor of breast-feeding are presented separately.

Food Sources: The Case for Organic Products to Reduce Pesticide Exposure

The consumption of organically grown food, especially fruit, vegetables, and grain produce, rather than conventionally grown equivalents, has been shown to significantly reduce pesticide exposure. Curl et al. (2003) were among the first groups to analyze pesticide metabolites in the urine of children eating organically grown produce as compared to children on conventional diets. The authors showed four-fold reductions of median total dimethyl metabolites of organophosphate (OP) pesticides in children eating organic produce. The authors concluded that if parents were to use organic produce it would be a simple way of reducing their children's OP exposure. This paper, published in a reputable journal, drew praise but also criticism (Charnley, 2003; Krieger et al., 2003). The main arguments advanced by the critics were, first, that some of the metabolites (potentially with lesser toxicity) were not actually generated by human metabolism but could have been produced by the plant and therefore were already in the food. Taking these metabolite levels to calculate exposure, therefore, could have inflated the estimates made by Curl and colleagues of exposure to the parent pesticide (but not the fact that organic food reduced metabolite levels). The second principal argument put forward was that pesticide use reduces plant stress responses and therefore reduces levels of toxins that plants may produce as defense mechanisms against insect attack or disease. Curl and colleagues replied to each of these criticisms. They put forward three arguments in response to the idea that plant-produced metabolites could inflate exposure estimates, including the fact that many of the plant-produced metabolites would not have affected the data, and the absence of data on metabolite levels in produce, as well as absence of information on the absorption and fate of these metabolites in humans. As to the second argument on plant stress, in their reply Curl and colleagues noted the critic had put forward the overly simplistic idea that organic farming methods are simply "conventional methods without pesticides," and their reply argued that this concept was not only reductionist but erroneous. They note that organic methods differ from industrial practices by the employment of a spectrum of techniques and that these practices do not necessarily increase plant stress.

Among others, one paper from a series arising from a well-designed set of experiments well illustrates reduction of pesticide exposure by use of organic food. Lu and colleagues (2006) recruited 23 schoolchildren, aged between 3 and 11, in Washington in the summer of 2003. None of the families participating in the study used pesticides at home, another major source of potential contamination. Again, the experimental setup was a longitudinal study that involved collecting evening and morning urine samples from the children for a 3-day period on control diets; a 5-day period on organic fruit, vegetables, and grain; followed by another 6-day period on control diets again. Meat and milk produce were not changed during the experiment, as these foodstuffs contain less of the pesticides monitored. Two main classes of organophosphate pesticides were monitored, chlorpyrifos and malathion, by measuring their metabolites in the urine. Just to recall, as described in Chapter 5, not only has chlorpyrifos been shown to modulate TH signaling in human and in animal models (De Angelis et al., 2009), but prenatal exposure to chlorpyrifos is associated with reduced IQ and working memory (Rauh et al., 2011). Similar TH-disrupting effects of malathion have also been described in animal models, including fish, amphibians, birds, and rodents. Returning to the data of Lu and colleagues, when the children consumed organic food, the levels of the pesticides dropped immediately and significantly, remaining low for the 5 days of organic produce consumption and increasing as soon as the children were provided with conventional fruit, vegetables, and grain. When on control, standard diets the mean levels of the malathion pesticide metabolites were in the ranges of 3–4 µg/L urine and maximum levels reached 263 µg/L, whereas on the organic diet, mean levels were close to undetectable at 0.3 µg/L with maximum levels being only 7.4 µg/L. Similarly, for the chlorpyrifos metabolites, a five-fold decrease was observed on the organic diet. As for the earlier study by Curl et al. (2003), this paper drew criticism from commentators (Krieger, Keenan, Li, & Vega, 2006), though this time the principal criticism was overdramatization of results and lack of associated risk of disease with exposure. Both of these arguments were countered by the authors of the original paper, in particular by providing data on cases of acute pesticide poisoning and on the longer term, nonacute effects of pesticide exposure and links with neurobehavioral disorders and cancer incidence. Lu, Toepel, and collaborators have used this longitudinal study design, alternating days on control, conventional produce, with a period on organic food to assess exposure to pyrethroid pesticides (2006). As pyrethroids are used domestically to control insects, the main exposure route was found to be household use. However, though less marked than with OP pesticides, effects of diet showed the same pattern as for the OP data.

In the debate about the need for pesticide usage, one argument that is often brought forward is the greater need for pest control to increase yield so as to feed a growing world population. However, as mentioned in Chapter 5, many studies have documented that pesticide reduction does not necessarily mean reduced production (Normile, 2013; Pimentel, 2012; Pretty et al., 2006) nor lower quality or nutritional value. The debate is also rendered more complex by the argument that introduction of genetically modified (GM; or genetically engineered [GE]) plants that can resist insects can reduce pesticide usage. Multiple social and environmental ramifications need to be taken into account in these discussions, with concern about health and biodiversity risks engendered by GM use being expressed by groups of consumers and scientists (see Lemaux, 2008, for review). In Europe, concern about the environmental and health risks of consuming GE products has led many EU countries to ban farming and importing GE crops. In other countries, specific health concerns, such as lack of vitamin A and consequent blindness, seem reasonable arguments for the introduction of GE rice bearing a daffodil gene for synthesis of a vitamin A precursor, even if natural supplies of vitamin A would seem preferable. The rice is effective (Tang et al., 2012), but local politics and broader policy concerns are delaying introduction (Hvistendahl & Enserink, 2012; Potrykus, 2010).

Thus, it seems reasonable to suggest that pregnant women should try to replace as much conventional produce as possible with organically grown equivalents. Although we can go on adding more and more epidemiological data on exposure as a function of organic versus conventional sources, the associative data on the effects of exposure on neurodevelopment, particularly in children of agricultural workers or women living near agricultural areas, argue strongly for the application of the precautionary principle in reducing the pesticide exposure of pregnant and nursing mothers. Drawing parallels from the history of medicine, there are many examples, particularly on infectious diseases such as cholera and puerperal fever, where without understanding of the underlying mechanisms of transmission a change in behavior could halt disease spread.[2] One paper showing strong associative data with pesticide exposure in areas close to agricultural sites and incidence of ASD is that of Roberts and colleagues (Roberts et al., 2007). The authors show that the greatest risk is incurred in the first 2 months of pregnancy. This observation underlines the particular sensitivity of the early stages of the developing brain in utero. Unfortunately, current pesticide neurotoxicity tests are most often carried out on adult animals and rarely on the more sensitive developing or embryonic stages (Lanphear, Vorhees, & Bellinger, 2005).

---

2  An often-quoted example is that of the British physician John Snow (1813–1858), who predicted that a water pump was the source of a cholera outbreak. As this was prior to both the demonstration of the waterborne nature of cholera and the germ theory of disease, he resorted to removing the handle from the pump and the epidemic ceased. The case of Ignaz Semmelweis (1818–1865) and his analysis of the cause of puerperal, or childbed, fever is perhaps more tragic. Despite ingenious demonstrations and statistics, but no knowledge of mechanisms, he could never convince colleagues to wash their hands between carrying out autopsies on rotting bodies and tending to women in childbirth.

Food choices for pregnant and nursing mothers are not by any means limited to the dichotomy of organic versus conventional produce. Many other factors can enter the equation, including the risk-benefit analysis of amounts and sources of fish and seafood to be eaten, as well as the possibility of choosing dairy products, such as cheese, in the forms that have the lowest natural fat contents. Many reliable Web sites (such as the British Cardiac Patients Association) give appropriate advice on these subjects.[3]

Taking the question of fish and seafood consumption first, it is important to note that such food categories, particularly marine fish and shellfish, remain major sources of both iodine and selenium. These elements along with other nutritional factors, such as high-protein and long-chain polyunsaturated fatty acids (such as omega 3 fatty acids), all enter the "benefit" side of the equation. The risk elements include contamination with mercury, TBT, and dioxins/polychlorinated biphenyls (PCBs), each of which generally increases with consumption of fish species that are higher up the food chain. In the case of the dioxins and PCBs, the higher the lipid content of the fish, the higher the level of contamination (Szlinder-Richert, Barska, Mazerski, & Usydus, 2009), with herring, mackerel, trout, and salmon being examples of the most "oily fish." However, despite these risks, the general benefit of eating fish has been shown to outweigh the risks. One particularly interesting study in this context comes from the group of Philippe Grandjean (Choi et al., 2008), who studied Faroe islanders and examined associations of neurodevelopmental outcomes with consumption of fish, including pilot whale meat that can be notoriously high in mercury. The authors were interested in the potential protective effects of selenium against mercury (see Chapter 2) in the fish and based their calculations on levels of these elements in cord blood and the neurodevelopmental status of children at 7 years of age. The authors conclude (Choi et al., 2008) that as fish consumption can be associated with beneficial effects on neurodevelopmental outcome, fish should be eaten during pregnancy, but that it is better to avoid sources of fish that are high in mercury contamination, such as whale meat. A similar conclusion, that regular (e.g. once or twice a week) consumption of oily fish is beneficial, was reached by a European consortium studying dietary fat requirements during pregnancy and lactation (Koletzko, Cetin, & Brenna, 2007). These authors also emphasized one exception to the benefit over risk argument, and highlighted the need to avoid Baltic herring or wild salmon from this region while pregnant or nursing (Koletzko et al., 2007). Despite reductions in pollution of the Baltic environment, these fish still show high levels of PCBs, leading to a general recommendation for pregnant women in Scandinavia (and elsewhere) to avoid this food source. These precautions are probably the basis for the RCOG suggesting that eating oily fish (notably tuna) should be avoided or limited to once a week. A final point is to remember that one easy-to-apply factor that can significantly reduce intake of most of

3   http://www.bcpa.co.uk/factsheets/FatContentOfCheeses.htm

the principal contaminants when eating oily fish is to remove the skin (Zhang, Gandhi, Bhavsar, & Ho, 2013).

Drinking Water: Bottled or Tap, Filtered or Non-Filtered

The public health issues and economics of water are far-ranging causing concern among consumers and even leading to international conflict in some cases. The debates are complex and go far beyond the scope of this chapter. To maintain a focus on the question discussed here, namely what an individual can do to limit exposure to endocrine-disrupting chemicals (EDCs), we consider the arguments for and against tap versus bottled water. Neither source is fully satisfactory. Probably the most effective action depends on the characteristic of your house, particularly the pipes that carry the water to the tap and its water supply. Information on water supply quality should be available and if the quality is questionable, the most effective action will be to contact associations addressing these questions at local and national levels.

The information relating to decisions on whether to use bottled or tap water and whether home-based filtering systems can remove significant amounts of contaminants is complex. Currently, most households in developed countries are using the same water they drink to shower, water the garden, wash clothes, and even wash the car. It is becoming increasingly evident that this situation is wasteful and that if drinking water standards are to be maintained, more rational use of supply has to be instigated. It has been suggested that a potential solution that would combine health benefits and economic advantage would be to deliver two liters of glass-bottled purified water per person to each household every day, in the same way that milk was once delivered to the door in postwar United Kingdom. In the meantime those in independent dwellings can collect rainwater from roof runoff to water the garden, run the washing machine, and flush the toilet, thereby reducing waste of drinking water. Others living in apartment blocks need to consider the tap versus bottle option more closely.

A number of methods exist for purifying wastewater and disinfecting tap water, including sand filtration or ultrafiltration (UF), powdered activated carbon (PAC), chlorination, ion exchange resins, use of ultraviolet (UV) light, and ozonization. Individual households can apply adaptations of some of these methods, including filtration by reverse osmosis and activated carbon (charcoal) filtration. In most developed countries water supply to houses is highly regulated and tap water is a safe and ecologically sounder option than bottled water, at least with respect to two of the major groups of EDCs, namely bis-phenol A (BPA) and phthalates (Amiridou & Voutsa, 2011). Besides the transport cost and the carbon footprint incurred, other drawbacks of bottled water vary as a function of source and of container. Plastic bottles are lighter and therefore incur less transport costs but have higher plasticizer content, in particular BPA from polycarbonate bottles. Though the amounts of BPA and phthalates from plastic bottles are not the major sources of exposure to these factors (phthalates not being added to the plastic used for water bottles but potentially entering during the manufacturing process; Al-Saleh, Shinwari, & Alsabbaheen, 2011), water from plastic bottles does contain more chemicals with estrogenic activity (probably these chemicals) than glass bottled water (Wagner & Oehlmann, 2011) or tap water.

Other chemicals with significantly different levels between tap and bottled water depending on the measurement site are two products with strong antithyroid actions: perchlorate and nitrates (the latter largely derived from intensive agricultural practices). Taking perchlorate first, different countries and, within the United States, individual states, apply, or simply recommend, varying limits for perchlorate in drinking water supplies. Drinking water can contain perchlorate from two sources: the ground water supply itself or chlorination disinfection methods, notably the addition of hypochlorite. The current general ruling in the United States, set by the Environmental Protection Agency (EPA), is 15 µg/L. However, Massachusetts has a much lower limit. At the turn of the century, high levels of perchlorate in drinking water supply to a residential area, and the lack of state or federal rulings on admissible levels at that time (2001–2002), led local authorities to convene an independent committee for guidance. Using a weight of evidence approach, consideration of sensitive life stages and the risk of iodine insufficiency brought the limit down to 2 µg/L (Zewdie, Smith, Hutcheson, & West, 2010). The EPA is currently working on measuring and removing perchlorate from drinking water. It is also expected to issue a statement in the coming year about the risk/benefits of introducing a ruling to regulate the perchlorate levels in drinking water. As it stands, there is no recommended limit for perchlorate levels in the EU directive for drinking water.

Nitrate levels vary significantly according to agricultural intensity. In France, a World Wildlife Fund (WWF) study published in 2011 reported that about half of the tap water sources had values over 20 mg/L, with some over the maximum permitted limit of 50 mg/L. As emphasized in Chapter 5, both nitrate and perchlorate inhibit uptake of iodide by the thyroid gland. Even though nitrate is more than a hundred-fold less active as a competitor for iodide transport by the thyroid than perchlorate, the fact that it is present at thousand-fold greater concentrations (nitrate is found in the milligram per liter range, and perchlorate in the microgram per liter range) means that both represent significant thyroid-inhibiting capacity, which argues, yet again, for the importance of iodine supplementation, especially during pregnancy (see Box 8.1).

Unfortunately, many water treatment plants do not remove all traces of organic substances, such as pesticides, perchlorate, and nitrate, so according to site and time of year, tap water can contain significant amounts of these molecules. Much research focuses on comparing methods for removing these compounds that represent the most common organic micropollutants of drinking water and the subject of increasing concern of the public and their suppliers. Although combinations of filtration and treatment will remove most contaminants, the questions of cost and who should foot the bill inevitably arise. In the meantime some householders apply a precautionary approach and look at methods to purify their home drinking water supply.

---

**Box 8–1. Preventing Irreversible Damage: Iodine Supplementation in Pregnancy**

---

As the Royal College of Obstetricians and Gynecologists (RCOG) report focuses on avoidance of unnecessary exposure, it does not mention the need of the pregnant mother for increased iodine (and selenium) intake. As emphasized earlier, the medical profession needs to have greater awareness of the risks undergone by women entering pregnancy in a state of even mild iodine lack. In the first half of 2013 no fewer than 17 papers have demonstrated yet again (Hynes, Otahal, Hay, & Burgess, 2013) or discussed the risk of maternal iodine lack on children's later neurodevelopment, one of them being wisely titled "Sufficient Iodine Intake During Pregnancy: Just Do It" (Leung, Pearce, & Braverman, 2013), and another "Iodine and Pregnancy: A Call to Action" (Stagnaro-Green & Pearce, 2013). Much of the debate concerns regional differences, with certain authors arguing that in many regions iodine intake is sufficient and supplementation unnecessary. However, many medical authorities consider that prevention is vital and recommend iodine supplementation during pregnancy.

Some antenatal vitamin and mineral preparations include both iodine and selenium. Alternatively, iodine can be provided in the form of injections every 3 months—but preferentially starting before conception.

Ensuring that women have sufficient iodine to avoid even transient and mild hypothyroidism is vital throughout pregnancy but also during the first months before the fetal thyroid is formed. This period has been shown repeatedly to be a particularly sensitive window of vulnerability for associations between chemical load and later neurodevelopmental and behavioral outcomes.

---

Four main types of home water treatment methods are available, each with its drawbacks. The most commonly used method is a carbon or charcoal filter, usually in the form of a jug or an on-tap appliance. They can also be installed as an "at-source" or under-sink appliance at the entry of the main drinking water supply. These filters must be changed regularly and therefore create landfill waste. Although the waste is probably not as voluminous as plastic bottles, for an equivalent amount of water, their recycling is more difficult. Carbon filters remove mainly chlorine and some chlorinated compounds, estrogen, lead, and copper. According to certain sources, they also can remove some PCBs, as well as pesticides and herbicides. They do not remove nitrate or perchlorate.

Reverse osmosis systems can be installed by specialized companies. These systems use power to membrane filter the water under pressure. From some points of view, the water quality is better than filtering, perchlorate and nitrate being removed by this method. However, they are exceedingly wasteful, both in terms of energy and water, with between five and ten times more water lost than filtered. The two other methods are home-based UV sources to kill bacteria and distillation units that are not only energy consuming but also require regular cleaning maintenance.

Overall, given the limited spectrum of chemicals removed and/or the ecological cost of these household devices, a reasonable guideline would be to draw water for drinking the night before and leave the chlorine to evaporate. However, nitrate does not evaporate, even during boiling; hence, boiling concentrates nitrate as water is lost. To avoid nitrate buildup, boiled water should not be subjected to a second round of boiling. With regard to perchlorate, probably the most effective immediate measure is to ensure adequate supply of iodine (see section on "Political and Regulatory Levels"). A longer term objective is associative action and lobbying to ensure that perchlorate levels in drinking water are regulated.

Packaging and Fresh Food Versus Prepared Meals

Many studies have shown that reducing the consumption of processed and packaged food can strongly diminish body levels of plasticizers, and use of organic food can reduce that of pesticides. Many will say that the cost of organic produce is prohibitive, but then the savings that result from the switch to preparing one's food rather that buying prepacked ready-to-eat microwave produce can be considerable. To this one can add the reduced generation of plastic, metal, and paper packaging associated with processed food. This is not to say that no packaging of any kind is required. Most foodstuffs need some protection during transport and shelf display; otherwise damage can lead to degradation and food wastage. However, a better balance between protection and marketing ploys needs to be sought, in the interests of the consumer and the environment. Simply put, consumers benefit immediately from the lower exposure to unnecessary plasticizers and in the longer term by a less polluted environment.

Taking the case of BPA exposure, a recent study from the NHANES group in the United States showed that the main factors increasing exposure to this chemical were soft drinks (soda) and food prepared outside the home, including school meals (Lakind & Naiman, 2011). Canned foods, particularly canned fish, corn, and soups (Cao et al., 2011), are a major source of BPA exposure in food. One notorious category of canned products that increase BPA exposure is canned sodas or soft drinks, such as juices and colas that leach BPA from their plastic linings. These canned drinks are not only a major source of BPA in the diet (Lakind & Naiman, 2011) but also of excess sugar. The consumption of soft drinks has often been incriminated as contributing to the epidemics of obesity and type 2 diabetes (James & Kerr, 2005). Although it is difficult to determine causality and to separate the obesogenic effects of chemicals from those of the superfluous sugar, urinary levels of BPA and phthalates have been associated repeatedly with obesity in population studies and in experimental models (Desvergne, Feige, & Casals-Casas, 2009; Trasande, Attina, & Blustein, 2012; Wang et al., 2012).

The case of phthalates is particularly puzzling, as this category of plasticizer is not generally added to food wrappings nor used in plastic water bottles made of polyethene terephthalate (PET), at least not in the United States (Enneking, 2006). Apparently, confusion arises from the chemical terms; the plasticizer phthalates are orthophthalates, which are distinct from PET (Enneking, 2006). Yet phthalate levels in foodstuffs, particularly those that are lipid rich, such as dairy products, display increased levels as a function of packaging and preparation (Fierens, Van Holderbeke, Willems, De Henauw, & Sioen, 2013). PVC used to be a starting material for the clear food wrapping commonly referred to as cling film, but today most of the cling film marketed appears to be made of polyethylene, which does not require addition of plasticizers. However, many reports make mention of, and measure (Goulas, Zygoura, Karatapanis, Georgantelis, & Kontominas, 2007), another food packaging additive, di(2-ethylhexyl) adipate, or DEHA, that is also found in cosmetics and deodorants (Zhou et al., 2013). The endocrine-disrupting properties of DEHA have rarely been researched. However, in 2009 the Canadian government carried out an assessment of this chemical and concluded that it was harmful to health (http://www.chemical-substanceschimiques.gc.ca).

Choice of Furnishings and Household Products and Equipment

The main worry about household furnishings, insulating materials, and electronic equipment is their brominated and chlorinated flame retardant content. This problem is particularly acute in some countries and states with stringent flammability standards for furniture components, especially cushions and sofas. This is the case for the United States in general and particularly California. However, this year the California state administration announced that it was modifying the rulings for flammability, originally drawn up in the 1970s. The basic idea is to change the flammability test from an open flame test, which requires high levels of brominated or chlorinated flame retardants to resist ignition, to a "smolder" test. This new ruling, resisted by the chemical industry, which argues that public safety is at risk, is based on the fact that most domestic fires are caused by smoldering objects, such as cigarettes or electrical cables. One of the reasons given in defense of the new rulings was that increased evidence was linking neurodevelopmental and behavioral disorders to environmental pollution—another example of belated action decades after introducing virtually untested chemicals and allowing them to accumulate in the environment. Although the flammability standards for furniture in California are more stringent than those of other administrations, they are often applied on a wider scale. Products manufactured for export will meet the most stringent requirements, even if imported into a country with less stringent regulations. This fact, along with the persistence of the chemicals concerned in the environment, contributes to the universal contamination from one of the main categories of brominated flame retardants (BFRs), the PDBEs (see Chapter 5, section on "Brominated Flame Retardants"). Although many new flame retardants are being introduced to replace the BFRs, there is little toxicity data available and so it is wise to apply a precautionary principle until more is known. As mentioned in Chapter 5, in 2013/2014, the EPA, within its Toxic Substance Control Act, is focusing on close testing of 23 substances of concern,[4] including no fewer than 20 flame retardants. Most of these chemicals are listed, but at least four are covered by company confidentiality, precluding independent assessment.

Not only household furniture is covered by flammability requirements but also car seats and electrical components. A recent US study showed that car dust contains 10 times higher levels of a new chlorinated flame retardant than house dust (Fang et al., 2013). Hence, perhaps the logic for the suggestion made by the RCOG (see earlier) that pregnant and nursing mothers should avoid buying a new vehicle, but rather stick to an older one in which, potentially, the main flush of flame retardants is gone. The authors of the car and house dust study (Fang et al., 2013) also found the chemical "V6" in the foam present in baby products, where it represented over 4% of the foam weight. Last but not least, a banned flame retardant and carcinogen, tris-(2-chloroethyl) phosphate (TCEP), was a consistent co-contaminant of V6, probably being introduced as a side product during manufacture. There are very little toxicity data on V6 and virtually nothing on its potential endocrine-disrupting properties.

One way of avoiding flame retardants in bedding is to use pure wool mattresses. Wool, like many natural products (e.g., hemp that can be used for insulation and cotton for clothing) is far less flammable than synthetic foam. This means that pure wool mattresses (and cushions) can be used without the addition of flame retardants. Given the sorry state of the Welsh wool industry and Welsh sheep farmers who cannot make a decent living because of the low price of wool, perhaps it is time to promote their products on this basis.[5]

It is somewhat unrealistic today to suggest that we should limit our exposure to electronic equipment, such as computers, e-book readers, and mobile phones. Air and dust levels of flame retardants are highest in offices, probably in large part due to the concentration of such equipment. Thus, apart from the energy savings, it is wise to shut down electronic equipment at night, especially in the home environment and if devices are in the bedroom. The reason they contain flame retardants is because they heat up during use. In turn, heat favors the release of volatile components.

Reduction of Household Pesticide Use

Pesticide use in the home can involve limiting parasites on domestic pets or wider use against household pests, particularly in lower income or dense communal dwellings (Lu et al., 2013). Some of the studies on exposure levels comparing organic versus conventional food also looked at levels of pesticides in children's urine as a function of use of pesticides at home (Lu, Barr, Pearson,

---

4   http://www.epa.gov/oppt/existingchemicals/pubs/assessment_chemicals_list.html
5   I cannot resist commenting (and revealing my Welsh heritage) that such an effort would hopefully have the extra benefit of encouraging the breeding and training of the magnificent Welsh sheep dogs!

Walker, & Bravo, 2009), while many others have examined this exposure route (Quiros-Alcala et al., 2011) as a component of environmental exposure from multiple sources. As might be expected, long-term and/or acute use increases exposure as judged by urine levels, leading many authors to argue that better management strategies are required to reduce use of potentially damaging pesticides in the home. For instance, studies in New York City have shown inverse relationships between maternal blood levels of chlorpyrifos due to residential pesticide use and infant birth weight (Whyatt et al., 2004). In turn, as emphasized earlier, low birth weight is a risk factor for many neurodevelopmental disorders. Thus, even if personal choice can be a factor in limiting use and therefore exposure of pregnant women and children in individual settings, legislation is required to protect those in areas of high residential density from unnecessary exposure.

Other, avoidable, sources of pesticide use around the house include flypapers, flea powders, shampoos for dogs and cats, and garden products, including insecticides and fungicides (such as antigreenfly or antimold sprays).

The Case for Breast-feeding Versus Formula

A number of times in discussions on the effect of chemicals on thyroid function and neurodevelopment the concept of sensitive developmental windows has been emphasized. One of these windows corresponds to the early stages of pregnancy, a stage that previously was understudied as most focus was placed on a second period of vulnerability, namely the first years of postnatal life. This focus is explained primarily by the undeniable importance of TH to the growing brain and secondly by the fact that, if detected and corrected rapidly, the otherwise irreversible effects of TH lack after birth can be prevented. In turn, much of the focus on the effects of chemical exposure on brain development has concentrated on the perinatal period and exposure during breast-feeding. It is only more recently that epidemiological and experimental studies have identified the period of early fetal growth as a vulnerable window, to both TH deficiency and chemical exposure. Many examples were given in Chapter 7. To illustrate the point, we can mention two of the most studied TH-disrupting chemicals (i.e., methylmercury and PCBs), for which many epidemiological reports show greater association of exposure during early pregnancy with adverse effects on neurological development, rather than exposure during breast-feeding (see, for example, Bjornberg et al., 2005 and Jacobson & Jacobson, 1996).

The overriding opinion in the field today is that the enormous benefits of breast-feeding override the risk of transferring chemicals to the child. Evolution has honed human breast milk composition to provide maximum nutritional and immunological benefit to the baby, with physiologically appropriate changes occurring in composition during the early postnatal period. Many reviews have covered the advantages for the child (Heinig & Dewey, 1996), to which it can be added that breast-feeding is associated with a reduced risk of breast cancer (Woodman, 2002) and ovarian cancer (Jordan, Cushing-Haugen, Wicklund, Doherty, & Rossing, 2012) for the mother.

**Box 8–2. Some Environmentally Friendly, Precautionary Actions to Limit Individual Exposure to Endocrine-Disrupting Chemicals**

- Consume organically grown grain, vegetables, fruit, and dairy produce, if possible.
- Limit the use of commercially prepared and packaged foods.
- Avoid storing food, particularly fatty foods, in plastic containers; use glass, silicone, or ceramic whenever possible.
- Do not microwave food in flexible plastic containers.
- Do not give flexible plastic teething toys to babies and use glass feeding bottles.
- Avoid use of pesticides and similar products in the home, on pets, and in the garden.
- Do not use household products containing antibacterial agents.
- Limit the use of spray-on impermeablizing agents.
- Choose cast iron or stainless steel pans instead of nonstick varieties.
- Do not overuse sunscreens and cosmetics, especially those containing parabens, when pregnant and/or breast-feeding.
- Avoid use of PVC flooring and carpets, particularly in children's rooms. Air rooms regularly. If choosing insulation materials, look at natural products such as hemp.
- If pregnant, avoid buying new sources of foam-filled furniture or seating (such as in new cars).
- Choose natural wool mattresses instead of foam products, especially for children.
- Wash clothes that may have been treated with flame retardants before wearing.
- Do not feel obliged to have the biggest flat-screen television possible, and if you do have one, switch it off when not in use, especially if sleeping in the same room.
- The same precautionary principles apply for computers and mobile phones,[10] so as to avoid heat-dependent release of flame retardants into the bedroom atmosphere.
- During pregnancy, limit the use of over-the-counter drugs and painkillers, as prolonged use of paracetamol has been associated with childhood respiratory problems (Andersen, Farkas, Mehnert, Ehrenstein, & Erichsen, 2012; Bakkeheim et al., 2011) and reproductive disorders in boys (Snijder et al., 2012).

Breast milk also contains high levels of iodine (on condition that the mother is iodine sufficient, taking iodine supplementation if necessary). In contrast, even in countries such as Switzerland, where iodination of salt ensures iodine

10 Also use of hands-free devices will reduce electromagnetic field exposure (WHO http://www.who.int/mediacentre/factsheets/fs193/en/)

sufficiency of school children and adults, babies who are being weaned can sometimes suffer from iodine lack (Andersson et al., 2010). As explained in Box 8.1 and as will be discussed in the section "Political and Regulatory Levels" on actions that can be taken by the medical profession, if a woman is planning pregnancy it is advisable to take not only folic acid and vitamin supplements but also to ensure an adequate supply of iodine, before, during, and after pregnancy (especially if breast-feeding). In the absence of any thyroid disorder, a sufficient iodine intake ensures normal production of TH. In turn, adequate TH levels in the mother and then in the developing child will lessen concomitant effects of chemicals affecting brain growth, irrespective of whether such chemicals act directly through TH disruption or through other related mechanisms.

## Nongovernmental and Associative Actions

### Associations With Wide Environmental Scope of Action

A good way to act more effectively is to work with others toward a common goal, either within an association or through a political party. What is more, according to researchers at the Erasmus University in the Netherlands, this can actually improve one's subjective feeling of happiness (http://worlddatabaseof-happiness.eur.nl/). So get involved!

A number of nongovernmental organizations (NGOs) have activities linked to the more responsible regulation and use of chemicals, environmental contamination, and the consequent deleterious effects on human health. The examples of the WWF (http://www.wwf.org) studies on chemical exposure in two different European populations were cited in Chapter 6. Greenpeace (http://www.greenpeace.org/) is clearly a forerunner in defending the environment, and their current priorities include actions on sustainable agriculture and reduction of chemical exposure by research into safer products.

More specifically, the Chemicals, Health and Environment Monitoring Trust or ChemTrust (http://www.chemtrust.org.uk) is a UK-based NGO set up in 2007 that focuses on effects of persistent organic pollutants on biodiversity and health. The organization is active in promoting legislation on better use of chemicals. In the United States, one nonprofit organization working toward more environmentally friendly and sustainable solutions for chemical production and usage is the GreenBlue Institute (http://www.ceres.org/).

Another means of group action, which is especially relevant in the context of the US legal framework, is class action. The Master Settlement Agreement exemplifies the effectiveness of this form of action. The agreement resolved the case brought by a group of state attorney generals against the tobacco industry in the United States in 1999 and awarded not only billions of dollars to health care services toward the cost of caring for smokers but also changed legislation on the advertising and sale of tobacco products (Jones & Silvestri, 2010). In the context of environmental pollution and effects on public health, examples of successful class action include those of residents living near a chemical plant producing perfluorooctanoic acid (PFOA) required for manufacturing nonstick pans (Lopez-Espinosa, Mondal, Armstrong, Bloom, & Fletcher, 2012). This settlement included the initiation of a project to follow the health of children exposed by contamination of drinking water with PFOA, now known to interfere with TH signaling.

Flame Retardants

It is hardly surprising, given the high use of flame retardants in the United States, that it has a number of associations researching and providing information on the (lack of) testing and use of flame retardants. One of them, the Green Science Policy Institute (greensciencepolicy.org/about-us/), was founded in 2008 by Arlene Blum. Her work on the action of BFRs was described in Chapters 1 and 5. This organization has already contributed to reducing significantly the use of flame retardants by modifying legislation.

This institute and other associations working toward more environmentally sustainable and less health-endangering approaches are up against strong lobbying by well-organized industries. *The Chicago Tribune* (currently) has an excellent site relating the collusion of various industrial groups toward the promotion of unnecessary use of toxic BFRs. The site lists examples of lobbying by tobacco companies[6] and the bromine industry and distortion of scientific information by representatives of the chemical industry and scientists alike (http://media.apps.chicagotribune.com/flames/index.html). A number of scientific publications have argued against the unnecessary and excessive use of flame retardants (DiGangi et al., 2010) that has led to their unrelenting buildup in the environment, even in sites at great distances from regions of high usage (Bogdal et al., 2008).

Biocides and Pesticides

Production of pesticides increased seven-fold between 1950 and 2000, reaching over 3.5 million tons per annum. More investment in sustainable agricultural practices is required for humankind to benefit from, and not further degrade, ecosystem potential. Numerous factors have to be taken into account to improve sustainability, but many have emphasized the need to reduce and rationalize herbicide, pesticide, and fertilizer use (Tilman, Cassman, Matson, Naylor, & Polasky, 2002). Multiple demonstrations show that reducing pesticide use is not necessarily associated with lower yields, but may often increase them (see, for example, Normile, 2013, and Pretty et al., 2006). To the arguments on sustainability of yields can be added the cost of the negative impacts on human health (Fantke, Friedrich, & Jolliet, 20142) and biodiversity. Further,

---

6   Apparently, tobacco companies had representatives in key committees who argued that making furniture safer was a better way to prevent fires than modifying the way cigarettes are made. To this one can add that the risk of smoking causing house fires in the United States and the European Union has dropped dramatically with increased awareness of the health risks associated with tobacco, and the associated reduction in smoking, notably smoking indoors and around children.

as Joe Thornton emphasized in his excellent analysis of the organo-chlorine industry and its effects (Thornton, 2000), when transiting to organic methods, reduction of pesticides requires putting something else into the equation, that is, work and information on crops and biodiversity. It is obviously a difficult exercise to calculate the longer term socioeconomic cost-benefits of reductions in herbicide/pesticide usage to embrace not only direct health and biodiversity benefits but also other multifactorial inputs such as land management, farm-labor employment possibilities, and the impact of urbanization of populations, but perhaps it is time to work these interactions and their consequences into the calculations.

Returning to actions by individuals, many policy changes in pesticide usage are driven by public concerns about health. These can be usefully channeled through NGOs such as the Pesticide Action Network (PAN) that has groups working in North America (http://www.panna.org) and Europe (http://www.pan-europe.info). Just in the context of this book, a recent expert opinion published by the European Food Safety Authority[7] showed that over a third of pesticides tested had TH-disrupting activity. Currently the European Union has delayed taking action on the endocrine-disrupting effects of pesticides. Public opinion can help NGOs, such as PAN Europe, be effective.

## Political and Regulatory Levels

### Ensuring Sufficient Iodine Supplies for Children and Pregnant Women at National Levels

One of the main messages of this book has been that iodine deficiency, rather than being a thing of the past, is not only present in mild forms in many parts of Europe but that intake is falling in many parts of the world. A second idea is that such iodine insufficiency could exacerbate the consequences of TH-disrupting chemicals on brain development.

Severe iodine lack causes cretinism. Although the distressing phenotypes of cretinism are rarely seen in developed countries today, mild to moderate iodine lack, with or without adverse chemical exposure, may be reducing the intellectual potential of large proportions of national populations. Not only have experts estimated that a third of the world's population has insufficient iodine supply, but numerous studies have also shown that lower maternal iodine intake is associated with reduced intellectual performance in children (Bath, Steer, Golding, Emmett, & Rayman, 2013; Zimmerman, 2009a, 2009b). Zimmerman has reviewed a number of meta-analyses of the effects of iodine supplementation during pregnancy on children's intellectual outcome and concludes that chronic iodine deficiency can result in a loss of 12–13 IQ points. Such findings can be explained by the essential roles, first, of iodine in TH synthesis and, second, the critical need for TH at many stages of brain development. To these figures one can add the IQ loss attributable to single classes of

7   *EFSA Journal* 2013, *11*(7), 3293.

chemical exposure, such as the 5–10 points seen in the PCB exposure studies of Jacobson (Jacobson & Jacobson, 1996) discussed in Chapter 1.

Many have argued that mental disability due to iodine insufficiency is the most easily prevented form of intellectual disadvantage, to which one could add its low cost and risk. Today it seems logical to ensure that women do not enter pregnancy with any risk of iodine lack. Two principal arguments can be put forward: first, the disastrous economic consequences of the loss of a few IQ points at a population level (see Chapter 1 for figures on cost estimates) and, second, the risk of exposure to such a wide spectrum of chemicals that can exacerbate the adverse effects of iodine lack on TH signaling. Thus, governments have the responsibility to guarantee sufficient iodine levels in their populations. The cost-benefit in the long term is immense at national levels, in both social and economic terms. For the individual, governmental failure to act is a form of social injustice.

Iodine sufficiency at the population level can be achieved either by legislation covering the iodization of salt (not only for sale in households but also for use in the food and agricultural industries) and/or by increased awareness in the medical profession. In the latter case, the recommendations of the World Health Organization (WHO) need to be taken into account. This organization, along with UNICEF and the International Council for the Control of Iodine Deficiency Disorders (ICCIDD), has increased the recommended iodine intake for pregnant and lactating women from 200 to 250 µg/d. As iodine is efficiently stocked in the thyroid gland, one way of ensuring iodine supply for women of child-bearing age is to provide iodine injections every 3 months, or even to give a dose of iodine-enriched oil once a year (Zimmerman, 2009b). Doctors and nurses need to be made more aware of the need for iodine supplementation, and medical associations should inform governments of the importance of implementing methods for preventing iodine lack.

The Need for International Cooperation on Chemical Regulation

As for problems related to climate change in the context of regulating chemicals, particularly those that persist and accumulate in the environment, little progress can be made at the level of individual states. Many international bodies have committees and activities aimed toward reaching agreement on different aspects of chemical regulation. The Organization for Economic Cooperation and Development (OECD) has an overriding role in proposing and ratifying testing procedures. In the field of endocrine disruption the OECD has committees on reproductive endocrinology and physiology as well as thyroid signaling. One committee that has recently been set up reflects the terminology of the WHO definition of endocrine disruption (WHO, State of the Science of Endocrine disrupting Chemicals 2013, Section 1.3, p.13). This definition, originally proposed by the IPCS reads as ". . . an exogenous substance or mixture that alters function(s) of the endocrine system and consequently causes adverse health effects in an intact organism, or its progeny, or (sub) populations." The term "adverse" is much debated and to many can be seen as a means of stalling action. How long-lasting, or to what extent, does a change in a hormone level, gene response, or physiological process need to be for it to be adverse? Clearly the answer depends on the time of exposure and the tissue considered. A small change in TH availability during early development in the brain can have irreversible consequences, while in an adult a transient change will be less harmful. To grapple with these complexities, the OECD has set up its Adverse Outcome Pathway committee, the members of which have to propose and determine which tests can be used to determine adverse effects in different settings, for a spectrum of signaling pathways. However, despite the best intentions of many OECD officials and time invested by many committee members, given the time needed for the OECD to discuss and ratify tests, it will require at least another decade before any concrete action can be taken.[8] The Endocrine Society in their statement on EDCs (Zoeller et al., 2012) found the use of the term "adverse" so ambiguous that, having discussed the terminology and its implications in detail, they proposed changing the wording of the text to "An endocrine disruptor is an exogenous chemical, or mixture of chemicals, that interferes with any aspect of hormone action."

An example of successful international cooperation came in May 2013 when a joint UN convention was signed to promote synergy and strengthen cooperation between the Basel, Rotterdam, and Stockholm conventions (http://synergies.pops.int/Secretariat/VisionStatement/), so as to better protect the environment and human health from toxic chemicals. The agreement can be consulted as the "Geneva Statement on Sound Management of Chemicals and Waste." At the outset, each of these conventions covered, respectively, transport of hazardous waste, trading of hazardous chemicals and pesticides, and persistent organic pollutants (POPs).

Other examples of international cooperation are less satisfying. One recent example includes the failure of the European Food Safety Association (EFSA) to take a sufficiently clear position on the need for testing the endocrine-disrupting potential of chemicals (http://www.efsa.europa.eu/en/efsajournal/pub/3132.htm), including pesticides. This decision was criticized by a number of parties for pandering to industry and failing to recognize the dangers of endocrine disruption, notably by flirting with the idea that low doses, mixture effects, and nonmonotonic dose–response curves were not fully established by science. Certain associations drew historical parallels with the ways in which politicians had failed to counter lobbying by the tobacco, lead, and asbestos industries in previous decades.

The EFSA statement in early 2013 is related to REACH enforcement and the discussion about its extension to cover pesticides. Both the EU and US regulations have specific provisions for pesticides. As described at the end of Chapter 5, the US EPA TSCA list currently includes over 84,000 chemicals, each of which is produced in quantities over 10 tons, but this list excludes pesticides

8  As a member of certain of these committees, I can vouch that this is an optimistic scenario.

(as well as drugs and cosmetics) that are covered by other legislation. Similarly, in the European Union, requirements to test chemicals for potential endocrine-disrupting action currently exclude pesticides. The pesticide exemption should have been revisited at the end of 2013, as the 4 years that the commission was given to find a solution to the problem have elapsed. But the decision has been delayed yet again, clearly due to lobbying by the chemical industry.

The Need for Testing While Respecting Ethics in Animal Research

Today we are faced with a major predicament. Thousands of chemicals are produced at significant tonnage, but because of the current regulatory scenarios,[9] the large majority of them have not been tested for their toxicological or endocrine-disrupting effects before being released onto the market. Testing the effects of chemicals on biodiversity or human health requires biological systems, most often cells or animals. There are, of course, numerous ethical problems with animal research and every effort must be made to apply the principles of the three "Rs": reduce, refine, and replace animals in testing. Yet another criticism of animal research often heard is that no animal model can predict what will happen in humans. The choice of testing thalidomide on rats is often cited, as these rodents, unlike highly sensitive species such as rabbits and humans, are insensitive to the teratogenic effects of the drug, due to interspecies differences in metabolic capacity (Chung et al., 2004). This is an important point, since many toxic or endocrine-disrupting effects are not exerted by the primary or parent compound but by a metabolite, produced in the organism itself. Many examples can be given. For instance, the fungicide vinclozolin is metabolized in vivo to numerous metabolites, two of which, M1 and M2, exert antiandrogenic actions directly at the level of the androgen receptor (Wolf, LeBlanc, Ostby, & Gray, 2000). Vinclozolin has become notorious for its effects on sperm seen in male pups born to exposed gestating rats (Anway, Memon, Uzumcu, & Skinner, 2006). Most disquieting, these effects can be transgenerational, even being seen in the great grandsons of the female rat exposed.

Given these interspecies differences in metabolism, it is often suggested that one has to use either human cells in culture or multiple animal models or potentially multiple in silico approaches upstream of a range of in vitro animal cell lines. Certainly the principles of comparative physiology teach us that although many processes are evolutionarily conserved and common to all vertebrates, there are many differences in metabolism, sensitivity, and timing of processes such as receptor or enzyme expression. Examples of processes that are largely conserved extend from the basic principles of gene regulation to complex endocrine processes, such as TH synthesis and action.

---

9  See the end of Chapter 5 for a comparison of current US and European regulations of chemical registration and authorization procedures, notably underlining the fact that in the United States it only takes 3 months to obtain clearance to produce or import a chemical and 30 years to ban it.

No doubt, future testing strategies will involve multiple layers of tests that incorporate both new animal models and in vitro approaches using both animal and human cells, all of which can be coupled to computer-based, or in silico, analysis. However, in the case of human cell lines, the question must be asked as to where one finds the first human cells to test or to derive the lines. Many cell lines have been derived from patients or fetuses without appropriate ethical consent from the person or parents concerned. Many think that a less problematic answer lies with cloning, possibly by transforming and multiplying easily obtainable cells such as some blood cells. Recent advances enable biologists to generate pluripotent stem cells from a variety of sources and then reprogram them into another tissue. The original work (Takahashi & Yamanaka, 2006) led to a Nobel Prize for the senior author. The different tissue types derived can be used for testing effects of chemicals across a variety of cell phenotypes. However, deriving human cells for chemical testing by cloning means that the tests are carried out on cells that are not really representative of the initial cells (cloning, by any means, introduces changes and errors in chromosomal number and/or organization). Furthermore, tests will most usually be carried out on a single type of cell: neurons or liver or skin cells. This situation, using cell types in isolation, is a long way from the complexity of an intact organism such as the human body. In all physiological systems there is continual communication between organs, tissues, and cells. Moreover, the chemical signals used for communication undergo continual metabolism and recycling, producing new molecules from old.

This concept is not just limited to the endogenous hormones. In the field of toxicology and endocrine disruption, it is known that many products with deleterious effects on human health need to be metabolized in the body, and it is the molecule that results from this metabolism that is active, not the parent compound. So studying the effects of chemicals in a cell such as a skin cell or a specialized neuron will not provide a full picture or indicate that chemical's potential toxicity and will need to be complemented by metabolic studies.

Not surprisingly, alternative models are continually sought to resolve this conundrum. One of the most explored is the use of fish and amphibian embryos (Scholz et al., 2013). These embryos have various advantages. Unlike mammalian embryos, fish and amphibian eggs are laid in water and the embryos hatch as free-living organisms, independent from the mother. They are usually available in larger numbers, with batches of hundreds or thousands of eggs being laid simultaneously. In contrast, working on mammalian embryos raises the major experimental problem of development inside the mother and the ethical problem of using the adult mother to obtain the embryos. As vertebrates, amphibians and fish have high homologies to mammals in terms of organ development and signaling molecules, particularly endocrine signaling. As mentioned previously, TH is exactly the same in fish, amphibians, birds, and mammals, including humans, with high homologies in the processes and molecules implicated in hormone production and signaling. There are also two other main advantages. First, these early fish and amphibian embryos are virtually transparent, allowing the use of fluorescent markers to follow gene transcription and organ development. Second, their small size means that screening methods, such as robot plate readers, primarily developed for in vitro methods, can sometimes be applied to embryos. This feature means that many more chemicals can be tested in greater detail, more rapidly, and at lower cost than if larger animals were used.

## FINAL COMMENTS: INDIVIDUAL ACTION CANNOT SUBSTITUTE FOR POLICY

Examples have been provided demonstrating that individuals can act to help reduce their exposure (summarized in Box 8.2) and to lobby industry and regulators into action. But what about people who are unaware of the dangers? Or the societal cost of those who choose to ignore recommendations? Or people who have no choice but to be subjected to exposure? Many factors enter a debate that covers numerous political and ethical considerations and weighs up arguments about who is responsible and who should act. Numerous studies have demonstrated the greater efficiency of policy over lifestyle choices (Horton et al., 2013). Simply taking the case of children growing up in disadvantaged areas, such as, but not only, those in farming communities (Sexton, Ryan, Adgate, Barr, & Needham, 2011), underlines the need for legislation. Such children can be doubly exposed to pesticides, both from intensive agriculture and from the excessive use of pesticides to control insects in substandard dwellings, not to mention the higher levels of iodine-uptake blocking nitrates found in the water of such areas with intensive agriculture. Unsurprisingly, in view of what has been argued in this and preceding chapters, children in these communities, prenatally exposed to cocktails of thyroid-disrupting chemicals, tend to have more behavioral problems, do less well at school, and have fewer career opportunities. In extreme cases they can become a burden on society. The causes of their disadvantages are specific, material, identifiable, and, given political will to introduce and enforce appropriate legislation, preventable. Failure to correct future injustices is also a failure to recognize that human intelligence and ingenuity have been responsible for the creation and production of a vast array of untested and potentially dangerous substances. It should be possible for human intelligence and ingenuity to find the means to control and eliminate their nefarious consequences. If not, then future generations could well find themselves lacking the intelligence and ingenuity ever to do so.

## REFERENCES

Aben, K. K., van Gaal, C., van Gils, N. A., van der Graaf, W. T., & Zielhuis, G. A. (2012). Cancer in adolescents and young adults (15–29 years), a population-based study in the Netherlands 1989–2009. *Acta Oncologica*, 51(7), 922–933.
Al-Saleh, I., Shinwari, N., & Alsabbaheen, A. (2011). Phthalates residues in plastic bottled waters. *Journal of Toxicological Sciences*, 36(4), 469–478.

Amiridou, D., & Voutsa, D. (2011). Alkylphenols and phthalates in bottled waters. *Journal of Hazardous Materials, 185*(1), 281–286.

Andersen, A. B., Farkas, D. K., Mehnert, F., Ehrenstein, V., & Erichsen, R. (2012). Use of prescription paracetamol during pregnancy and risk of asthma in children: A population-based Danish cohort study. *Clinical Epidemiology, 4,* 33–40.

Andersson, M., Aeberli, I., Wüst, N., Piacenza, A. M., Bucher, T., Henschen, I., ... Zimmermann, M. B. (2010). The Swiss iodized salt program provides adequate iodine for school children and pregnant women, but weaning infants not receiving iodine-containing complementary foods as well as their mothers are iodine deficient. *Journal of Clinical Endocrinology and Metabolism, 95*(12), 5217–5224.

Anway, M. D., Memon, M. A., Uzumcu, M., & Skinner, M. K. (2006). Transgenerational effect of the endocrine disruptor vinclozolin on male spermatogenesis. *Journal of Andrology, 27*(6), 868–879.

Bakkeheim, E., Mowinckel, P., Carlsen, K. H., Haland, G., & Carlsen, K. C. (2011). Paracetamol in early infancy: The risk of childhood allergy and asthma. *Acta Paediatrica, 100*(1), 90–96.

Bath, S. C., Steer, C. D., Golding, J., Emmett, P., & Rayman, M. P. (2013). Effect of inadequate iodine status in UK pregnant women on cognitive outcomes in their children: Results from the Avon Longitudinal Study of Parents and Children (ALSPAC). *Lancet, 382*(9889), 331–337.

Bjornberg, K. A., Vahter, M., Berglund, B., Niklasson, B., Blennow, M., & Sandborgh-Englund, G. (2005). Transport of methylmercury and inorganic mercury to the fetus and breast-fed infant. *Environmental Health Perspectives, 113*(10), 1381–1385.

Bogdal, C., Schmid, P., Kohler, M., Müller, C. E., Iozza, S., Bucheli, T. D., ... Hungerbühler, K. (2008). Sediment record and atmospheric deposition of brominated flame retardants and organochlorine compounds in Lake Thun, Switzerland: Lessons from the past and evaluation of the present. *Environmental Science and Technology, 42*(18), 6817–6822.

Cao, X. L., Perez-Locas, C., Dufresne, G., Clement, G., Popovic, S., Beraldin, F., ... Feeley, M. (2011). Concentrations of bisphenol A in the composite food samples from the 2008 Canadian total diet study in Quebec City and dietary intake estimates. *Food Additives and Contaminants Part A: Chemistry, Analysis, Control Exposure, and Risk Assessment, 28*(6), 791–798.

Charnley, G. (2003). Pesticide exposures and children's risk tradeoffs. *Environmental Health Perspectives, 111*(13), A689; author reply A689–691.

Choi, A. L., Budtz-Jørgensen, E., Jørgensen, P. J., Steuerwald, U., Debes, F., Weihe, P., & Grandjean, P. (2008). Selenium as a potential protective factor against mercury developmental neurotoxicity. *Environmetnal Research, 107*(1), 45–52.

Chung, F., Lu, J., Palmer, B. D., Kestell, P., Browett, P., Baguley, B. C., ... Ching, L. M. (2004). Thalidomide pharmacokinetics and metabolite formation in mice, rabbits, and multiple myeloma patients. *Clinical Cancer Research, 10*(17), 5949–5956.

Curl, C. L., Fenske, R. A., & Elgethun, K. (2003). Organophosphorus pesticide exposure of urban and suburban preschool children with organic and conventional diets. *Environmental Health Perspectives, 111*(3), 377–382.

De Angelis, S., Tassinari, R., Maranghi, F., Eusepi, A., Di Virgilio, A., Chiarotti, F., ... Mantovani, A. (2009). Developmental exposure to chlorpyrifos induces alterations in thyroid and thyroid hormone levels without other toxicity signs in CD-1 mice. *Toxicological Sciences, 108*(2), 311–319.

Deary, I. (2008). Why do intelligent people live longer? *Nature*, *456*(7219), 175–176.

Desvergne, B., Feige, J. N., & Casals-Casas, C. (2009). PPAR-mediated activity of phthalates: A link to the obesity epidemic? *Molecular and Cellular Endocrinology*, *304*(1–2), 43–48.

DiGangi, J., Blum, A., Bergman, A., de Wit, C. A., Lucas, D., Mortimer, D.,... Webster, T. F. (2010). San Antonio Statement on brominated and chlorinated flame retardants. *Environmental Health Perspectives*, *118*(12), A516–518.

Enneking, P. A. (2006). Phthalates not in plastic food packaging. *Environmental Health Perspectives*, *114*(2), A89–90.

Fang, M., Webster, T. F., Gooden, D., Cooper, E. M., McClean, M. D., Carignan, C.,... Stapleton, H. M. (2013). Investigating a novel flame retardant known as v6: Measurements in baby products, house dust, and car dust. *Environmental Science and Technology*, *47*(9), 4449–4454.

Fantke, P., Friedrich, R., & Jolliet, O. (2012). Health impact and damage cost assessment of pesticides in Europe. *Environment International*, *49*, 9–17.

Fierens, T., Van Holderbeke, M., Willems, H., De Henauw, S., & Sioen, I. (2013). Transfer of eight phthalates through the milk chain--a case study. *Environment International*, *51*, 1–7.

Goulas, A. E., Zygoura, P., Karatapanis, A., Georgantelis, D., & Kontominas, M. G. (2007). Migration of di(2-ethylhexyl) adipate and acetyltributyl citrate plasticizers from food-grade PVC film into sweetened sesame paste (halawa tehineh), kinetic and penetration study. *Food Chemistry and Toxicology*, *45*(4), 585–591.

Heinig, M. J., & Dewey, K. G. (1996). Health advantages of breast feeding for infants: A critical review. *Nutrition Research Review*, *9*(1), 89–110.

Horton, M. K., Bousleiman, S., Jones, R., Sjodin, A., Liu, X., Whyatt, R.,... Factor-Litvak, P. (2013). Predictors of serum concentrations of polybrominated flame retardants among healthy pregnant women in an urban environment: A cross-sectional study. *Environmental Health*, *12*(1), 23.

Hvistendahl, M., & Enserink, M. (2012). GM research. Charges fly, confusion reigns over golden rice study in Chinese children. *Science*, *337*(6100), 1281.

Hynes, K. L., Otahal, P., Hay, I., & Burgess, J. R. (2013). Mild iodine deficiency during pregnancy is associated with reduced educational outcomes in the offspring: 9-year follow-up of the gestational iodine cohort. *Journal of Clinical Endocrinology and Metabolism*, *98*(5), 1954–1962.

Jacobson, J. L., & Jacobson, S. W. (1996). Intellectual impairment in children exposed to polychlorinated biphenyls in utero. *New England Journal of Medicine*, *335*(11), 783–789.

James, J., & Kerr, D. (2005). Prevention of childhood obesity by reducing soft drinks. *International Journal of Obesity (London)*, *29*(Suppl 2), S54–S57.

Jones, W. J., & Silvestri, G. A. (2010). The Master Settlement Agreement and its impact on tobacco use 10 years later: Lessons for physicians about health policy making. *Chest*, *137*(3), 692–700.

Jordan, S. J., Cushing-Haugen, K. L., Wicklund, K. G., Doherty, J. A., & Rossing, M. A. (2012). Breast-feeding and risk of epithelial ovarian cancer. *Cancer Causes and Control*, *23*(6), 919–927.

Koletzko, B., Cetin, I., & Brenna, J. T. (2007). Dietary fat intakes for pregnant and lactating women. *British Journal of Nutrition*, *98*(5), 873–877.

Krieger, R. I., Dinoff, T. M., Williams, R. L., Zhang, X., Ross, J. H., Aston, L. S., & Myers, G. (2003). Correspondence: Preformed biomarkers in produce inflate human organophosphate exposure assessments. *Environmental Health Perspectives, 111*(13), A688–689; author reply A689–691.

Krieger, R. I., Keenan, J. J., Li, Y., & Vega, H. M. (2006). OP pesticides, organic diets, and children's health. *Environmental Health Perspectives, 114*(10), A572; author reply A572–573.

Lakind, J. S., & Naiman, D. Q. (2011), Daily intake of bisphenol A and potential sources of exposure: 2005–2006 National Health and Nutrition Examination Survey. *Journal of Exposure Science and Environmental Epidemiology, 21*(3), 272–279.

Lanphear, B. P., Vorhees, C. V., & Bellinger, D. C. (2005). Protecting children from environmental toxins. *PLoS Medicine, 2*(3), e61.

Lemaux, P. G. (2008). Genetically engineered plants and foods: A scientist's analysis of the issues (Part I). *Annual Review of Plant Biology, 59*, 771–812.

Leung, A. M., Pearce, E. N., & Braverman, L. E. (2013). Sufficient iodine intake during pregnancy: Just do it. *Thyroid, 23*(1), 7–8.

Lopez-Espinosa, M. J., Mondal, D., Armstrong, B., Bloom, M. S., & Fletcher, T. (2012). Thyroid function and perfluoroalkyl acids in children living near a chemical plant. *Environmental Health Perspectives, 120*(7), 1036–1041.

Lu, C., Adamkiewicz, G., Attfield, K. R., Kapp, M., Spengler, J. D., Tao, L., & Xie, S. H. (2013). Household pesticide contamination from indoor pest control applications in urban low-income public housing dwellings: A community-based participatory research. *Environmental Science and Technology, 47*(4), 2018–2025.

Lu, C., Barr, D. B., Pearson, M., Bartell, S., & Bravo, R. (2006). A longitudinal approach to assessing urban and suburban children's exposure to pyrethroid pesticides. *Environmental Health Perspectives, 114*(9), 1419–1423.

Lu, C., Barr, D. B., Pearson, M. A., Walker, L. A., & Bravo, R. (2009). The attribution of urban and suburban children's exposure to synthetic pyrethroid insecticides: A longitudinal assessment. *Journal of Exposure Science and Environmental Epidemiology, 19*(1), 69–78.

Lu, C., Toepel, K., Irish, R., Fenske, R. A., Barr, D. B., & Bravo, R. (2006). Organic diets significantly lower children's dietary exposure to organophosphorus pesticides. *Environmental Health Perspectives, 114*(2), 260–263.

Normile, D. (2013). Vietnam turns back a "tsunami of pesticides." *Science, 341*(6147), 737–738.

Pimentel, D. (2012). Silent Spring: The 50th anniversary of Rachel Carson's book. *BMC Ecology, 12*, 20.

Potrykus, I. (2010). Lessons from the "Humanitarian Golden Rice" project: Regulation prevents development of public good genetically engineered crop products. *New Biotechnology, 27*(5), 466–472.

Pretty, J. N., Noble, A. D., Bossio, D., Dixon, J., Hine, R. E., Penning De Vries, F. W., & Morison, J. I. (2006). Resource-conserving agriculture increases yields in developing countries. *Environmental Science and Technology, 40*(4), 1114–1119.

Quiros-Alcala, L., Bradman, A., Nishioka, M., Harnly, M. E., Hubbard, A., McKone, T. E.,… Eskenazi, B. (2011). Pesticides in house dust from urban and farmworker households in California: An observational measurement study. *Environmental Health, 10*, 19.

Rauh, V., Arunajadai, S., Horton, M., Perera, F., Hoepner, L., Barr, D. B., & Whyatt, R. (2011). Seven-year neurodevelopmental scores and prenatal exposure to chlorpyrifos, a common agricultural pesticide. *Environmental Health Perspectives*, *119*(8), 1196–1201.

Roberts, E. M., English, P. B., Grether, J. K., Windham, G. C., Somberg, L., & Wolff, C. (2007). Maternal residence near agricultural pesticide applications and autism spectrum disorders among children in the California Central Valley. *Environmental Health Perspectives*, *115*(10), 1482–1489.

Scholz, S., Renner, P., Belanger, S. E., Busquet, F., Davi, R., Demeneix, B. A.,...Embry, M. R. (2013). Alternatives to in vivo tests to detect endocrine disrupting chemicals (EDCs) in fish and amphibians--screening for estrogen, androgen and thyroid hormone disruption. *Critical Reviews in Toxicology*, *43*(1), 45–72.

Sexton, K., Ryan, A. D., Adgate, J. L., Barr, D. B., & Needham, L. L. (2011). Biomarker measurements of concurrent exposure to multiple environmental chemicals and chemical classes in children. *Journal of Toxicology and Environmental Health A*, *74*(14), 927–942.

Snijder, C. A., Kortenkamp, A., Steegers, E. A., Jaddoe, V. W., Hofman, A., Hass, U., & Burdorf, A. (2012). Intrauterine exposure to mild analgesics during pregnancy and the occurrence of cryptorchidism and hypospadia in the offspring: The Generation R Study. *Human Reproduction*, *27*(4), 1191–1201.

Stagnaro-Green, A., & Pearce, E. N. (2013). Iodine and pregnancy: A call to action. *Lancet*, *382*(9889), 292–293.

Szlinder-Richert, J., Barska, I., Mazerski, J., & Usydus, Z. (2009). PCBs in fish from the southern Baltic Sea: Levels, bioaccumulation features, and temporal trends during the period from 1997 to 2006. *Marine Pollution Bulletin*, *58*(1), 85–92.

Takahashi, K., & Yamanaka, S. (2006). Induction of pluripotent stem cells from mouse embryonic and adult fibroblast cultures by defined factors. *Cell*, *126*(4), 663–676.

Tang, G., Hu, Y., Yin, S. A., Wang, Y., Dallal, G. E., Grusak, M. A., & Russell, R. M. (2012). Beta-Carotene in golden rice is as good as beta-carotene in oil at providing vitamin A to children. *American Journal of Clinical Nutrition 96*(3), 658–664.

Thornton, J. (2000). *Pandora's poison: Chlorine, health, and a new environmental strategy*. Cambridge, MA: MIT Press.

Tilman, D., Cassman, K. G., Matson, P. A., Naylor, R., & Polasky, S. (2002). Agricultural sustainability and intensive production practices. *Nature*, *418*(6898), 671–677.

Trasande, L., Attina, T. M., & Blustein, J. (2012). Association between urinary bisphenol A concentration and obesity prevalence in children and adolescents. *Journal of the American Medical Association*, *308*(11), 1113–1121.

Wagner, M., & Oehlmann, J. (2011). Endocrine disruptors in bottled mineral water: Estrogenic activity in the e-screen. *Journal of Steroid Biochemistry and Molecular Biology*, *127*(1–2), 128–135.

Wang, T., Li, M., Chen, B., Xu, M., Xu, Y., Huang, Y.,...Ning, G. (2012). Urinary bisphenol A (BPA) concentration associates with obesity and insulin resistance. *Journal of Clinical Endocrinology and Metabolism*, *97*(2), E223–227.

Whyatt, R. M., Rauh, V., Barr, D. B., Camann, D. E., Andrews, H. F., Garfinkel, R.,...Perera, F. P. (2004). Prenatal insecticide exposures and birth weight and length among an urban minority cohort. *Environmental Health Perspectives*, *112*(10), 1125–1132.

Wolf, C. J., LeBlanc, G. A., Ostby, J. S., & Gray, L. E., Jr. (2000). Characterization of the period of sensitivity of fetal male sexual development to vinclozolin. *Toxicological Sciences*, *55*(1), 152–161.

Woodman, I. (2002). Breast feeding reduces risk of breast cancer, says study. *BMJ* *325*(7357), 184.

Zewdie, T., Smith, C. M., Hutcheson, M., & West, C. R. (2010). Basis of the Massachusetts reference dose and drinking water standard for perchlorate. *Environmental Health Perspectives, 118*(1), 42–48.

Zhang, X., Gandhi, N., Bhavsar, S. P., & Ho, L. S. (2013). Effects of skin removal on contaminant levels in salmon and trout filets. *Science of the Total Environment, 443*, 218–225.

Zimmermann, M. B. (2009a). Iodine deficiency. *Endocrine Review, 30*(4), 376–408.

Zimmermann, M. B. (2009b). Iodine deficiency in pregnancy and the effects of maternal iodine supplementation on the offspring: A review. *American Journal of Clinical Nutrition, 89*(2), 668S–672S.

Zoeller, R. T., Brown, T. R., Doan, L. L., Gore, A. C., Skakkebaek, N. E., Soto, A. M.,... Vom Saal, F. S. (2012). Endocrine-disrupting chemicals and public health protection: A statement of principles from The Endocrine Society. *Endocrinology, 153*(9), 4097–4110.

Zhou, S. N., Moody, R. P., Aikawa, B., Yip, A., Wang, B., & Zhu, J. (2013). In vitro dermal absorption of di(2-ethylhexyl) adipate (DEHA) in a roll-on deodorant using human skin. *Journal of Toxicology and Environmental Health A, 76*(3), 157–166.

# Index

Note: *f* denotes figure; *n* denotes note.